MW01196123

2019

The Complete Directory of
Antique Farm Equipment Events

Jan. 1 – Dec. 31, 2019

☞ Contents ☜

Show Listings 33

Recommened Products for the Vintage Farm Collector 178

Show Advertising 182

National Clubs/Publications 253

Show Features 257

Reference 267

On the cover: CASE high-crop tractor from the collection of Doug & Barb Deshaw (Hopkinton, IA) at the 47th Annual Albert City, IA Thresherman & Collectors Show in 2017

Photo by: Loretta Sorensen

Every possible effort has been made to ensure the accuracy of the content of this directory. However, before traveling, please verify dates and locations.

Ogden Publications Inc.
1503 S.W. 42nd St. • Topeka, KS 66609 • (866) 624-9388
Publishers of *Farm Collector* and *Gas Engine Magazine*
ISBN: 978-1-948734-03-5

MAFMCA
EST 1991

find us on Facebook!
www.facebook.com/mafmca

VISIT OUR WEBSITE!
www.mafmca.org

Montour Antique Farm Machinery Collectors Association
PRESENTS THE **28**TH ANNUAL

Antique Farm Machinery Show

August 30 - September 1, 2019

* Labor Day weekend * Family Fun *

* 2019 Feature * ALLIS CHALMERS *

Equipment Parades
Fireworks
Chicken BBQ
Hay Wagon Rides
Ice Cream
Barrel Train Rides
Toy Displays
Working Machinery
Pedal Tractor Pulls
Flea Market
Tractor Games
Hit & Miss Engines
Kids Play Area
Breakfast Sat/Sun
Stone Crusher
Shingle Mill
Tractor
Teeter Totters
Chinese Auction

Free Admission!

Friday, Aug 30

Registration starts at Noon
4 pm—Parade of Equipment
7 pm—Double-Tree & Powder Puff Tractor Pulls
Classes: 3250; 3500; 3750; 4000; 4250;
4500; 5000; 5500; 6000

Saturday, Aug 31

6:30 am—Breakfast
11 am—Pedal Tractor Pull—All Ages Welcome!
12 noon—Tractor Games & Chicken BBQ
2 pm—Parade of Equipment
4pm—Tractor Pulls
Classes: 2750; 3250; 3750; 4000; 4250;
4500; 5000; 5500; 6000
9 pm—FIREWORKS

Sunday, Sept 1

6:30 am—Breakfast
8:30 am—Church Services (main building)
11 am—Parade of Equipment
12:30 pm—Tractor Games
1:30 pm—Tractor Pulls
Classes: 6500; 7000; 7500; 8000; 8500; 9000; 10000;
11000; 12000; 13000; 14000

FLEA MARKET
held Fri, Sat & Sun!

HELD AT:
Montour Delong Fairgrounds
Washingtonville, PA
Montour County
exit 215 off I-80, go East on Rt 254
or exit 224 off I-80 then go West
on Rt 54 & then left on Rt 254

FIREWORKS!
held Sat 9pm

MAFMCA hosts the
Antique Truck Show of
America—Short Way Chapter!

Show Schedule subject to Change
MAFMCA is not responsible for accidents or injuries

General Info - *Pres. Ken Cotner Jr*---------------------570-437-2264 -*email* cotnerkc@verizon.net
Flea Market - *April & Clark Shuman* ----------- 570-847-4850 or 570-274-0403 -*email* amsbubba@yahoo.com
Tractor Pulls - *Gus Jones* ---------------------- 570-412-5195 -*email* jonesweldingandrepair@gmail.com
Truck Chapter - *Pam Karnes* --570-458-6228
Website - *Jason Bird* ---*email* info@mafmca.org

2020 Show Feature:
Silver King
Sept 4, 5 & 6, 2020

42nd Annual
McCRACKEN COUNTY FFA ALUMNI
ANTIQUE GAS ENGINE
& TRACTOR SHOW

IN COOPERATION WITH:
McCracken Co. Farm
Bureau Federation &
Purchase Area Antique
Tractor Association

SEPTEMBER 19-21, 2019
CARSON PARK FAIR GROUNDS • PADUCAH, KY
McCRACKEN COUNTY FARM BUREAU

6th Annual **FFA FALL ON THE FARM**

FREE to the Public with Paid Admission to the Show
(Farm Animals. Agriculture Exhibitors. Agriculture Games)

BRiNG THE KiDS! (Daily)
and Make a Day of Agriculture History and Education

GRAND STAND ATTRACTIONS

THURSDAY, SEPT. 19 • Gates Open • 8:00 am DAILY

FRIDAY, SEPT. 20
5:00 pm – Sanctioned Antique Tractor Pull #1

SATURDAY, SEPT. 21
9:00 am - Sanctioned Antique Tractor Pull #2
12 noon PARADE (starts as soon as weather permits)
1:30 pm KIDDIE TRACTOR PULL- Grandstand
(Children weighing 1 lb. to 70 lbs.)
2:00 pm GARDEN TRACTOR PULL - Grandstand

FOOD SERVICE
Starts at 6:30am
BREAKFAST
Biscuits, Gravy,
Sausage & Eggs
LUNCH & DINNER
BBQ Pork Plates
Brisket & Butt
Fries, BBQ Frito Pie,
Hamburgers,
Hotdogs, Catfish,
BBQ Bologna

GENERAL ADMISSION $5.00
(3 day access pass $10)

Children Under 12 FREE When Accompanied By An Adult

ARTS & CRAFTS/ FLEA MARKET:
$30 Fee for Thurs., Fri. & Sat.
WED. MORNING 10am-Set-Up
SPACES 18' x 20'
NO ALCOHOL • NO PORNOGRAPHY

FLEA MARKET
Jeff Lambert, SUPERINTENDANT
270-519-8572
jeff.lambert.vendor@gmail.com

ANTIQUE GAS ENGINES
Rob Gill, SUPERINTENDANT
270-559-1203
robgill2008@aol.com

ANTIQUE TRACTORS
Danny Thompson, SUPERINTENDANT
270-559-1848
doallexcavating@gmail.com

ANTIQUE TRACTOR PULLS
Kale Manke, SUPERINTENDANT
618-830-4992

MICHAEL WOOD
SHOW CHAIRMAN
270-832-1167
Email:
michael.wood@mccracken.kyschools.us

PULLING ON THE DIRT IN 2019

THE 27TH ANNUAL RUMELY PRODUCTS COLLECTORS EXPO

Hosted by the
**White Pine Logging & Threshing Show
as part of their 41st Annual Show in
McGrath, Minnesota on Labor Day Weekend**

AUGUST 31- SEPTEMBER 2, 2019

DIRECTIONS: The showgrounds are 85 miles north of Minneapolis/St. Paul. Take I-35 Exit #195 Finlayson/Askov to State Highway 18, then go 20 miles west to Aitkin County Rd 61 North for 1.5 miles

**Daily Admission $12.00, children under 12 free.
Weekend Pass: $20.00
Gates open 7:00 am till Midnight**

ACTIVITIES:

Daily Parade at 1 pm
Grain Threshing and Clover Hulling,
Corn Shredding and Shelling,
Water Wheel-Powered Feed Mill
Working Blacksmith Shop, Barrel Making Shop,
Print Shop, Shingle Mill, Sawmill and Lathe Mill
250 hp Nordberg Steam Engine
5 Large Operating Fairbanks Morse Diesel Engines
150 hp Bessemer Natural Gas Engine
60 hp Patton Hit-N-Miss Engine

Barn Dances: Saturday night 8 pm to Midnight
Sunday night 7 pm -11 pm
Pancake Breakfast 7-9 am • Dinners served daily

**CONTACTS: White Pine Show: John Langenbach at
(651)433-5067 • www.whitepineshow.webs.com
Rumely Products Collectors: Keith R. Kuhlengel at
(717)917-8659 • www.rumelycollectors.com**

The International J.I. Case Heritage Foundation
33rd Annual Exposition

Aug. 30 - Sept. 2, 2019
HOST
WESTERN MINNESOTA STEAM THRESHERS
ROLLAG, MINNESOTA

Local Contacts: Eric Nelson
(701) 261-5171

JI Case Heritage Foundation contacts:

Jim Voyles
(417) 683-1470
www.caseheritage.org

Mark Corson
caseheritage@aol.com

The International J.I. Case Heritage Foundation cordially invites anyone interested in J.I. Case equipment, toys, cars and history to join one of North America's finest heritage organizations and receive the quarterly magazine, *The Heritage Eagle*.

SEND:　U.S.A. - $25.00
Canada - $30.00 (US Funds)
Overseas - $40.00 (US Funds)

TO:　The International J.I. Case
Heritage Foundation
P.O. BOX 801156
Racine, WI 53408-1156

www.CaseHeritage.org

J.I. CASE
THRESHING MACHINE CO.
RACINE WIS.
U.S.A.

35th Annual Moon Lake Threshermen's Association, Inc.

THRESHING BEE & MINNEAPOLIS MOLINE SUMMER CONVENTION

Sat. & Sun., August 17 & 18, 2019

EXHIBITOR SET-UP - FRIDAY, AUGUST 16

ALL EXHIBITORS WELCOME!! LUNCH AVAILABLE ON GROUNDS

Banquet will be held Saturday, August 17th at Das Lach Haus in Cumberland at 7:00 p.m.
Reserve your tickets now for $20.
For information contact Craig Nelson at 715-822-8329

PANCAKE BREAKFAST 8:00 - 10:30 a.m. SATURDAY & SUNDAY

For lodging information visit:

EXPERIENCE Barron COUNTY

VisitBarronCounty.com

CAMPING NEARBY NO CARRY-ONS

FLEA MARKET
Bring Your Own Table
$30.00 for weekend. Includes one button
For information contact Ericka
MLTAFleaMarket@yahoo.com
Shaded Exhibit Area

Check out MoonLakeShow.org for any updates and applications

TRAIN RIDES FOR KIDS

Face Painting
Sawdust Pile - Treasure Hunt
SENIOR CITIZEN SUNDAY
FREE Admission to 65 & older
if accompanied by grandchild

GRILLED CHICKEN DINNER
Sunday beginning at 11:00 a.m.

GATES OPEN 8:00 - 5:00
Steam Threshing
Stone Flour Mill
Steam Powered Saw Mill
Steam Powered Rock Crushing
Rope Making

DEMONSTRATIONS:
Rug Loom • Blacksmith • Hay Loader • Antique Baler • Silo Filler • Corn Sheller • Feed Grinding • Shingle Mill • Snowfence Making Machine • Door Mat Making • Antique Combine • Lumber Planing • Corn Shredder • Lath Mill • Clover Huller • Antique Sewing Machines • Spinning Wheel

DISPLAYS:
Antique Tractors • Antique Cars & Trucks • Antique Snowmobiles • Gas Engines • Large Miniature Farm Display • Fire Trucks • Collector Shingles • Clayton Fire Dept. Smokehouse • Antique Lamp & Lantern Collection

Company C 8th Wisconsin
Volunteers Display - Civil War Camp

FOR MORE INFORMATION CALL (715) 948-2533 OR (715) 781-5566
LOCATION: George Sollman's - Five miles south of Turtle Lake, Wisconsin on Hwy. K
862 2-3/8 St. Clayton, WI 54004 • Lat. 45° 19' 56" N Long. 92° 06' 27" W
ADMISSION - $5.00 per day - includes Button, Under 12 Free • FREE PARKING

Golf Carts, ATVs, etc. must have MLTA as an additional insured and state handicap tag
Not Responsible for Accidents. – SERVICE DOGS ONLY – ALL BOILERS MUST BE STATE INSPECTED

FREE SHUTTLE SERVICE
From Turtle Lake to the Show Grounds.
Every Hour - Both Days
Parking at St. Croix Casino Annex Parking Lot behind Austad's Super Valu

MINNEAPOLIS-MOLINE COLLECTORS

DOUBLE D LIVING HISTORY FARM

located on the beautiful 650 acre

TOPLANDS FARM

(home of Tops quality pasture raised meats and fresh eggs)

102 Painter Hill Road, Roxbury, CT 06783

OPEN SEASONALLY APRIL 1 - OCTOBER 31

CONTACT: NIKKI, 860-354-0649

$5 PER CAR

6TH ANNUAL

SPRING TRACTOR SHOW AND FARM OPEN HOUSE

SUNDAY, JUNE 2, 2019 • 11 AM-4 PM

FEATURING:

- Over 200 restored tractors from 1899-1954
- Tractor Parade
- Gas Engines and Implements
- Working Displays
- Farm Animals, Draft Horses
- Country Life Artifacts
- Activities for Kids

- Wagon Rides
- Food and Food Vendors featuring Toplands Farm Meats
- Exhibitors of old tractors, cars, engines and trucks welcome
- Sawmill
- Rock Crusher
- Baker Fan

Watch our website: toplandsfarm.com for updates and info
Like us on Facebook: Toplands Farm LLC

Memorial Day Weekend
Ixonia Vintage Tractor Expo

New Location

New Location

Ashippun Fireman's Park
Hwy O Ashippun, WI 53036

Friday, Saturday & Sunday May 24 - 26, 2019
Accepting Consignments for Sunday's Auction

J.I. Case
Collectors'
Association
National Spring
Convention

FUN FOR ALL!

 Tractor Drives * Flea Market * Raffle Tractor * Consignment Auction
Silent Auction * Great Food * Crafts, Demonstrations * Kids Events
Live Music All Week-end * Model Train Displays * Sunday Church

For Show info, Auction Consignments
                    & Flea Market Call : Curt Pernat 920 988-0857
Tractors & Tractor Drives   Call : Tom Triplett 920 925-3414
        Join us on Facebook: Ixonia Vintage Tractor Expo

No admission charge

TEXAS EARLY DAY **TRACTOR and ENGINE ASSOC.** TEMPLE, TEXAS ESTABLISHED 1971

• 2019 •
Featured Tractor
ALLIS-CHALMERS
Featured Engine
WITTE ENGINE

2019
TEMPLE **48TH** TEXAS
ANNUAL STATE

Tractor, Truck and Engine Show

SATURDAY
OCT. 5TH
twenty nineteen

9:00 IN THE MORNING | COME *early* STAY *late*

1717 EBERHARDT ROAD | TEMPLE, TEXAS

It's a day packed full of fun for the whole family!

TRACTOR PULL&PARADE   FLEA MARKET   ARTS&CRAFTS

HOMEMADE ICE CREAM   FOOD TRUCKS   CORN SHELLING

WHEAT THRESHING   BLACKSMITHING   BIG ENGINE CRANK

 ★**FREE**★ KIDS 12 & UNDER

 $**10** ADMISSION

 Flea Market SPACES AVAILABLE

 EXHIBITORS *free* ADMISSION

 RV SPACES WATER+ELECTRICITY **AVAILABLE**

 DRYCAMPING *free*

☞ **TEXASEDTEA.ORG** ☜

August 22-25, 2019

SANCTIONED TRACTOR PULLS THURSDAY, FRIDAY & SATURDAY

LARGEST VINTAGE WORKING FARM SHOW
PARADES DAILY   ALL BRANDS WELCOME
FIELD DEMONSTRATIONS DAILY

INFO 217-595-5000

halfcenturyofprogress.com

HISTORIC
FARM DAYS
PENFIELD, ILLINOIS
JULY 11-14, 2019
Featuring
International Harvester

INFO 217-595-5000
historicfarmdays.com

BLUE MOUNTAIN ANTIQUE GAS & STEAM ENGINE ASSOCIATION INC.

JACKTOWN GROVE
1229 Richmond Rd – Bangor, Pa. 18013
www.jacktown.org

33rd ANNUAL SWAP MEET/FLEA MARKET   **MAY 18-19, 2019**

GAS, STEAM, TRACTOR, CAR & RELATED ITEMS
BUY, SELL, SWAP
Saturday – Entertainment from 1-4 p.m.
Sunday – Entertainment from 1-4 p.m.

48th ANTIQUE GAS ENGINE & TRACTOR SHOW   **JULY 19-21, 2019**

GAS • STEAM • TRACTORS • MODELS • SHINGLE MILL SAWMILL • CRAFTS • FLEA MARKET • TRAIN RIDES

Friday Night – Antique Tractor Pull • Entertainment 6-9 p.m.
Saturday – Antique Tractor Pull • Entertainment from 12-3 p.m.
Saturday Night – Entertainment from 6-9 p.m.
Sunday – Antique Car Show • Kids Pedal Tractor Pull
Garden Tractor Pull 10 a.m.
Entertainment 1-4 p.m.
Tractor Parade

40th ANNUAL FALL HARVEST & SAWMILL SHOW   **OCT. 19-20, 2019**

AMERICAN SAWMILL • AMERICAN WOOD SPLITTER • CASE STEAM ENGINE, SHINGLE MILL IN OPERATION • DRAGSAW, CORD WOOD SAWING • 25 HP MESSINGER & NAGLE STATIONARY STEAM ENGINES • TRACTORS • GAS ENGINES AND FEED GRINDERS

Saturday - Antique Tractor Pull • Entertainment from 1-4 p.m.
Sunday - Entertainment from 1-4 p.m.
Garden Tractor Pull Sunday 10 a.m.
Kids Pedal Tractor Pull
Fall foods such as apple butter, apple dumplings, cider and homemade soups.

AT ALL EVENTS
Blue Mountain Railway – 110 hp watts – Campbell steam engine
Good food served on grounds • Friendly family atmosphere
Jacktown ice cream • Primitive camping
Train rides • Free parking • Free admission

All Shows Rain or Shine
FOR MORE INFORMATION CALL:
Robert Rowe .....(570) 897-6893 • Grove Rental, Tom .....(610) 588-7360
For flea market or membership information, Tom....(610) 588-7360 or tbbuist@frontiernet.net
SHOWTIME: (610) 588-6900
Hope to see you at "The Friendly Show in the Grove!!"
Additional information on show, go to www.jacktown.org

2020 JANUARY GET-TOGETHER - JANUARY 18, 2020

BOS BROTHERS
OLD FASHIONED
THRESHING BEE

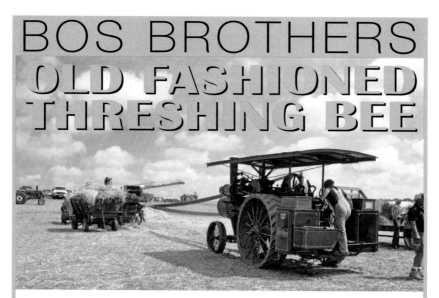

SHOW DATES:
JULY 26-28, 2019
8-5 FRI., SAT. & 8-3 SUN.

William Rutherford Farm,
29265 Co. Hwy. 1, Erie, IL

DEMONSTRATIONS INCLUDE: harvesting standing wheat to baking bread from milled grain, plowing, blacksmithing, rock crushing, shingle making and more.

Sunday morning church service.

Parking and admission are free.

Food available on the grounds.

Displays of tractors and equipment are welcome.

Contact us to include a working display or to participate in field demonstrations.

Kevin Bos...**309-945-8117**

Chuck Bos...**309-781-6394**

"FALL HARVEST DAYS" RETURNS IN 2020

49TH ANNUAL
CENTRAL KENTUCKY ANTIQUE MACHINERY ASSOCIATION
PARIS, KENTUCKY

est.1970 Central Kentucky Antique Machinery Association

JULY 26-27, 2019
FEATURING
ALLIS-CHALMERS TRACTORS

Longest Running Show in the State of Kentucky
Partnered with:
Bluegrass Chapter of the American Truck Historical Society

EVENTS
Events Subject to Change

- Farm & Garden Tractors
- Antique Farm & Semi Truck
- Free Admission
- Tractor Parade
- Free Parking
- Free Camping (electric first come, first serve)
- Kids Activities
- No Vendor Fees

- Flywheel Engines
- Friday Night Live Band
- Free Entertainment
- Equipment Demonstrations
- Craft Vendors
- Silent Auction
- Great Food Vendors
- Farm Machinery

PRESIDENT & VENDOR CONTACT:	TRACTOR CONTACT:	FLYWHEEL ENGINES:
Steve Persinger	Allen Bennett	Aaron Biddle
(859) 588-2000	(859) 954-3222	(859) 707-9877

 Like & Follow us on Facebook @CentralKentuckyAntiqueMachineryAssociation

FREE Admission/Parking

TIOGA COUNTY EARLY DAYS

54th Annual

FALL FESTIVAL

Tioga County Fairgrounds
Whitneyville, PA

facebook

October 11-13, 2019

Featured Tractor – Orphans and Odd Motorized Farm Equipment
Friday's Opening Ceremony will Honor FHA, FFA and 4H Groups
Gas Engines • Model Engines • Steam Engines • Tractor Pulls • Garden Tractor Pulls
Hit and Miss Engines • 4th US Light Artillery • Craft & Flea Market • Quilting
Live Music • Cider Mill • Shingle Mill • Homemade Food • Apple Dumplings
Largest Hammer Collection in the area • Saw Mill (one of the oldest operating on East Coast)
Weekend Camping: $25/with electric or $10/no electric

Contacts - Gary Comfort: 607-259-6234, Tom Cuneo: 570-835-5634
Tractor Pulls - Jay Shabloski: 570-439-2555
Craft & Flea Market - Barb Johnson: 607-535-2261

Limited vendors and exhibitors on Sunday

The **Tioga County Historical Society Farm, Mine and Lumber Museum**
is located just above the steam run sawmill. There are hundreds of early farm, mine,
lumber and household items on display. Among the artifacts is a dog powered child's hay
wagon, a fanning mill made in Wellsboro, spinning wheels and a wooden washing machine!

tiogachs.weebly.com • tiogachs@gmail.com • 📘 **@Tioga1904**

Visit POTTER-TIOGA *Pennsylvania*

For Lodging and Area Information:
VisitPotterTioga.com
1-888-846-4228

Field Day of the Past

Sept. 20, 21, 22, 2019

**Heritage Crafts, Antique Vehicles, Machinery, Tractors and
Construction Equipment, Tractor Pulls, Music, Kids' Events,
4-H Livestock Shows, Equestrian Events, Historic Buildings, Va. High
School Rodeo, Historic Re-enactments, Arts & Crafts, Church Services
on Sunday & Much More! Food Available; Free Parking**
*Admission: $10 Friday & Sunday; $15 Saturday; Seniors: $8;
Children under 13: Free*
**Displays & Exhibits: Fri, Sat. 8-6; Sun. 8-5; Truck Pulls Fri. & Sat.
14 miles west of Richmond, VA, off I-64, Exit #173
For Information: (804) 741-8468
fielddayofthepast@gmail.com; fielddayofthepast.net**
Tickets available online

Wallow in the Fun!

ROUGH & TUMBLE ENGINEERS
71st Annual

Threshermen's Reunion
August 14 - 17, 2019

Lots of Things To See & Do For All Ages!

Special Feature
MINNEAPOLIS MOLINE & WATER PUMPING EQUIPMENT

THE MOST COMPLETE STEAM & GAS SHOW IN THE EAST
BUS GROUPS WELCOME • RAIN or SHINE
Enjoy the Rough & Tumble Experience!

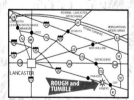

4997 Lincoln Hwy. East
P.O. Box 9
Kinzers, PA 17535

No ATM on site. Any video taken at R&T must have Board approval before being offered for resale. NO bikes of any kind, firearms or alcoholic beverages are permitted on grounds.

2019 CALENDAR

February 9 .... Mid-Winter Get Together
April 27 .... Antique Tractor Pull
May 10-11 .... Spring Steam-Up
June 21-22 .... IHC Spring Show and R&T Tractor Pull
July 26-27 .... John Deere Days
August 14-17 .... 71st Annual Threshermen's Reunion
October 11-12 .... "A Time of Harvest"

20th Annual
Empire Expo

1946   1950

Held by The Empire
Tractor Owners Club
in conjunction with the
71st Annual
Threshermen's Reunion
August 14 - 17, 2019

National Pike Steam, Gas & Horse Association

39th Annual Show
Annual Show August 9, 10 & 11 2019

August 2019 Feature: **Jeep**

"The Sun Never Sets on The Mighty Jeep"

Spring Show May 18-19 2019

Largest Digging Show in the USA!
Fun for the Whole Family!

- Antique Tractors
- Antique Gas Engines
- Threshing & Baling
- Rope Making
- Shingle Mill
- Sawmill
- Crafts
- Flea Market
- Antique Construction Equipment
- Antique Trucks and Cars
- 1914 Porter 060 Steam Locomotive
- Working Blacksmith Shop
- Oil Well Derrick
- Off-road Parking & Camping Area
- Great Food Booths
- Live Daily Entertainment
- Daily Parades
- Something for Everyone

Admission:
Spring Show - FREE
August Show: $5, under 12 FREE
Friday $3 Seniors

Information:
(724) 785-6855

Email:
info@nationalpike.com

Like us on Facebook

**Fairgrounds located just off Route 40
4 miles west of Brownsville, PA at 222 Spring Road**

www.nationalpike.com

Ford Fordson
COLLECTORS ASSOCIATION, INC.

28TH ANNUAL F/FCA SHOW & MEETING

Will be hosted by

ALUM BANK COMMUNITY FIRE CO. ANTIQUE CLASSIC WEEKEND ALUM BANK, PA

JULY 11-14, 2019

FOR SHOW INFORMATION CONTACT:

Jim Claycum......................814-276-3533

Ted Foster 269-470-3888

tfoster@triton.net

WEBSITES: www.alumbankvfc.org
www.ford-fordson.org

OLD THRESHERS REUNION

AUG. 29 - SEPT. 2, 2019
MOUNT PLEASANT, IOWA

HARRISON STEAM ENGINE

JOHN DEERE GARDEN TRACTORS

OVER 2,000 EXHIBIT & ATTRACTIONS!

MACK AND FORD TRUCKS & CARS

ON-SITE CAMPING AVAILABLE

JOHN DEERE GAS ENGINES

JOHN DEERE TRACTORS

OLDTHRESHERS.COM

EMAIL: INFO@OLDTHRESHERS.ORG * 319-385-8937

GREATER IOWA SWAP MEET & FLEA MARKET
MAY 24 & 25, 2019
MCMILLAN PARK, MOUNT PLEASANT, IOWA

JOIN US FOR OUR HUGE 25th ANNIVERSARY SHOW

2019

THE GREAT

Franklin County

Antique Machinery
Show

11225 **COUNTY PARK RD.**

BROOKVILLE, INDIANA

SEPT. 26-27-28-29

FEATURING

Allis-Chalmers Tractors and

Equipment Plus Stover Engines

**Brian Baxter From Classic Tractor
Fever Will Be Filming Our 25th
Anniversary Show**

Hosting

More Information
www.facebook.com/fcamc
www.fcamc.org

CAMPING

Greg Pflum	765-265-1404
Mark Lang	513-502-2750

Featured Equipment

Information

Chuck Van Meter   765-265-2883
Keith Van Meter   765-265-3568
Susan Van Meter   765-265-2882

Club President	765-265-6541
Susan Van Meter	765-265-2882
FLEA MARKET	765-265-6245

$5.00 Gate Fee

HUGE 2019 SWAP MEET

11225 COUNTY PARK RD. BROOKVILLE, INDIANA

SATURDAY APRIL 6, 2019 7:00am-3:00pm

$5.00 Per Person

Franklin County Convention, Recreation
& Visitors Commission
www.franklincountyin.com

Greensburg Power of the Past

Greensburg, Indiana
Decatur Co Fairgrounds
(812) 662-4723 or (812) 593-8977

30th Annual Reunion
August 15-18, 2019

*"BRINGING PEOPLE OF THE PRESENT,
A GLIMPSE OF THE PAST"*

Featured Tractors: Ford, Orphans,& Oddballs
Featured Steam Engine: T.B.D.
Featured Hit-Miss Engine: Bessemer
Featured Garden Tractor: Ford

Tractor Games	Threshing	Spark Show
Old-Time Music	Parade	Fiddle Contest
Farm Machinery	Children's Games	Woodcarving
Wagon Train	Horse Pull	Antique Tractor Pull
Consignment Auction	Steam Engines	Antique Gas Engines
Arts & Crafts	Flea Markets	Horse-Drawn Machinery
Field Demonstrations	Bingo	Toy Show (Sat. & Sun.)

Contacts:

President, Clark Martin: (812) 662-4723   V.P. Aaron Morgan: (812) 614-1566
Decatur Co Tourism: (812) 222-8733
Crafts & Flea Market: Rick & Kim Carpenter (812) 593-2917
Camping: Clark Martin (812) 662-4723
Auction: Tom Cherry (812) 593-8977
Toy Show: Frank Narwold (812) 614-5300
Tractor Pull: Darren Scutter: (812) 593-0434
Horse Pull: Cory Crafton (812) 569-7128
Lodging:
Baymont Inn, Greensburg, IN (812) 663-6055
Hampton Inn, Greensburg, IN (812) 663-5000
Holiday Inn Express, Greensburg, IN (812) 663-5500
Nana's B&B, Greensburg, IN (812) 663-6607
Quality Inn, Greensburg, IN (812) 663-9998

When making hotel reservations, mention the Greensburg Power of the Past.

Admission - $5 per person • Children under 12 free
Golf Carts-$10.00 w/Proof of Insurance
greensburgpowerofthepast.com

Coming In 2019! The 26th Annual Appalachian Antique Farm Show & Farmer's Reunion!

Tri-State Antique Power Association

Presents

BATTLE OF THE BRANDS

Ford

Cub Cadet

John Deere

Attention All Tractor, Engine & Lawn & Garden Tractor
Exhibitors! Bring Your Equipment To See Which Brand Will Win?
Be Sure To Register So Your Brand Will Be Counted!

April 25-28, 2019

Appalachian Fairgrounds
100 Lakeview Street Gray, TN 37615
www.tsapa.com
Admission: $5.00
Senior Admission on Thursday: $4.00
Children 12 & Under FREE
Gates Open:
Thursday thru Saturday 8 AM till dark
Sunday 8 AM-2 PM

International

Oliver

Silver King

Allis Chalmers

Fairbanks Morse

Economy

Minneapolis Moline

Large Craft & Antique Flea Market
Parts Dealers-Special Area For Lawn &
Garden Tractors-Parade of Power-
Food Vendors-Demonstrations-Pedal
Tractor Race & Pull-Much More!

Hercules

Cockshutt

Massey Ferguson

Corporate Sponsor

FOOD CITY

Show Information:
Dave Gross: 423-341-7241
Paul Helvey: 423-612-1332
**Vendor & Public
Relations:**
Melissa Milner: 423-794-6672
Food Vendors:
Kyle Shell
Camping:
Paul Helvey

THE AMERICAN THRESHERMAN ASSOCIATION, INC.

60th Annual Steam, Gas, & Threshing Show

★ August 14-18, 2019 ★ Wednesday Evening through Sunday

Home Of The American Thresherman Association

PINCKNEYVILLE, ILLINOIS

State Hwy. 154, 127 & 13 ~ Pinckneyville • GPS Address: 711 Fairground Road
Exit 77 On I-57 To 154 To Pinckneyville • Exit 50 On I-64, Then 127 South To Pinckneyville

Featuring

Oliver,
Hart-Parr
ALL Crawler
Tractors

Hartland Oliver Collectors
Heartland Earth Movers
(CAT-Collectors)
Heartland Ropemakers Guild

Gas Engine Hill
Vertical
Hit & Miss
Engines

Wednesday, Aug. 14 Tractor Parade Through Town at 5:00pm | Farm Horse Pull and Competition at 7pm

Daily Activities

Blacksmithing
Steam Engines
Wheat Threshing
Veneer Mill ~ Saw Mill
Grist Mill ~ Dynamometer

Gas Engines & Tractors
Baker Fans ~ Corn Shelling
Tractor Activities
Plowing W/Steam Engines,
Tractors & Horses

Rope Making
Broom Corn Threshing
& Broom Making
Feature Tractor Plowing
Events

Sunday, Aug. 18

Antique Auto Show & Swap Meet

Sponsored by:
The Egyptian Antique Auto Club
Featured Car: Hudson-Essex Terraplane
(Cars on display to be 50 years and older)

Worship And Memorial Service at 8am

Antique Tractor Pulls at 10am

3 Big Nights of Tractor Pulls

Thursday, Aug. 15 - Illinois Hot Farm Stock & ITPA
Friday, Aug. 16 - ITPA
Saturday, Aug. 17 - ITPA
at 7:00pm
50/50 Drawing Nightly

Vintage Lawn/ Garden Tractors

Steam Train Rides
American & Southern Illinois Railroad

KIDS' PEDAL TRACTOR PULL
TRACTOR PROVIDED
Saturday, Aug.17
10am

LARGE FLEA MARKET

GENERAL INFO
(618) 318-0745
Phone For Show Days Only
(618) 357-6643
Email: americanthresherman@gmail.com

GROUNDS ADMISSION $7
Children Under 12 Free
Additional Charge for Evening Shows
Children 6 & Under Are Free

Horse Farming Activities
(618) 318-5543

Flea Market Info
(618) 830-0878
lcbabysis2@gmail.com

Gas Engine Info
(217) 821-2665

ITPA Tractor Pull Info
Wayne (618) 967-6448
Richard (618) 927-3597

IL Hot Farm Stock Puller Info
Dwayne (618) 559-8057

Reserve Camper Hook-Ups
(217) 273-9793

Concessions
(573) 768-9300
mbrickhaus@yahoo.com

Antique Tractor Pull Info
Danny (618) 967-6718

Antique Auto/Car Show Info
Ron/Clara (618) 687-2235

Fall Show Dates:
★ October 18 - 20, 2019 ★

ILLINOSouth TOURISM

A GOOD CLEAN INTERESTING SHOW THE WHOLE FAMILY WILL ENJOY

ILLINOIS ARE YOU UP FOR AMAZING?

★ www.americanthresherman.com ★

46TH ANNUAL REUNION & SHOW

Tuckahoe Steam & Gas Assn. Inc.

JULY 11-14, 2019

Show grounds located 5 miles north of Easton, Md., on U.S. Route 50.

Gates will open at 12 p.m. on Thursday with activities as listed.

Horse Pull Competition – Friday at 7:30 p.m.
Country Music Entertainment – Saturday Evening
Large Crafts Pavilion & Home Arts Building
Large Outdoor Flea Market

FEATURING: ORCHARD & HI-CROP TRACTORS, WHEEL HORSE GARDEN TRACTORS, DOMESTIC GAS ENGINES

Old steam traction engines, antique tractors and gas engines of all sizes, antique cars and trucks, wheat threshing demonstrations, two operating sawmills, lumber planing, rock crushing, shingle sawing, plowing with horses, steam engines and antique tractors. Large crafts pavilion, indoor home arts demonstrations including spinning, weaving, soap making and more. Colonial crafts, broom making, basket weaving, blacksmith shop and more. Large stationary steam engines in operation plus many working models. If you have models, bring them along. Hot air pumping engines, large 150 HP Corliss engine. Large building full of stationary gas and diesel engines of all sizes. Acres of exhibitors with all sizes of gas engines operating antique equipment of all kinds. A 3-foot gauge passenger train with nearly 1 mile of track and a smaller train for the younger kids. Indoor Rural Life Museum full of displays including turn-of-the-century country store and kitchen, plus an array of other items found on farms and in rural towns.

**Parade of Equipment Daily • Horse-Drawn Equipment Building
Large Machine Shop Museum with Line Shaft Driven Machine Tools
Auction Sale Saturday at 10 a.m.
Antique Tractor Pull Sunday at 12 p.m.
Church Services Sunday at 9 a.m. on the Grounds**

Plenty of good Maryland Eastern Shore Cooking. Breakfast Friday - Sunday from 7 - 10 a.m. Full menu plus chicken dinners starting at 10:30 a.m. Sub shop, ice cream, popcorn, peanuts, snow cones and funnel cakes. Plenty of shade and clean, modern restrooms.

Admission: $6 donation for adults (under 12 free)
No donation necessary for exhibitors and colonial crafts.

FOR MORE INFORMATION CALL: (410) 822-9868
Or write: P.O. Box 636, Easton, MD 21601
Visit our website: www.tuckahoesteam.org
An All-Volunteer, Non-Profit Organization

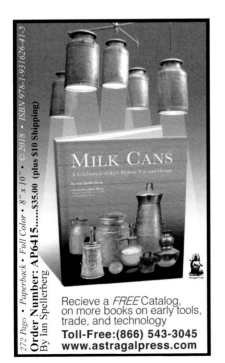

FARM COLLECTOR
SHOW DIRECTORY
2019

SHOW
LISTINGS

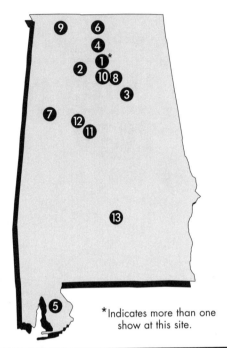

*Indicates more than one
show at this site.

ALABAMA

① Southland Flywheelers Spring Show and Swap Meet
March 16   Hartselle
1715 Hwy 36 E., I-65 east 3-1/2 miles, showgrounds on the right, just past Sparkman Elementary School.
Contact: Larry Lemmond, 1358 Community Ln., Hartselle, AL 35640; 256-773-2692;
email: larrylemmond@aol.com
www.southlandflywheelers.org

② April Fest - Sponsored by Lawrence County Tractor Club
April 13   Moulton
Lions Club Fairgrounds, 455 School St.
Contact: Dwight Bowling, 1998 CR 327, Danville, AL 35619;
256-353-5167; 256-565-0129;
email: dbowling.2@charter.net
Facebook: Lawrence County Tractor Club

③ Snead Case IH Show
April 20   Snead
Contact: Joe Criswell, 205-466-3500

④ 41st Annual Alabama Jubilee
May 25   Decatur
Point Mallard Park.
Contact: Larry Lemmond, 1358 Community Ln., Hartselle, AL 35640; 256-773-2692;
email: larrylemmond@aol.com
www.southlandflywheelers.org

⑤ SAATEC Plow Days
May 31-June 1   Summerdale
George Underwood Farm.
Contact: Lloyd Dillon, 251-978-3152;
email: dillon471@gmail.com
www.saatec.org

⑥ Piney Chapel American Farm Heritage Days
Aug. 2-3   Athens
2 miles north of Athens, 20147 Elkton Rd.
Contact: Steve Garner, 28208 Mitchell Loop, Ardmore, AL 35739;
334-750-2545;
email: rgarner557@aol.com

1 **Hartselle Depot Days**
Sept. 20-21   Hartselle
Downtown, 110 Railroad St.
Contact: Andrea Owensby,
256-773-4370

7 **Winfield Mule Day**
Sept. 27-28   Winfield
Contact: Debbie Killingsworth,
205-487-4265;
www.winfieldcity.org

8 **Eva Frontier Days**
Sept. 28   Eva
I-65 South, take exit 322. Take
Hwy 55 east for 10 miles to Eva 4-way,
turn right at 4-way and showgrounds
are on the left.
Contact: Jerriel Patton, 245-636-0864

9 **October Fest**
Oct. 5-6   Saint Florian
St. Florian City Park, 1 mile north of
Florence on County Road 47.
Contact: Malcolm Wilkes, 1567
CR 124, Florence, AL 35633;
256-766-7698;
email:
pawpawmawmaw2015@gmail.com

10 **Falkville Festival**
Oct. 12   Falkville
Contact: Tom Summerford,
256-227-2911

11 **Jean's on the River
Antique Tractor Show**
Oct. 12   Cordova
Feature: International Harvester
Tractors.
From Hwy 78, take River Road south.
Contact: Becky Johnson, PO Box 214,
Sumiton, AL 35148;
205-483-0024;
email: shermanihc@yahoo.com

12 **Jasper Heritage Festival**
Oct. 19   Jasper
Feature: Farmall Tractors.
Downtown on the Square.
Contact: Sherman Roberts,
10766 Hwy 78, Jasper, AL 35501;
205-275-4895;
email: shermanihc@yahoo.com

13 **Old Tyme Farm Days**
Oct. 26   Greenville
2828 Sandcutt Rd.
Contact: Carey Thompson,
334-382-2295; 334-406-0427;
www.oldtimefarmdays.com

1 **Southland Flywheelers Fall Festival
and Harvest Exhibits**
Oct. 26   Hartselle
Feature: All IH Products.
1715 Hwy 36 E., I-65 exit 328, east
3-1/2 miles, showgrounds on right.
Contact: Larry Lemmond, 1358
Community Ln., Hartselle, AL 35640;
256-773-2692;
email: larrylemmond@aol.com
www.southlandflywheelers.org

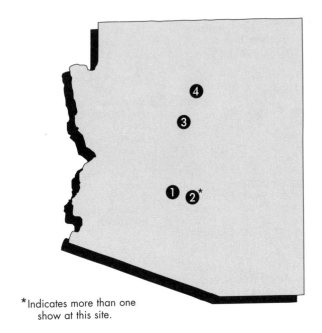

*Indicates more than one
show at this site.

ARIZONA

① Sahuaro Ranch Park Winter Show
Feb. 9-10   Glendale
9802 N. 59th Ave., 1/2 mile between
Olivia and Peoria avenues on 59th
Avenue.
Contact: Tom Trainor, 623-435-3955

**② 2019 Winter Meeting -
Apache Junction**
March 9-10   Apache Junction
Feature: BF Avery.
Contact: Gary Duff, 2030 Wood Rd.,
Marlette, MI 48453; 989-635-2619;
810-357-2673;
email: redtractorman@yahoo.com
www.aedgeta.org

② Arizona Junction Spring Show
March 9-10   Apache Junction
Apache Junction Rodeo Park,
1590 E. Lost Dutchman Blvd.,
intersection of Tomahawk and Lost
Dutchman Boulevard.
Contact: Tim Brain, 623-435-3955

**② Vintage Garden Tractor Club of
America Southwest Regional Show**
March 9-10   Apache Junction
Apache Junction Rodeo Grounds,
1590 E. Lost Dutchman Blvd.
Contact: Kathleen Lawson, Mansfield,
OH 44906; 623-435-3955;
email: dtallman@accnorwalk.com

**③ 35th Annual Arizona Flywheelers
Show**
March 15-16   Cottonwood
Verde Valley Fairgrounds, Cherry and
12th streets.
Contact: Gary Covert, 975 E. Bow
Maker, Cottonwood, AZ 86326;
928-301-0649;
email: gcovert3@gmail.com
www.arizonaflywheelers.com

④ Beat the Heat
July 27-28   Flagstaff
8.5 miles north of Flagstaff Mall
on North Hwy 89.
Contact: Walt and Janet Hanf,
928-699-0837;
email: wjmd111343@gmail.com

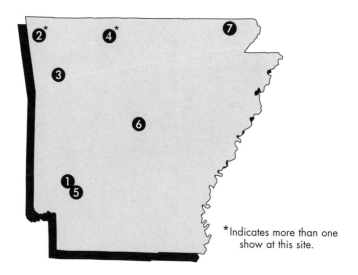

*Indicates more than one show at this site.

ARKANSAS

1 Rusty Wheels Old Engine Club Jonquil Festival
March 16   Old Washington
I-30, exit 30, north 8 miles from Hope.
Contact: Bryan Boyce, 13194 S.W.
296, Texarkana, AR 71854;
903-733-5545;
email: bboyce@swat.coop;
Butch James, 870-640-4337

2 26th Annual Spring Show
April 19-20   Gentry
Features: Moline and Mayrath Garden
Tractors and Waterloo Engines.
From Gentry or Siloam Springs, follow
signs to show grounds at 13344 Taylor
Orchard Rd.
Contact: Johnny Burger,
479-215-6050;
email: jburger370@gmail.com;
Jerry Friend, 1640 E. Stewart,
Fayetteville, AR 727703;
479-283-5287;
email: jerryprice0369@att.net
www.tiredironoftheozarks.org

3 20th Annual Tractor, Implement and Engine Show
May 31-June 1   Ozark
Features: International Harvester
Tractors and Engines.
Turn off Hwy 64 and go to the North
Franklin County Fairgrounds.
Contact: Clyde Traylor, 12111 James
Fork Rd., Hartford, AR 72938;
479-650-0768;
email: tractorhauler47@gmail.com
www.edgeta.org (Branch 90)

4 North Arkansas Rusty Wheels Old Engine Club Spring Show
June 7-8   Harrison
5722 Hwy 65S, 6 miles south
on Hwy 65S.
Contact: Ken Clements, 870-743-2017;
email: alaska8838@gmail.com
www.rustywheels.com

5 **42nd Annual Rusty Wheels Engine and Tractor Show**
Aug. 9-10   Hope
I-30, exit 30, Fair Park.
Contact: Bryan Boyce, 13194 S.W. 296,
Texarkana, AR 71854; 903-733-5545;
email: bboyce@swat.coop;
Butch James, 870-648-4337

2 **27th Annual Fall Show**
Sept. 6-8   Gentry
Features: Moline and Mayrath Garden
Tractors and Waterloo Engines.
From Gentry or Siloam Springs, follow
signs to show grounds at 13344 Taylor
Orchard Rd.
Contact: Johnny Burger,
479-215-6050;
email: jburger370@gmail.com;
Jerry Friend, 1640 E. Stewart,
Fayetteville, AR 72703; 479-283-5287;
email: jerryprice0369@att.net
www.tiredironoftheozarks.org

6 **27th Annual Antique Tractor and Engine Show**
Sept. 7   Scott
Plantation Agriculture Museum State
Park, from Little Rock, I-440, exit 7
(Hwy 165), east on Hwy 165 S.,
5 miles south, right on Hwy 161.
Contact: Betty Coors, PO Box 151,
Scott, AR 72142; 501-961-1409;
email: betty.coors@arkansas.gov
www.arkansasstateparks.com/
plantationagriculturemuseum

4 **North Arkansas Rusty Wheels Old Engine Club Fall Show**
Oct. 11-12   Harrison
5722 Hwy 65 S, 6 miles south
on Hwy 65 S.
Contact: Ken Clements,
870-743-2017;
email: alaska8838@gmail.com
www.rustywheels.com

7 **Corning Harvest Festival**
Oct. 26   Corning
Wynn Park, Hwy 67 W.
Contact: Daniel E. Moore, 701 N.
Missouri Ave., Corning, AR 72422;
870-857-3931;
email:
haroldimplement@centurytel.net

CALIFORNIA

① Table Top Auction
Jan. 26   Vista
2040 N. Santa Fe Ave.
Contact: Megan Tessicini, 2040
N. Santa Fe Ave., Vista, CA 92083;
760-941-1791;
email: agsemoffice@gmail.com
www.agsem.com

② World AG Expo
Feb. 12-14   Tulare
Features: Case and International
Harvester Tractors.
S. Laspina Avenue off Hwy 99.
Contact: Roger Lubiens, 113 Econome
Ct., Folsom, CA 95630;
916-983-6415;
email: r_lubiens@juno.com

① Table Top Auction
Feb. 23   Vista
2040 N. Santa Fe Ave.
Contact: Megan Tessicini, 2040
N. Santa Fe Ave., Vista, CA 92083;
760-941-1791;
email: agsemoffice@gmail.com
www.agsem.com

③ Winter Meeting
Feb. 23   Dos Palos
Feature: International Harvester
Red Tractors.
Bertao Farms, 5781 Mint Rd.
Contact: Roger Lubiens, 113 Econome
Ct., Folsom, CA 95630;
916-983-6415;
email: r_lubiens@juno.com

❶ Table Top Auction
March 23　　　　　Vista
2040 N. Santa Fe Ave.
Contact: Megan Tessicini, 2040
N. Santa Fe Ave., Vista, CA 92083;
760-941-1791;
email: agsemoffice@gmail.com
www.agsem.com

**❷ California Antique
Farm Equipment Show**
April 12-14　　　　　Tulare
Feature: John Deere.
4500 S. Laspina St. From Hwy 99
take Paige Avenue exit, turn right on
Laspina Street and head south to the
parking entrance at gate A.
Contact: Jennifer Fawkes, 4500
S. Laspina St., Tulare, CA 93274;
559-688-1030;
email: waesales@farmshow.org
www.antiquefarmshow.org

❷ California Antique Farm Show
April 12-14　　　　　Tulare
Feature: International Harvester and
FFA Restored Tractors by youth.
S. Laspina Avenue off Hwy 99.
Contact: Roger Lubiens, 113 Econome
Ct., Folsom, CA 95630;
916-983-6415;
email: r_lubiens@juno.com
www.ihcc14.org

**❹ Early Day Gas Engine and Tractor
Association Spring Gas-Up**
April 26-28　　　　　Red Bluff
At the Tehama District Fairgrounds,
650 Antelope Blvd.
Contact: Steve Zane, 530-597-2253;
John Aspesi, 831-234-1279

❺ ATHS Show
April 27　　　　　Plymouth
Feature: International Harvester
Trucks.
Fairgrounds.
Contact: Roger Lubiens, 113 Ecomome
Ct., Folsom, CA 95630; 916-983-6415;
email: r_lubiens@juno.com

❶ Antique Engine & Tractor Show
June 15-16　　　　　Vista
2040 N. Santa Fe Ave.
Contact: Meg Tessicini, 2040
N. Santa Fe Ave., Vista, CA 92083;
760-941-1791;
email: agsemoffice@gmail.com
www.agsem.com

❶ Antique Engine & Tractor Show
June 22-23　　　　　Vista
2040 N. Santa Fe Ave.
Contact: Meg Tessicini, 2040
N. Santa Fe Ave., Vista, CA 92083;
760-941-1791;
email: agsemoffice@gmail.com
www.agsem.com

❶ Outdoor Consignment Auction
July 28　　　　　Vista
2040 N. Santa Fe Ave.
Contact: Megan Tessicini, 2040
N. Santa Fe Ave., Vista, CA 92083;
760-941-1791;
email: agsemoffice@gmail.com
www.agsem.com

**❻ International Harvester Sierra Fall
Rallye**
Oct. 4-6　　　　　Grass Valley
Feature: International Harvester
Products.
Nevada County Fairgrounds, 11228
McCourtney Rd. Enter at Gate 4.
Contact: Jeff Ismail, 119 E. McKnight
Way, Grass Valley, CA 95949;
530-274-1795;
email: info@ihsfr.org
ihsfr.org

❶ Antique Engine & Tractor Show
Oct. 19　　　　　Vista
2040 N. Santa Fe Ave.
Contact: Meg Tessicini, 2040
N. Santa Fe Ave., Vista, CA 92083;
760-941-1791;
email: agsemoffice@gmail.com
www.agsem.com

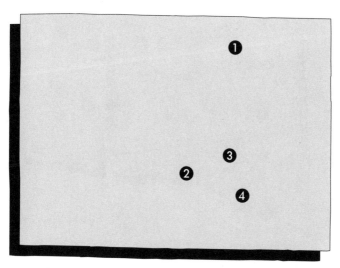

*Indicates more than one show at this site.

COLORADO

❶ Ault Engine and Machinery Show
Aug. 2-3   Ault
Highland High School grounds
by Liberty Park.
Contact: Bert Herrera and John
Widerman, 2015 W CR 82 E,
Livermore, CO 80536;
970-224-3957; 970-371-8753;
email: jwengineman01@gmail.com

**❷ Chaffee County Fair Tractor Pull and
Engine Show**
Aug. 3-4   Salida
10165 CR 120.
Contact: Steve Stratman,
285 28th Ln., Pueblo, CO 81001;
719-250-7279;
email: stevestratman@yahoo.com
www.avflywheelers.com

**❸ Pikes Peak Antique Machinery Days
Show and Museums Makers Fair**
Aug. 10-11   Colorado Springs
Western Museum of Mining and
Industry, between Colorado Springs
and Denver, I-25, exit 156.
Contact: Harold Hopkins Jr.,
719-634-0862;
email: harold.hopkinsjr@yahoo.com
www.frapa.us.com
www.avflywheelers.com
www.wmmi.org

**❹ Arkansas Valley Flywheelers
Antique Farm Equipment Show
and Tractor Pull**
Oct. 12-13   Pueblo
Millberger Farms, 28570 Business
Hwy 50 E.
Contact: Wes and Donna Stratman,
1506 29th Ln., Pueblo, CO 81006;
719-948-2778; 719-250-5646;
James Perry (tractor pull),
719-641-2692; Wes Stratman (tools
and equipment), 719-250-5646;
www.avflywheelers.com

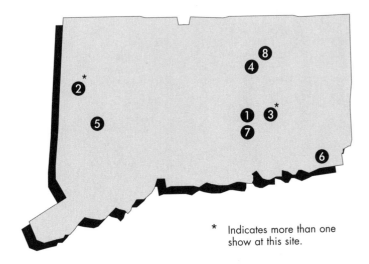

* Indicates more than one show at this site.

CONNECTICUT

❶ 45th Annual Belltown Antique Engine & Tractor Meet
April 28   East Hampton
Show location in lower CT River Valley area TBA.
Contact: Alan Carlson, PO Box 211, East Hampton, CT 06424;
860-267-9894;
email: belltowncarclub@gmail.com
www.belltownantiquecarclub.org

❷ Annual Spring Power-Up
May 4-5   Kent
1 mile north of Kent on Rt. 7.
Contact: John Pawloski, PO Box 425, Kent, CT 06757; 860-927-0050;
email: j.a.pawloski@att.net
www.ctamachinery.com

❸ Zagray Farm Museum Spring Gas-up and Swap Meet
May 4-5   Colchester
544 Amston Rd. On right, 1.5 miles north of Colchester center on Rt. 85.
Contact: Arthur Chester, 180 S. Plumb Rd., Middletown, CT 06457;
860-982-5158;
email: art.chester@rjillc.com
www.zagrayfarmmuseum.org

❹ 42nd Antique Machinery Show
May 18   Vernon
Tolland County Agricultural Center, 24 Hyde Ave. (Rt. 30). From I-84, exit 67, onto Rt. 31 toward intersection of Rts. 30 and 31. 150 yards east on Rt. 30 toward Tolland. Show is on the right.
Contact: Mark Wheldon, 32 Rolocut Rd., Broad Brook, CT 06016;
860-519-7831;
email: markwheldon@gmail.com
www.svaec.com

5 6th Annual Spring Tractor Show and Farm Open House
June 2　　　　Roxbury
I-84 exit 15. North on Rt. 67 to Roxbury, right on 317, left on Painter Hill Road to Toplands Farm at the top of the hill.
Contact: Nikki Hine, 102 Painter Hill Rd., Roxbury, CT 06783; 860-354-0649; email: ddlivinghistory@aol.com www.toplandsfarm.com
See our ad on page 10

3 Zagray Farm Museum Summer Show
July 20-21　　　　Colchester
544 Amston Rd. On right, 1.5 miles north of Colchester center on Rt. 85.
Contact: Arthur Chester, 180 S. Plumb Rd., Middletown, CT 06457; 860-982-5158; email: art.chester@rjillc.com www.zagrayfarmmuseum.org

2 Annual Antique Engine Show
July 27　　　　Kent
1 mile north on Rt. 7.
Contact: John Pawloski, PO Box 425, Kent, CT 06757; 860-927-0050; email: j.a.pawloski@att.net www.ctamachinery.com

6 Annual Antique Marine Engine Exposition
Aug. 17-18　　　　Mystic
Feature: Hydroplane Boat with a Quincy Looper Engine
75 Greenmanville Ave. Exit 90 off of I-95, south on County Road 27, museum is on right side at second and third traffic lights.
Contact: Scott Noseworthy, PO Box 6000, Mystic Seaport, Shipyard, Mystic, CT 06355; 860-572-5343; email: scott.noseworthy@mysticseaport.org www.mysticseaport.org

7 39th Annual Gas, Steam and Machinery Meet
Sept. 13-15　　　　Haddam
Features: Farm and Garden Tractors and Fairmont and Flywheel Engines. Haddam Meadows State Park, 820 Rt. 154 Saybrook Rd. Take exit 7 off CT 9, turn left at end of ramp, follow Rt. 154 north approximately 3 miles. Park is on the right. Gates open at noon on Friday for setup.
Contact: Randy Root, 100 Saddle Hill Dr., Middletown, CT 06457; 860-301-6933; email: tvf301@yahoo.com www.oldengine.org/members/tvf

2 Annual Fall Festival
Sept. 27-29　　　　Kent
1 mile north on Rt. 7.
Contact: John Pawloski, PO Box 425, Kent, CT 06757; 860-927-0050; email: j.a.pawloski@att.net www.ctamachinery.com

8 11th Fall Tractor Ride and Tractor Show
Sept. 28　　　　Tollan
Country Butcher, 1032 Tolland Stage Rd. From I-84 take exit 69, west on Tolland Stage Road (Rt. 74), 2 miles on the left.
Contact: Archie Tanner, 693 Buff Cap Rd., Tolland, CT 06084; 860-818-6601; email: archie.tanner@gmail.com www.svaec.com

3 Zagray Farm Museum Fall Festival and Swap Meet
Oct. 5-6　　　　Colchester
544 Amston Rd. On right, 1.5 miles north of Colchester center on Rt. 85.
Contact: Arthur Chester, 180 S. Plumb Rd., Middletown, CT 06457; 860-982-5158; email: art.chester@rjillc.com www.zagrayfarmmuseum.org

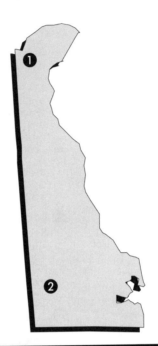

DELAWARE

1 German Vehicle Display
To be announced   Newark
Off St. Rt. 273 east of town
at 49 Salem Church Rd.
Contact: Mr. or Mrs. A.K. Kissell,
Box 7583, Newark, DE 19714;
302-731-5862

**2 First State Antique Tractor Club
Show**
June 14-15   Seaford
Feature: Allis-Chalmers Tractors.
Governor Ross Mansion and
Plantation, 23669 Ross Mansion Rd.
(off Rt. 20).
Contact: Martin Evans, 302-519-9133;
email: martinevans7119@yahoo.com
www.firststateantiquetractorclub.com

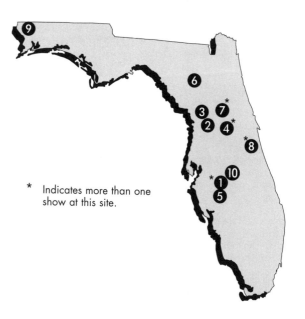

* Indicates more than one show at this site.

FLORIDA

❶ International Harvester Collectors Club, Florida Chapter 27 at the 32nd Annual Antique Engine and Tractor "Swap Meet" Show
Jan. 16-19   Fort Meade
Feature: International Harvester.
7000 Avon Park Cutoff Rd., 8 miles southeast of Fort Meade, or 10 miles northwest of Avon Park.
Contact: Charles G. Stevenson, 4800 Tiger Ln., Mims, FL 32754; 321-268-5072; 863-285-9121; email: cstevenson14@cfl.rr.com info@floridaflywheelers.org www.fl27ihc.com www.floridaflywheelers.org

❷ 20th Annual Tractor and Truck Pull
Jan. 25-26   Inverness
3600 S. Florida Ave.
Contact: Paul McPherson, 3600 S. Florida Ave., Inverness, FL 34450; 352-726-2993; email: citruscountyfair@embarqmail.com www.citruscountyfair.com

❸ 2nd Annual Dunnellon Farm Days Antique Tractor and Engine Show
Feb. 8-9   Dunnellon
19737 SE 127th Terrace, 6 miles west of town on CR 40 at the Withlacoochee Bluegrass Festival Park.
Contact. Dave Elliot, 5311 W. Riverbend Rd., Dunnellon, FL 34433; 352-472-2703; email: tinroofshack@gmail.com tinroofshack.com

❹ International Harvester Collectors Club, Florida Chapter 27 at the 12th Annual Tractor Show at Paquette's Historical Farmall Museum
Feb. 14-16   Leesburg
Feature: International Harvester.
615 S. Whitney Rd. GPS coordinates: north 28.909268 west 81.9414464. From I-75, take Wildwood exit 329 heading east on Hwy 44 approximately 9 miles.
Contact: Stewart Paquette, 615 S. Whitney Rd., Leesburg, FL 34748; 352-728-3588; email: stewsstuff@gmail.com www.stewsihstuff.com

4 **12th Annual Tractor Show at Paquette's Historical Farmall Museum**
Feb. 14-16   Leesburg
Feature: International Harvester Tractors.
615 S. Whitney Road. From I-75 take Wildwood exit east on Hwy 44 approximately 9 miles. Look for sign at Whitney Road. From I-95 exit on Hwy 44 head west through Leesburg 1 mile.
Contact: Stewart Paquette, 615 S. Whitney Rd., Leesburg, FL 34748; 352-728-3588; 352-267-4448; email: stewsstuff@gmail.com
www.stewsihstuff.com

1 **International Harvester Collectors Club, Florida Chapter 27 at the 27th Annual Florida Flywheelers Engine and Tractor Show**
Feb. 20-23   Fort Meade
Features: International Harvester, Case IH, Case, & New Holland.
7000 Avon Park Cutoff Rd., 8 miles southeast of Fort Meade, or 12 miles northwest of Avon Park.
Contact: Ron Zobel, 6672 SE 56th St., Okeechobee, FL 34972; 863-610-3068; 863-357-3495; email: ancientoaks1@comcast.net
info@floridaflywheelers.org
www.fl27ihc.com
www.floridaflywheelers.org

5 **51st Annual Pioneer Park Days**
Feb. 28-March 2   Zolfo Springs
Intersection of St. Rt. 64 and U.S. Hwy 17.
Contact: Opal Wilkerson, 863-773-2161; email: opal.wilkerson@hardeecounty.net
www.hardeecounty.net

6 **North Florida Antique Tractor Club with the Dudley Farms Florida State Park**
March 1-2   Newberry
Feature: John Deere.
State Road 26, 5 miles west of Gainesville.
Contact: Larry Shannon, 2500 NW 46th St., Bell, FL 32619; 386-935-2207; email: larginfarm@aol.com

7 **Mid-Florida Antique Machinery Club Display of Antique Machines & Tractors Spring Show**
March 2-3   Belleview
The Market of Marion, 12888 S.E. U.S. Hwy 441.
Contact: Info/Reservations, 6530 S.E. 135th St., Summerfield, FL 34491; 352-266-3990; 352-854-2259
See our ad on page 183

8 **International Harvester Collectors Club, Florida Chapter 27 3rd Annual Fort Christmas School Students Farm Show**
Oct. 3-4   Christmas
Feature: International Harvester.
1300 Fort Christmas Park. Travel 7 miles west from I-95 or 15 miles east from Orlando on Hwy. 50, then 3 miles north on Fort Christmas Road (CR 420) on left side.
Contact: Charles Stevenson, 4800 Tiger Ln., Mims, FL 32754; 321-268-5072; 407-254-9312; email: cstevenson14@clf.rr.com
andrea.etevenson@ocfl.net
www.fl27ihc.com
www.organgecountyparks.net

9 **30th Annual Jay Peanut Festival - Sponsored by Gabbert Farm**
Oct. 5-6   Jay
Gabbert Farm, 3604 Pine Level Church Rd., 4-1/2 miles south off Hwy 89.
Contact: Brenda Gabbert, PO Box 578, Jay, FL 32565; 850-675-6823

10 **International Harvester Collectors Club, Florida Chapter 27 Lake Wales Pioneer Days**
Oct. 26-27   Lake Wales
Features: International Harvester and John Deere Tractors and International Harvester and Fairbanks Morse Engines.
On shores of Lake Wales. From U.S. 27 take West Central Avenue east for approximately 1 mile directly to park.
Contact: Susan Cunningham, 464 H L Smith Rd., Haines City, FL 33844; 863-438-9052; email: jerrycunningham2@hotmail.com
www.fl27ihc.com

7 **Mid-Florida Antique Machinery Club Display of Antique Machines & Tractors Fall Show**
Nov. 2-3   Belleview
The Market of Marion, 12888 SE US Hwy 441.
Contact: Info/Reservations, 6530 S.E. 135th St., Summerfield, FL 34491; 352-266-3990; 352-854-2259
See our ad on page 183

1 **International Harvester Collectors Club, Florida Chapter 27 at the 24th Annual Florida Flywheelers Fall Fuel Up**
Nov. 6-9   Fort Meade
7000 Avon Park Cutoff Rd., 8 miles southeast of Fort Meade, or 10 miles northwest of Avon Park.
Contact: Charles G. Stevenson, 4800 Tiger Ln., Mims, FL 32754; 321-268-5072; 863-285-9121;
email: cstevenson14@cfl.rr.com info@floridaflywheelers.org www.fl27ihc.com www.floridaflywheelers.org

1 **24th Annual Florida Flywheelers Fall Fuel-Up**
Nov. 6-9   Fort Meade
7000 Avon Park Cutoff Rd.
Contact: Tom Simco-Cason, 7000 Avon Park Cutoff Rd., Fort Meade, FL 33841; 863-285-9121;
email: flywheelerpresident@yahoo.com www.floridaflywheelers.org
See our ad on page 183

8 **International Harvester Collectors Club, Florida Chapter 27 Cracker Christmas Antique Engine and Tractor Show**
Dec. 7-8   Christmas
Feature: International Harvester.
1300 Fort Christmas Park. Travel 7 miles west from I-95 or 15 miles east from Orlando on Hwy 50, then 3 miles north on Fort Christmas Road (CR 420) on left side.
Contact: Charles Stevenson, 4800 Tiger Ln., Mims, FL 32754; 321-268-5072;
email: cstevenson14@clf.rr.com andrea.stevenson@ocfl.net www.fl27ihc.com

1 **Florida Flywheelers Antique Engine Club Christmas in the Village**
Dec. 13-14 & 20-21   Fort Meade
7000 Avon Park Cutoff Rd., 8 miles southeast of Fort Meade, or 8 miles northwest of Avon Park.
Contact: Flywheelers Club, 7000 Avon Park Cutoff Rd., Fort Meade, FL 33841; 863-285-9121;
www.floridaflywheelers.org
See our ad on page 183

1 **Florida Flywheelers Antique Engine Club 33rd Annual Antique Engine and Tractor "Swap Meet"**
Jan. 15-18, 2020   Fort Meade
7000 Avon Park Cutoff Rd.
Contact: Tom, 7000 Avon Park Cutoff Rd., Fort Meade, FL 33841; 863-285-9121;
email: flywheelerpresident@yahoo.com; Tomi Simco-Cason, 909 Brooker Rd., Brandon, FL 33511; 863-285-9121;
email: ffwadvertise@yahoo.com www.floridaflywheelers.org
See our ad on page 183

1 **Florida Flywheelers Antique Engine Club 28th Annual Antique Engine and Tractor Show**
Feb. 19-22, 2020   Fort Meade
7000 Avon Park Cutoff Rd.
Contact: Tom, 7000 Avon Park Cutoff Rd., Fort Meade, FL 33841; 863-285-9121;
email: flywheelerpresident@yahoo.com www.floridaflywheelers.org
See our ad on page 183

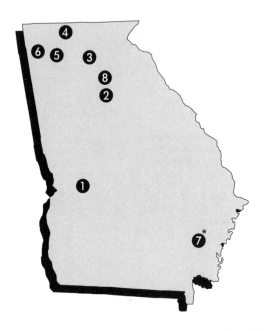

GEORGIA

1 Hog Killing at Old South Farm Museum
Feb. 2   Woodland
80 Pleasant Valley Rd. Hwy 41
between Manchester and Woodland.
Contact: Paul Bulloch, 706-975-9136;
www.oldsouthfarm.com

2 Trains, Trucks and Tractors
Aug. 2-4   Duluth
Southeastern Railway Museum, 3595
Budford Hwy. I-85 to exit 104, west
(pass Gwinnett Place mall) to Buford
Hwy, north 1/4 mile. Museum is on
the left (across from Howard Bros.
Hardware).
Contact: Randy Pirkle, PO Box 1267,
Duluth, GA 30096; 678-765-9208;
email: admin@train-museum.org
www.train-museum.org

3 Farm Days of Yesteryear
Sept. 13-14   Jasper
Lee Newton Park. 599 Stegall Dr.
Contact: Alan Proudfoot, 31 W. Eden
Way, Jasper, GA 30143; 561-723-4119;
email: swampones@etcmail.com

4 2nd Annual Antique Tractor Show
Sept. 20-21   Chatsworth
10 Peeples Farm Rd.
Contact: Brady Bagwell, 64 Little
Mountain Rd. South, Dawsonville, GA
30534; 706-531-6071;
email:
northgatractorshow@yahoo.com

5 13th Annual Gordon County Antique Engine and Tractor Show
Oct. 18-19   Calhoun
Features: All Brands of Lawn and
Garden Tractors.
Cherokee Capital Fairgrounds. Hwy 53
and Liberty Road S.W., I-75, exit 312,
4 miles west on Hwy 53, 3-1/2 miles
west of downtown.
Contact: Ricky Matthews, PO Box
1871, Calhoun, GA 30703;
770-527-5346;
email: kwprimmer1@mindspring.com
www.gcaeatc.com
Facebook: GCAEATC

6 **Fall Colors Tractor Ride**
Oct. 26   Trion
5146 E. Broomtown Rd.
Contact: Michael Wallace, 2092
Red Belt Rd., Chickamauga, GA
30707; 423-316-3708;
email: ihman70@yahoo.com

7 **Wayne County Cruser Arch Fest**
Oct. 26   Jesup
Downtown.
Contact: Donald Sloan, PO Box 146,
Screven, GA 31560; 912-294-0901

8 **19th Annual Cumming Steam,
Antique Tractor and Gas Engine
Show**
Nov. 8-9   Cumming
235 Castleberry Rd. Cumming
Fairgrounds, from Atlanta Hwy 400
N., exit 15, left to fourth stoplight, left
again, straight to show on right.
Contact: 770-316-2925;
www.capa-ga.com
See our ad on page 184

7 **"Crusin' Into Christmas" Car Show**
Dec. 14   Jesup
Lane Memorial Park, 865 S. First St.
Contact: Donald Sloan, PO Box 146,
Screven, GA 31560; 912-294-0901;
email:
crusinintochristmascarshow@gmail.com
Facebook: Crusin' Into Christmas

Show Listings

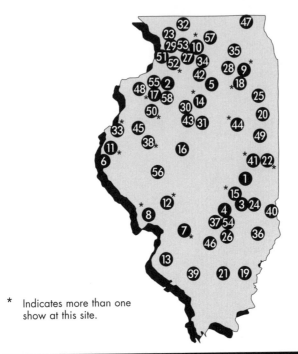

* Indicates more than one show at this site.

ILLINOIS

1 Illini Farm Toy Show and Auction
Jan. 4-5   Urbana
Wyndham Garden Urbana Champaign
Hotel, 1001 W. Killarney St. From I-74,
take Lincoln Avenue exit south towards
Urbana. Hotel is on right.
Contact: Lynn Doran, 801 N. Country
Fair Dr., Champaign, IL 61821;
970-420-4765;
email: doranlynn@gmail.com
Facebook: Champaign County Farm
Bureau Young Ag Leaders

**2 26th Annual ROWVA FFA and
Alumni Toy Show Auction**
March 3   Oneida
346 E. Rova Dr.
Contact: Rodney Main, 346 E. Rova
Dr., Oneida, IL 61467; 309-483-6371;
email: rmain@rowva.k12.il.us
www.rowvaffa.com

3 ECIA Antique Tractor Show
March 8-10   Mattoon
Cross County Mall.
Contact: Greg Rhoads, 7067 ECR
1100 N, Mattoon, IL 61938;
217-254-1489;
email: gregrhoads@ymail.com
www.eciafec.org

**4 25th Annual Antique Tractor Show
Sponsored by the Triple A Tractor
Club Inc.**
March 14-17   Effingham
Feature: Allis-Chalmers & all brands.
Village Square Mall, Rt. 45 S.
Contact: Rich Raber, 217-536-6315;
Steve Miller, 618-483-6241; Bob &
Carolyn Hollar, 618-238-4775;
email: buttons.hollar@gmail.com
Facebook: Triple A Tractor Club, Inc.

5 **Sublette Farm Toy and Antique Tractor Show**
March 16-17   Sublette
Feature: John Deere Tractors.
Main and John streets.
Contact: Don Dinges, PO Box 12,
Sublette, IL 61367; 815-713-5675;
www.subletteweb.com

6 **Corn Items Collectors Spring Meeting**
April 12-13   Quincy
Contact: David Vandenboom,
641-919-2042

7 **American Farm Heritage Museum Annual Swap Meet and Spring Fling Festival**
May 4   Greenville
1395 Museum Ave., 45 minutes east of
St. Louis, MO at I-70 exit 45, south 1/4
mile on St. Rt. 127, first left on Museum
Avenue.
Contact: Steve Loos, 1395 Museum
Ave., Greenville, IL 62246;
618-667-9140;
email: steve.loos@sbcglobal.net
www.americanfarmheritagemuseum.org

8 **Swap Meet**
May 4-5   Dow
23946 St. Hwy 3. 9 miles south of
Jerseyville to junction of St. Hwy 9
and St. Hwy 3, then 2 miles west on
St. Hwy 3.
Contact: Alex Harris, 31361 Bartlett
Rd., Brighton, IL 62012;
618-535-8575;
email: aharris@618connect.com
www.tricountyantiqueclub.org

9 **Spring at the Farm**
May 5   Montgomery
IL 47, 2 miles north of Yorkville, east on
U.S. 30 1 mile to Dickson Road, south
1 mile to the Dickson-Murst Farm.
Contact: Ken Wolf, PO Box 445,
Oswego, IL 60543; 630-816-0604;
email: jwolf_308@yahoo.com

10 **10th Annual AJ's Garden Tractor Jamboree**
May 18   Oregon
1675 S. Columbian Rd. From I-39:
Take Rt. 64 West to Oregon. At the
intersection of Tr. 2, turn left. Take a
right on W. Pines Road. Follow the
red and white signs to the show. WE
ARE 1 MILE EAST OF WHITE PINES
STATE PARK.
Contact: Andy & Lisa Hinrichs, 1675
S. Columbian Rd., Oregon, IL 61061;
815-732-6551; 815-262-6358;
email:
hinrichscustomwoodworking@gmail.com
www.hinrichscustomwoodworking.com

11 **Adams County Olde Tyme Spring Swap Meet and Flea Market**
May 18-19   Mendon
9 miles northeast of Quincy on Hwy
336, fairgrounds exit.
Contact: Paul Woodworth, PO Box 4,
Ursa, IL 62376; 217-219-0272;
email: pcwood@adams.net

12 **Spring Festival**
May 25-26   Carlinville
Features: Massey-Harris, Ferguson
and Ford Tractors.
Breckenridge Street, 12 miles west
from I-55 exit 60.
Contact: Nancy Lange, 13917 Lange
Rd., Carlinville, IL 62626;
217-825-7631;
email: langebillnancy@gmail.com;
PJ Rosentreter, 217-854-4439;
Facebook: Macoupin Agricultural
Antique Association

13 **27th Annual Gateway Two Cylinder Club Antique Tractor, Gas Engine and Toy Show**
June 2   Waterloo
Monroe County Fairgrounds, IL Rt. 3
to Hwy 156 W.
Contact: John Meier, 3462 Trout Camp
Rd., Waterloo, IL 62298;
314-608-4212;
email: jmmeier@htc.net

⑭ 32nd Annual Marshall-Putnam Antique Tractor and Engine Show
June 8-9   Lacon
Features: Ford Tractors and Sattley Engines.
Johnson's Grover Park, 700 S. Prairie St.
Contact: Marshall-Putnam Antique Association, 815-223-1877;
309-238-7058;
email: mpaa_info@yahoo.com
www.marshallputnamaa.com
See our ad on page 183

⑮ 10th Annual Amish Country Tractor Cruise
June 15   Arthur
9 miles west of I-57 (exit 203) on St. Hwy 133.
Contact: Jim Fleming, 830 E. Columbia, Arthur, IL 61911;
217-791-1026;
email: fbjf1964@consolidated.net
Facebook: Amish Country Tractor Cruise

⑯ Marbold Farmstead Antique Show & Farm Fest
June 22-23   Greenview
21722 St. Hwy 29, 20 miles north of Springfield.
Contact: Charlotte Wohler, 26725 Wohler Ave., Greenview, IL 62642;
217-341-8293;
email: cawhlr64@gmail.com
www.historic-marbold-farmstead.org

⑰ 15th Annual Railroad Days Spoon River Antique Agriculture Association Toy and Tractor Show
June 28-29   Galesburg
Galesburg Athletic Field House, Dayton Street.
Contact: Myron Hovind, 309-335-3619;
email: myronhovind@gmail.com
www.spoonrivertractor.com

⑱ Tractor Parade Through Sandwich
June 28   Sandwich
Sandwich Fairgrounds, 1401 Suydam Rd.
Contact: Ryan Anderson, 12091 Lisbon Rd., Newark, IL 60541;
815-354-5549;
email:
sandwichengineclub@yahoo.com
www.sandwichengineclub.com

⑱ 48th Annual Engine, Tractor and Toy Show
June 29   Sandwich
Feature: John Deere.
Historic Sandwich Fairgrounds, 1401 Suydam Rd. (1 block north of Rt. 34).
Contact: Ryan Anderson, 12091 Lisbon Rd., Newark, IL 60541;
815-354-5549;
email:
sandwichengineclub@yahoo.com
www.sandwichengineclub.com

⑱ Tractor Ride - Sandwich Early Day Engine Club
June 30   Sandwich
Sandwich Fairgrounds, 1401 Suydam Rd.
Contact: Ryan Anderson, 12091 Lisbon Rd., Newark, IL 60541;
815-354-5549;
email:
sandwichengineclub@yahoo.com
www.sandwichengineclub.com

⑲ 12th Annual Carmi Lions Tractor, Truck and Car Show
July 4   Carmi
White County Fairgrounds, located between St. Rt. 1 and St. Rt. 14 on the west side of town.
Contact: Don Ridenour, 409 E. Main St., Carmi, IL 62821; 618-382-5711;
email: donsbump@newwavecomm.net

⑳ Thee Olde Time Farm Show
July 5-7   Bradley
Features: Allis-Chalmers and Oliver Tractors and David Bradley Engines.
Rt. 45-52, Bourbonnais, IL.
Contact: Carol Churilla, 259 N. Fulton Ave., Bradley, IL 60915;
815-939-1485, leave a message;
email: marksmyboy@comcast.net
www.oldetimefarmshow.com

㉑ Hamilton County Ageless Iron
July 6   McLeansboro
Feature: John Deere Tractors.
St. Rt. 14 West.
Contact: Andy Miller, 13295 CR 1200 E., McLeansboro, IL 62859;
618-231-2556

㉒ Historic Farm Days
July 11-14　　　　　Penfield
Feature: International Harvester
Tractors.
10 miles east of Rantoul, just south of
Rt. 136.
Contact: JC Reitmeier, 217-595-5000;
email: halfcenturyofprogress.com
www.halfcenturyofprogress.org
See our ad on page 15

㉒ I&I Antique Tractor and Gas Show
July 11-14　　　　　Penfield
Feature: Corn Items Collectors
Association Inc. will be there.
800 Busey.
Contact: David Vandenboom,
641-919-2042

**㉓ Rock Falls Antique Tractor and
Engine Show**
July 13　　　　　Rock Falls
Feature: Farmall.
1206 Diesel. Triple P BBQ, 3312
W. Rock Falls, Rt. 30.
Contact: Stephanie & Jason Kersten,
22580 Hickory Hills Rd., Sterling, IL
61081; 309-530-9209;
email: stecowir@hotmail.com

㉔ 21st Annual ECIA Summer Show
July 18-20　　　　　Charleston
Feature: Allis-Chalmers Tractors.
Coles County Fairgrounds, 803 W.
Madison Ave.
Contact: Greg Rhoads, 7067
E. CR 1100 N., Mattoon, IL 61938;
217-254-1409,
email: gregrhoads@ymail.com
www.eciafec.org

**㉕ 57th Annual Reunion of the Will
County Threshermen's Association**
July 18-21　　　　　Manhattan
Features: Oliver and Cletrac Tractors.
14151 W. Joliet Rd., 1/2 mile east of
Wilton Center on Rt. 52.
Contact: Alan Heatherwick,
815-545-4928;
www.steamshow.org
See our ad on page 184

**㉖ 23rd Annual County Line
Sod Busters Prairie Days**
July 19-21　　　　　Bible Grove
Features: Ford and Massey-Harris
Tractors.
South Rt. 45, east on Bible Grove
Road, 20 miles south of Effingham on
Rt. 45 to Bible Grove, watch for signs.
Contact: Carolyn M. Hollar, 3453
Edgewood Rd., Edgewood, IL 62426;
618-238-4775;
email: buttons.hollar@gmail.com
Facebook: County Line Sod Busters
See our ad on page 187

**㉗ 41st Annual Bureau Valley Antique
Club Ol' Fashun Threshun Days**
July 20-24　　　　　Ohio
2 miles south of Ohio or 8 miles north
of Princeton (I-80), then 3/4 mile west
to Albrecht's Grove.
Contact: Ray Forrer, PO Box 43,
Somonauk, IL 60552; 815-498-2013;
815-824-6810;
email: rncforrer@juno.com

**㉘ Waterman Lions Summerfest and
Antique Tractor and Truck Show**
July 20　　　　　Waterman
Waterman Lions Park.
Contact: Leonard Johnson,
PO Box 276, Waterman, IL 60556;
815-757-5065;
email: lenj9635@yahoo.com
www.watermantractorshow.com

**⑪ Adams County Olde Tyme
Threshing Show**
July 26-29　　　　　Mendon
Features: Massey-Ferguson and
Ferguson Tractors.
9 miles northeast of Quincy on
Hwy 336, fairgrounds exit.
Contact: Paul Woodworth, PO Box 4,
Ursa, IL 62376; 217-219-0272;
email: pcwood@adams.net

Show Listings

7 Annual Heritage Days Show
July 26-28   Greenville
Features: International Harvester and
McCormick-Deering Tractors.
1395 Museum Ave., I-70 (exit 45),
45 minutes east of St. Louis, MO. Turn
south off interstate and make first left
onto Museum Avenue.
Contact: Brent Adkins, 1395 Museum
Ave., Greenville, IL 62246;
217-836-4180;
email: amheritagemuseum@yahoo.com
www.americanfarmheritagemuseum.org
See our ad on page 186

**29 Bos Brothers Old Fashioned
Threshing Bee**
July 26-28   Erie
Bill Rutherford Farm, 29265 County
Hwy 1. Between Geneseo and Erie on
Springhill Road.
Contact: Chuck Bos or Kevin Bos,
309-781-6394; 309-945-8117;
email: chuck@bosmachine.com
See our ad on page 17

30 Summer Harvest
July 26-27   Princeville
Features: Morse and Monitor Engines
and "Fields of Steel" Tractors.
325 N. Ostrom Ave., 20 minutes north
of Peoria, 45 minutes south of I-80.
Contact: Kevin Engquist, 2103
E. Rome Rd., Chillicothe, IL. 61523;
309-579-3293;
email: enky65@gmail.com
www.princevilleheritagemuseum.com
www.citractorclub.com

31 Grandpa's Day
July 27   Tremont
11810 Miller Rd. I-155 exit 22
(Townline Road), east 1/4 mile,
follow signs.
Contact: Vernon Koch, 11810 Miller
Rd., Tremont, IL 61568; 309-925-5493;
email: rmkoch96@gmail.com

15 3rd Annual Steam Threshing Days
Aug. 2-3   Arthur
284 E St. Hwy 133, 6.3 miles west of
Arcola at Chesterville. Exit 203 off I-57.
Contact: Jim Fleming, 830 E. Columbia,
Arthur, IL 61911; 217-791-1026;
email: fbjf1964@consolidated.net
www.illinoisamish.org

**7 43rd Annual Bond County
Antique Machinery Expo**
Aug. 2-4   Greenville
Features: Oliver White and
Minneapolis-Moline Tractors.
In conjunction with Bond County Fair.
I-70 exit 45.
Contact: Leroy Brave, 396 Browns Mill
Ave., Pocahontas, IL 62275;
618-664-2732; 618-558-3902;
email: ihleroy39@yahoo.com;
Larry Harnetiaux, 618-292-8383;
Bob Loos, 618-887-4483
See our ad on page 187

**32 50th Annual Old-Time Threshing
and Antique Show**
Aug. 2-4   Freeport
Features: Stover and Rawleigh
Engines. Stephenson County
Fairgrounds, 1 mile south of town.
Contact: The Stephenson County
Visitors Bureau, 800-369-2955;
815-235-2195;
email:
thefreeportshow@thefreeportshow.com
www.thefreeportshow.com
See our ad on page 187

**33 52nd Annual Western Illinois
Thresher's Bee, Craft Show and
Flea Market**
Aug. 2-4   Hamilton
Feature: International Harvester
Tractors.
2 miles north on 19th Street.
Contact: Ed Hartweg, 217-845-3041;
www.westernillinoisthreshers.org
See our ad on page 186

33 Western Illinois Threshers
Aug. 2-4   Hamilton
Feature: Corn Items Collectors
Association Inc. will be there.
1570 North CR 900 (N. 19th Street).
Contact: Steve Link, 309-338-2727;
westernillinoisthreshers.org

**34 Living History Antique Equipment
Association Show**
Aug. 3-4   Franklin Grove
1674 Whitney Rd.
Contact: Don Hopper, 1285 Killmer
Rd., Amboy, IL 61310; 815-288-6185;
email: bdhopper@grics.net
www.lhaea.org

35 63rd Annual Northern Illinois Steam Power Club Sycamore Steam Show
Aug. 8-11   Sycamore
Taylor Marshall Farm, Plank Road.
1-1/2 miles north on Rt. 23, 2 miles
east on Plank Road.
Contact: Dan Kocher, 630-222-5138;
815-895-9388 (site);
www.threshingbee.org
See our ad on page 185

36 33rd Annual Oblong Antique Tractor and Engine Assn. Show
Aug. 9-11   Oblong
Features: Oliver Hart-Parr Tractors and
Novo Engines.
Crawford County Fairgrounds, Hwy 33.
Contact: Mike Garrard, 303 S. White
St., Robinson, IL 62454; 618-546-5615
See our ad on page 186

37 38th Annual Mill Road Thresherman's Show
Aug. 9-11   Altamont
Features: Allis-Chalmers and
Minneapolis-Moline Tractors.
I-70, exit 82, 1 mile north to 4-way
stop. 3/4 mile on Hwy 40.
Contact: Jim Schroeder, PO Box 35,
Altamont, IL 62411; 217-821-1426;
email: kschroeder@mcswireless.net
www.millroadthresherman.org
See our ad on page 185

38 18th Annual South Fulton Antique Tractor Show (Sunday Tractor Ride)
Aug. 10   Vermont
Contact: Dick Russell, 309-254-3770;
David Brockley, 309-784-6111

39 60th Annual Steam, Gas and Threshing Show
Aug. 14-18   Pinckneyville
Features: Oliver, Hart-Parr and
Crawler Tractors, and Vertical Hit-and-
Miss Engines.
711 Fairground Rd.
Contact: 618-318-0745;
www.americanthresherman.com
See our ad on page 28

40 18th Annual Clark County Antique Power Club Tractor and Engine Show
Aug. 16-18   Marshall
Feature: Allis-Chalmers Tractors.
Clark County Fairgrounds, North
Second Street.
Contact: Joe McManus, 1006 Poplar
St., Marshall, IL 62441; 217-264-6052;
email: vmac1@charter.net

9 Day at the Farm
Aug. 18   Montgomery
IL 47, 2 miles north of Yorkville, east on
U.S. 30, 1 mile to Dickson Road, south
1 mile to the Dickson-Murst Farm.
Contact: Ken Wolf, PO Box 445,
Oswego, IL 60543; 630-816-0604;
email: jwolf_308@yahoo.com

41 I&I Antique Tractor and Gas Engine Club at the Half Century of Progress Show
Aug. 22-25   Rantoul
Rantoul National Aviation Center
Airport, south of Rt. 136 and east of
Rt. 45.
Contact: JC Reitmeier, 217-595-5000;
email: halfcenturyofprogress.com
www.halfcenturyofprogress.org
See our ad on page 14

41 Rantoul Half Century of Progress Show
Aug. 22-25   Rantoul
Features: Allis-Chalmers Tractors.
Rantoul Airport, 6 Aviation Center Dr.
Contact: Randy Freshour, 12407
E. Stringtown Rd., Idaville, IN 47950;
574-870-9901;
email: rfreshour@hotmail.com

42 Amboy Depot Days Tractor Show
Aug. 24   Amboy
Feature: Farmall.
Downtown. Hwy 52 to Main Street.
(8 a.m. to 1 p.m.).
Contact: John Pierce, 131 S. Appleton
Ave., Amboy, IL 61310; 815-973-4676;
www.depotdays.com

8 Olden Days
Aug. 24-25   Dow
Features: Massey-Harris and Massey-
Ferguson Tractors and Massey-
Ferguson and Fairbanks-Morse
Garden Tractors.
23946 St. Hwy 3. 9 miles south of
Jerseyville to junction of St. Hwy 9 and
St. Hwy 3, then 2 miles west on St.
Hwy 3.
Contact: Alex Harris, 31361 Bartlett
Rd., Brighton, IL 62012; 618-535-8575;
email: aharris@618connect.com
www.tricountyantiqueclub.org

43 River Valley Antique Tractor Show
Aug. 24-25   Mapleton
Feature: Case Tractors.
9424 S. Mapleton Rd.
Contact: Bob Hunnicutt, 309-745-9102;
email: jh12487@frontier.com
www.rvaatractors.com

**44 71st Annual Central States
Threshermen's Reunion**
Aug. 29-Sept. 2   Pontiac
Features: Hart-Parr Oliver, Massey-
Harris, Pre 35 Tractors and Equipment.
2 miles north of I-55 on Rt. 23 (exit
201).
Contact: Bill Carroll, 815-848-4985;
Dave Herz, 219-616-2016;
www.threshermensreunion.org
See our ad on page 185

**44 Illinois Massey Collectors
State Show**
Aug. 29-Sept. 2   Pontiac
In conjunction with Central States
Threshermen's Reunion. Exit 201 on
I-55, 2 miles north on Rt. 23.
Contact: Wayne Wolf, 217-722-1664;
email: wwolf1947@gmail.com

**45 43rd Annual Argyle Antique Gas
Engine Show**
Aug. 30-Sept. 2   Colchester
Features: Ford and Fordson Tractors.
2 miles north at Argyle Lake State Park.
Contact: Dan Savage, 6064 Madison
Ave., Burlington, IA 52601;
309-850-6786;
email: ems1920@yahoo.com
Facebook: Argyle Antique Gas Engine

**46 30th Annual Southern Illinois
Antique Power Club Antique Power
Days**
Sept. 5-8   Salem
Features: McCormick-Deering and
International Harvester Tractors.
Marion County Fairgrounds, Rt. 37 S.
Contact: Sean Earle, 632 S. Pine St.,
Centralia, IL 62801; 618-322-3978;
email: antiquepowerdays@yahoo.com;
Doug Telford, 618-267-6384;
Rick Garner, 618-339-4518;
www.antiquepowerdays.com
See our ad on page 186

**17 Stearman Fly-In with Spoon River
Antique Agriculture Association
Show**
Sept. 6-7   Galesburg
Galesburg Municipal Airport, 1 mile
west of town.
Contact: Myron Hovind, 309-335-3619;
email: myronhovind@gmail.com
www.spoonrivertractor.com

47 15th Annual Tractors for Charity
Sept. 7-8   McHenry
3709 Miller Rd.
Contact: Vernon Stade, 3709 W. Miller
Rd., McHenry, IL 60051;
815-482-3191;
email: thefarm@stadefarm.com
www.stadesfarmandmarket.com

48 1st Annual Viola Heritage Fest
Sept. 7-8   Viola
Miles Memorial Park, follow signs.
Contact: Mike Lester, 1110 Norlawn
Dr., Viola, IL 61486; 309-221-9573;
email: bearsluver1@yahoo.com

**49 Slow Boys Antique Tractor & Farm
Equipment Show**
Sept. 7   Gilman
I-57, exit 283 to Rt. 24 to downtown.
Contact: Russell Schuler, 326 N. Secor
Ave., Gilman, IL 60938; 815-265-7712;
email: russmaryann@sbcglobal.net
www.slowboys.org

50 58th Annual Antique Engine and Tractor Working Farm Show
Sept. 13-15   Geneseo
Feature: Case Tractor and Related Equipment.
9 miles north of Geneseo at 13451 St. Hwy 92. I-88, exit 6, east 3 miles on St. Hwy 92. Watch for signs.
Contact: Phil Jordan, c/o AETA, PO Box 112, Geneseo, IL 61254; 309-314-5000;
email: pm.jordan2591@gmail.com;
Randy Goddard, c/o AETA, PO Box 112, Geneseo, IL 61254; 309-314-5000;
email: rgoddard1947@gmail.com
www.ae-ta.com

50 Corn Items Collectors Association Inc. at the Antique Engine and Working Farm Show
Sept. 13-15   Geneseo
13451 St. Hwy 92.
Contact: David Vandenboom, 641-919-2042;
www.ae-ta.com

51 Moline Universal Tractor and Plow Co. Reunion
Sept. 13-15   Joslin
Features: Moline Universal Tractors and Moline Plow Co. Engines.
To be held at the Geneseo AE&T annual working farm show at 13457 IL-92, or due east of the I-88 Joslin exit or 10 miles north of Geneseo I-80 exit.
Contact: Paul Searl, 3630 S Macobach Rd., Stockton, IL 61085; 309-781-2896;
email: psearl13@yahoo.com
molineplowco.com

52 5th Annual Vintage Farm Equipment Show
Sept. 14-15   Atkinson
Feature: Vintage Garden Tractor Club of America.
19030 E. 2120 St. (Rock Island Avenue).
Contact: Dave Carton, 11493 Wolf Rd., Geneseo, IL 61254; 309-441-5915;
email: davidcarton2015@gmail.com
www.vintagefarmequipmentshow.com

53 Farm and Family Day
Sept. 14   Sterling
1801 Ave. G.
Contact: Kim Muller, 1801 Ave. G, Sterling, IL 61081; 815-626-1121;
email: parkwaycenteract@att.net

52 Vintage Garden Tractor Club of America Illinois Regional Show
Sept. 14-15   Atkinson
Bridge Park, 19030 E. 2120 St. (Rock Island Avenue).
Contact: Doug Tallman, 804 N. Trimble Rd., Mansfield, OH 44906; 419-545-2609;
email: dtallman@accnorwalk.com
www.vgtcoa.com

54 6th Annual "All About Allis-Chalmers" Farm Days
Sept. 15-16   Watson
Percival Springs, south of Effingham on Rt. 45.
Contact: Ron Repking, 9318 N. 1675th Rd., Effingham, IL 62401; 217-240-6206;
email: rrepking@frontiernet.net
Facebook: Triple A Tractor Club, Inc.
See our ad on page 187

55 34th Annual Edwards River Antique Engine Show
Sept. 21-22   New Windsor
Features: Ford and Ferguson.
Biggest Little Rodeo Grounds and Park. St. Hwy 17
Contact: Les Brasmer, 111 E 5th St., Sherrard, IL 61281; 309-593-2207;
email: mr_magneto@hotmail.com

11 Adams County Olde Tyme Fall Swap Meet and Flea Market
Sept. 21-22   Mendon
9 miles northeast of Quincy on Hwy 336, fairgrounds exit.
Contact: Paul Woodworth, PO Box 4, Ursa, IL 62376; 217-219-0272;
email: pcwood@adams.net

⑫ Fall Festival
Sept. 21-22   Carlinville
Features: Massey-Harris, Ferguson
and Ford Tractors.
Breckenridge Street, 12 miles west
from I-55 exit 60.
Contact: Nancy Lange, 13917 Lange
Rd., Carlinville, IL 62626;
217-825-7631;
email: langebillnancy@gmail.com;
PJ Rosentreter, 217-854-4439;
Facebook: Macoupin Agricultural
Antique Association

**㊌ 50th Annual Steam Show and
Fall Festival**
Sept. 27-29   Jacksonville
Features: Ferguson, Massey-Ferguson
and Massey-Harris Tractors.
Corner west Michigan and Lincoln
Avenue, South Jacksonville.
Contact: Hank Pool, PO Box 754,
South Jacksonville, IL 62651;
217-473-7431;
www.prairielandheritage.com

**㊄ Stillman Valley Fall Festival Hit and
Miss Engine and Antique Tractor
Show**
Sept. 27-29   Stillman Valley
Route 72 to North Walnut Street.
Contact: Brent Pearson, 111 West
Roosevelt Rd., Stillman Valley, IL
61084; 815-997-2295;
email: brentandjess2014@gmail.com

**㊅ 43rd Annual Knox County Scenic
Drive Spoon River Antique
Agriculture Association Show**
Oct. 5-6 & 12-13   Knoxville
Knox County Fairgrounds, Knox Hwy 9.
Contact: Myron Hovind, 309-335-3619;
email: myronhovind@gmail.com
www.spoonrivertractor.com

⑩ Autumn on Parade Tractor Show
Oct. 5   Oregon
Oregon Park East. U.S. Route 64.
Contact: Stan Eden, 1781 N. Daysville,
Oregon, IL 61061; 815-732-7746;
email: edensre@msn.com

**⑭ Marshall-Putnum
Antique Swap Meet**
Oct. 5   Lacon
Johnson's Grove Park, 700 S. Prairie St.
Contact: 815-223-1877; 309-238-7058;
email: mpaa_info@yahoo.com
Facebook: Marshall Putnam Antique
Association
See our ad on page 183

⑮ 2nd Annual Harvest To Home
Oct. 18-19   Arthur
284 E. St. Hwy 133, 6 miles west of
Arcola at Chesterville. Exit 203 off I-57.
Contact: Jim Fleming, 830 E. Columbia,
Arthur, IL 61911; 217-791-1026;
email: fbjf1964@consolidated.net
www.illinoisamish.org

㊳ 33rd Annual Fall Show and Festival
Oct. 18-20   Pinckneyville
711 Fairground Rd.
Contact: 618-318-0745;
www.americanthresherman.com
See our ad on page 28

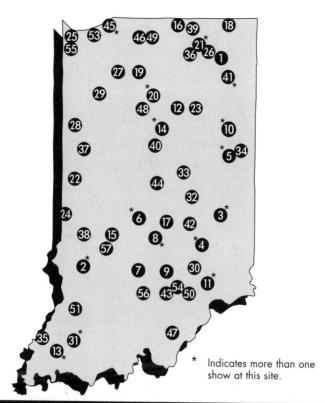

* Indicates more than one
show at this site.

INDIANA

1 **Winter Tractor and Gas Engine Show**
March 14-16　　　　　Auburn
Feature: Prairie Gold Rush
Minneapolis-Moline Tractors.
Indoors at Auburn Auction Park,
I-69 and CR 11A, exit 326.
Contact: Bruce Bell, 5535 CR 45,
Auburn, IN 46706; 260-925-0855
See our ad on page 190

2 **16th Annual White River Valley Antique Swap Meet and Barn Market**
April 5-6　　　　　Elnora
220 Indian St., one block south
of Hwy 57 on the Daviess County
Fairgrounds.
Contact: Ben Chestnut, 12275 E. 1650
N., Odon, IN 47562; 812-257-1668;
email: benrchestnut@gmail.com
www.wrvaa.org

3 **Franklin County Antique Machinery Club Swap Meet**
April 6　　　　　Brookville
11225 County Park Rd., U.S. 52 & 101.
Contact: Dale Hertel, 765-220-1615;
email: fcamcinc@yahoo.com
www.fcamc.org
See our ad on page 25

4 **S.E. Indiana F.A.R.M. Club's Spring Swap Meet**
April 13　　　　　Osgood
Ripley County Fairground, West
Beech Street. Go 2 blocks west of
the intersection at U.S. 421 and
St. Rt. 350.
Contact: Chuck Heck, 18372
Collier Ridge Rd., Aurora, IN 47001;
812-926-3654;
email: deeringheck@yahoo.com
www.farmclubonline.com
See our ad on page 191

5 4th Annual Crank-Up Gas Engine Show
April 20 Winchester
Randolph County Antique Club grounds on U.S. Hwy 27 south of town. GPS: 201 E 700 S.
Contact: Jeff Boyer, 6230 N. St. Rd. 1, Farmland, IN 47340; 765-744-1390; email: jboyer1020@gmail.com
www.randolphcountyantiqueclub.com

6 Morgan County Antique Machinery Spring Swap Meet
April 20 Martinsville
Morgan County Fairgrounds, St. Rt. 37 and 252.
Contact: John Schoolcraft, 765-318-7571
See our ad on page 195

7 Spring Show
April 26-27 Bedford
Lawrence County 4-H Fairgrounds, 1 mile west of junction Hwy 37 and 50 E.
Contact: Sonja Mills, PO Box 557, Mitchell, IN 47446; 812-797-6251; email: mills_sonja@yahoo.com

8 23rd Annual Brown County Antique Machinery Spring Swap Meet
May 4 Nashville
Brown County 4-H Fairgrounds, east old Hwy 46.
Contact: Randy C. Barrett, 9611 E. St. Rd. 46, Bloomington, IN 47401; 812-325-6722;
email: rbarret1967@gmail.com
www.bcama.net
See our ad on page 195

9 10th Annual Jackson County Antique Machinery Show
May 9-11 Brownstown
Features: Massey-Harris and Massey-Ferguson Tractors and Indiana-built Engines.
Jackson County Fairgrounds. 476 East CR 100 South.
Contact: Robert Bishop, 4514 South CR 700 E., Crothersville, IN 47229; 812-523-3246;
email: bishoprepair@c3bb.com
See our ad on page 194

10 37th Annual Tri-State Gas Engine and Tractor Swap and Sell
May 15-18 Portland
At the Club Grounds adjacent to the Jay County Fairgrounds.
Contact: Shirley Karn, 8123 E. 200 S., Portland, IN 47371; 260-251-9971; email: shirleykarn@gmail.com
www.tristategasenginetractor.com
See our ad on page IFC

11 13th Annual Tractor Supply Show
May 18 Madison
405 E. Clifty Dr., Tractor Supply parking lot.
Contact: Jeff Shepherd, 7430 W. Ramsey Creek Rd., Lexington, IN 47138; 812-866-5883; email: jshepf@gmail.com

11 3rd Annual Kent Vintage Tractor Drive
June 1 Madison
Route to be announced at a later date.
Contact: Jeff Shepherd, 7430 W. Ramsey Creek Rd., Lexington, IN 47138; 812-866-5883; email: jshepmf@gmail.com

12 La Fontaine Ashland Days
June 7-8 La Fontaine
Community building.
Contact: Duane Davis, 202 N. Wabash Ave., La Fontaine, IN 46940; 765-517-1944;
Jerry Wilson, 765-981-4928;
Tom Willcox, 765-981-2329

13 Cast Iron Seat Club Annual Meeting
June 7-9 Evansville
In conjunction with Southern Indiana's Antique and Machinery Club Classic Iron Show. Vanderburgh 4-H Center, 201 E. Boonville-New Harmony Rd., 6 miles north of town on Hwy 41.
Contact: Tom Wilson, 563-210-6836; email: qctrax@frontiernet.net

⑬ Southern Indiana's Antique and Machinery Club Classic Iron Show
June 7-9   Evansville
Features: John Deere Tractors, Hercules and other Evansville-built Engines.
Vanderburgh 4-H Center, 201 E. Boonville-New Harmony Rd.; 6 miles north of town on Hwy 41.
Contact: Brad Fromm, 812-983-3300; www.siamclassiciron.com
See our ad on page 196

⑭ Wildcat Creek Antique Tractor and Engine Show
June 7-9   Greentown
Feature: Allis-Chalmers.
610 E. Payton St., Howard County 4-H Fairgrounds.
Contact: Bill Johnson, 13413 E. 500 N-34, Converse, IN 46919; 765-437-2624;
email: bill4103@att.net

⑮ Owen County Antique Machinery Show
June 8-9   Spencer
Owen County Fairgrounds.
Contact: Olen Dickson, president, 5598 Drunkards Pike, Gosport, IN 47433; 812-821-0047;
email: ddstorage@bluemarble.net

⑯ 14th Annual Collector Show
June 13-15   Shipshewanna
Chups Auction House, 809 South Van Buren St.
Contact: Doug De Shazer, 105 W. Main St., Crofton, NE 68730; 402-510-8845;
email: doug_deshazer@yahoo.com
www.haytrolleyheaven.com

⑰ 28th Annual Johnson County Antique Machinery Show
June 13-16   Edinburgh
Features: All Muscle Tractors, Construction and Industrial Equipment; Oil Field Engines.
Johnson County Park, I-65 exit 80, 4 miles west on St. Rt. 252, follow signs at U.S. Hwy 31 and St. Rt. 252.
Contact: Dwayne Hansford, 2364 S. 625 W., Shelbyville, IN 46176; 317-512-0493;
email: rusticredacres@yahoo.com
www.jcamach.org
See our ad on page 192

⑱ 24th Annual Steuben County Antique Power Association Antique Farm Equipment Show
June 14-15   Angola
Features: Cockshutt, Coop, Ford and New Holland Tractors and Pennsylvania-built Engines.
Prairie Heights School Farm, 395 S. 1150 E., LaGrange, IN 46761. 11-1/2 miles west of town on U.S. 20 to flashing light.
Contact: Steve Shank, 5920 N. 500 W, Angola, IN 46703; 260-833-1216;
Facebook: Steuben County Antique Power

⑲ Fulton County Historical Power Show
June 14-16   Rochester
Features: Lesser-known Classics and Oddballs.
37E 375N, 4 miles north of town on U.S. 31 and County Road 375 N.
Contact: Melinda Clinger, 37E 375N, Rochester, IN 46975; 574-223-4436;
email: melinda@rtcol.com
www.fultoncountyhistory.org
See our ad on page 196

❺ Randolph County Antique Garden Tractor Pull, Show, and Old Iron Swap Meet
June 15   Winchester
Randolph County Antique Club grounds on U.S. Hwy 27 south of town. GPS: 201 E 700 S.
Contact: Keith Snyder, 4688 W. 300 N., Winchester, IN 47394; 765-969-4904;
email: keithsnyder55@gmail.com
www.rcaconline.com

❻ 27th Annual Morgan County Antique Machinery Show
June 22-23   Martinsville
1749 Hospital Dr.
1/4 mile west of junction of St. Rd. 37 and St. Rd. 252. Morgan County Fairgrounds.
Contact: Dave Zoller, president, 765-318-1493;
email: rcoffman6670@yahoo.com
See our ad on page 195

20 29th Annual Hoosier Flywheelers Show
June 26-29   Peru
Show grounds.
Contact: Ken or Wendy Wolf, 3474 W.
200 N., Peru, IN 46970; 765-473-3904

4 23rd Annual S.E. Indiana F.A.R.M. Club's Antique Machinery Show
June 27-29   Osgood
Features: Massey Family Tractors and
Economy Engines.
Ripley County Fairground, West Beech
Street, 3 blocks west of the traffic light
at U.S. 421 and St. Rt. 350.
Contact: Chuck & Sherri Heck, 18372
Collier Ridge Rd., Aurora, IN 47001;
812-926-3654;
email: deeringheck@yahoo.com
www.farmclubonline.com
See our ad on page 191

21 Olde Time Engine and Tractor Show
June 28-29   Albion
1426 W. 300 N.
Contact: Jerry, 260-450-0044;
Mark, 260-239-5081

22 17th Annual Covered Bridge Antique Power Tractor Tour
June 29-30   Rockville
Parke County Fairgrounds, U.S. 41 N.
Contact: Bob Rennick, 765-562-2616;
email: bjrennick99@yahoo.com;
Joe Warters, 765-362-0910

23 27th Annual Warren Area Antique Tractor and Engine Show
July 4-6   Warren
Features: Massey-Harris, Ferguson,
Wallis and Massey-Ferguson Tractors.
The Daugherty Companies,
534 E. First St.
Contact: Mike Daugherty,
260-375-6018

24 Vigo County Fair Antique Tractor, Threshing and Gas Engine Show
July 6-7   Terre Haute
Wabash Valley Fairgrounds, 1/2 mile
south of I-70 on Hwy 41.
Contact: Bill or Chris Nicoson, 16176
S. Sullivan Pl., Farmersburg, IN 47850;
812-898-2128

24 Vigo County Fair
July 7-13   Terre Haute
Washbash Valley Fairgrounds,
1/2 mile south of I-70 on Hwy 41.
Contact: Bill or Chris Nicoson, 16176
S. Sullivan Pl., Farmersburg, IN
47850; 812-898-2128

14 Greentown Lions Club Pioneer Village Tractor & Engine Show
July 8-13   Greentown
Feature: Allis-Chalmers.
Howard County 4-H Fairgrounds.
Contact: Bill Johnson, 13413
E. 500 N. 34, Converse, IN 46919;
765-437-2624;
email: bill4103@att.net

25 35th Annual Antique Farm & Tractor Show
July 12-14   Crown Point
Lake County Fairgrounds,
889 S. Court St.
Contact: Bill Wiater Jr., 14332 Riskin
Rd., Cedar Lake, IN 46303;
219-779-5965;
email: billw@chs.com
www.slcahs.org

26 37th Annual Noble County Gas and Steam Show and Noble County Community Fair
July 14-20   Kendallville
Features: Case and International
Harvester Tractors.
In conjunction with Noble County
Community Fair, Hwy 6 E.
Contact: Larry Palmer, 4187 N. St.
Rd. 9, Albion, IN 46701;
260-636-2605

27 42nd Annual Northern Indiana Power from the Past Antique Show
July 18-21   Winamac
Features: Graham Bradley Tractors
and Hit-and-Miss Engines.
City Park.
Contact: Chris Smith, 574-946-3712;
email: catfishm@pwrtc.com
www.winamacpowershow.com
See our ad on page 196

28 **38th Annual Illiana Antique Power Association Show**
July 19-21   Rainsville
Features: Ford Tractors and Waterloo-built Engines.
986 W. Briscoe Rd., Williamsport, IN. Pine Creek Valley, 8 miles south of Boswell, or 12 miles north of Attica on U.S. Hwy 41, east on Warren CR 650.
Contact: Tom Swanson, 272 N. St. Rd. 55, Attica, IN 47918; 765-585-8371;
email: cfswan@att.net
www.illianaantiquepower.com

5 **Randolph County Antique Club Tractor, Gas Engine, and Equipment Show**
July 19-23   Winchester
Randolph County Antique Club grounds on U.S. Hwy 27 south of town.
GPS: 201 E 700 S.
Contact: Jeff Boyer, 6230 N St. Rd. 1, Farmland, IN 47394; 765-744-1390;
email: jboyer1020@gmail.com
www.rcaconline.com

29 **White County 4-H Fair and Antique Power Show**
July 19-25   Reynolds
White County Road 25 E., 1/4 mile north of U.S. Hwy 24.
Contact: Keith Snowberger, 765-414-1776;
www.wcantiquepower.com

30 **4th Annual Orscheln's Tractor Show at North Vernon**
July 20   North Vernon
2110 N. St. Rd. 3. Orscheln's parking lot.
Contact: Jeff Shepherd, 7430 W. Ramsey Creek Rd., Lexington, IN 47138; 812-866-5883;
email: jshepmf@gmail.com

31 **Antique Steam and Gas Engine Club Summer Show**
July 26-28   Boonville
Features: Allis-Chalmers Tractors and Kitten Steam Engines.
Thresherman's Park, 2144 New Harmony Rd., 1/4 mile off Hwy 61.
Contact: Clara Broshears, 807 S. Third St., Boonville, IN 47601; 812-897-2683;
email: wanddaugh90@gmail.com
See our ad on page 191

20 **Hoosier Heritage Fest**
July 26-28   Peru
Features: Case and Minneapolis-Moline.
Miami County 4-H Fairgrounds, 1029 W. 200 North. 2 miles north of U.S. 24 on Business 31/Mexico Road.
Contact: Jodie Schmitt, 103 S. 440 W., Kokomo, IN 46901; 765-438-3835;
email: pioneerpower@comcast.net
www.hoosierheritagefest.com

32 **71st Annual Reunion Pioneer Engineers**
Aug. 1-4   Rushville
Features: Case Tractors, Case Steam Engines and Oil Field Engines.
Caldwell Pioneer Acres, 3707 S. 200 W.
Contact: Mark Herbert, 596 W. SR. 24, Milroy, IN 46156; 765-629-2924;
email: mherbert1359@gmail.com;
Carolyn Sorber, 7687 E. 900 S., Rushville, IN 46173; 765-561-4958;
email: dcsorber@gmail.com
www.pioneerengineers.com
See our ad on page 193

33 **Markleville Jamboree**
Aug. 1-3   Markleville
Feature: Case.
St. Rts. 38 and 109, follow signs.
Contact: George Mock, 757 N. 500 E., Anderson, IN 46016; 765-748-3543;
email: bubblingsprings2@aol.com

34 **Randolph County Antique Club State Line Heritage Days**
Aug. 1-3   Union City
North of St. Rt. 571 at the Indiana-Ohio state line to the railroad park.
Contact: Larry Wiley, 1015 N. 700 E., Union City, IN 47390; 765-964-7442;
937-459-9804

35 **29th Annual Keck Gonnerman Antique Machinery Association Show**
Aug. 2-4   New Harmony
Feature: Case Tractors.
Posey County Fairgrounds, 9 miles south of I-64, exit 4.
Contact: Brian Pierce, 975 Durlin Rd., New Harmony, IN 47631; 812-568-4256;
email: farmallcubfan@hotmail.com

36 8th Annual Wolf Lake Onion Days Farm and Garden Tractor Show
Aug. 2-3   Wolf Lake
Feature: Allis-Chalmers Tractors.
One block from intersection of
St. Rd. 109 and U.S. Hwy 33 at the
Wolf Lake Elementary School.
Contact: Mark Beck, 2795
S. Washington Rd., Columbia City, IN
46725; 260-239-5081;
email: mbeckmh44@yahoo.com

37 Wingate Antique Tractor, Gas Engine and Old Truck Show
Aug. 3   Wingate
At the town park on south edge of
town on St. Rd. 25. 5 miles north of
I-74 at exit 25 north.
Contact: Glenn Lawson, 9714 N. St.
Rd. 25, Wingate, IN 47994;
765-275-2576;
email: gblawson@tctc.com

38 YesterYear Power Club Tractor and Engine Show
Aug. 3   Clay City
Features: Orphans and Oddball
Tractors and International Engines.
Clay City Goshorn Park, 12 miles
south of I-70 on St. Rd. 59.
Contact: Ron Miller, 276
S. Montgomery St., Bowling Green, IN
47833; 812-986-2829; 812-585-1814;
email: ronm@ccrtc.com
Facebook: Yesteryear Power Club

39 38th Annual Northeast Indiana Steam and Gas Antique Farm Power Show
Aug. 8-10   LaGrange
Features: Lesser-known Classics,
Doodlebugs and Port Huron.
LaGrange County 4-H Fairgrounds.
Contact: Jim Eberly, 401 S. Sherman
St., LaGrange, IN 46761;
260-463-3639;
LaGrange County Convention and
Visitors Bureau, 888-277-3184;
www.visitshipshewana.org
See our ad on page 192

40 45th Mid-America Threshing and Antiques
Aug. 8-11   Tipton
Feature: Case.
Tipton County Fairgrounds, 1200
S. Main St.
Contact: Terry Dunn, PO Box 576,
Arcadia, IN 46030; 317-966-2539;
email: deere1950b@comcast.net
See our ad on page 195

41 42nd Annual Summer Show - Maumee Valley Steam and Gas Association
Aug. 15-18   New Haven
Feature: John Deere, Massey-Harris,
Ferguson and Wheel Horse Tractors.
1720 Webster Rd., east of town
between U.S. 24 and U.S. 30.
Contact: Roger Schuller, 3728
Webster Rd., Woodburn, IN 46797;
260-749-0169;
email: rschuller7640@gmail.com
www.maumeevalley.org
See our ad on page 195

42 Greensburg Power of the Past 30th Annual Reunion
Aug. 15-18   Greensburg
Features: Ford Orphans, Ford Garden
and Oddballs Tractors and Bessemer
Hit-and-Miss Engines.
Decatur County Fairgrounds,
West Park Road.
Contact: Tom Cherry, 812-593-8977;
email: tom@ekova.com
www.greensburgpowerofthepast.org
See our ad on page 26

10 54th Antique Engine and Tractor Show
Aug. 20-24   Portland
Features: Lesser-known Tractors and
Michigan Engines.
Jay County Fairgrounds, 1010
N. Morton St.
Contact: Shirley Karn, 8123 E. 200 S.,
Portland, IN 47371; 260-251-9971;
email: shirleykarn@gmail.com
www.tristategasenginetractor.com
See our ad on page IFC

⑩ Tri-State Gas Engine Show and Tractor Show
Aug. 20-24   Portland
Feature: Corn Items Collectors Association Inc. will be there.
1010 N. Morten St.
Contact: David Vandenboom, 641-919-2042

㊸ 37th Leota Country Frolic
Aug. 23-24   Leota
2976 S. Bloomington Trl., 3 miles west and 2 miles south of Scottsburg.
Contact: Charles Murphy, 812-752-3636

㊹ 29th Annual Toy Truck-N Construction Show and Auction
Aug. 23-25   Indianapolis
Wyndham Indianapolis West Hotel.
Contact: Lori Aberle, 7496 106th Ave. S.E., La Moure, ND 58458; 701-883-5206; 800-533-8293; email: laberle@toyfarmer.com
www.toyfarmer.com

㊺ Hesston Steam & Power Show
Aug. 30-Sept. 2   LaPorte
1201 E. 1000 N, Hesston, IN; exit 1 off I-94 then south, OR Indiana toll road exit 49 then north to CR 1000 N, turn at billboard. See interactive map at www.hesston.org/plan.
Contact: Ted Rita, 1201 E. 1000 N, Laporte, IN 46350; 269-449-7391; email: ted.rita@hesston.org
www.hesston.org

② 35th Annual White River Valley Antique Show
Sept. 5-8   Elnora
Features: Co-op, Cockshutt and Leader Tractors and Reeves Engines.
Daviess County Fairgrounds, Hwy 57, 3 blocks east of Hwy 58.
Contact: 812-692-7800;
www.wrvaa.org
See our ad on page 189

㊻ Rentown Old Fashion Days
Sept. 6-7   Bremen
2640 Birch Rd.
Contact: Jason Helmuth, 1510 2B Rd., Bremen, IN 46506; 574-546-1246; email: jasonrhelmuth@gmail.com

㊼ 44th Annual Lanesville Heritage Weekend
Sept. 12-15   Lanesville
Features: Massey-Harris, Ferguson, Massey-Ferguson Lawn and Garden Tractors, Oddballs & Orphans Steam Engines, and Sandow Gas Engines.
2800 Memory Lane.
Contact: Kenny Acton, PO Box 313, Lanesville, IN 47136; 812-952-2027; email: lanesvilleheritage@gmail.com
www.lanesvilleheritageweekend.com
See our ad on page 188

⑧ Brown County Antique Engine and Tractor Show
Sept. 13-14   Nashville
Feature: International Harvester Tractors.
1/4 mile east of Nashville on Old St. Rd. 46 at Brown County 4-H Fairgrounds.
Contact: Randy C. Barrett, 9611 E. St. Rd. 46, Bloomington, IN 47401; 812-325-6722; email: rbarret1967@gmail.com
www.bcama.net
See our ad on page 195

㊽ Tip Wa Antique Tractor and Engine Show
Sept. 14-15   Walton
402 S. Main St.
Contact: Dean A. McCloskey, 8224 S. CR 1000 E., Galveston, IN 46932; 765-432-7844;
flea market info, 574-753-7390

㊾ Nappanee Apple Festival Antique Tractor, Engine and Toy Show
Sept. 19-21   Nappanee
The Farm at Amish Acres, 1600 W. Market St. Located 1 mile west of historic downtown off U.S. 6 and County Road 3.
Contact: Brian Metzler, 71593 CR 100, Nappanee, IN 46550; email:
admin@nappaneepowerfromthepast.org
www.nappaneepowerfromthepast.org

45 Rumely Allis Chalmers La Porte Heritage Center Tractor Show
Sept. 20-22   La Porte
Features: Rumely and Allis-Chalmers Tractors.
2859 West St. Rd. 2.
Contact: Randy Freshour, 12407 E. Stringtown Rd., Idaville, IN 47950; 574-870-9901;
email: rfreshour@hotmail.com
www.rumelyallis.com

21 21st Annual Albion Harvest Fest
Sept. 21-22   Albion
Saddle Club Grounds, State Road 8 E.
Contact: Larry Palmer, 4187 N. St. Rd. 9, Albion, IN 46701; 260-636-2605

50 8th Annual Kent Vintage Tractor Show at Leroy's
Sept. 21   Lexington
7887 E. Main St.
Contact: Jeff Shepherd, 7430 W. Ramsey Creek Rd., Lexington, IN 47138; 812-866-5883;
email: jshepmf@gmail.com

51 From the Seat of a Tractor - Tractor Drive
Sept. 21   Petersburg
I-69 exit 46.
Contact: David Yager, PO Box 205, Lynnville, IN 74619; 812-483-9532;
email: dlyager66@aol.com
Facebook: Pike County Indiana Tractor Group

3 25th Annual Franklin County Antique Machinery Show
Sept. 26-29   Brookville
Features: Allis-Chalmers Tractors and Stover Engines.
11225 County Park Rd., U.S. 52 & 101.
Contact: Dale Hertel, 765-220-1615;
email: fcamcinc@yahoo.com
www.fcamc.org
See our ad on page 25

53 43rd Annual Northern Indiana Historical Power Association Fall Harvest Festival and Antique Equipment Show
Sept. 27-29   Valparaiso
Feature: John Deere Tractors and Engines.
Sunset Hill Farm County Park, 775 N. Meridian Rd.
Contact: Nick Misch, president, 219-309-0417;
Jack Kashak, 219-241-5991;
www.nihpa.org
See our ad on page 193

54 3rd Annual Orscheln's Tractor Show at Scottsburg
Oct. 5   Scottsburg
1326 N. Gardner.
Contact: Jeff Shepherd, 7430 W. Ramsey Creek Rd., Lexington, IN 47138; 812-866-5883;
email: jshepmf@gmail.com

10 15th Annual Tri-State Gas Engine and Tractor Fall Swap Meet
Oct. 10-12   Portland
At the Club Grounds adjacent to the Jay County Fairgrounds.
Contact: Shirley Karn, 8123 E. 200 S., Portland, IN 47371; 260-251-9971;
email: shirleykarn@gmail.com
www.tristategasenginetractor.com
See our ad on page IFC

20 Annual Hoosier Flywheelers Fall Swap Meet
Oct. 10-12   Peru
Show grounds.
Contact: Ken or Wendy Wolf, 3474 W. 200 N., Peru, IN 46970; 765-473-3904

31 Antique Steam and Gas Engine Club Fall Show
Oct. 11-13   Boonville
Features: Allis-Chalmers Tractors and Kitten Steam Engines.
Thresherman's Park, 2144 New Harmony Rd., 1/4 mile off Hwy 61.
Contact: Clara Broshears, 807 S. Third St., Boonville, IN 47601; 812-897-2683;
email: wanddaugh90@gmail.com
See our ad on page 191

41 **19th Annual Model Engine, Gas Engine, and Tractor Pull Fall Show**
Oct. 12   New Haven
1720 Webster Rd.
Contact: John Schambr, 260-485-9104;
Tony Herman, 260-414-9489;
www.maumeevalley.org
See our ad on page 195

55 **Buckley Homestead Fall Festival**
Oct. 12-13   Lowell
I-65, west 4 miles on Rt. 2, 1/4 mile
south on Hendricks Road.
Contact: Chris Orange, 3606 Belshaw
Rd., Lowell, IN 46356; 219-696-0769;
email: grandkankakeechris@gmail.com

8 **23rd Annual Brown County Antique Machinery Fall Swap Meet**
Oct. 26   Nashville
Brown County 4-H Fairgrounds,
east old Hwy 46.
Contact: Randy C. Barrett, 9611
E. St. Rd. 46, Bloomington, IN 47401;
812-325-6722;
email: rbarret1967@gmail.com
www.bcama.net
See our ad on page 195

56 **Farm Toy Show**
Dec. 7   Orleans
Robinson's Auction and Gathering
Building, 8620 N. St. Rd. 37.
Contact: Sonja Mills, PO Box 557,
Mitchell, IN 47446; 812-797-6251;
email: mills_sonja@yahoo.com

57 **2019 Hendricks County Antique Tractor and Machinery Show**
July 14-20   Newark
In conjunction with the Hendricks
County 4-H and Agricultural Fair.
Hendricks County 4-H Fair and
Conference Complex, 1900 E. Main St.
Contact: Bert Thralls, 317-626-857;
Brad Beson, 317-432-8196;
email: btat294@att.net
email: brad5812@sbcglobal.net

47 **2019 Indiana Massey Collectors Association State Show**
Sept. 12-15   Lanesville
Features: Massey-Ferguson, Massey-
Harris and Ferguson and Wallis
Tractors.
In conjunction with the 44th Annual
Lanesville Heritage Weekend.
Lanesville Heritage Park, 2800
Memory Ln.
Contact: John Bush, 317-605-3361;
email: jwbush53@hotmail.com;
Gary Emsweller, 317-745-7949;
email: masseyh@aol.com
www.lanesvilleheritageweekend.com
www.masseycollectors.com

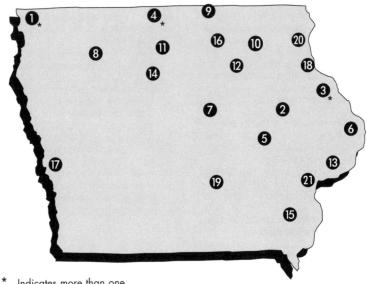

* Indicates more than one
show at this site.

IOWA

1 27th Annual Swap Meet
May 17-18   Granite
7 miles west, 1-1/2 miles north
of Larchwood.
Contact: Darrel Hansen, 1138 125th
St., Larchwood, IA 51241;
605-261-9270;
email: farmall@alliancecom.net
www.granitethreshingbee.com

2 MAGETA Steam & Gas Engine Show
May 18-19   Springville
Springville Tractor Pull Association
Grounds, 162 JR Barnes Pkwy.
Contact: John Johnston Jr., 2855
Springville Rd., Springville, IA 52336;
319-560-2109

3 Summer Farm Toy Show
June 7-8   Dyersville
From Hwy 20 take exit 294 to 1110
16th Ave. Ct. S.E. Free parking at
Beckman High School or National
Farm Toy Museum. Show is at both
locations.
Contact: Amanda Schwartz, 1110
16th Ave. Ct. S.E., Dyersville, IA 52040;
563-875-2727;
email: farmtoys@dyersville.com
www.summerfarmtoyshow.com

**4 36th Annual Steam Threshing
Festival**
June 7-9   Forest City
Features: Minneapolis Threshing
Machine Co. Products and Sheppard
Diesel Tractors.
1811 Sage Ct.
Contact: Jerred Ruble, 612-860-9830;
email: steamthreshingfestival@
heritageparkofnorthiowa.com
www.heritageparkofnorthiowa.com
See our ad on page 197

**5 28th Annual The Allis Connection
"All Allis" Father's Day Weekend
Show**
June 15-16   Middle Amana
Feature: Allis-Chalmers Tractors.
Middle Amana Community Park.
Contact: Mike Anderson, 913 N. Main
St., Abingdon, IL 61410;
309-462-3517;
email: barma@frontier.com
www.theallisconnection.com

1 **20th Annual Tractor Tour**
July 13   Granite
7 miles west, 1.5 miles north
of Larchwood.
Contact: Darrel Hansen, 1138
125th St., Larchwood, IA 51241;
605-261-9720;
email: farmall@alliancecom.net
www.granitethreshingbee.com

6 **Threshing Day**
July 13   Miles
Southeast corner of town.
Contact: Larry Jepsen, 582
Breezy Point Dr., Clinton, IA 52732;
563-242-3865;
email: sljepsen@aol.com
www.milesiowa.org

1 **35th Annual Threshing Bee**
July 19-21   Granite
Features: International Harvester
Tractors and Engines.
7 miles west, 1.5 miles north
of Larchwood.
Contact: Darrel Hansen, 1138
125th St., Larchwood, IA 51241;
605-261-9720;
email: farmall@alliancecom.net
www.granitethreshingbee.com

7 **35th Annual Steam Threshing and
Plowing Show**
Aug. 2-4   Marshalltown
Feature: International Harvester
Tractors and Equipment.
2373 Jessup Ave. 8 miles west of town
on Hwy 3.
Contact: Paul Sams, 2614 260th St.,
Marshalltown, IA 50158; 641-751-7600;
email: psams2614@gmail.com
www.miapa.org

8 **49th Annual Albert City
Threshermen and Collectors Show**
Aug. 9-11   Albert City
Feature: Massey.
2 miles west, 1/2 mile north of town.
Contact: Karen, PO Box 333,
Albert City, IA 50510; 712-843-2076;
email:
info@albertcitythreshermen.com
www.albertcitythreshermen.com

9 **24th Annual Cedar Valley Memories**
Aug. 10-11   Osage
Feature: Oliver Tractors.
2 miles west of town on Hwy 9.
Contact: Gary, 641-330-2017;
Facebook: Mitchell County
See our ad on page 196

10 **Northeast Iowa Antique Engine and
Power Show**
Aug. 10-11   Fredericksburg
Features: Farmall and International
Harvester Tractors.
2732 Stanley Ave., 1/2 mile south
of Shawver Well.
Contact: Chuck Stone, 402 Birch Dr.,
Box 264, Fredericksburg, IA 50630;
319-231-4666; Roger Burgart (tractor
pull), 563-920-8522

11 **30th Annual Prairie Homestead
Antique Power Tractor Show**
Aug. 16-18   Belmond
Feature: Minneapolis-Moline Tractors.
2 miles north on Hwy 69, 1 mile east.
Contact: Dave Nelson, 515-571-6838;
www.belmondartscenter.org
See our ad on page 197

12 **55th Annual Antique Acres Old Time
Power Show**
Aug. 16-18   Cedar Falls
Feature: Oliver Tractor.
7610 Waverly Rd.
Contact: Antique Acres, 319-987-2380;
www.antiqueacres.org
See our ad on page 197

13 **Farm Days in the Village**
Aug. 24-25   Davenport
2123 E 11th St.
Contact: Ed Vieth, 563-271-3551;
Tom Largomarcino, 309-235-6765;
3436 N. Sturdevant St., Davenport,
IA 52806;
www.deervalleycollectors.com
www.villageofeastdavenport.com

4 **Heritage Park of North Iowa
Horse and Mule Event**
Aug. 24-25   Forest City
1811 Sage Ct.
Contact: Keith Kyle;
email: kwkyle@wctatel.net
www.heritageparkofnorthiowa.com
See our ad on page 197

⑭ Homer Threshing Bee
Aug. 24-25　　　　　　Webster City
Features: Cockshutt, CO-OP, Gambles
and Farmcrest Tractors and Stationary
Engines.
405 Homer Second St. (8 miles north
of Stratford on Rt. 21).
Contact: Don Lamb, 405 Homer
Second St., Webster City, IA 50595;
505-408-0664;
Facebook: West Central Region
Cockshutt & CO-OP Club

⑮ Midwest Old Threshers Reunion
Aug. 29-Sept. 2　　　　Mount Pleasant
Feature: John Deere.
405 E. Threshers Rd.
Contact: Terry McWilliams, 405
E. Threshers Rd., Mount Pleasant, IA
52641; 319-385-8937;
email: info@oldthreshers.org
www.oldthreshers.com
See our ad on page 24

**⑯ Cedar Valley Engine Club
Threshers Reunion**
Aug. 31-Sept. 2　　　　Charles City
Features: Minneapolis-Moline Tractors
and Economy Engines.
2097 210th St., 7 miles west of town
on Hwy 14.
Contact: Kelly Barnett, 1013 Hawthorne
Ave., Plainfield, IA 50666;
641-257-8171;
email: cvec.threshers@gmail.com
www.cedarvalleyengineclub.com

⑰ Carstens Farm Days
Sept. 7-8　　　　　　　Shelby
Feature: Minneapolis-Moline Tractors.
1-1/2 miles southwest of town, I-80
exit 34.
Contact: Mel Hursey, PO Box 302,
Shelby, IA 51570; 712-544-2341;
email: info@carstensfarm.com
www.carstensfarm.com

⑱ Plagman Barn Show Days
Sept. 20-22　　　　　　Garber
Plagman Barn, 28384 Garber Rd.
Contact: Larry Moser, 34834 Mesquite
Rd., Colesburg, IA 52035;
563-880-1604;
email: dlmoser@alpinecom.net
www.plagmanbarn.com

⑲ 54th Annual Fall Festival
Sept. 21　　　　　　　Oskaloosa
Nelson Pioneer Farm, 2211 Nelson
Ln. From Hwy 63, turn east on Old
Glendale Road, 2 miles to the farm
museum.
Contact: Margaret Stiegel,
PO Box 578, Oskaloosa, IA 52577;
641-672-2989;
email: curator@nelsonpioneer.org
www.nelsonpioneer.org

**⑳ Fall-der-all Antique Tractors and
Engines Festival**
Sept. 28-29　　　　　　Froelich
Feature: John Froelich's Tractors.
Froelich Foundation and Museum,
24397 Froelich Rd., 4 miles east of
Monona on Hwy 15/52.
Contact: Denise Schutte, 24397
Froelich Rd., Froelich, IA 52157;
563-880-1525; 563-536-2841;
email: froelichtractor1892@yahoo.com
www.froelichtractor.com

**❸ 42nd Annual National Farm Toy
Show**
Nov. 1-3　　　　　　　Dyersville
Beckman High School, 1325
Ninth St. S.E.
Contact: Lori Aberle, 7496
106th Ave. S.E., LaMoure, ND 58458;
800-533-8293; 701-883-5206;
email: laberle@toyfarmer.com
www.toyfarmer.com
See our ad on page 194

㉑ 26th Annual Massey Days
June 6-7　　　　　　　Muscatine
Features: Massey-Ferguson, Massey-
Harris and Ferguson and Wallis
Tractors.
1624 Thayer Ave.
Contact: Tim and Connie Pace,
563-263-9122;
email: tkpace89@gmail.com
www.masseycollectors.com

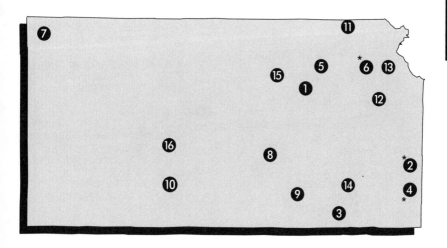

> * Indicates more than one
> show at this site.

KANSAS

1 Spring Crank Up! Tractor Show
April 20   Alta Vista
103 S. Main, 15 minutes south of I-70.
Contact: Connie Larson, 620 Warpole
Rd., Olsburg, KS 66520;
785-468-3640;
email: agheritagepark@gmail.com
www.agheritagepark.com

2 Pioneer Harvest Fiesta Swap Meet
May 10-11   Fort Scott
Bourbon County Fairgrounds, west off
Hwy 69 on 23rd Street.
Contact: Allen Warren, 1906 Maple
Rd., Fort Scott, KS 66701;
620-224-7761;
email: awarren@cebridge.net;
Peggy Niles, treasurer, 620-223-0391;
www.pioneerharvestfiesta.com
See our ad on page 198

**3 Caney Valley Antique Power
Association Pioneer Days**
May 31-June 2   Caney
Features: International Harvester
Tractors and Engines.
3 1/2 miles north on Hwy 75.
Contact: Don Clifford, 111 S. Seminole,
Bartlesville, OK 74003; 918-327-3293;
www.cvapa.com

**4 31st Annual Tractor and Engine
Show**
June 21-22   Pittsburg
Features: McCorminick Deering 10-20
Tractors and International Engines.
On the outer road just off the 69 Hwy
Bypass between 20th Street and
Atkinson Drive.
Contact: Andy Smith, 620-238-9345;
email: a_smitty_@hotmail.com
www.sekgasenginetractorclub.com

5 **Kaw Valley Engine Truck and Tractor Club**
July 4   Wamego
Corner park at Locust and Fourth Street.
Contact: G. Wayne Walker Jr., 14820 Arispie Rd., Onaga, KS 66521; 785-889-4667; email: kcjunior@bluevalley.net

6 **43rd Annual Threshing Show**
July 19-21   Meriden
Features: Massey-Harris Tractors and New Holland Engines.
8275 K-4 Hwy.
Contact: Jess Noll, 8275 K-4 Hwy, Meriden, KS 66512; 785-633-9706; email: lazyjn77@yahoo.com
www.meridenthreshers.org
See our ad on page 199

7 **66th Annual Tri-State Antique Engine and Thresher Show**
July 25-27   Bird City
U.S. Hwy 36.
Contact: Brendon Haack, PO Box 9, Bird City, KS 67731; 785-734-2291; email: bmhaack@eaglecom.net
www.threshershow.org
www.birdcity.com
See our ad on page 198

8 **Goessel Country Threshing Days**
Aug. 2-4   North Newton
Feature: John Deere Tractors.
Wheat County Show Grounds behind the Goessel Grade School.
Contact: Bruce, PO Box 84, 2310 Berry Ave., North Newton, KS 67117; 316-734-2861; email: bfunk457@gmail.com
www.wheatco.org

9 **38th Annual Kansas and Oklahoma Steam and Gas Engine Association Show**
Aug. 16-18   Winfield
Feature: Massey-Harris Tractors.
Winfield Fairgrounds, 1105 West Ninth.
Contact: Billy Metzinger, 620-506-7246;
Les Yung, 620-441-8320;
www.kosgeclub.com
See our ad on page 198

10 **55th Annual SouthWest Kansas Antique Engine and Thresher Show**
Aug. 23-24   Haviland
502 E. Walnut St.
Contact: Andrew Kimble, PO Box 62, Mullinville, KS 67109; 620-408-5600; email: havilandthreshershow@yahoo.com
Facebook: SouthWest Kansas Antique Engine & Thresher Show

11 **Old Albany Days**
Sept. 7-8   Sabetha
Feature: Moline Tractors & Equipment.
U.S. Hwy 75 N, west 1 mile on 192nd Road, north 1-1/2 miles on X Road, east 1/2 mile on 204th Road.
Contact: Doyle Bechtelheimer, PO Box 62, Sabetha, KS 66534; 785-284-3446

12 **25th Annual Power of the Past Antique Engine and Tractor Show**
Sept. 13-15   Ottawa
Features: Ford Tractors and Cushman Engines.
Forest Park, 302 N. Locust.
Contact: David Reeves, Ottawa, KS 66067; 785-241-0834

13 **62nd Annual McLouth Threshing Bee**
Sept. 20-22   McLouth
Feature: John Deere Tractors.
Intersection of K-16 and K-92.
Contact: Austin Chapman, PO Box 63, McLouth, KS 66054; 785-691-6749; email: contactus@mclouththreshingbee.com
www.mclouththreshingbee.com

14 **21st Annual Wilson County Old Iron Days**
Sept. 26-29   Fredonia
Feature: Oliver Hart-Parr Tractors.
Close to intersection of U.S. 400 and KS-47, 1 mile south of KS-47 on Jade Road.
Contact: Jeff Walker, 620-212-8309; email: oldironclub@gmail.com
www.oldironclub.org
See our ad on page 199

6 41st Annual Fall Festival and Swap Meet
Sept. 28-29   Meriden
Features: Massey-Harris Tractors and New Holland Engines.
8275 K-4 Hwy.
Contact: Jess Noll, 8275 K-4 Hwy, Meriden, KS 66512; 785-633-9706;
email: lazyjn77@yahoo.com
www.meridenthreshers.org
See our ad on page 199

15 Heritage Day Festival
Oct. 5   Abilene
Feature: International Harvester.
412 S. Campbell St., I-70 exit 275, south 1.5 miles on Buckeye Avenue, east on southeast Sixth Street.
Contact: Austin Anders, 412 S. Campbell St., Abilene, KS 67410; 785-263-2681;
email: heritagecenterdk@sbcglobal.net
www.heritagecenterdk.com

4 Annual Swap Meet
Oct. 11-12   Pittsburg
On the outer road just off the 69 Hwy Bypass between 20th Street and Atkinson Drive.
Contact: Andy Smith, 620-238-9345;
email: a_smitty_@hotmail.com
www.sekgasenginetractorclub.com

16 19th Annual Santa Fe Trail Tired Iron Show
Oct. 12-13   Larned
1349 K-156 Hwy, 2 miles west of town.
Contact: Santa Fe Trail Center Museum, 1349 K-156 Hwy, Larned, KS 67550; 620-285-2054;
email: museum@santafetrailcenter.org
www.santafetrailcenter.org
See our ad on page 199

2 63rd Annual Pioneer Harvest Fiesta
Oct. 18-20   Fort Scott
Feature: Hercules Engines.
Bourbon County Fairgrounds, west off Hwy 69 on 23rd Street.
Contact: Allen Warren, 1906 Maple Rd., Fort Scott, KS 66701; 620-224-7761;
email: awarren@cebridge.net;
Peggy Niles, treasurer, 620-223-0391;
www.pioneerharvestfiesta.com
See our ad on page 198

17 3rd Annual K.A.E.S.S.A Steam School
April 27-28   Goessel
Wheat County Show Grounds, behind Goessel Elementary School
Contact: Sherry Housos; 785-488-6727;
email: sherryhousos@gmail.com
www.kssteamassoc.com

Show Listings

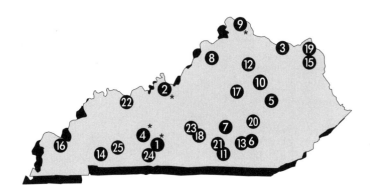

* Indicates more than one
show at this site.

KENTUCKY

❶ Winter Antique Tractor Show
Jan. 12   Bowling Green
Western Kentucky University
Agriculture Expo Center, 406 Elrod
Rd., 1/4 mile south of Natcher
Parkway, exit 6.
Contact: Bill Kratts, 1289 Rockfield
Browning Rd., Rockfield, KY 42274;
931-220-0490;
email: wkratts@gmail.com
www.wcatec.us

**❷ 25th Annual Meade County Farm
Toy Show & Sale**
March 1-3   Brandenburg
Meade County Fairgrounds
Community Building.
Contact: Melody Dodson, 2835
Hardesty Raymond Rd., Webster, KY
40176; 270-547-6443;
email: nmdodson@bbtel.com

**❸ 5th Annual Tollesboro Treasure
Days and Flea Market**
March 1-3   Tollesboro
Tollesboro Lions Club Fairgrounds,
214 Lions Club Rd.
Contact: Clinton Applegate,
PO Box 123, Tollesboro, KY 41189;
606-782-2884;
Facebook: Tollesboro Lions Club

**❹ 23rd Butler County FFA Farm Toy
and Antique Tractor Show**
March 9   Morgantown
Butler County High School, 1852
Main St. Exit 28 off William Natcher
Parkway.
Contact: Ryan Pendley, 270-999-0767;
Lee Ann Daugherty, 270-791-0113

**❺ 17th Annual Hillbilly Flywheelers
Gas Engine and Tractor Show**
April 25-27   Irvine
Estill County Fairgrounds.
Contact: Phillip Sparks, 525
Cedar Grove Rd., Irvine, KY 40336;
606-723-3811; 606-975-5550

6 14th Annual Shopville Community Park Antique Tractor and Small Engine Show
May 4　　　Shopville
Feature: Ford Tractors.
Shopville Community Park, intersection of E. Hwy 80 and 692.
Contact: Larry Price, 1900 Piney Grove Rd., Somerset, KY 42501; 606-416-6080

7 11th Annual Sycamore Flats Flywheelers Show at the Ag Center
May 10-11　　　Liberty
Feature: Allis-Chalmers.
Central Kentucky Ag/Expo Center, 678 S. Wallace Wilkinson.
Contact: Glen Whitis, PO Box 1874, Russell Springs, KY 42642; 270-585-1968;
email: gswhitis@duo-county.com
Facebook: Sycamore Flats Flywheelers

8 5th Annual Salt River Antique Power Tractor Drive
June 1　　　Eminence
Henry County, Kentucky, Fairgrounds.
Contact: Jerry Smith, 71 Goose Creek Ct., Taylorsville, KY 40071; 502-477-6675;
email: snufysmith@att.net

9 Antique Farm Machinery & Craft Show
June 7-8　　　Alexandria
Knights of Columbus Grounds, 11186 S. Licking Pike.
Contact: Greg Rawe, 859-620-1069

10 Clark County Antique Tractor & Machinery Show
June 15　　　Winchester
4980 Ironworks Rd. From I-64 take exit 96 and go south to the first light. Turn left on Veteran's Memorial Parkway (KY 1958). Go for 1.6 miles then turn left on KY 15 (third light). Travel 3.2 miles, Clark County Fairgrounds on the left.
Contact: Ernest Barnes, 2244 Irvine Rd., Winchester, KY 40391; 859-556-0155;
email: ffbarnes@yahoo.com
Facebook: Clark County Antique Tractor and Machinery Club

11 Sycamore Flats Flywheelers Lakefest Historic Machinery Show
July 6　　　Jamestown
43 West Cumberland Ave.
Contact: Glen Whitis, PO Box 1874, Russell Springs, KY 42642; 270-585-3227;
email: gswhitis@duo-county.com
Facebook: Sycamore Flats Flywheelers

2 27th Annual Antique Tractor and Engine Show
July 20-21　　　Brandenburg
Features: Massey-Harris and Ferguson Tractors.
Meade County Fairgrounds in conjunction with Meade County Fair.
Contact: Alan Thomas, 12555 Hwy 60, Guston, KY 40142; 270-547-7505;
email: abthomas@bbtel.com

12 49th Annual Central Kentucky Antique Machinery Association Show
July 26-27　　　Paris
Feature: Allis-Chalmers Tractors.
Bourbon County Fairgrounds, 30 Legion Rd.
Contact: Amber Biddle, 234 Creekview Dr., Paris, KY 40361; 859-588-0478;
email: amberjane2100@gmail.com
See our ad on page 18

4 13th Annual Tractor Show
Aug. 2-3　　　Morgantown
Features: Allis-Chalmers, Allis-Chalmers/Simplicity, and Lawn and Garden Tractors and Almo Engines.
Charles Black City Park. 150 Helm Ln. Exit 28 and 29 off Natcher Parkway North.
Contact: Roger Tanner, 1193 Caney Fork Rd., Lewisburg, KY 42256; 270-726-5155;
Facebook: Butler County Antique Tractor & Engine Club
See our ad on page 200

⑬ 2nd Annual Sycamore Flats Flywheelers Tractor Show and Farmer's Market
Aug. 10   Somerset
Somerset Mall Farmer's Market.
Contact: Glen Whitis, PO Box 1874,
Russell Springs, KY 42642;
270-585-3227;
email: gswhitis@duo-county.com
Facebook: Sycamore Flats
Flywheelers

❶ 15th Annual Vette City Lions Motor Fest
Aug. 17   Bowling Green
From Bowling Green, exit 6 from
Natcher Parkway, south on 31 W
6 miles to Chaney's Dairy Barn, 9191
Nashville Rd.
Contact: Lyndell Graven, 6299
Louisville Rd., Bowling Green, KY
42101; 270-843-1556;
email: lyndellgraven@twc.com

❶ Warren County Antique Tractor & Engine Club at the 15th Annual Vette City Lions Motorfest
Aug. 17   Bowling Green
From Bowling Green, exit 6 from
Natcher Parkway, south on 31W,
6 miles to Chaney's Dairy Barn, 9191
Nashville Rd.
Contact: Lyndell Graven, 6299
Louisville Rd., Bowling Green, KY
42101; 270-843-1556;
email: lyndellgraven@twc.com

⑭ Hopkinsville Antique Tractor and Small Engine Show
Sept. 6-7   Hopkinsville
Cherokee Park Show Grounds, 1599
Shawnee Dr. Take exit 8 off Pennyrile
Parkway, turn west, travel past first
stop light, Shawnee Drive is the next
right. Look for signs.
Contact: Howard Jones, 6250
Greenville Rd., Hopkinsville,
KY 42240; 270-348-5883;
email: christyjo20@hotmail.com
Facebook: Hopkinsville Antique Tractor
and Small Engine Show

⑮ Old Time Machinery Show
Sept. 6-7   Grayson
South of town on St. Rt. 7.
Contact: Brenda Eldridge, 509
Eldridge Rd., Grayson, KY 41143;
606-474-8189;
email: brendaeldridge8189@yahoo.com

⑯ 42nd Annual McCracken County FFA Alumni Antique Gas Engine and Tractor Show
Sept. 19-21   Paducah
Carson Park, 300 N 30th St.
Contact: Michael Wood, 7020
Old Mayfield Rd., Paducah, KY 42003;
270-832-1167;
email:
michael.wood@mccracken.kyschools.us
Facebook: Paducah Antique Tractor &
Gas Engine Show
See our ad on page 4

⑰ Tractor and Engine Show
Sept. 20-21   Nicholasville
Feature: Allis-Chalmers Tractors.
Jessamine Co. Fairgrounds, 95 Park
Dr. From South Main Street, turn east
onto Longview Drive across from
Kroger, turn right at stop sign, follow
through subdivision to fairgrounds.
Contact: Chris Riggs, 859-396-3650;
email: info@jcafeinc.com
www.jcafeinc.com

⑱ Greensburg Rotary Club's Cow Days, Antique Tractor and Gas Engine Show
Sept. 21   Greensburg
Downtown Greensburg.
Contact: Jon Darnell, 3415 Hwy 88,
Greensburg, KY 42743; 270-932-1249

⑲ 20th Annual Greenup Old Tractors, Engines and Machinery Show
Oct. 3-5   Greenup
Features: Case Tractors and Michigan-
built Engines.
Intersection U.S. 23 and Washington
Street; Greenup Farm Bureau
showgrounds.
Contact: Mike Bryant, 3938 Dickerson
Rd., Ashland, KY 41102;
606-324-0191;
email: mike32844@yahoo.com

㉓ 24th Annual South East Kentucky Antique Tractor Show
Oct. 3-5   Renfro Valley
Features: Allis-Chalmers and Oliver Hart-Parr Tractors.
I-75, exit 62.
Contact: Dennis Elliot, 662 Elliot Acres, Yosemite, KY 42566; 606-706-3888; www.southeastkentuckytractor.com

㉑ 12th Annual Show at the Park
Oct. 5   Russell Springs
Feature: Allis-Chalmers.
Russell Springs City Park, 130 Milton Heights.
Contact: Glen Whitis, PO Box 1874, Russell Springs, KY 42642; 270-585-3227;
email: gswhitis@duo-county.com
Facebook: Sycamore Flats Flywheelers

㉒ 33rd Annual Farm Festival
Oct. 5-6   Philpot
Features: International Harvester Tractors and Engines.
Lampkin Farm, 8284 Short Station Rd. Go east of Owensboro on Hwy 54, 2 miles past Philpot to Karns Grove Road, then follow the signs.
Contact: Dennis Hutchinson, 3780 N. Old State Rd., Rockport, IN 47635; 812-660-2192;
email: 31stlnd@gmail.com
www.kyantiquefarmmachinery association.com

❾ Campbell County Log Cabin History and Farm Heritage Museum
Oct. 12   Alexandria (Grants Lick)
890 Clayridge Rd. U.S. Hwy. 27 to Grants Lick (Rt. 1936). Follow signs, 1 mile up the hill.
Contact: Kenneth A. Reis, 890 Clayridge Rd., Alexandria, KY 41001; 859-466-0638;
email: kennethareis@yahoo.com

㉓ Summersville Fun Days Tractor and Old Engine Show
Oct. 12   Summersville
Call for directions.
Contact: David Milby, 379 V D Milby Rd., Greensburg, KY 42743; 270-932-1573

㉔ Woodburn Antique Tractor, Engine, Truck and Car Show
Oct. 12   Woodburn
From Bowling Green, take exit 6 off Natcher Parkway, south on 31. Drive 9 miles to Woodburn. Left on Hwy 240 E., 1 mile on right.
Contact: Linda Dickerson, 2286 Woodburn-Allen Springs Rd., Woodburn, KY 42179; 270-784-0170;
email: didfarm@bellsouth.net

㉕ 14th Annual Clifty Tractor 7 Car Show
Oct. 18-19   Clifty
Clifty School Park, intersection of Hwy 181 and 890.
Contact: Darrell Keeling, PO Box 213, Clifty, KY 42216; 270-604-2804;
email: meganpeg1234@gmail.com
www.cliftytractorclub.webs.com

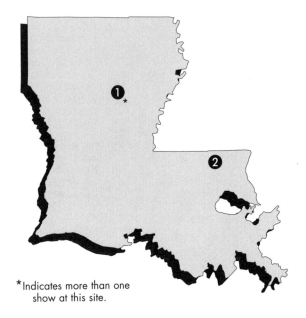

*Indicates more than one
show at this site.

LOUISIANA

❶ Jena Spring Tractor Show and Pull
March 16   Jena
Jena Fairgrounds.
Contact: Roselea Cooper,
318-992-2206;
email: roseleacooper@yahoo.com

**❷ IHC LA Chapter #31 Tractor and
Engine Show**
May 2-4   Franklinton
Features: International Harvester and
Farmall Tractors.
Washington Parish Fairgrounds,
100 Main St.
Contact: Buddy Banks, 13364
Hwy 21 S., Bogalusa, LA 70427;
985-732-3950;
email: bhbanks@bellsouth.net

❶ Jena Fall Tractor Show and Pull
Oct. 19   Jena
Jena Fairgrounds.
Contact: Roselea Cooper,
318-992-2206;
email: roseleacooper@yahoo.com

MAINE

1 Antique Engine and Outboard Meet
July 6   Boothbay
586 Wiscasset Rd., 7 miles south
of Rt. 27 S.
Contact: Margaret Hoffman,
PO Box 123, Boothbay, ME 04537;
207-633-1727;
email: staff@railwayvillage.org
www.railwayvillage.org

**2 24th Eliot Antique Tractor and
Engine Show**
July 26-28   Eliot
Features: Ford Tractors and
Old Engines.
2077 St. Rd. (Rt. 103). Only 45 minutes
from Portland, ME or Boston, MA. Take
Rt. 236 north from I95 at exit 2 or 3 in
Maine, go 5 miles until you see Rt. 103
(State Road), take a left and it will be
on the right.
Contact: Tom and Lisa Raitt, 2077
St. Rd., Eliot, ME 03903;
207-748-3303;
email: info@raittfarmmuseum.org
www.raittfarmmuseum.org

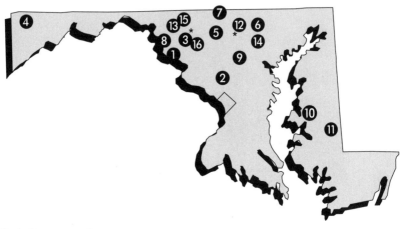

*　Indicates more than one
show at this site.

MARYLAND

❶ Annual Toy Auction and Toy Show
Feb. 9-10　　　　　　　　　　Brunswick
Brunswick Volunteer Fire Co. Hall,
1500 Volunteer Dr.
Contact: Mike Driver, PO Box 212,
Mount Airy, MD 21771; 301-829-9275;
email: cmatc@comcast.net
www.cmatc.org

**❷ Friends of the Agricultural History
Farm Park Gas and Steam Engine
Show**
April 6-7　　　　　　　　　　Derwood
18400 Muncaster Rd.
Contact: Maurice Ward, 634 Blossom
Dr., Rockville, MD 20850;
301-738-9892;
email: msward20850@yahoo.com
www.friendsofthefarmpark.org

❸ 28th Annual Antique Tractor Show
May 4-5　　　　　　　　　　Frederick
Gladhill Tractor, 5509 Mount Zion Rd.
Take Rt. 15 to Rt. 340 W., second exit
at Mount Zion Road N. On right.
Contact: Howard Salan, 12113
Merricks Ct., Monrovia, MD 21770;
443-677-8928;
email: hjsalan@comcast.net

**❹ Farm Toy Show and Sale
and Antique Tractor, Truck and
Car Show**
May 18　　　　　　　　　　Accident
86 Pride Pkwy.
Contact: Becky Yost, 86 Pride Pkwy.,
Accident, MD 21520;
email:
becky.yost@garrettcountyschools.org

5 Johnsville Ruritan Spring Show
May 18-19   Johnsville
11375 Green Valley Rd.,
Union Bridge, MD.
Contact: Robin Ibex, 11704 Keymar
Rd., Keymar, MD 21757;
410-775-2390;
email: daisey11704@msn.com

6 Hampstead Day Tractor Show
May 25   Upperco
Features: John Deere and Farmall
Tractors, and International McCormick
and John Deere Engines.
16020 Carnival Ave., held at the
Upperco Fire Co. Show Grounds;
same location as the Maryland Steam
Show in September.
Contact: Gary "Tadpole" Snyder,
443-257-0823

**7 42nd Annual Kingsdale
Gas Engine Show**
June 1-2   Harney
Features: Oliver Hart-Parr Tractors,
Equipment, and Associated Gas
Engines.
Harney Volunteer Fire Co., 5130
Harney Rd., Taneytown, MD.
5 miles south of U.S. Rt. 15 on Rt. 134.
Contact: Steve Harmon, 3341 Blacks
Schoolhouse Rd., Taneytown, MD
21787; 410-346-7327; 443-953-0119;
John Harmon, 443-605-6752;
email: ihcjon@aol.com

**3 41st Annual Central Maryland
Antique Tractor Club Gas Engine
and Tractor Show**
June 7-9   Frederick
Gladhill Tractor, 5509 Mount Zion Rd.
Contact: Jeremiah Herbst, 8104
Ray Smith Rd., Frederick, MD 21704;
443-286-7843;
email: cmatc@comcast.net
www.cmatc.org
See our ad on page 199

8 Strawberry Festival
June 8-9   Rohrersville
21023 Rohrersville School Rd.
Contact: J.R. Smith, 240-818-1038;
email: lumpymck@myactv.net

9 Howard County Summer Fest
June 22-23   West Friendship
12985 Frederick Rd. 1/2 mile west
of Rt. 32 and Rt. 144 intersection.
Across from Howard County
Fairgrounds Road.
Contact: Virginia Frank, 11785
Triadelphia Rd., Ellicott City, MD
21042; 410-531-2569;
email: jsrstar@verizon.net
www.farmheritage.org

**10 46th Annual Tuckahoe Steam and
Gas Engine Reunion and Show**
July 11-14   Easton
Features: Orchard and H. Corp., Wheel
Horse Garden Tractors; Domestic Gas
Engines.
5 miles north on U.S. Rt. 50, between
mile markers 58-59.
Contact: PO Box 636, Easton, MD
21601; 410-822-9868;
www.tuckahoesteam.org
See our ad on page 29

**11 59th Annual Eastern Shore
Threshermen and Collectors Assn.
Old-Time Wheat Threshing, Steam
and Gas Engine Show**
Aug. 2-4   Federalsburg
5806 Federalsburg Hwy, Rt. 313
between Denton and Federalsburg.
Contact: Brenda Stant, 6101 Harmony
Rd., Preston, MD 21655;
410-673-2414;
email: threshermen@gmail.com
www.threshermen.org
See our ad on page 202

3 12th Annual Wheat Threshing
Aug. 3-4   Frederick
Rose Hill Park, 1161 N. Market St.
Contact: Dan Herbst, 8104 Ray Smith
Rd., Frederick, MD 21704;
301-343-5093;
email: mdihcc39@comcast.net
www.mdihcc39.org

⓬ Gravely Tractor Club of America Mow-In 2019
Aug. 22-24   Westminster
Feature: Gravely.
Carroll County Farm Museum, 500 South Center St. In conjunction with the 57th Annual Mason-Dixon Historical Society Steam and Gas Round-Up.
Contact: Doug Hoelscher, 403 S. Mill St., New Knoxville, OH 45871; 419-296-0812;
email: dhoelscher@nktelco.net
www.gtcoa.com

⓭ Rural Heritage Spud Fest & Antique Tractor Show
Aug. 24-25   Boonsboro
Features: International Harvester and Farmall Tractors.
Agricultural Education Center, 7303 Sharpsburg Pike.
Contact: Joel Reynolds, 11328 Whitehall Rd., Smithsburg, MD 21783; 240-217-5093;
email: jreynolds@jrservisesmd.com; Howard Thomas (for vendors), 20641 Millers Church Rd., Hagerstown, MD 21742; 301-790-2422;
www.wcatc.org

⓬ 57th Annual Steam and Gas Round-Up Mason-Dixon Historical Society
Sept. 6-8   Westminster
Features: Minneapolis-Moline, Sears and David Bradley Tractors.
500 S. Center St.
Contact: Shane Ey, PO Box 67, Westminster, MD 21158; 410-913-5627;
email: shane.ey@hotmail.com; Joe Rogers (flea market info), 410-274-0447;
See our ad on page 200

⓮ 64th Annual Steam and Gas Engine Show
Sept. 12-15   Arcadia
Fire Company Grounds, 16060 Arcadia Ave., Rt. 30, 5 miles north of Reisterstown, 3 miles south of Hampstead.
Contact: Jodi Rill, 3720 Millers Station Rd., Manchester, MD 21102; 443-375-1273;
email: mdsteamhistoricalsociety@gmail.com
www.marylandsteam.org
See our ad on page 201

⓯ Catoctin Antique Gas Engine Show
Oct. 5-6   Wolfsville
Wolfsville Ruritan Club Park, 2708 Brandenburg Hollow Rd.
Contact: David Fogle, 3835 Brethren Church Rd., Myersville, MD 21773; 301-606-9130;
email: caseyo6@verizon.net

⓰ 11th Annual Fall Harvest
Oct. 19-20   Ijamsville
Murphy's Farm,11502 Browningsville Rd.
Contact: Jerry Murphy, 11502 Browningsville Rd., Ijamsville, MD 21754; 301-418-0635;
email: mdihcc39@comcast.net
www.mdihcc39.org

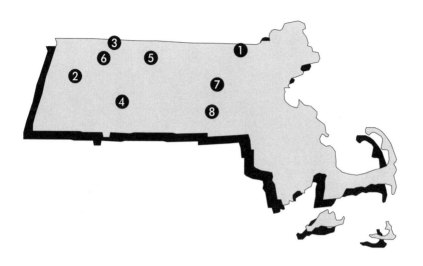

MASSACHUSETTS

❶ Dunstable Show
May 5   Dunstable
From the junction of U.S. 3 and
Rt. 113, 1 mile west on Rt. 113.
Follow signs.
Contact: David Beard, 584
S. Mammoth Rd., Manchester, NH
03109; 603-623-2217;
email: dl.beard@comcast.net

❷ 12th Annual Hillside Tractor Ride
May 19   Cummington
Rt. 9 to Fairgrounds Road, t
o Cummington Fairgrounds.
Contact: Francis Judd, 145
Berkshire Trail W., Goshen, MA 01032;
413-268-3264;
email: juddsgoshenstone@gmail.com

**❸ Bernardston Gas Engine Show
and Flea Market**
May 25-26   Bernardston
Pratt's Field.
Contact: Vickie Ovitt (engine show),
413-834-0103; Harvey Phelps (flea
market), 413-648-9551;
www.unitedchurchofbernardston.org

**❹ Charter Day Antique Tractor Pull
and Show**
June 9   Granby
Feature: Friday, Case and Massey.
Dufresne Recreation Park, Taylor
Street entrance of Rt. 202.
Contact: George Randall, 52 Taylor
St., Granby, MA 01033; 413-530-5218;
email: george.randall3@comcast.net

5 **43rd Annual Central Mass Steam Gas and Machinery Association Yankee Engine-uity Show**
June 29-30   Orange
Feature: Moline Tractors.
80 Airport St.
Contact: Grover Ballou, PO Box 32, Orange, MA 01364; 413-249-2895; email: info@cmsgma.com
www.cmsgma.com

6 **Retired Iron Tractor Show**
July 6-7   Greenfield
Features: Farmall H and Bolens Garden Tractors and John Deere Engines.
89 Wisdom Way at the Fairgrounds. Exit 26 off Rt. 91, follow Rt. 2A east to right at Dunkin' Donuts, turn right onto River Street and third right (approximately 1/2 mile) onto Wisdom Way. Signs will be posted.
Contact: Mike Scranton, 109 Shelburne Line Rd., Colrain, MA 01340; 413-834-8208; email: retiredironshow.org
www.retirediron.org

7 **40th Annual Straw Hollow Engine Works Show**
Aug. 10-11   Boylston
100 Cross St. off Rt. 70.
Contact: Daniel Moore, 125 Linden St., Boylston, MA 01505; 508-869-2722

8 **40th Annual Waters Farm Days Fall Festival**
Oct. 19-20   Sutton
53 Waters Rd.
Contact: Ken Ethier, 4 Uxbridge Rd., Sutton, MA 01590; 508-832-6678; email: emethier5@charter.net
www.watersfarm.com

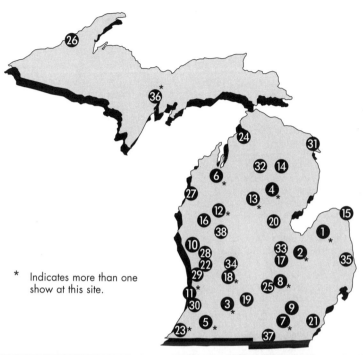

* Indicates more than one show at this site.

MICHIGAN

1 16th Annual Farm Collectibles and Toy Show
Feb. 23　　　　　　　　　　　Caro
Feature: Ford,
The Brentwood, 178 Park Dr.
Contact: Dale Will, 2100 W. Sanilac Rd.,
Caro, MI 48723; 989-673-3430;
email: dswill@centurytel.net
www.carotractorshow.com
See our ad on page 208

2 43rd Spring Swap Meet
April 19-20　　　　　　　　　　Clio
Clio Fireman's Park, 1170 W. Wilson Rd.
Contact: Bob Watson, 14055 Vassar
Rd., Millington, MI. 48746;
810-513-0369; 989-871-2467;
email: mmamaclio@gmail.com
www.mmama.org

3 Olde Tyme Plow Days and Swap Meet
April 27-28　　　　　　　　　Scotts
Features: Oliver Hart Parr Tractors and
Fairbanks and Morse Engines.
Scotts Mill Park, 8451 S. 35th St.,
follow the signs.
Contact: Marian Beardsley-Gibbs,
7920 S. 36th St., Scotts, MI 49088;
269-779-1972;
www.sotpea.org
See our ad on page 211

4 Pioneer Power Antique Tractor and Gas Engine Swap Meet
May 2-4　　　　　　　　　West Branch
302 W. M-55. 5 miles east of town or
1 mile west of M-33.
Contact: Walt Sappington, president,
989-240-3637;
Facebook: Pioneer Power
See our ad on page 210

5 35th Annual Michiana Antique Engine and Tractor Swap Meet
May 3-4   Jones
Boot Hill Ranch, 1-1/2 miles east of
Jones on Bair Lake Street.
Contact: Tim Rossman, 269-651-4878;
David Machan, 269-625-7232
See our ad on page 204

6 37th Annual Buckley Old Engine Spring Swap Meet
May 17-18   Buckley
Buckley Show Grounds, M-37.
Contact: Jim Luper, 231-499-6574;
email: tractornutjim@yahoo.com
www.buckleyoldengineshow.org
See our ad on page 207

7 26th Annual Farmer's Antique Tractor and Engine Spring Show
May 17-19   Adrian
Feature: International Harvester Tractors.
5 miles west of Adrian, corner of
U.S. Hwy 223 and Forrister Road.
Contact: Jackie Salsbury, 11803
Wegner Rd., Riga, MI 49276;
517-673-5104; Jim Opersal & Lois
Tuberville (flea market), 517-673-6522;
567-454-7412;
www.adrianfatea.org
See our ad on page 209

8 28th Annual Hudson Mills Old Power Antique Gas Engine and Tractor Show
May 31-June 2   Fowlerville
8800 W. Grand River Ave. I-96 exit 129,
north to W. Grand River Avenue, west
to fairgrounds.
Contact: Joe (pull), 517-545-0322;
Judi (vendor), 248-804-8507; or Jenny
(camping), 517-223-8186;
www.hmopc.com
See our ad on page 211

9 Clinton Summerfest and Antique Tractor Show
June 1   Clinton
Tate Park, 475 W. Michigan Ave. or
U.S. 12.
Contact: Basil Greenleaf, 4505
Pennington Rd., Clinton, MI 49236;
517-423-6371;
email: greenleafbg@ymail.com

10 28th Annual Antique Farm Power Club Antique Tractor and Engine Show
June 6-8   Fruitport
Feature: Oliver Hart-Parr Tractors,
Garden Tractors and Trucks for
the Decades.
Muskegon County Fairgrounds,
6621 Heights Ravenna Rd.
Contact: Mark Scholten, 616-293-1961;
www.antiquefarmpowerclub.biz
See our ad on page 202

11 Swap Meet & Flea Market
June 7-8   South Haven
06285 68th St.
Contact: Patrick Ingalls, 64958 M-43
Hwy, Bangor, MI 49013; 269-639-2010;
email:
michiganflywheelers@yahoo.com
www.michiganflywheelers.org
See our ad on page 202

12 Big Rapids Antique Farm and Power Club Swap Meet and Flea Market
June 7-8   Big Rapids
Features: Allis-Chalmers Tractors,
Gamble and Noble Engines, and
Hit-and-Miss Engines.
15422 Old Mill Pond Rd.
East of town on M-20; at corner of Old
Mill Pond and M-20.
Contact: Gordon Oliver, 14851
230th Ave., Big Rapids, MI 49307;
231-408-2393;
email: gordonoliver@hotmail.com
www.bigrapidstractorclub.com

13 Twenty Lakes Antique Engine and Tractor Show
June 19-23   Harrison
Features: Minneapolis-Moline Tractors
and Hercules and Onan Engines.
2411 Temple Dr. 4-1/2 miles west on
M-61 from stoplight.
Contact: Nathan and Nancy Blakemore,
2523 W. Arnold Lake Rd., Harrison, MI
48625; 989-339-0764;
email: nancyblakemore357@gmail.com

14 AuSable Valley Engine and Tractor Show
June 28-29   Mio
Oscoda County Fairgrounds, 1889
Caldwell Rd., north on Caldwell Road
off M-33 between Mio and Fairview.
Contact: Lynn Roemer, president,

8550 S. Black River Rd., Onaway, MI
49765; 989-370-5471;
email: ausablevalleytractors@gmail.com

**⑮ Port Hope Antique Gas Engine and
Tractor Show**
July 5-7   Port Hope
Feature: Economy Tractors.
Contact: Roy Reinke, 4128 Main St.,
Port Hope, MI 48468; 989-428-4838

**⑯ Jugville Old Engine Club
Annual Show**
July 11-13   Jugville
Feature: Engines in Their Work Clothes.
The Shack on Robinson Lake. 50 miles
north of Grand Rapids.
Contact: Butch, 231-250-6873;
www.theshackbedandbreakfast.com
See our ad on page 211

**⑰ 3rd Annual Heart of Michigan
Antique Tractor Club Show**
July 12-13   Owosso
Bennington Township Hall,
5849 S. M52.
Ron, 517-282-6761; Lee, 517-202-5921;
or Floyd, 517-896-7134;
4400 W. Lovejoy Rd., Perry, MI 48872

**⑱ Vintage Garden Tractor Club of
America National Expo 2019**
July 12-13   Hastings
2545 S. Charlton Park Rd.
Contact: Doug Tallman, 804 N. Trimble
Rd., Mansfield, OH 44906;
419-545-2609;
email: dtallman@accnorwalk.com
www.vgtcoa.com

**⑲ 3rd Annual Antique Tractor and
Equipment Show**
July 12-14   Marshall
Features: Alternative Fuels, LP, All Fuel,
Rare Gas and Diesel Tractors.
189 15-1/2 Mile Rd.
Contact: Alex Woodward, 425 E Bristol
Rd., Delton, MI 49046; 517-795-7824;
email: ccyatractors@gmail.com
www.calhouncountyyesteryear
association.com

**⑱ 48th Annual Antique Gas and Steam
Engine Show**
July 12-14   Hastings
Feature: International Harvester
Tractors.
Historic Charlton Park Village,
2545 S. Charlton Park Rd.
Contact: Dan Patton, 269-945-3775;
email: info@charltonpark.org;
Russ Yage (flea market & swap),
616-299-4223;
www.charltonpark.org
See our ad on page 209

⑳ 31st Annual Midland Antique Engine
July 12-14   Midland
3226 S. Meridian Rd., 6 miles south
of M-20 or 5 miles north of M-46 on
Meridian Road.
Contact: Riggie, 152 N. Homer Rd.,
Midland, MI 48640; 989-859-6480;
email: hsriggie@gmail.com;
Sharon Riggie, 989-859-0206;
www.maeai.org

**⑱ Summer Show at the
Barry County Fair**
July 14-20   Hastings
Barry County Fairgrounds, 4 miles
north of town on M-37.
Contact: Chad Furrow, 269-804-9881

**㉑ 30th Annual Southeast Michigan
Antique Tractor & Engine Show**
July 18-20   Monroe
Features: Minneapolis Moline 7
Cockshutt Tractors and Hit-and-Miss
Gas Engines.
Nike Park, Newport Road. Exit 21 off
I-75, 2-1/2 miles west to park.
Contact: Lee Eggert, president,
734-279-1202; Brian Hoppert, vice
president & flea market, 734-777-9611;
www.smatea.org
See our ad on page 210

㉒ Riverbend Steam & Gas Show
July 18-20   Allendale
9853 56th Ave. 12 miles west of
Grand Rapids on M-45 to 56th
Avenue, then south 1-1/2 miles to the
Lee Scholma Farm.
Contact: Richard L. Gilder, 2222
92nd SW, Byron Center, MI 49315;
616-878-0846;
email: brljgilder@att.net
www.riverbendshow.com

④ 26th Annual Pioneer Power Antique Tractor and Gas Engine Show, Flea Market and Crafts
July 18-21   West Branch
5 miles east of West Branch on M-55 or 1 mile west of M-33.
Contact: Walt Sappington, president, 989-240-3637;
Facebook: Pioneer Power
See our ad on page 210

❸ Olde Tyme Tractor and Steamer Show
July 19-21   Scotts
Scotts Mill Park, 8451 S. 35th St.
Contact: Marian Beardsley-Gibbs, 7920 S. 36th St., Scotts, MI 49088; 269-779-1972;
www.sotpea.org
See our ad on page 211

㉓ River Valley Antique Summer Show
July 20-21   Three Oaks
7816 Warren Woods Rd., 3 miles north, 2 miles west of town.
Contact: Delbert Kelver, 52671 Lilac Rd., South Bend, IN 46628; 574-272-1145;
email: delbert1929@att.net

㉔ 32nd Annual Show
July 25-28   Walloon Lake
00145 US-131, Boyne Falls, 4 miles south of town on U.S. Hwy 131.
Contact: Debra L. Matthew,
03017 Coash Rd., Vanderbilt, MI 49795; 231-675-7434;
email: flywheelersclub@gmail.com
www.walloonlakeflywheelers.com
See our ad on page 210

⑫ 21st Annual Big Rapids Antique Farm and Power Club Swap Meet and Flea Market
July 26-27   Big Rapids
Features: Allis-Chalmers Tractors, Gamble and Noble Engines, and Hit-and-Miss Engines.
15422 Old Mill Pond Rd., east of town on M-20; at corner of Old Mill Pond and M20.
Contact: Gordon Oliver,
14851 230th Ave., Big Rapids, MI 49307; 231-408-2393;
email: gordonoliver@hotmail.com
www.bigrapidstractorclub.com

㉕ 61st Annual Michigan Steam Engine and Threshers Club Reunion
July 26-28   Mason
Contact: Todd Luks, 517-628-2635;
email: toddluks@aol.com
See our ad on page 205

㉖ Michigan/Wisconsin Antique Power Association
July 27-28   Greenland
Ontonagon County Fairgrounds.
Contact: Rob Drier, 906-224-7251;
email: rdrier@up.net

㉗ 46th Annual Old Engine and Tractor Show
Aug. 1-3   Scottville
Scottville Riverside Park, 700 S. Scottville Rd.
Contact: Bruce Patterson, 231-843-2483;
www.oldengineclub.org

❺ 59th Annual St. Joe Valley Old Engine Association Show
Aug. 2-4   Jones
Features: Allis-Chalmers and Rumely Tractors.
1 1/2 miles east of town on Blair Lake St.
Contact: Tim Rossman, 71026 Miller Rd., Sturgis, MI 49091; 269-651-4878;
email: bakertow1@mail.com
www.sjvoea.org
See our ad on page 204

㉘ 21st Annual Coopersville Tractor Show
Aug. 7-10   Coopersville
Features: International Harvester and Farmall.
Coopersville Farm Museum, 375 Main St. Take either 19 or 16 off 96 and follow signs to downtown. Coopersville is located halfway between Grand Rapids and the Lakeshore.
Contact: Coopersville Farm Museum, PO Box 64, Coopersville, MI 49404; 616-997-8555;
email:
info@coopersvillefarmmuseum.org
www.coopersvillefarmmuseum.org

㉙ Rust n Dust Antique Steam and Gas Show
Aug. 8-11   Zeeland
8427 Taylor St.
Contact: Emily Ferwerda, 8354 Stanton St., Zeeland, MI 49464; 616-218-0780;

email:
rustnduststeamshow@yahoo.com
www.rustnduststeamandgasshow.
weebly.
com
See our ad on page 211

30 **22nd Annual Hartford Old Engine and Tractor Show**
Aug. 30-Sept. 1   Hartford
Feature: Fords.
Van Buren County Fairgrounds,
Red Arrow Highway.
Contact: Bill Yankovich, PO Box 116,
Lawrence, MI 49064; 269-503-4510;
email: yankovichbill@gmail.com
www.hartfordtractorshow.com

1 **44th Annual Thumb Area Old Engine and Tractor Association Show**
Aug. 9-11   Caro
Feature: Ford.
Tuscola County Fairgrounds,
188 Park Dr.
Contact: Corey Will, 4425 Leix Rd.,
Mayville, MI 48744; 989-325-1176;
email: deereboy87@hotmail.com
www.carotractorshow.com
See our ad on page 208

31 **Alpena Antique Tractor and Steam Engine Show**
Aug. 9-11   Alpena
Take U.S. 23 north out of town,
approximately 3 miles to 6850 French
Rd., near intersection of Naylor Road.
Contact: Nathan Wojda, 1150 Halley
Rd., Alpena, MI 49707; 989-358-0380;
email: alpenatractor@gmail.com
www.alpenaantiquetractor.com

32 **Wellington Antique Tractor & Engine Club**
Aug. 9-11   Grayling
Feature: Allis-Chalmers.
6940 S. Military Rd. Exit 251 from
I-75, west 3 miles to Military Road, left
(south) 1 mile to Wellington Farm's
west side.
Contact: Carl Hunt, 9065 E. Houghton
Lake Rd., Merritt, MI 49667;
989-915-1872;
email: mafd102@hotmail.com

6 **52 Annual Buckley Old Engine Show**
Aug. 15-18   Buckley
1 mile west of town on M-37.
Contact: Jim Luper, 231-499-6574;
email: tractornutjim@yahoo.com
www.buckleyoldengineshow.org
See our ad on page 207

33 **45th Annual Mid-Michigan Old Gas Tractor Show**
Aug 16-18   Oakley
Feature: International Harvester Tractors.
17180 W. Ferden Rd.
Contact: Jody Schlicklin, 896
West Braden Rd., Perry, MI 48872;
517-625-3263;
email: jschlicklin71@gmail.com
www.mmogta.org
See our ad on page 206

34 **30th Annual Clarksville Steam and Gas Engine Tractor Show**
Aug. 22-24   Clarksville
Feature: John Deere.
I-96 exit 69 (Clarksville), go through
town across railroad tracks to Robbins
Road, west to the show grounds, watch
for signs.
Contact: Vickie, 616-893-5545

35 **35th Annual St. Clair County Farm Museum Fall Harvest Days**
Aug. 23-25   Goodells
Feature: J.I. Case Tractors & Equipment.
Goodells County Park, 8310 County
Park Dr., Wales, MI. Hosting the
International Harvester Collectors Club
Chapter 11 of Michigan.
Contact: Mark Schwab, 1747 Ditty
Rd., Kimball, MI 48074; 810-367-3470;
email: markschwab@yahoo.com
www.stclaircountyfarmmuseum.org
See our ad on page 207

36 **44th Annual U.P. Steam and Gas Engine Show**
Aug. 30-Sept. 2   Escanaba
Features: John Deere Tractors and
Flywheel Engines.
U.P. State Fairgrounds, U.S. Hwys 2
and 41.
Contact: Robert Willis, 4880 11.5 Rd.,
Escanaba, MI 49829; 906-789-1257;
email: robwillis@charter.net
www.upsteamandgasengine.org
See our ad on page 208

8 Hudson Mills Old Power Fall Antique Tractor Pulls
Aug. 31-Sept. 1   Fowlerville
8800 W. Grand River Ave. I-96 exit 129, north to W. Grand River Avenue, west to fairgrounds.
Contact: Joe (pull), 517-545-0322; Judi (vendor), 248-804-8507; or Jenny (camping), 517-223-8186;
www.hmopc.com
See our ad on page 211

37 Waldron Antique Tractor Show
Aug. 31-Sept. 2   Waldron
Feature: Silver King.
Hwy 127 to Camden Road, turn left on Waldron Road, take to Water Street, turn right. Water tower in the background.
Contact: Phil Siegel, 10511 Tuttle Rd., Pittsford, MI 49271; 517-383-2936; 517-673-1623

11 Antique Engine & Tractor Show
Sept. 5-8   South Haven
06285 68th St.
Contact: Patrick Ingalls, 64958 M-43 Hwy, Bangor, MI 49013; 269-639-2010;
email: michiganflywheelers@yahoo.com
www.michiganflywheelers.org
See our ad on page 206

7 34th Annual Farmer's Antique Tractor and Engine Fall Show
Sept. 20-22   Adrian
Feature: International Harvester Tractors.
5 miles west, corner of U.S. Hwy 223 and Forrister Road.
Contact: Jackie Salsbury, 11803 Wegner Rd., Riga, MI 49276; 517-672-5104; Jim Opersal & Lois Tuberville (flea market), 517-673-6522; 567-454-7412;
www.adrianfatea.org
See our ad on page 209

2 43rd Annual Fall Show
Sept. 20-22   Clio
Clio Fireman's Park, 1170 W. Wilson Rd.
Contact: Bob Watson, 14055 Vassar Rd., Millington, MI 48746; 989-871-2467; 810-513-0369;

email: mmamaclio@gmail.com
www.mmama.org
See our ad on page 210

38 Harvest Festival Tractor Show
Sept. 21   Howard City
Downtown next to the fire barn, Shaw and White streets.
Contact: David Saucier, 655 N. Orton St., Howard City, MI 49329; 231-629-1873;
email: hausrx@yahoo.com
www.howardcity.org

13 35th Annual Fall Swap Meet
Sept. 26-28   Harrison
42411 Temple Dr. 1/2 mile west on M-61 from stoplight.
Contact: Nathan & Nancy Blakemore, 2523 W. Arnold Lake Rd., Harrison, MI 48625; 989-339-0764;
email: nancyblakemore357@gmail.com

18 6th Annual Fall Harvest Festival & Tractor Show
Sept. 27-29   Hastings
Historical Charlton Park, 5 miles west of Nashville on M-79.
Contact: Chad Furrow, 269-804-9881

23 Fall Festival and Swap Meet
Oct. 5-6   Three Oaks
7816 Warren Woods Rd., 3 miles north, 2 miles west.
Contact: Delbert Kelver, 52671 Lilac Rd., South Bend, IN 46628; 574-272-1145;
email: delbert1929@att.net

3 Olde Tyme Harvest Festival
Oct. 5-6   Scotts
Scotts Mill Park, 8451 S. 35th St., follow the signs.
Contact: Marian Beardsley-Gibbs, 7920 S. 36th St., Scotts, MI 49088; 269-779-1972;
www.sotpea.org
See our ad on page 211

36 Christmas in the Village
Dec. 7-8   Escanaba
U.P. State Fairgrounds, U.S. Hwys 2 and 41.
Contact: Robert Willis, 4880 11.5 Rd., Escanaba, MI 49829; 906-789-1257;
email: robwillis@charter.net
www.upsteamandgasengine.org

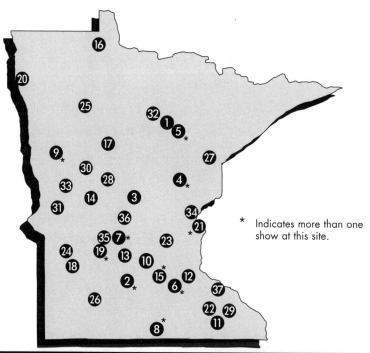

MINNESOTA

❶ North Central Minnesota Farm and Antique Association Horse-Drawn Sleigh Rides
Feb. 23   Grand Rapids
25313 U.S. Hwy 2, 7 miles east on Hwy 2, behlnd Blackberry Store.
Contact: Bruce Gould, 20240 St. Hwy 200, Jacobson, MN 55752; 218-244-2932;
email: allis1@frontiernet.net

❷ Le Sueur County Pioneer Power Swap Meet
April 26-28   Le Sueur
6 miles east of town.
Contact: Julie Bluhm, 507-934-5841;
email: julieb5841@gmail.com
www.pioneerpowershow.com
See our ad on page 213

❸ 27th Annual Field Days, Swap Meet and Auction
May 4-5   Little Falls
Features: John Deere Tractors and Walk-Behind Garden Tractors.
Morrison County Fairgrounds, 15575 Hawthorne Rd. From Hwy 10, east on Hwy 27, 1 mile, left on Hawthorne Road, go 3/4 mile. Show on left.
Contact: Lee Mortensen, 8675 River Rd. N.E., Rice, MN 56367; 320-249-0331;
email: lamortenson@jetup.net
www.gmntcc.com

❹ Spring Meeting Minnesota Association of Antique Power Shows (MAAPS)
May 11   McGrath
White Pine Logging and Threshing Show.
Contact: Jody Hicks, president, 612-940-5588; Karen Kuhnau, secretary, 218-943-5631
See our ad on page 214

⑤ Annual Flea Market and Swap Meet
May 25   Blackberry
25313 U.S. Hwy 2, 7 miles east
of Grand Rapids on Hwy 2.
Contact: Bruce Gould, 20240
St. Hwy 200, Jacobson, MN 55752;
218-244-2932;
email: allis1@frontier.net

**⑥ 19th Annual Rice County Steam
and Gas Engines Swap Meet and
Flea Market**
May 25-26   Dundas
11988 Faribault Blvd. 7 miles east
of I-35 (exit 69) on Hwy 19, 4 miles
south of Northfield on Hwy 3.
Contact: Carmen Sevcik, secretary,
507-663-0882;
email: highcrop@msn.com;
Roger Janak, president,
952-652-2062;
www.ricecountysteamandgas.com

**⑦ Forest City Threshers Spring
Antique Tractor Pull**
May 26   Litchfield
64917 309th St., 5 miles north
on Hwy 24, across from Forest City
Stockade.
Contact: Dave Jutz, 320-535-0656;
or Maynard Theis, 320-693-8773;
www.forestcitythresher.com

**⑧ Farming of Yesteryear Horse and
Mule Show**
June 15-16   Kiester
1736 600th Ave., 2 miles east, then
2 miles south.
Contact: Jake Jacobson, 57015 35th
St., Kiester, MN 56051; 507-383-1966

**⑨ University of Rollag Steam Traction
Engineering Course**
June 15-16   Rollag
Registration required. 35 miles
southeast of Fargo, ND, just off I-94.
This course is filled for 2019.
Contact: Tom Hall, PO Box 999,
Moorhead, MN 56561; 218-233-1771;
www.rollag.com

⑩ Waverly Daze Tractor Show
July 12-14   Waverly
Railroad Park, 405 Elm Ave. 1/2 block
north of Hwy 12.
Contact: David DeLude, 405 Elm Ave.,
PO Box 214, Waverly, MN 55390;
763-670-0128;
email: delud80@gmail.com

**⑤ North Central Minnesota Farm
and Antique Association Gearhead
Car Show**
July 13   Blackberry
25313 U.S. Hwy 2, 7 miles east
of Grand Rapids on Hwy 2.
Contact: George Funk, 16246 Lake St.,
Pengilly, MN 55755; 218-360-1483

**⑪ 37th Annual Antique Engine &
Tractor Show**
July 19-21   Spring Valley
Features: Case and Track Tractors.
78715 255th St., 15 miles south of
Rochester on Hwy 63. Next to Deer
Creek Speedway.
Contact: Les Radcliffe, 507-254-0622;
email: lesradcliffe@yahoo.com

**⑫ 29th Annual Little Log House
Antique Power Show**
July 26-28   Hastings
Feature: John Deere Tractors.
21889 Michael Ave., 6 miles south on
Hwy 61, east 1 mile on 220th Street.
Contact: Sylvia Bower, 13746
220th St. E., Hastings, MN 55033;
651-437-2693;
email: info@littleloghouseshow.com
www.littleloghouseshow.com
See our ad on page 213

⑬ Orange Spectacular
July 26-28   Hutchinson
Feature: Allis-Chalmers 220 Tractors.
McLeod County Fairgrounds.
Contact: Darrell Grams Sr.,
612-280-3397;
www.orangespectacular.com
See our ad on page 214

14 **Rose City Threshing and Heritage Festival**
July 27-28　　　　　　　　Miltona
From Miltona: 4 miles east, turn left on CR 66, 1-1/2 miles north around curve one and 1/2 mile east you will see signs at the show grounds. From Brownerville: about 14 miles west you will come to Rose City, CR 66, keep going west about 2 miles, you will see signs at the show grounds.
Contact: Karen Kuhnau, 13883 Spruce Hill Park Rd. N.E., Miltona, MN 56354; 218-943-5631;
email: kmkuhnau@midwestinfo.net
www.rosecitythreshing.org

15 **56th Annual Scott-Carver Threshers Harvest Festival**
Aug. 2-4　　　　　　　　　Jordan
Features: Allis-Chalmers Tractors and Fairbanks-Morse Engines.
Threshers Park east of Scott County Fairgrounds. Take U.S. Hwy 169 to CR 9 (stop lights), go north 2 blocks to W. 190th Street, turn left to Fairview Lane, turn left.
Contact: Wes Boettcher, 952-687-7687;
www.scottcarverthreshers.org
See our ad on page 213

16 **Lake of the Woods Steam and Gas Show**
Aug. 3-4　　　　　　　　Roosevelt
9 miles north on Rocky Point Road, CR 17.
Contact: William Olson, 4628 Rocky Point Rd. N.W., Roosevelt, MN 56673; 218-442-6381;
email: weolson@wiktel.com
www.wiktel.net/lowsteam

17 **Park Rapids Antique Tractor and Engine Club Field Days**
Aug. 3-4　　　　　　　Park Rapids
Feature: Allis-Chalmers Tractors and Equipment.
1008 Eighth St. East. East side of town: From St. Hwy 34, go 1/2 mile south on CR 6.
Contact: Noel Allard, 14155 Briarwood Dr., Menahga, MN 56464; 218-732-5100;
email: nallard@unitelc.com

18 **Pioneer Power Good Old Days & Threshing Show**
Aug. 3-4　　　　　　　Hanley Falls
Features: Massey-Harris Tractors and Hercules and Economy Engines.
Minnesota's Machinery Museum, St. Hwy 23.
Contact: 507-768-3522;
email: agmuseum@frontiernet.net
www.mnmachinerymuseum.com
See our ad on page 213

19 **Lake Lillian Fun Days Tractor Pull**
Aug. 4　　　　　　　　Lake Lillian
South City Park.
Contact: Chuck Molitor, 881 First St. E., Lake Lillian, MN 56253; 320-905-4674;
email: cmcasec@gmail.com
www.wcapc.org

20 **Heritage Days**
Aug. 8-11　　　　　　East Grand Forks
Hwy 220 North.
Contact: Kim Nelson, 218-779-3034;
email: kim.nelson3034@gmail.com
www.egfheritage.com

21 **2019 Annual Almelund Threshing Show**
Aug. 9-11　　　　　　　　Almelund
Feature: Cockshutt Tractors.
17760 St. Croix Trail, Taylors Falls, MN. Between Taylors Falls and North Branch.
Contact: Mark Strand, 12217 250th St., Chisago City, MN 55013; 651-829-1242;
email: mstrand1242@gmail.com
www.almelundthreshingco.org
See our ad on page 214

5 **35th Annual Steam and Threshing Show**
Aug. 10-11　　　　　　　Blackberry
25313 U.S. Hwy 2, 7 miles east of Grand Rapids on Hwy 2.
Contact: Bruce Gould, 20240 St. Hwy 200, Jacobson, MN 55752; 218-244-2932;
email: allis1@frontiernet.net

㉒ Days of Yesteryear
Aug. 10-11 Rochester
Feature: Allis-Chalmers Tractors.
Contact: Marlys Ohnstad,
PO Box 7386, Rochester, MN 55903;
507-288-2790;
email: mlohnstad@outlook.com
www.mhrt.org

㉓ 49th Annual Nowthen Historical Power Threshing Show
Aug. 16-18 Nowthen
Feature: Massey-Harris Tractors.
7415 Old Viking Blvd. N.W., or 6 miles northeast of Elk River.
Contact: Joe Lewerenz, 26 Sioux Trail, Otsego, MN 55330; 763-744-7290;
email: joelewerenz@gmail.com
www.nowthenthreshing.com
See our ad on page 212

㉔ Heritage Hill Threshing Show
Aug. 16-18 Montevideo
Features: Ford and Fordson Tractors.
4 miles east on Hwy 7.
Contact: Chip Grube, 8025
190 Ave. NW, Appleton, MN 56208;
320-815-5791;
email: chipgrube@yahoo.com
www.heritagehill.us

㉕ Lake Itasca Region Pioneer Farmers 44th Annual Show
Aug. 16-18 Bagley
Intersection of St. Hwy 200 and north entrance to Itasca State Park.
Contact: Earl Hemmerich,
P.O. Box 385, Nisswa, MN 56468;
218-963-4495;
email: ejhem1958@gmail.com
www.itascapioneerfarmers.com

㉖ Butterfield Steam and Gas Engine Show
Aug. 17-18 Butterfield
Feature: John Deere.
West on CR 2, just off St. Hwy 60.
Contact: David Buhler, PO Box 277, Butterfield, MN 56120; 507-380-3290;
email: ddbuhler@frontiernet.net
www.butterfieldmn.com

❼ Forest City Threshers Show
Aug.17-18 Litchfield
Feature: Case Tractors.
64917 309th St., 5 miles north on Hwy 24, across from Forest City Stockade.
Contact: Dale Loch, 65636 355th St., Watkins, MN 55389; 320-535-0656;
320-693-8773;
email: brokenwheelfarms@gmail.com
www.forestcitythresher.com

❷ 46th Annual Le Sueur County Pioneer Power Show
Aug. 23-25 Le Sueur
Features: Hart-Parr, Oliver and Cletrac Tractors.
6 miles east of town.
Contact: Bill Thelemann,
952-994-2743;
email: bthelemann@yahoo.com
www.pioneerpowershow.com
See our ad on page 213

㉗ 58th Annual Lakehead Harvest Show
Aug. 23-25 Esko
4 miles north on St. Louis River Road (halfway between Duluth and Cloquet).
Contact: Bill Ritchie, 3025 E. Milchesky Rd., Foxboro, WI 54836;
218-310-1345;
email: ritchiew96@gmail.com
www.lakeheadharvest.org

㉘ England Prairie Pioneer Days
Aug. 23-25 Verndale
4229 CR 1. From U.S. Hwy 10 S., approx. 1 mile on Wadena CR 23, 2-1/2 miles west on CR 1.
Contact: Shelly Dukowitz, PO Box 221, Verndale, MN 56481; 218-296-2611;
email: pioneer@england-prairie.org;
Marietta Matthews, 218-639-4511;
www.england-prairie.org

㉙ St. Charles Gladiola Days Tractor Show
Aug. 23-25 St. Charles
Winona County Fairgrounds.
Contact: Tim or Terry Jones, 378 W. 12th, St. Charles, MN 55972;
507-251-4565; 507-259-6014;
email: tim.jones.1@hotmail.com;
tjones@semaequip.com

㉚ 44th Annual Finn Creek Summer Folk Festival
Aug. 24-25   New York Mills
3 miles east on Hwy 10 to Hwy 106, south 2-1/2 miles, 1/2 mile west on 340th Street.
Contact: David Witikko, 55738 County Hwy 58, New York Mills, MN 56567; 218-385-3439; www.finncreek.org

㉛ 54th Annual Donnelly Threshing Bee
Aug. 24-25   Donnelly
East edge of town.
Contact: Harry Kruize, 48898 150th St., Donnelly, MN 56235; 320-246-3337; email: chkruize@runestone.net www.donnellythreshingbee.com

㉜ White Oak Antique Farm Show
Aug. 24-25   Deer River
1655 Division St., 1 mile north on Hwy 6.
Contact: Stanley Grunenwald, 26124 Dove Ln., Grand Rapids, MN 55744; 218-326-5134; email: smgrun1966@gmail.com www.whiteoaktractorclub.org

❾ Western Minnesota Steam Threshers Reunion
Aug. 30-Sept. 2   Rollag
12 miles south on Hwy 32.
Contact: Peter Mandt, 701-212-2034; email: secretary@rollag.com www.rollag.com
See our ad on page 214

❻ 45th Annual Rice County Steam and Gas Engines Show
Aug. 30-Sept. 1   Dundas
Features: Farmall and International Harvester Tractors.
11988 Faribault Blvd. 7 miles east of I-35 (exit 69) on Hwy 19, 4 miles south of Northfield on Hwy 3.
Contact: Carmen Sevcik, secretary, 507-663-0882; Roger Janak, president, 952-652-2062; www.ricecountysteamandgas.com

❾ 33rd Annual JI Case Exposition
Aug. 30-Sept. 2   Rollag
Hosted by Western Minnesota Steam Threshers, local contact is Eric Nelson, 701-261-5171.
Contact: Mark Corson, 9374 Roosevelt St., Crown Point, IN 46307; 219-663-6234; 219-669-6319; email: caseheritage@aol.com; Jim Voyles, 417-683-1470; www.caseheritage.org
See our ad on page 7

❹ 27th Annual Rumely Products Collectors Expo
Aug. 31-Sept. 2   McGrath
Feature: Rumely Tractors.
Hosted by the 41st Annual White Pine Logging and Threshing Show. 85 miles north of Minneapolis/St. Paul. Take I-35 exit 195 (Finlayson/Askov) to St. Hwy 18, go 20 miles west to Aitkin CR 61, north 1.5 miles. Or Junction St. Hwy 65 & 18, 2 miles east on 18 to Aitkin County 61, north 1.5 miles.
Contact: Keith Kuhlengel, 5455 Elizabethtown Rd., Palmyra, PA 17078; 717-917-8659; email: krkhulengel@comcast.net www.rumelycollectors.com www.whitepineshow.webs.com
See our ad on page 6

❹ 41st Annual White Pine Logging and Threshing Show
Aug. 31-Sept. 2   McGrath
Feature: Rumely Tractors.
85 miles north of Minneapolis/St. Paul. Take I-35 exit 195 (Finlayson/Askov) to St. Hwy 18. Go 20 miles west to Aitkin CR 61, north 1.5 miles, or Junction St. Hwy 65 & 18, 2 miles east on 18 to Aitkin County 61, north 1.5 miles.
Contact: John Langenbach, 10951 Mayberry Trail N., Marine St. Croix, MN 55047; 651-433-5067; email: whitepinewoodman@frontiernet.net www.whitepineshow.webs.com

33 66th Annual Lake Region Pioneer Thresherman - LRPTA - Dalton Threshing

Sept. 6-8   Dalton
Feature: Ford.
I-94 exit 67, 2 miles north on CR 35.
Contact: John Halvorson, 17169
County Hwy 35, Dalton, MN 56324;
218-770-5584;
email: lrptadalton@yamil.com
www.lrpta-dalton.org

8 36th Annual Farming of Yesteryear Threshing Festival

Sept. 7-8   Kiester
Feature: Allis-Chalmers.
2 miles east, then 2 miles south.
Contact: Bryan Linder, 507-525-2345

34 Andersons' Rock Creek Relics Threshing and Sawing Show

Sept. 7-8   Rush City
I-35 exit 165, east 1 mile to 4-way stop,
right 2-1/2 miles to showgrounds on
the left.
Contact: Duane Anderson, 54433
Forest Blvd., Rush City, MN 55069;
320-358-4844;
www.andersonsrockcreekrelics.com

35 Atwater Threshing Days

Sept. 7-8   Atwater
Feature: International Harvester
Tractors.
1 mile east of Atwater on U.S. Hwy 12,
then 1/4 mile south on Kandi-Meeker
Road. Watch for signs.
Contact: Adam Bosch, PO Box 77,
Kandiyohi, MN 56251; 320-382-6184;
email: adamcherib@frontiernet.net
www.atwaterthreshingdays.com
Facebook: Atwater Threshing Days

36 45th Annual Pioneer Days Threshing Show

Sept. 13-15   Albany
Features: Case Tractors and
Galloway Engines.
21565 360th St. I-94 exit 147, Hwy 238
north 1 mile, follow signs.
Contact: Lee Mortenson, 8675
River Rd. N.E., Rice, MN 56367;
320-249-0331;
email: lamortenson@jetup.net
www.albanypioneerdays.com

19 23rd Annual West Central Antique Power Collectors Tractor Pull

Sept. 22   Lake Lillian
South City Park.
Contact: Chuck Molitor, 881 First St. E.,
Lake Lillian, MN 56253; 320-905-4674;
email: cmcasec@gmail.com
www.wcapc.org

37 20th Annual Corn Shredding Autumn Harvest Days

Sept. 28-29   Oak Center
64245 355th Ave. 25 miles north of
Rochester on Hwy 63, or 15 miles
southwest of Lake City on Hwy 63,
follow signs.
Contact: Dwain Gerken, 64245 355th
Ave., Lake City, MN 55041;
507-753-2543 home; 507-951-4348 cell;
email:
farming@cornshreddingharvest.com
www.cornshreddingharvest.com

15 Fall Meeting Minnesota Association of Antique Power Shows (MAAPS)

Oct. 5   Jordan
Scott-Carver Threshers' Association.
Contact: Jody Hicks, president,
612-940-5588; Karen Kuhnau,
secretary, 218-943-5631
See our ad on page 214

21 Minnesotans Go-Pher Cockshutt Club 10th Annual Regional Show at the Almelund Threshing Show

Aug. 9-11   Almelund
Features: Cockshutt, Co-Op and
Gambles Tractors.
17760 St. Croix Trail, Taylors Falls.
On Hwy 95 about halfway between
North Branch and Taylors Falls.
Contact: Gordy Lefebvre, MN Go-Pher
Cockshutt Club, 5132 46th Ave. S.,
Minneapolis, MN 55417; 612-210-9668;
email: kay@aesupportsystems.com
www.mngophercockshutt.com

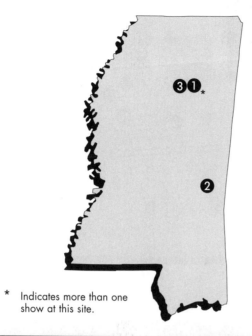

* Indicates more than one show at this site.

MISSISSIPPI

1 **Mississippi Valley Flywheelers Spring Show**
April 26-27   Houston
Houston City Park.
Contact: Harry Collins, PO Box 2883, Tupelo, MS 38803; 662-401-9252; email: harry@plnktrucks.com

1 **Mississippi Valley Flywheelers Fall Show**
Sept. 27-28   Houston
Houston City Park.
Contact: Harry Collins, PO Box 2883, Tupelo, MS 38803; 662-401-9252; email: harry@pinktrucks.com

2 **Soulé Live Steam Show**
Nov. 1-2   Meridian
Soule Steam Feed Works Factory Complex, 1808 4th St.
Contact: Greg Hatcher, 601-693-9905; email. soulelivesteam@comcast.net
www.soulelivesteam.com
See our ad on page 215

3 **Vardaman Sweet Potato Festival's Annual Antique Tractor Show**
Nov. 2   Vardaman
205 Sweet Potato St.
Contact: Mary Tutor, 662-682-7594; email: mtutor65@gmail.com
www.vardamansweetpotatofestival.com

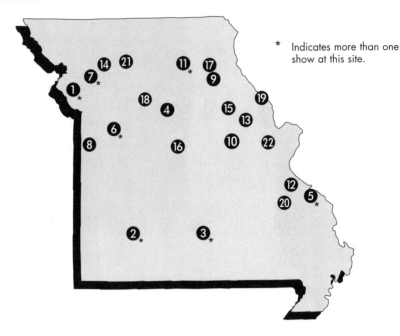

* Indicates more than one
show at this site.

MISSOURI

1 PC Antique Swap and Flea Market
April 12-13   Tracy
Platte County Fairgrounds, First and
Trebble streets.
Contact: Alan Goodwin, 16130 Mona
Ln., Platte City, MO 64079;
816-550-0481;
email: kidinus2@aol.com
www.plattecountysteamandgasshow.com

**2 Early Day Gas Engine and Tractor
Association Branch 16 Swap Meet**
April 13   Republic
7175 W. Farm Rd. 170.
Contact: Jeff Ruth, 8984 St. Hwy U,
Rogersville, MO 65742;
417-767-4632;
email:
thesteampowerman@hotmail.com
www.steamorama.com

3 Spring Show - Ozarks Older Iron
May 10-11   Cabool
310 Cannaday Ln., take 181 exit off 60
Hwy, north, go to Shelton Drive and
follow signs.
Contact: David Melton, Rt. 1 Box 47G,
Mountain Grove, MO 65711;
417-259-0395;
email: dm.lsmo_mg@yahoo.com

**4 Missouri River Valley Steam Engine
Ozark Flint Knappers Spring Show**
May 15-19   Boonville
24200 Hwy 179.
Contact: Bob Hunt, 24200 Hwy 179,
Kansas City, MO 65233;
816-807-1334;
www.mrvsea.com

5 43rd Old Timers' Day
May 25-26   Perryville
Feature: International Harvester Tractors.
Seminary Grounds. I-55 exit 129, north
on 51 to St. Joseph Street, turn left on
St. Joseph Street, go about 1/4 mile,
grounds will be on the right.
Contact: Jerry Davis, 573-547-4556;
Marty Conrad, 573-450-4847

⑥ CAFMO June Tractor Pull and Swap Meet
June 1   Chilhowee
38 SW 1125 Rd. 13 miles south of Warrensburg on 13 Hwy to 2-13 junction, west on Hwy 2, 1.5 miles to SW 151 Road.
Contact: Leah Daugherty, 1401 South Pine St., Holden, MO 64040; 816-732-6690;
email: 1dayg77@hotmail.com

⑦ 41st Annual Lathrop Antique Car, Tractor and Engine Show
June 13-16   Lathrop
Features: Allis-Chalmers Tractors and Advance Steam and IH Gas Engines. 30 miles north of Kansas City, 3 miles west of I-35, south edge of city limits on Hwy 33.
Contact: Jim Plowman, Box 335, Lathrop, MO 64465; 816-896-5546; email: gmolsen@windstream.net
See our ad on page 216

⑧ Western Missouri Antique Tractor & Machinery Association
June 28-30   Adrian
Features: John Deere Tractors and Gas Engines and Harrison Machine Works Steam Engines.
SE corner of I-49 and Hwy 18.
Contact: Gib Thurman, 816-738-9432; email: gibthurman@gmail.com
www.frontiervillagemissouri.com

⑨ Mark Twain Old Threshers
July 11-13   Paris
Feature: International Harvester Tractors.
423 E. Locust St., Paris Fairgrounds.
Contact: Mary Curtright, 106 Hill St., Paris, MO 65275; 573-473-5487;
www.marktwainoldthreshers.com

⑩ Gasconade County Threshers, aka Owensville Threshers 57th Steam and Threshing Show
July 19-21   Rosebud
Hwy 44W to Hwy 50W, about 30 miles to Rosebud, 1 block south at grounds.
Contact: Joe Hendon, 4195 Hwy T, Cuba, MO 65453; 319-540-5639

⑪ 39th Annual Macon County Flywheel
July 25-28   Macon
Feature: Allis-Chalmers.
Macon County Fairgrounds, 1303 Missouri St.
Contact: Paul Schumann, 20316 Empire Rd., Callao, MO 63534; 660-346-8000;
email: paulschumann_ih@hotmail.com
www.macon-flywheel.com

⑤ 17th Annual River Hills Antique Tractor Club Adventure Ride
July 27   Perryville
East Perry Fairgrounds, take U.S. Hwy 61 south to Hwy A in Perry County, east to Altenburg. Go through Altenburg, grounds will be on the right.
Contact: Jerry Davis, 573-547-4556; Marty Conrad, 573-450-4847

⑫ Weingarten Picnic, Antique Tractor and Steam Engine Expo
July 28   Weingarten
10 miles west of Ste. Genevieve on Hwy 32.
Contact: Robert A. Wolk, PO Box 452, Ste. Genevieve, MO 63670; 573-883-0470;
email: robert.mwolk@farmersagency.com

❶ Platte County Steam Engine Show
Aug. 8-11   Tracy
Feature: Statc Massey Collectors.
Platte County Fairgrounds, First and Trebble streets.
Contact: Jim McClung, email: pcsteamshow1961@gmail.com;
www.plattecountysteamandgasshow.com
See our ad on page 216

⑬ Warren County Farm Heritage Days
Aug. 10-11   Warrenton
29550 Palmyra Rd.
Contact: Alan Emge, 25553 Schuetzenground Rd., Warrenton, MO 63383; 636-359-8397;
email: alanemge@gmail.com
www.warrenco-mothreshers.org

Show Listings

⑭ 55th Annual Northwest Missouri Steam and Gas Engine Association Annual Show
Aug. 16-18   Hamilton
Features: Case Tractors, Implements and Mowers, and Sandwich Engines. From Hwy 36 take Hwy 13 north 1 mile then west on CC Hwy 1 mile to 834 NW Osage Dr.
Contact: Robert Blades, 1509 SW Hollow Rd., Kingston, MO 64650; 816-390-0199;
email: bobblades@earthlink.net
www.northwestmissouristeam
andgas.com

⑮ 43rd Annual Montgomery County Old Threshers Show
Aug. 16-18   Montgomery City
Montgomery County Fairgrounds, South Hwy 19.
Contact: Valerie Johnson, 300 Cemetery Rd., Wellsville, MO 63384; 573-999-5741;
email: vrj91@earthlink.net;
Howard Hollensteiner, 573-684-2645;
www.montgomerycounty
oldthreshers.org
See our ad on page 216

⑯ Osage River Antique Power Engine Show
Aug. 23-25   Eldon
Features: Ford-Fordson and Ferguson Tractors.
Eldon Fairgrounds, off Old 54 and Eighth Street.
Contact: Howard Vann, 3479 Hwy 52 W., Eldon, MO 65026; 573-375-3703;
www.orapa.org

⑰ 32nd Annual Northeast Missouri Old Threshers
Aug. 23-25   Shelbina
Feature: John Deere Tractors.
1/2 mile north of Hwy 36 on Hwy 15 to show grounds.
Contact: Jim Peters, 17644 Hwy 24, Holliday, MO 65258; 573-489-2149;
email: mcdeering@windstream.net
www.nemooldthreshers.com

② Steam-O-Rama
Sept. 12-15   Republic
Features: Rumely Oilpull and Wheelhorse Tractors and Scale Model Steam and Maytag Gas Engines.
7175 W. Farm Rd. 170.
Contact: Jeff Ruth, 8984 St. Hwy U, Rogersville, MO 65742; 417-767-4632;
email:
thesteampowerman@hotmail.com
www.steamorama.com

⑱ Mid-Missouri Antique Power and Collectible Show
Sept. 19-21   Marshall
South edge of town.
Contact: Harold Eddy, 26780 Thompson Ln., Slater, MO 65349; 660-529-2708;
email: heeddy@socket.net

⑲ 50th Annual Lincoln County Old Threshers
Sept. 19-22   Elsberry
Feature: Hercules Built Engines. Walnut Grove Farm, junction of Hwy B and NN.
Contact: Erin Tapley, Elsberry, MO 63343; 573-986-8990;
email: sportsman7301@gmail.com
www.lincolncountyoldthreshers.org

⑥ CAFMCO Fall Show
Sept. 20-22   Chilhowee
138 SW 1125 Rd. 13 miles south of Warrensburg on 13 Hwy to 2-13 junction, west on Hwy 2, 1.5 miles to SW 151 Road.
Contact: Leah Daugherty, 1401 S. Pine, Holden, MO 64040; 816-694-2690;
email: ldaug77@hotmail.com
Facebook: Chilhowee Antique Farm Machinery Collectors Organization

⑳ JP's 18th Midwest Cub-Arama
Sept. 26-28   Fredericktown
Features: International Harvest Cubs and Cub Cadets Tractors.
85 miles south of St. Louis at Priest and Jaycee Parks.
Contact: Jamie Hargis, 1860 Madison 417, Fredericktown, MO 63645; 573-561-4524;
email: jamiehargis573@gmail.com
www.cub-a-rama.com

㉑ Livingston County Steam and Gas Association Old Time Harvest Days
Sept. 27-28   Chillicothe
Feature: John Deere Tractors.
Livingston County Fairgrounds.
Contact: Mike Williams, 31292
Hwy DD, Browning, MO 64630;
660-359-7333;
email: dukduster@yahoo.com
www.livcosteamandgas.com

❸ Fall Show - Ozarks Older Iron Club
Oct. 11-12   Cabool
310 Cannaday Ln., take 181 exit off
60 Hwy, north, go to Shelton Drive
and follow signs.
Contact: David Melton, Rt. 1 Box 47G,
Mountain Grove, MO 65711;
417-259-0395;
email: dm.lsmo_mg@yahoo.com

❼ 27th Antique Car, Tractor and Steam Engine Association
Oct. 11-13   Lathrop
I-35 and 116 Hwy to 33 Hwy South
(south edge of city limits on Hwy 33).
Contact: Jim Plowman, Box 335,
Lathrop, MO 64465; 816-796-5546;
email: gmolsen@windstream.net

㉒ Cedar Hill Tractor and Engine Show
Oct. 19   Cedar Hill
6771 Mall Dr., one block off Hwy 30.
Contact: Del Viehland, PO Box 522,
Cedar Hill, MO 63016; 636-274-3734;
email: hitandmiss@brick.net

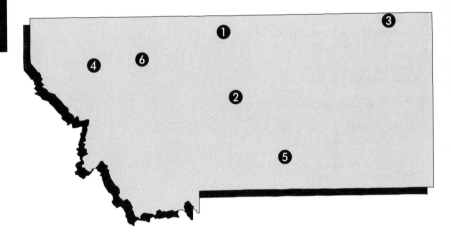

MONTANA

1 **North Central Montana Antique Show**
May 31-June 2   Havre
Feature: John Deere Tractors and Air Motors Engines.
1/2 mile west on U.S. Hwy 2.
Contact: Wally Duchscher, PO Box 590, Havre, MT 59501; 406-265-7314; email: wally@duchscherins.com

2 **Central Montana Flywheelers Pioneer Power Days**
June 8-9   Lewistown
Lewistown Airport.
Contact: Dan Mason, 912 Ninth Ave. North, Lewistown, MT 59457; 406-538-2767

3 **Pioneer Days**
June 29-30   Scobey
720 Second Ave. West.
Contact: Mike Thievin, PO Box 682, Scobey, MT 59263; 406-487-2024; email: dcmuseum@outlook.com

4 **Miracle of America Museum Live History Days**
July 20-21   Polson
36094 Memory Ln.
Contact: Gil Mangels, 36094 Memory Ln., Polson, MT 59860; 406-270-7895; email: info@miracleofamericamuseum.org
www.miracleofamericamuseum.org

5 **Huntley Project Threshing Bee**
Aug. 17-18   Huntley
Feature: Minneapolis Tractors.
770 Railroad Hwy, approximately 15 miles northeast of Billings, toward Worden on Hwy 312.
Contact: Dick Tombrink, 2250 N. 12th Rd., Worden, MT 59088; 406-967-6687; email: dicknsue@nemontel.net
www.antiquetractorclub.org

6 **TASGA Threshing Bee**
Sept. 21-22   Choteau
2 blocks south of City Park. Follow signs.
Contact: David Klette, Box 278, Choteau, MT 59422; 406-450-1803; email: dklette@outlook.com
tasga.org

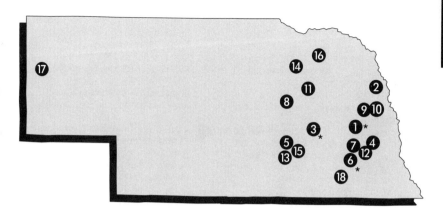

* Indicates more than one
show at this site.

NEBRASKA

1 Camp Creek Threshers Swap Meet
May 18   Lincoln
17200 Bluff Rd., Waverly. 2 miles
east of Waverly Middle School on
Bluff Road.
Contact: Pam Fleming, 2119 N. 58th
St., Lincoln, NE 68505; 402-786-3003;
email: nyorker71@hotmail.com
www.ccthreshers.org

2 Tractor Relay Across Nebraska
June 1-8   Blair
Tractor ride starts at Crofton and
will end at Falls City. Check website
for route.
Contact: Diane Case, 400 N. Fillmore,
Apt. #3, Mount Ayr, IA 50854;
641-340-3536;
email: charlie.dianecase@gmail.com
www.nebraskacowman.com/nafa

3 Planting Festival
June 8   York
5520 S. Lincoln Ave. 1 mile south of
I-80, exit 353.
Contact: Hillary Mundt, 5520
S. Lincoln Ave., York, NE 68467;
402-710-0682;
email: wesselsfarm@gmail.com
www.livinghistoryfarm.org
Facebook: Wessels Living History Farm

4 Windmiller's Trade Fair
June 12-14   Syracuse
Kimmel Ag Expo Center, 198 Plum St.
Contact: David Flatt, PO Box 46,
1416 Central Ave., Nebraska City, NE
68410; 402-873-1078;
email: david@kregelmuseum.org

5 All Nebraska Tractor Ride
June 14-15   Hastings
Pioneer Village in Minden.
Contact: Donna Wilton, 600
S. Baltimore Ave., Hastings, NE 68901;
402-469-4455;
email: djwilton12@gmail.com

6 **Homestead Days**
June 19-23　　　　　　　Beatrice
8523 West St. Hwy 4. 4 miles west on
St. Hwy 4.
Contact: Charlotte McDaniel, 8523
W. State Hwy 4, Beatrice, NE 68310;
402-223-1706;
email: charlotte_mcdaniel@nps.gov
www.nps.gov/home

6 **51st Annual JayHusker Swap Meet
and Show**
June 21-22　　　　　　　Beatrice
Chautauqua Park, Grable Avenue and
Hwy 77, 1 block south of Blue River
bridge.
Contact: Roger Mohling, 819
S. Sumner St., Beatrice, NE 68310;
402-239-4579;
email: nginz@windstream.net

7 **Cortland Antique Tractor Show**
June 22　　　　　　　　Cortland
Main Street.
Contact: Donelle Moormeier,
PO Box 63, Cortland, NE 68331;
402-429-2480;
email: dmoor53@yahoo.com
www.cortlandne.com

8 **Grover Cleveland Alexander Days
Antique Tractor Display, Games
and Parade**
July 6　　　　　　　　　St. Paul
City Park.
Contact: Donna Wilton, 600
S. Baltimore Ave., Hastings, NE 68901;
402-469-4455;
email: djwilton12@gmail.com

1 **43rd Annual Camp Creek Threshers
Association Show**
July 20-21　　　　　　　Lincoln
Feature: Oliver Tractors.
17200 Bluff Rd., Waverly. 2 miles
east of Waverly Middle School on
Bluff Road.
Contact: Pam Fleming, 2119 N. 58th
St., Lincoln, NE 68505; 402-786-3003;
email: nyorker71@hotmail.com
www.ccthreshers.org

9 **40th Annual Mid-States Antique
Tractor and Engine Show**
July 27-28　　　　　　　Ashland
Features: International (Red/Green)
and John Deere.
12601 262nd St.
Contact: Ashley Heitman, 12601
262nd St., Ashland, NE 68003;
402-440-6652;
email: ashboller@hotmail.com
www.mid-statesantiquetractorshow.org

10 **23rd Annual Antique Tractor and
Farm Machinery Show**
Aug. 2-4　　　　　　　Springfield
Features: Case, Ford and International
Harvester Tractors.
Sarpy County Fairgrounds, 90 Cedar St.
Contact: Jeff Meyer, 7108 N. 121st St.,
Omaha, NE 68142; 402-214-1541;
email: evapa.tractors@gmail.com
www.elkhornvalleytractors.com

11 **Heritage Power Association
Tractor Show**
Aug. 3-4　　　　　　　　Genoa
South Genoa City Park.
Contact: Rod Elm, Box 48052 St. Hwy
39, Genoa, NE 68640; 402-920-1156;
email: fulblast@live.com
Facebook: Heritage Power Association

3 **13th Annual Tractor Show and
Summer Fair**
Aug. 10　　　　　　　　York
5520 S. Lincoln Ave. 1 mile south of
I-80, exit 353.
Contact: Hillary Mundt, 5520 S. Lincoln
Ave., York, NE 68467; 402-710-0682;
email: wesselsfarm@gmail.com
www.livinghistoryfarm.org
Facebook: Wessels Living History Farm

12 **37th Annual Antique Machinery
Show**
Aug. 11　　　　　　　　Sterling
Features: Minneapolis-Moline Tractors
and Engine Lines M-N-O.
72927 610 Ave., 4-1/2 miles south.
Contact: Robert Wolff, 72973 610 Ave.,
Sterling, NE 68443; 402-239-2307;
email: sodbuster@diodecom.net
www.deercreeksodbusters.org
See our ad on page 217

⓭ 36th Annual Antique and Collector Show - Platte Valley Antique Machinery
Aug. 16-18　　　　　　　　　　Ayr
Crystal Lake Recreation Area, 10 miles south of Hastings on Hwy 281, 2 miles west to Ayr, 1 mile north.
Contact: Pam Arterburn, 501 W. Lancaster, Blue Hill, NE 68930; 402-460-0066;
email: pam@gtmc.net
pam@pvama.org
www.pvama.org
See our ad on page 217

⓮ Nebraska State Antique Tractor and Horse Plowing Bee/Rae Valley Old Threshers Reunion
Aug. 24-25　　　　　　　Petersburg
Feature: Minneapolis-Moline Tractors.
1951 135th St., Charlies Park. From Petersburg, north edge, Hwy 14, west 1-1/2 miles, follow signs.
Contact: Larry Petsche, 1249 St. Hwy 14, Petersburg, NE 68652; 402-841-7760;
email: camsofptbg@yahoo.com
www.raevalley.org
Facebook: Rae Valley Heritage Assn., Inc

⓯ 37th Annual Old Trusty Antique Engine and Collectors Show
Sept. 7-8　　　　　　　Clay Center
Feature: John Deere Tractors.
Clay County Fairgrounds, 705 N. Martin.
Contact: Joyce A. Schlick, 30551 Road G, Fairfield, NE 68938; 402-726-2487;
email: oldtrustyshow@yahoo.com
www.oldtrusty.org
See our ad on page 217

⓰ Pierce Old Time Threshers Bee
Sept. 7-8　　　　　　　　　Pierce
Features: International Harvester and Farmall.
Pierce County Fairgrounds, 713 N. Brown. 20 miles northwest of Norfolk.
Contact: John Schoenauer, 55192 849th Rd., Norfolk, NE 68701; 402-860-5104;
email: johnschoenauer@q.com
www.piercethreshersbee.com

❶ Camp Creek Threshers Miniature Railroad Show
Sept. 14-15　　　　　　　　Lincoln
17200 Bluff Rd., 2 miles east of Waverly Middle School on Bluff Road.
Contact: Pam Fleming, 2119 No. 58th St., Lincoln, NE 68505; 402-786-3003;
email: nyorker71@hotmail.com
www.ccthreshers.org

⓱ Harvest Festival
Sept. 21-22　　　　　　　　Gering
Legacy of the Plains Museum.
1 mile east of Scotts Bluff National Monument, 2930 Old Oregon Trail.
Contact: Amanda Gibbs, 2930 Old Oregon Trl., Gering, NE 69341; 308-436-1989;
email: info@legacyoftheplains.org
www.legacyoftheplains.org
See our ad on page 217

⓲ Tractors & Treasures
Sept. 21-22　　　　　　Steele City
Feature: Minneapolis-Moline Tractors.
12 miles southeast of Fairbury on Hwy 8.
Contact: Juliann Endorf, 2376 CR 400, Tobias, NE 68453; 402-446-7486

❸ Harvest Festival
Oct. 12　　　　　　　　　　York
5520 S. Lincoln Ave. 1 mile south of I-80, exit 353.
Contact: Hillary Mundt, 5520 S. Lincoln Ave., York, NE 68467; 402-710-0082;
email: wesselsfarm@gmail.com
www.livinghistoryfarm.org
Facebook: Wessels Living History Farm

Show Listings

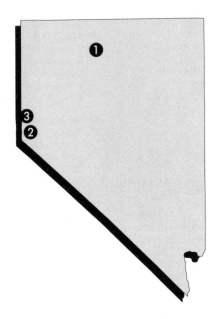

NEVADA

1 **ATHS National Convention and Truck Show**
May 31-June 2   Reno
Feature: 1,000+ Large and Small Antique/Vintage Trucks.
2500 E. Second St.
Contact: Lea Ann Reed, 10380 N. Ambassador Dr., Suite 101, Kansas City, MO 64153;
816-891-9900;
email: leaann@aths.org
www.aths.org

2 **25th Annual Northern Nevada Antique Power Show**
July 27-28   Carson City
701 Old Clear Creek Rd.
Contact: Dave Schneider, PO Box 21054, Carson City, NV 89721;
775-267-164; 775-546-3995;
www.edgeta.org/branch132

3 **Antique Tractor and Engine Show**
Aug. 30-Sept. 1   Winnemucca
Features: Ford Tractors and Fairbanks-Morse Engines.
Winnemucca Nevada Fairgrounds.
Contact: Dan Thompson, 6940 Rose Creek Rd., Winnemucca, NV 89445; 775-722-3207;
email: dthompson3207@gmail.com

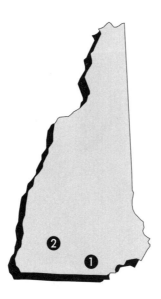

NEW HAMPSHIRE

1 **87th Annual Gas and Steam Spring Show**
June 1-2   Hollis
Features: Rusty, Red, Green and Blue;
Any Implements.
Hillsborough County Youth Center
Fairgrounds. Rt. 13 and Hilldale Lane.
Contact: Richard Keegan, 61 Conifer
Rd., Rindge, NH 03461;
603-899-5285;
email:
gsgassteamenginea@gmail.com
www.granitestategasandsteamengine
association.com

2 **48th Annual Dublin Engine Meet**
Sept. 6-8   Dublin
East of junction 101/137 on Rt. 101.
Contact: Bart Cushing, PO Box 668,
Walpole, NH 03608; 603-313-9970;
email: bart@cushingandsons.com
www.dublinnhgasenginemeet.com
See our ad on page 218

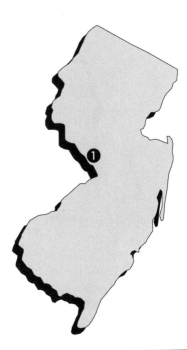

NEW JERSEY

❶ Days of the Past
Sept. 20-22   Titusville
Brick Yard Road (off Church Road).
Back corner of Washington Crossing
State Park. Church Road can be
accessed from either Rt. 29 or Rt. 579.
Contact: Sue Stokes, 1285 Rt. 179,
Lambertville, NJ 08530;
609-209-6400;
email: dvotpe@yahoo.com
www.daysofthepast.com

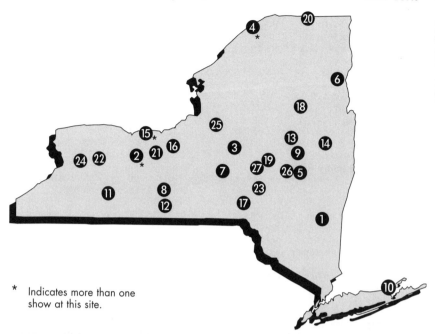

NEW YORK

❶ Century Museum Village and Collectors Association Antique Machinery and Motorcycle Show
To be announced　　　　　Rhinebeck
Dutchess County Fairgrounds, Rt. 9 N.
Contact: Bob Michaelis, PO Box 280,
Pleasant Valley, NY 12569;
845-223 5000,
email: jamichaelis@aol.com
www.cmvca.blogspot.com

❷ New York Steam Engine Spring Flea Market and Tractor Pull
May 25　　　　　　　Canandaigua
5 miles east on Gehan Road off Rts. 5
and 20.
Contact: Gary Love, 585-394-8102;
email: info@pageantofsteam.org
www.pageantofsteam.org
See our ad on page 218

❸ Mohawk Valley Power of the Past Ole Time Power Show
May 31-June 2　　　　　Oriskany Falls
Features: 41 Farmall M; 47 Farmall
MD; 1895 A-T Jone 15hp Hot Tube
Engines.
Rts. 26 and 12B.
Contact: Cole, 3096 Lumbard Rd.,
Clinton, NY 13323; 315-382-2277;
email: farmall4000@gmail.com
www.mohawkvalleypowerofthe
past.com

❹ 37th Annual Spring Antique Gas and Steam Engine Exhibition
June 8-9　　　　　　　Madrid
1755 St. Hwy 345. Near Canton and
Potsdam, where St. Rts. 310 and 345
intersect.
Contact: Alan Garrand, 299 CR 20,
Richville, NY 13681; 315-287-7225;
315-276-4533;
email: nagarrand@twcny.rr.com
slpowermuseum.com

Show Listings

5 **52nd Annual Hudson-Mohawk Chapter Pioneer Gas Engine Gas-Up Show**
June 8-9 & 15-16   Schoharie
106 Murphy Rd., west of Albany on Rt. 443. I-88, exit 23, follow signs.
Contact: Charlie Stuart, 518-605-1926; email: gasup1967@gmail.com
www.mysite.company/thegasup.html
See our ad on page 219

6 **20th Anniversary Barber Homestead Antique Tractor Show**
June 15   Westport
68 Barber Ln.
Contact: Billie Marsh, 68 Barber Ln., Westport, NY 12993; 518-962-8989; email: bhp@westelcom.com
www.barberhomesteadpark.com

7 **Kreiner/Loomis Antique Gas Engine and Tractor**
June 28-30   South Plymouth
3573 St. Hwy 23.
Contact: Margaret E. Kreiner, 3668 St. Hwy 23, South Plymouth, NY 13844; 607-334-8764; email: pkreiner@roadrunner.com

8 **Antique Tractors and Engines working for Diabetes**
July 5-7   Montour Falls
1525 Johnson Farm. South on Rt. 14.
Contact: Barbara Johnson, 1525 Rt. 14, Millport, NY 14864; 607-535-2261

9 **Tri-County Old Time Power Gas Engine Show Representing 42 Years**
July 6-7   Fort Hunter
129 Schoharie St.
Contact: Donald Bernaski, 113 Burber Rd., Amsterdam, NY 12010; 518-843-2709; email: wildraven62@yahoo.com

2 **New York State Two-Cylinder Expo XIV**
July 11-13   Canandaigua
Feature: John Deere Model M Series Tractors.
Gehan Road, off Rts. 5 and 20, 5 miles east of town.
Contact: Al Hain, 585-227-1864; email: alswife127@aol.com
www.newyorkstateexpo.com
See our ad on page 220

10 **26th Annual Long Island Antique Power Association Show**
July 13-14   Riverhead
Features: International Harvester and Case Tractors.
5942 Sound Ave.
Contact: Susan Young, 5942 Sound Ave., Riverhead, NY 11901; 631-404-2708; email: styoung@optonline.net
www.liapa.com

11 **Allegany County Fair**
July 15-20   Angelica
Allegany County Fairgrounds, I-86, exit 31.
Contact: Alan Wakefield, 7605 Peavy Rd., Angelica, NY 14709; 585-466-3110; email: aland.wakefield@gmail.com
www.alleganycountyfair.org

12 **42nd Annual Chemung Valley Old Timers Show**
July 19-21   Horseheads
Features: International Harvester Tractors, Engines and Equipment.
Chemung County Fairgrounds.
Contact: Randy Brigham, 607-745-7349; email: mccracken.cory@yahoo.com; Diana Henneman (flea market), 607-624-3834;
www.chemungvalleyoldtimers.com
See our ad on page 219

⑬ Coon Hollow Engine & Tractor Show
July 20-21　　　　　　　　Gloversville
K.C. Canary Building, 1719 St. Hwy 29.
Contact: Matthew Montgomery, 1041
St. Hwy 163, Fort Plain, NY 13339;
518-993-4371;
email: matratster@gmail.com
Facebook: Coon Hollow Engine Club Inc.

⑭ Saratoga County Fair
July 23-28　　　　　　　　Ballston Spa
162 Prospect St.
Contact: Sarah L. Welch, 378 Goode
St., Burnt Hills, NY 12027;
518-885-6269;
email: antiquewitch@nycap.rr.com

**⑮ 55th Annual Pioneer Gas Engine
Reunion Show**
July 24-27　　　　　　　　　　Marion
Marion Town Park, 4072 Park Dr.
Contact: Dani Salerno, 7497 Mount
Pleasant Rd., Lyons, NY 14489;
585-749-8741;
email: marionpgea@yahoo.com

⑯ Empire Farm Days
Aug. 6-9　　　　　　　　　Seneca Falls
Rodman Lott & Son Farms, 2907
Rt. 414, 2 miles south.
Contact: Alexandra Grimm, PO Box
566, Stanley, NY 14561;
585-526-5356;
email: alex@empirefarmdays.com
www.empirefarmdays.com

**❷ 59th Annual New York Steam Engine
Pageant of Steam**
Aug. 7-10　　　　　　　　　Canandaigua
Features: Rumley Oil Pull and New
York Built Equipment.
3349 Gehan Rd.
Contact: Rick Finley, 585-721-6172;
Gary Love, 585-394-8102;
email: info@pageantofsteam.org
www.pageantofsteam.org
See our ad on page 218

**⑰ 30th Annual Catskill Mountain
Antique Engine and Machinery
Show at the Delaware County Fair**
Aug. 12-17　　　　　　　　　Walton
Delaware County Fairgrounds.
Contact: Art Reed, 6411 Fall Clove Rd.,
Delancey, NY 13752; 845-676-4622;
email: artlindareed@catskill.net
See our ad on page 219

**⑱ Allen's Adirondack Gas Engine
Show**
Aug. 16-17　　　　　　　　Bakers Mills
1 mile off Rt. 8, 226 Edwards Hill Rd.
Contact: Kjerstia Allen, PO Box 41,
Bakers Mills, NY 12811; 518-251-2707;
email: kjarch2@juno.com

**⑲ 19th Annual Roseboom Antique
Power Days**
Aug. 17-18　　　　　　　　　Roseboom
Rt. 20 to Cherry Valley, corner of Rts.
166 and 165.
Contact: Jack Van Buren, John Deere
Road, Cherry Valley, NY 13320;
607-264-3015

⑳ The Way It Was Antique Club
Aug. 17-18　　　　　　　　Churubusco
88 Campbell Rd.
Contact: Oliver Sorrell, 88 Campbell
Rd., Churubusco, NY 12923;
518-521-4912;
email: sorrellshirley1955@gmail.com

**㉑ Yates Antique Tractor and
Engine Society**
Aug. 30-31　　　　　　　　　Geneva
61 Route 14A.
Contact: Dave Nielsen, 946 Voak Rd.,
Penn Yan, NY 14527; 315-481-3021;
email: economydave@yahoo.com

**❹ 37th Annual Fall Harvest Days
and Exhibition**
Aug. 31-Sept 1　　　　　　　Madrid
1755 St. Hwy 345. Near Canton and
Potsdam, where St. Rts. 310 and 345
intersect.
Contact: Alan Garrand, 299 CR 20,
Richville, NY 13681; 315-287-7225;
315-276-4533;
email: nagarrand@twcny.rr.com
slpowermuseum.com

**㉒ 53rd Annual Rally Western New York
Gas and Steam Engine**
Sept. 5-8　　　　　　　　　Alexander
Feature: Honoring Steam.
10294 Gillate Rd., I-90, exit 48, Rt. 98
S., U.S. 20 W., right on Gillate Road.
Contact: Bill Dellapenta, PO Box 75,
Alexander, NY 14005; 716-380-7061;
email:
president@alexandersteamshow.com
www.alexandersteamshow.com
See our ad on page 219

㉓ Dan Rion Memorial Antique Engine Jamboree and Powerfest
Sept. 7   East Meredith
51 County Hwy 12.
Contact: Kajsa Harley, 607-278-5744;
www.hanfordmills.org

㉔ 14th Annual Marilla Ag Day
Sept. 15   Marilla
Marilla Town Hall/Community Center,
1740 Two Rod Rd.
Contact: Earl Gingerich Jr., 1740
Two Rod Rd., Marilla, NY 14102;
716-652-7293, ext. 403

㉕ 17th Annual Oneida Lake Ole-Tymers Antique Engine and Tractor Show
Sept. 13-15   Bernhards Bay
Dave C. Webb Memorial Park, Rt. 49.
Contact: Mark Congden, 45 Phinney
Ln., Central Square, NY 13036;
315-708-2214;
email: oneidalakelogger@aol.com

⑮ 8th Annual Pioneer Gas Engine Fall Division Tractor Pull and Gas-Down Running Class A & C
Sept. 21   Marion
Marion Town Park, 4072 Park Dr.
Contact: Dani Salerno, 7497 Mount
Pleasant Rd., Lyons, NY 14489;
585-749-874;
email: marionpgea@yahoo.com

㉖ Antique Tractor and Engine Show
Oct. 5   Cobleskill
SUNY Cobleskill, Curtis Mott Hall.
176 Schoharie Pkwy N., just off exit 21
of I-88. Call for detailed directions.
Contact: Nick Testa, 176 Schoharie
Pkwy. N., Cobleskill, NY 12043;
518-255-5503;
email: testand@cobleskill.edu

㉗ The Farmers' Museum Tractor Fest
Oct. 12-13   Cooperstown
5775 St. Hwy 80.
Contact: Meg Preston, PO Box 30,
Cooperstown, NY 13326;
607-547-1452;
email: m.preston@farmersmuseum.org
www.farmersmuseum.org

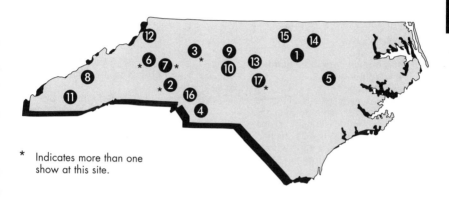

* Indicates more than one
  show at this site.

NORTH CAROLINA

① Southern Farm Show
Jan. 30-Feb. 1   Raleigh
North Carolina State Fairgrounds.
Contact: David J. Zimmerman,
PO Box 36859, Charlotte, NC 28236;
704-376-6594;
email: dzimmerman@southnshows.com
www.southernshows.com/ofs

② Cotton Ginning Days Swap Meet
March 30   Dallas
Hwy 321 N., exit 279/275, toward
Cherryville, west 1/2 mile, Dallas Park
on the left, across from Walmart.
Contact: Curt Holland, 241 Chestnut
Oaks Dr., Bessemer City, NC 28016;
704-860-6689;
email: curt@rustyiron.com
www.oldengine.org/members/gamtra

③ Spokes and Cleats Swap Meet
April 12-13   Turnersburg
2342 Turnersburg Hwy, 8 miles north
of Statesville on U.S. Hwy 21.
Contact: Ron Gooden, PO Box 40,
Turnersburg, NC 28688;
704-880-5507;
email: rongooden@gmail.com

**④ 10th Annual Union County Farm
Show and Festival**
April 13-14   Monroe
Union County Agricultural Center,
3230 Preston Rd., 1 mile east
on Hwy 74.
Contact: Jim Nolen, PO Box 336,
Marshville, NC 28103; 704-272-7502;
email: jncaseman@windstream.net
www.unioncountytractors.com

⑤ Antique Farm Equipment Days
May 2-3   Goldsboro
Wayne County Fairgrounds, U.S.
Hwy 117 South, 6 miles south.
Contact: Frankie Vinson, 190
Old Kenly Rd. N.W., Pikeville, NC
27863; 919-763-7694;
email: williamv7694@gmail.com
www.oilslingers.com

Show Listings

6 **12th Annual Spring Valley Hills Antique Power Club Swap Meet**
May 3-4　　　　　　　Morganton
Catawba Meadows Park.
Contact: Walt Garrison, 828-438-8987;
email: vhap2007@yahoo.com
Facebook: Valley Hills Antique
Power Club

7 **19th Annual Foothills Antique Power Show**
May 18-19　　　　　　　Newton
Hickory American Legion Fairgrounds.
I-40, exit 128, Fairgrove Church Road,
south to Hwy 70, light just beyond
Wendy's, turn left, right at the next light.
Contact: Ned Story, 4067 Story Rd.,
Newton, NC 28658; 828-461-0637;
email: nedjillstory@gmail.com
www.antiquepower.com

8 **24th Annual Ole Smoky Antique Tractor and Engine Show**
May 31-June 1　　　　　Waynesville
Haywood County Fairgrounds,
758 Crabtree Rd.
Contact: James Dickson, 828-775-5773;
Darren Wade, 828-593-8327;
www.olesmokytractorclub.com
See our ad on page 220

9 **1st Annual T-ville Vintage Power Show**
June 14-15　　　　　　Thomasville
Carolina Christian Academy,
367 Academy Dr.
Contact: Ben Rhoades, 336-247-0936

7 **Annual Harvest Wheat, Binding and Threshing Show**
June 15　　　　　　　Newton
Sigmon Farm Park, 420 E. N St.
Contact: John Sigmon, 420 E. N St.,
Newton, NC 28658; 828-850-4709;
email: sigmonjohn69@gmail.com
www.catawbavalleyharvest
association.com

10 **49th Annual Southeast Old Threshers' Reunion**
July 2-6　　　　　　　Denton
Feature: Earth Master.
1072 Cranford Rd., 5 miles southeast
off Hwys 49 and 109, follow signs.
Contact: Karen Miller, 1072 Cranford
Rd., Denton, NC 27239;
336-859-2755;
email: klm2567@windstream.net
www.dentonfarmpark.com

11 **27th Annual Early Farm Days Antique Engine and Tractor Show**
July 19-20　　　　　　Franklin
Macon County Fairgrounds (Wayne
Proffitt Agricultural Center), 1 mile
south of the 64 bypass on St. Rt. 441,
on the left.
Contact: Chuck or Joyce Hall, PO Box
554, Tiger, GA 30576; 706-490-5302;
email: tyrap554@windstream.net

12 **High Country Crank-Up**
July 25-27　　　　　　Boone
Approximately 5 miles south on
Hwy 421 S.
Contact: Betty Hodges, 828-264-4977;
email: flywheelernc@yahoo.com

3 **28th Annual Spokes and Cleats Antique Engine and Tractor Show**
Aug. 9-10　　　　　　Turnersburg
2342 Turnersburg Hwy, 8 miles north
of Statesville on U.S. Hwy 21.
Contact: Ron Gooden, PO Box 40,
Turnersburg, NC 28688;
704-880-5507;
email: rongooden@gmail.com

13 **41st Annual Old-Fashioned Farmers' Day**
Aug. 31-Sept. 1　　　　Siler City
Silk Hope Farm Heritage Park, Hwy 64
east 1 mile, left 4 miles on Silk Hope
Road.
Contact: Michael Rogers,
919-548-4912;
email: michael@rogersauction.com

⑭ 19th Annual Justice Community Antique Tractor, Car and Engine Show
Sept. 6-7　　　　　　　　　Louisburg
8 miles from town on Hwy 581.
Contact: Milton Shearin, 3193 NC 581 Hwy, Louisburg, NC 27549;
919-495-1644;
email: mmfshearin@embarqmail.com

❼ Foothills Antique Power Annual Swap Meet
Sept. 7-8　　　　　　　　　Newton
Hickory American Legion Fairgrounds. I-40, exit 128, Fairgrove Church Road, south to Hwy 70, light just beyond Wendy's, turn left, right at the next light.
Contact: Ned Story, 4067 Story Rd., Newton, NC 28658; 828-461-0637;
email: nedjillstory@gmail.com
www.foothillsantique.com

❻ 12th Annual Fall Valley Hills Antique Power Club Tractor Show
Oct. 4-5　　　　　　　　　Morganton
Catawba Meadows Park.
Contact: Walt Garrison, 828-438-8987;
email: vhap2007@yahoo.com
Facebook: Valley Hills Antique Power Club

⑮ 13th Annual Harvest Show Lord Granville Agricultural Heritage Association
Oct. 4-6　　　　　　　　　Butner
West G and 12th streets.
Contact: Al Gulvin, 2140 Cedar Creek Rd., Creedmoor, NC 27522;
919-528-1652;
email: agulvin@frontier.com
www.lgaha.com

❷ Cotton Ginning Days Show
Oct. 11-13　　　　　　　　　Dallas
Hwy 321 N., exit 279/275, toward Cherryville, west 1/2 mile, Dallas Park on the left, across from Walmart.
Contact: Curt Holland, 241 Chestnut Oaks Dr., Bessemer City, NC 28016;
704-860-6689;
email: curt@rustyiron.com
www.oldengine.org/members/gamtra

⑯ Hodges Farm Antique Tractor and Engine Show
Oct. 18-20　　　　　　　　　Charlotte
Hodges Farm, 3900 Rocky River Rd.
Contact: Eric Culp, 3900 Shelly Rd., Gold Hill, NC 28071; 704-202-3450;
email: bandec3900@yahoo.com
www.stumptowntractor.com

⑰ 100 Years of Progress
Nov. 1-3　　　　　　　　　Carthage
644 Niagara Carthage Rd.
Contact: Patti Eder, 644 Niagara Carthage Rd., Carthage, NC 28327; 919-708-8665;
www.edervillenc.com

⑰ 2019 ACMOC National Show
Nov. 1-3　　　　　　　　　Carthage
Features: Caterpillar Tractors and Engines.
644 Niagara Carthage Rd.
Contact: Tricia Pearson, 7501 N University, Ste. 117, Peoria, IL 61614; 309-691-5002;
email: cat@acmoc.org
www.acmoc.org

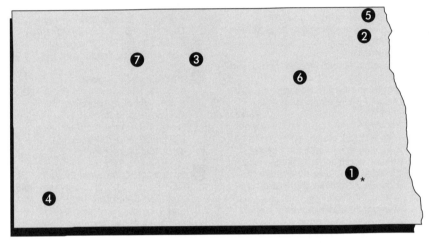

* Indicates more than one show at this site.

NORTH DAKOTA

❶ Fort Ransom Sodbuster Days
July 13-14   Fort Ransom
2 miles north of town.
Contact: Richard A. Birklid, 12128
59th St. S.E., Nome, ND 58062;
701-680-0916;
email: rjbirklid@ictc.com

❷ NE North Dakota Pioneer Machinery Threshing Show
Aug. 25   Park River
Southwest edge of town.
Contact: Teri Dahl, 101 Oak Ridge Pl.,
Park River, ND 58270; 701-284-6241;
email: theresa_dahl@hotmail.com

❸ Drake Threshing Show
Sept. 7-8   Drake
1/2 mile west on Hwy 52.
Contact: Warren Zakopyko,
3238 Hwy 53, Balfour, ND 58712;
701-626-7337

❶ Fort Ransom Sodbuster Days
Sept. 7-8   Fort Ransom
2 miles north of town.
Contact: Richard A. Birklid, 12128
59th St. S.E., Nome, ND 58062;
701-680-0916;
email: rjbirklid@ictc.com

❹ Yesterday's Farmers Threshing Bee
Sept. 7-8   Bowman
Field on west side of city.
Contact: Kenny Woodely,
701-523-3217

❺ 26th Annual Pembina County Historical Society Pioneer Machinery Show
Sept. 8   Cavalier
5 miles west on Hwy 5.
Contact: Zelda Hartje, 13572 Hwy 5,
Cavalier, ND 58220; 701-265-4941;
701-265-4691;
email: pchm@polarcomm.com

6 **Central North Dakota Steam Threshers Reunion**
Sept. 20-22   New Rockford
Feature: Steam Engines.
Southeast edge of town at the
Eddy County show grounds.
Contact: Verle Marsaa, 1232
Fourth Ave. N., New Rockford, ND
58356; 701-220-7770;
email: cndstr@yahoo.com
www.cityofnewrockford.com

7 **59th Annual Makoti Threshing Show**
Sept. 28-29   Makoti
St. Hwy 23, 43 miles southwest of
Minot (18 miles south on U.S. 83,
24 miles west on St. Hwy 23 and
1 mile south on Ward County 9).
Contact: Chris Huus, PO Box 6,
Makoti, ND 58756; 701-726-5200;
email: chris_run@yahoo.com
www.makotithreshingshow.org

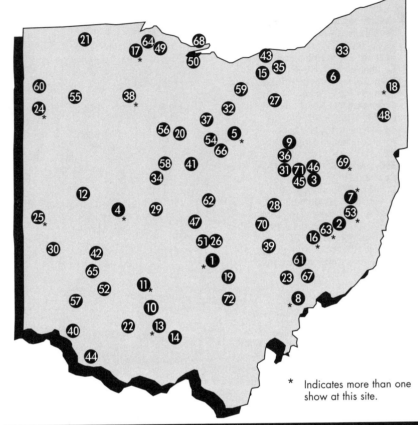

* Indicates more than one show at this site.

OHIO

❶ Fairfield County Antique Tractor Club Toy Show
Feb. 17   Lancaster
AAA Building at the Fairfield County Fairgrounds, 157 E. Fair Ave.
Contact: Doug Shaw, 4585 Crumley Rd. S.W., Lancaster, OH 43130;
740-407-2347;
email: stractorlover@sbcglobal.net
www.fairfieldcountytractorclub.com

❷ 28th Annual Union Local FFA Farm Toy Show
March 10   Belmont
Union Local High School, 66779 Belmont-Morristown Rd. Off I-70, exit 208.
Contact: Corey Betts, 41562 Brown Rd., Bethesda, OH 43719;
740-484-4112;
email: cbasbetts@att.net

❸ International Cockshutt Club Spring Meeting
April 12-14   New Philadelphia
The Schoenbrunn Inn, 186 W. High Ave.
Contact: Caleb Schwartz,
740-262-3987;
email: resshowtractors@yahoo.com
www.cockshutt.com
See our ad on page 230

❹ 33rd Annual Farm Toy Show
April 14   Urbana
Feature: Collector Toys.
Champaign County Fairgrounds, 384 Park Ave. Park Avenue goes east off of S. Main.
Contact: Lowell Morningstar, 1913 Chatfield Rd., Cable, OH 43009;
937-826-4201

5 **Ashland County Yesteryear Machinery Club Swap Meet**
April 20　　　　　　　　　Ashland
Ashland County-West Holmes Career Center, 1783 St. Rt. 60.
Contact: Tom Adams, 419-651-4109;
email: tkadams90@yahoo.com
www.yesteryearmachinery.org
See our ad on page 220

6 **Watch Fob and Vintage Equipment Show**
April 26-27　　　　　　　　Mantua
Features: Allis-Chalmers, Euclid and Terex.
Lakeside Sand and Gravel, 3540 Frost Rd.
Contact: Chuck Sword, 107 Karl St., Berea, Ohio 44017; 440-816-1882;
email: chuck@dhsdiecast.com
www.watchfob.com

7 **4th Annual Harrison Career Center FFA Tractor, Truck, Engine and Car Show**
May 5　　　　　　　　　　　Cadiz
Harrison County Fairgrounds, 550 Grant St. Held on the midway.
Contact: Alan Albright, Harrison Career Center FFA, 82500 Cadiz-Jewett Rd., Cadiz, OH 43907; 330-440-5578;
email: hccffa@yahoo.com
Facebook: HCCFFA

7 **25th Annual Harrison Coal and Reclamation Historical Park Dinner- Auction**
May 11　　　　　　　　　　Cadiz
Sally Buffalo Park's Wallace Lodge. 100 College Way or Industrial Park Road.
Contact: Dale Davis/HCRHP, 143 S. Main St., Cadiz, OH 43907; 740-391-4135;
email: info@hcrhp.org
www.hcrhp.org
www.coalpark.org
Facebook: HCRHP

8 **Dean Becker - Bill Atkinson Memorial Tractor Ride**
May 11　　　　　　　　　　Belpre
Call for directions.
Contact: Pat Tornes, 740-984-2516;
Blaine Melvin, 304-482-9305

9 **Kidron Antique Power Show**
May 11　　　　　　　　　　Kidron
Behind Lehman Hardware.
Contact: Tim Yoder, 7041 Brinker St. S.W., Navarre, OH 44662; 330-317-3883

10 **Spring Show - South Salem**
May 11　　　　　　　South Salem
From St. Rt. 41 turn east on Lower Twin Road. From St. Rt. 28 turn south on Lynden Road. From U.S. 50 west of Chillicothe, turn north on Lower Twin Road. Show is at the Bucksin School.
Contact: Jim Forsythe, 1383 N. Benner Hill Rd., South Salem, OH 45681; 740-634-2162;
email: teepeefroggy@aol.com

11 **Ashtabula County Antique Engine Club Annual Spring Gas-Up**
May 11　　　　　Wayne Township
4026 St. Rt. 322, Williamsfield. 3-1/2 miles east of Rt. 11 between Rts. 193 and 7.
Contact: Janet Lipps, 6 Hickory Ct., Jefferson, OH 44047; 440-576-5418;
email: lipps2@yahoo.com
www.ashtabulaantiqueengineclub.com
See our ad on page 229

12 **30th Annual Buckeye Farm Antiques Show**
May 24-26　　　　　　　　Sidney
Features: Allis-Chalmers Tractors and Indiana Engines.
Shelby County Fairgrounds, 655 S. Highland Ave.
Contact: President, 937-726-2485;
Beverly Kuck, 06020 Kettler Rd., New Bremen, OH 45869; 419-305-0997
dbkuck@nktelco.net www.buckeyefarmantiques.com
See our ad on page 223

13 **Historical Society and Paint Valley Antique Machinery Club Show**
May 25　　　　　　　　Bainbridge
202 N. Maple St., 2 blocks north of U.S. Rt. 50 on Maple Street.
Contact: Jim Forsythe, 1383 N. Benner Hill Rd., South Salem, OH 45681; 740-634-2162;
email: teepeefroggy@aol.com

⑭ Antique Tractor & Machinery Show
May 31-June 2　　　　　　Piketon
Features: Case and Wheel Horse
Garden Tractors.
Pike County Fairgrounds. From north,
turn right on Mill Street and cross
railroad tracks, directly across from
Comfort Inn. From south (on St. Rt.
23), turn left on Mill Street and cross
railroad tracks across from Comfort Inn.
Contact: Robin L., 1261 Smokey
Hollow Rd., Piketon, OH 45661;
740-708-6943;
email: jazzed2max@yahoo.com

⑧ 20th Annual Planting Time Show
June 1-2　　　　　　　　Belpre
Features: Allis-Chalmers Tractors and
Engines made in Michigan.
Howes Grove Park, 1600 block
of Washington Boulevard.
Contact: Pat Tornes, 740-984-2516;
Blaine Melvin, 304-482-9305

**⑮ 43rd Annual Columbia Station
Engine Show**
June 1-2　　　　　Columbia Station
Feature: International Harvester.
Columbia Park, 25496 Royalton Rd.,
8 miles west of I-71 on Royalton Road,
behind Columbia Station Fire Dept.
Contact: Tom Sampson, 12700 Cowley
Rd., Columbia Station, OH 44028;
440-225-9636;
email: hitnmiss@frontier.com

**⑯ 14th Annual Antique Tractor and
Power Show**
June 8　　　　　　　Quaker City
Lashley Tractor Sales, 24821 Lashley
Rd. (St. Rt. 313 in Kennonsburg).
Contact: Dennis Lashley, 24821
Lashley Rd., Quaker City, OH 43773;
740-679-2141;
email: lashleytractor@yahoo.com
www.lashleytractor.com

⑰ Power of Yesteryear Spring Show
June 8-9　　　　　Bowling Green
13660 County Home Rd. I-75 to U.S 6.,
exit 180; head east 1/2 mile to County
Home Road.
Contact: Allen Snyder, 6740 Holcomb
Rd., Pemberville, OH 43450;
419-819-9355;
email: accubs1@yahoo.com
www.powerofyesteryear.org

**⑱ Antique Tractor Club of Trumbull
County Ohio Tractor, Car, Truck and
Motorcycle Show**
June 9　　　　　　　　　Vienna
Feature: Ford.
1653 Ridge Rd.
Contact: Terrance Taylor, 4800 St. Rt. 46,
Cortland, OH 44410; 330-442-2430;
email: chiefttaylor@yahoo.com

**❺ 8th Annual Ohio Vintage Truck
Jamboree**
June 15-16　　　　　　　Ashland
Ashland County Fairgrounds,
2042 Claremont Ave.
Contact: Bill Peters, 592 Wadsworth Rd.,
Orrville, OH 44667; 330-682-1707;
email: wep515@gmail.com
www.ohvintrkjam.com

**⑲ Washboard Music Festival Antique
Tractor/Vehicle Show**
June 16　　　　　　　　　Logan
1 E. Main St., on courthouse parking
lot in center of town.
Contact: Bob Davis, 740-385-3131;
email: country3131@gmail.com
www.washboardmusicfestival.com

⑳ 19th Annual Crawford Farm Show
June 20-22　　　　　　　Bucyrus
Feature: John Deere Tractors and
Waterloo Engines.
Crawford County Fairgrounds,
870 Whetstone St.
Contact: Michael McCracken, 7879
St. Rt. 309, Galion, OH 44833;
419-689-0667

**㉑ 75th Annual National Threshers
Reunion**
June 27-30　　　　　　　Wauseon
Features: Port Huron Steam Engines,
Caterpillar Equipment and Novo Gas
Engines.
Fulton County Fairgrounds, Rt. 108
at Ohio Turnpike, exit 34/3.
Contact: Michele Johnson,
419-666-1884;
email: michele.johnson.nta@gmail.com
www.nationalthreshers.com
See our ad on page 228

㉒ Highland County Antique Machinery Show
June 28-30   Hillsboro
Amvets Park, North Shore Drive, near Rocky Fork Lake; from Rt. 50 and 124 East, follow signs.
Contact: Gene Malott, 4609 Abernathy Rd., Lynchburg, OH 45142; 937-288-2384;
email: jfmalott@att.net

㉓ 22nd Annual Beverly Lions Club Antique Tractor and Engine Show
July 4   Beverly
St. Rt. 60, behind Fort Frye High School.
Contact: Linda Schaad, 4725 Miles Ln., Waterford, OH 45786; 740-984-1819;
email: wschaad09@gmail.com

㉔ 43rd Annual Old Fashioned Farmers Days
July 4-6   Van Wert
Features: Ohio-built Orphans and Oddball Tractors, Hit-and-Miss Engines and Wheel Horse Lawn Mowers.
Van Wert County Fairgrounds, St. Rt. 127 on south side of town.
Contact: Dwight Sheets, PO Box 882, Van Wert, OH 45891; 419-203-2700;
email: willshirefd@frontier.com
www.oldfashionedfarmersdays.com
See our ad on page 226

㉕ 63rd Annual Darke County Steam Threshers Show
July 4-7   Greenville
Features: Ford, Jacobsen Lawn and Garden Tractors, Baker Steam Engines and Ford Fuller Gas Engines.
6129 Reed Rd., Ansonia.
Contact: Joanne Stuck, 937-417-3745;
www.darkecountysteamthreshers.com
See our ad on page 231

⑪ 38th Annual Ashtabula County Antique Engine Club Three-Day Show
July 5-7   Wayne Township
Features: Case Tractors and Wisconsin-built Engines.
4026 St. Rt. 322, Williamsfield.
3-1/2 miles east of Rt. 11.
Contact: Dave Cover, 29 S. Outer Dr., Vienna, OH 44473; 330-507-9078;
www.ashtabulaantiqueengineclub.com
See our ad on page 229

㉖ 14th Annual Outville Power Show
July 6-7   Outville
Harrison Township Complex, 6750 Outville Rd., between Kirkersville and St. Rt. 16 on Outville Road.
Contact: Dan Vanness, 3933 Morse Rd., Alexandria, OH 43001; 740-398-6611;
email:
buckeyeantiquepower@yahoo.com
www.buckeyeantiquepower.com

❺ 27th Annual Ashland County Yesteryear Machinery Club Show
July 6-7   Ashland
Features: Avery Tractors and Hercules Engines.
Ashland County-West Holmes Career Center, 1783 St. Rt. 60.
Contact: Tom Adams, 419-651-4109;
email: tkadams90@yahoo.com;
Ken Booth (vendors), 419-606-6504;
Jason Arnold (tractors), 419-685-2234;
email: massey444@zoominternet.net
arnoldjrfn@gmail.com
www.yesteryearmachinery.org
See our ad on page 220

❺ 2019 BF Avery Summer Show
July 6-7   Ashland
Feature: BF Avery.
Contact: Brian Duff, 166 Township Rd. 2650, Lakeville, OH 44638;
419-827-2169;
email: averyred1947@yahoo.com
www.bfavery.com

㉕ Greenville Farm Power of the Past
July 11-14   Greenville
Features: Allis-Chalmers Tractors, New Idea Farm Equipment and Fractional HP Engines.
800 Sweitzer St. Visitor entrances on St. Rt. 121 (Fort Jefferson Avenue) or Edison Road.
Contact: Von Oswalt, PO Box 57, Greenville, OH 45331; 937-547-1845;
email: voswalt@woh.rr.com
www.greenvillefarmpower.org
See our ad on page 224

⑯ Ohio Hills Folk Festival
July 12   Quaker City
Walton Field (tractor show and cruise);
Broadway Street (truck and car show).
Contact: PO Box 22, Quaker City, OH
43773; 740-685-6590

**㉗ Medina County Antique Power
Assn. Show (EDGETA branch 192)**
July 12-13   Medina
Feature: John Deere.
720 W. Smith Rd. Medina County
Fairgrounds, use gate 1 off West Smith
Road.
Contact: Josh Arnold, 4253 Paxton Rd.,
Akron, OH 44321; 330-352-3168;
email: olivercollector@gmail.com

**㉘ 12th Annual Coshocton County
Antique Power Association
Summer Show**
July 13-14   Coshocton
Features: Farmall and Case.
Coshocton County Fairgrounds,
707 Kenilworth Ave., Coshocton exit,
5 traffic lights to Seventh Street, right
3 traffic lights, on left after stop sign.
Contact: Ed Skerness, 740-575-1356;
Sam Wyler, 740-545-7792

**㉙ 70th Annual Miami Valley Steam
Threshers Show and Reunion**
July 18-21   Plain City
Feature: Oliver Hart-Parr Tractors.
Pastime Park, off St. Rt. 42 on North
Chilicothe.
Contact: Amber Martinez,
PO Box 364, Plain City, OH 43064;
614-270-0007;
www.mvsteam.com
See our ad on page 225

**㉚ 69th Annual Brookville
Community Picnic**
July 25-27   Brookville
Exit 21 to upper Lewisburg Road to
Golden Gate Park.
Contact: John Weist, 13919
Providence Pike, Brookville, OH
45309; 937-478-5835;
email: weistfarm@frontier.com
www.brookvilleareachamber.org

**㉛ Steam, Tractor and Gas Engine
Reunion**
July 25-27   Charm
5023 St. Rt. 557, Millersburg, between
Berlin and Charm.
Contact: JR Schrock, 330-763-0303

⑬ Summer Show - Bainbridge
July 26   Bainbridge
Features: John Deere and Wheelhorse
Lawn Tractors.
570 E. Main St., at the Paint Valley
Hardware Store.
Contact: Jim Forsythe, 1383
N. Benner Hill Rd., South Salem, OH
45681; 740-634-2162;
email: teepeefroggy@aol.com

**㉜ 24th Annual F.A.R.M. Inc. FARM
Tractor Show**
July 26-28   New London
Features: Oliver Hart-Parr and
Cockshutt Tractors.
New London Recreation Park.
Contact: Steve Metro, PO Box 172,
New London, OH 44851;
419-750-0709;
Deb Metro, 419-750-0711

**㉝ 49th Annual Historical Engine
Society's Antique Power Exhibition**
July 26-28   Burton
Features: Rumely, Wheel Horse,
and Garden Tractors; Fairbanks and
Morse Engines.
14653 East Park St.
Contact: Dean Kirby, PO Box 945,
Burton, OH 44021; 440-669-2578;
email: info@historicalengine.org
www.historicalengine.org
See our ad on page 224

**㉞ Mid-Ohio Antique Farm Machinery
Show**
July 26-28   Richwood
Features: Cockshutt and CO-OP
Tractors.
Richwood Independent Fairgrounds,
Gill Street.
Contact: Tom Myers, 17330 Yoakum
Rd., Richwood, OH 43344;
740-225-2301
See our ad on page 229

35 DHS Annual Open House
July 27-28   Berea
Features: Peterbilt and Kenworth.
DHS World Headquarters, 107 Karl St.
Contact: Chuck Sword, 107 Karl St.,
Berea, OH 44017; 440-816-1882;
email: chuck@dhsdiecast.com
www.dhsdiecast.com

**36 Holmes County Steam and
Engine Show**
Aug. 1-3   Mount Hope
Features: Massey-Harris and Massey-
Ferguson.
Mount Hope Auction Grounds, I-77 to
St. Rt. 39 west, to CR 77, north to town.
Contact: Roy Miller, 7777 St. Rt. 241,
Millersburg, OH 44654; 330-231-1111;
email: rmiller@cvwltd.com
www.hcsea.com

37 Silver King Festival
Aug. 1-3   Plymouth
Downtown, behind Sheets In The Wind.
Setup day is July 31.
Contact: Frank Ousley, 4306 Opdyke
Rd., Plymouth, OH 44865;
419-687-6241;
email: frousley@gmail.com

**38 48th Annual Northwest Ohio
Antique Machinery Show**
Aug. 1-4   Findlay
Features: Case Tractors and Vertical
Shaft Engines.
Hancock County Fairgrounds, 1017
E. Sandusky St.
Contact. Christy Rettig, 4680 TRL 39,
Rawson, OH 45881; 419-722-4698;
email: crettig@aol.com
www.nwohioantiquemachinery.com
See our ad on page 225

**39 3rd Annual Chandlersville
Homecoming Tractor and
Power Show**
Aug. 2-4   Chandlersville
8775 Chandlersville Rd.
Contact: Joe Alut, 107 Radnor Dr.,
Zanesville, OH 43701; 740-297-3586;
email: mudthumpin@gmail.com

**40 29th Annual Clermont County
Antique Machinery Show**
Aug. 2-4   Owensville
Features: Odd Balls and Orphans.
Clermont County Fairgrounds.
Contact: Jon Carpenter, 1761
Steward Harbough Rd., Williamsburg,
OH 45176; 513-404-9617;
email:
jcarpenter@clermontcountyohio.gov
Facebook: Clermont County Antique
Machinery Club

**41 30th Annual Morrow County Antique
Tractor and Equipment Farm Days**
Aug. 2-4   Mount Gilead
Feature: Allis-Chalmers Tractors.
Morrow County Fairgrounds, St. Rt. 42.
Contact: Larry Welch, 6077 CR 57,
Galion, OH 44833; 419-946-2277;
email: gduryea@att.net
www.morrowcountytractor.com
See our ad on page 221

42 18th Annual Vintage Truck Show
Aug. 3   Yellow Springs
Young's Dairy on Rt. 68, north of town.
Contact: Vintage Truck Show,
PO Box 838, Yellow Springs, OH
45387; 937-767-1433;
email: jamielee@ertelpublishing.com
www.youngsdairy.com/truck-show

**24 Jon Amundson Crossroads
of America Memorial
Antique Tractor Tour**
Aug. 3   Van Wert
Contact: Ray Etzler, 11277 Union
Pleasant Rd., Van Wert, OH 45891;
419-605-6002;
email: retzler@watchtv.net
www.vanwert.com/museum

**43 Olmsted Historical Society Antique
Engine Show**
Aug. 4   North Olmsted
Cleveland Metroparks Rocky River
Reservation, 24101 Cedar Point Rd.
Contact: John Baker, 6651 Charles Rd.,
North Olmsted, OH 44070;
440-734-3124;
email: jbbaker1962@gmail.com
www.lagrangeengineclub.com

44 49th Annual Reunion Ohio Valley Antique Machinery Show
Aug. 8-11   Georgetown
Feature: International Harvester Tractors, Garden Tractors and Engines. 1 mile west at intersection of St. Rt. 125 and Winfield Drive.
Contact: Jeff Smith, 112 N. East St., Bethel, OH 45106; 513-734-6272; email: camper8790@yahoo.com
www.ovams.com
See our ad on page 226

45 Annual Car and Power Show
Aug. 11   Ragersville
Contact: Raymond Hisrich, 8800 Crooked Run Rd. SW, Sugarcreek, OH 44681; 330-897-9204; email: ragersville@gmail.org
www.ragersville.org

46 56th Annual Dover Steam Show
Aug. 16-18   Dover
Feature: Massey-Harris Tractors. Tuscarawas County Fairgrounds, 259 S. Tuscarawas Ave.
Contact: Emily Weldon, 330-844-5415; www.doversteamshow.com
See our ad on page 230

18 Antique Tractor Club of Trumbull County Ohio Fall Show
Aug. 16-18   Vienna
Feature: Ford Tractors and Implements. 1653 Ridge Rd.
Contact: Terry Taylor, 4800 St. Rt. 46, Cortland, OH 44410; 330-442-2430; email: chiefttaylor@yahoo.com; Linda Silvernail, 7690 St. Rt. 534, West Farmington, OH 44491; 440-693-4687; tractorgrandma@gmail.com

1 Fairfield County Antique Tractor Club and Truck Show
Aug. 16-18   Lancaster
Feature: Allis-Chalmers. Fairfield County Fairgrounds, 157 E. Fair Ave.
Contact: Doug Shaw, 4585 Crumley Rd., Lancaster, OH 43130; 740-407-2347; email: dstractorlover@sbcglobal.net
www.fairfieldcountytractorclub.com
See our ad on page 230

47 Harlem Township Days Annual Show
Aug. 17-18   Center Village
Harlem Township Park on St. Rt. 605, 5 miles north of New Albany.
Contact: John Yeagle, 740-965-4442

48 58th Annual Canfield Fair Antique Equipment Pageant
Aug. 28-Sept. 2   Canfield
Canfield Fairgrounds.
Contact: Jim Brown, PO Box 250, Canfield, OH 44406; 330-533-4107; www.canfieldfair.com

49 31st Annual Antique Tractor and Engine Show
Aug. 30-Sept. 2   Gibsonburg
960 Township Rd. 60.
Contact: Elwood Dick, 512 CR 214, Fremont, OH 43420; 419-307-4265; email: earnhardt@woh.rr.com
www.s-c-r-a-p-inc.org
See our ad on page 227

50 14th Annual Mad River and Nickel Plate Railroad Museum Truck and Car Show
Aug. 31   Bellevue
253 Southwest St.
Contact: Mad River & Nickel Plate Railroad Museum, 253 Southwest St., Bellevue, OH 44811; 419-483-2222; email: madriver@onebellevue.com
www.madrivermuseum.org
Facebook: Mad River NKP Museum

51 6th Annual Capital City Chrome and Customs Special Olympics Benefit Truck Show
Aug. 31-Sept. 1   Pataskala
50 Park Ave. (off St. Rt. 16 on west side of town).
Contact: Capital City Chrome and Customs, 50 Park Ave., Pataskala, OH 43062; 740-964-2766; email: capitalcitychrome@yahoo.com
www.capitalcitychrome.com

52 Clinton County Corn Festival
Sept. 6-8   Wilmington
Features: Case and JI Case Tractors. Clinton County Fairgrounds, 958 W. Main St.
Contact: Dale Mayer, 937-383-5676; email: cccornfestivalchairman@gmail.com
www.cornfestivalonline.com

53 16th Annual Old Construction and Mining Equipment Show
Sept. 7-8　　　　　　　New Athens
St. Rt. 519 between New Athens and U.S. Rt. 22., 43672 Stumptown Rd., Cadiz.
Contact: Bryan Coulson, PO Box 116, Holloway, OH 43985; 740-312-5385; email: oldironshow@yahoo.com
Facebook: OCMES

54 22nd Annual Antique Tractor and Gas Engine Show and 64th Annual Richland County Steam Threshers
Sept. 7-8　　　　　　　Mansfield
Feature: Wheel Horse.
Richland County Fairgrounds, 750 N. Home Rd.
Contact: Bill Gardner, 419-347-3981; Derek Rehberg, 419-565-1996; Barry Naugle, 419-747-3829;
www.buckeyeironwillclub.org
See our ad on page 231

53 57th Annual Stumptown Steam Threshers Club Reunion and Show
Sept. 7-8　　　　　　　New Athens
Harrison County Fairgrounds, 550 Grant St.
Contact: Gary Wellendorf, 8465 Valleybrook St. S.E., East Canton, OH 44730; 330-265-3659;
email: welleglz@aol.com
See our ad on page 228

53 Ohio Antique Power Club Gathering
Sept. 7-8　　　　　　　New Athens
St. Rt. 519 between U.S. 22 and New Athens. Just over 1 mile west of town.
Contact: Ohio Antique Power Club, 2361 Pleasant Valley Rd. N.E., New Philadelphia, OH 44663; 330-401-5129;
email: ohioantiquepowerclub@yahoo.com

55 Pioneer Days Tractor & Machinery Show
Sept. 7　　　　　　　　Kalida
Downtown Kalida.
Contact: Paul Schulte, 16732 Road J, Ottawa, OH 45875; 419-538-6087

56 Wyandot County Fair Show
Sept. 10-15　　　　　Upper Sandusky
Wyandot County Fairgrounds, Rt. 67/53 N.
Contact: Glenn Wickham, 9984 Township Hwy 122, Upper Sandusky, OH 43351; 419-294-4829;
email: glj@thewavz.com

57 Old Machinery Days
Sept. 12-15　　　　　　　Morrow
1369 U.S. Rts. 22 & 3.
Contact: Jim Hurst, 9600 Pleasant Renner Rd., Goshen, OH 45122; 513-877-2765;
email: chrisrolke@fuse.net
www.thefarmclub.org

17 34th Annual International Convention and Old Equipment Exposition
Sept. 13-15　　　　　　Bowling Green
Feature: International Harvester, also hosting Power of Yesteryear's Annual Show.
National Construction Equipment Museum, 16623 Liberty Hi Rd.
Contact: Thomas Berry, 16623 Liberty Hi Rd., Bowling Green, OH 43402; 419-352-5616
See our ad on page 222

58 Green Camp Fireman's Festival Tractor and Car Show
Sept. 14　　　　　　　Green Camp
5 miles southwest of Marion on St. Rt. 739.
Contact: Cork Crawford, PO Box 142, Green Camp, OH 43322; 740-528-2587

59 49th LaGrange Engine Club Show
Sept. 20-22　　　　　　Wellington
Features: White, Oliver Hart-Parr and Minneapolis-Moline.
Lorain County Fairgrounds, 1 mile west of Rt. 58 on Rt. 18.
Contact: see website; PO Box 91, LaGrange, OH 44050;
email: jschmitkons@
www.lagrangeengineclub.com

60 Flat Rock Creek Fall Festival
Sept. 20-22   Paulding
Features: Oliver Hart-Parr and
Cockshutt.
Paulding County Fairgrounds,
503 Fairgrounds Dr.
Contact: Mikayla Pieper, chamber
director, or Mike Hunt, PO Box 237,
Paulding, OH 45879; 419-399-5215;
email: pauldingchamber@gmail.com
www.flatrockcreekfestival.com
See our ad on page 227

**11 Ashtabula County Antique Engine
Club 23rd Annual Fall Show**
Sept. 21-22   Wayne Township
4026 St. Rt. 322, Williamsfield. 3-1/2
miles east of Rts. 11 and 322, between
Rts. 193 and 7.
Contact: Dave Cover, 29 S. Outer Dr.,
Vienna, OH 44473; 330-507-9078;
www.ashtabulaantiqueengineclub.com
See our ad on page 229

**61 Old Iron Power Club and
Appalachian Foot Hills Fall Festival**
Sept. 21-22   Caldwell
Features: Minneapolis-Moline,
Cockshutt and Oil Pull Tractors and
New Holland Engines.
Exit 25 off I-77 at Noble County
Fairgrounds.
Contact: Taylor Winland, 740-934-2258;
email: oldironpower@live.com
www.oldironpowerclub.com

62 Oldtime Farming Festival
Sept. 21-22   Centerburg
Community Memorial Park, corner of
St. Rts. 314 and 3.
Contact: Wilbur Buxton, 2174 Ball Rd.,
Centerburg, OH 43011; 740-625-5397;
www.oldtimefarmingfestival.org

**63 56th Annual Barnesville
Pumpkin Festival**
Sept. 26-29   Barnesville
Downtown.
Contact: Barnsville Pumpkin Festival,
PO Box 5, Barnesville, OH 43713;
740-425-2593;
email:
info@barnesvillepumpkinfestival.com
www.barnesvillepumpkinfestival.com

64 37th Annual Luckey Fall Festival
Sept. 27-29   Luckey
Basic Park, corner of Adams Street
and Gilbert Road.
Contact: Terry Rothenbuhler, 5920
Cloverdale Rd., Cygnet, OH 43413;
419-575-3617;
email: rothy1957@gmail.com
www.luckeyfallfestival.com

**65 49th Annual Old Timers Club
Old Timer's Days**
Sept. 27-29   Xenia
Features: Oliver Hart-Parr,
Minneapolis-Moline and White
Tractors.
Greene County Fairgrounds.
Contact: Lester Davis, president,
3125 Tobias Rd., Cedarville, OH
45314; 937-789-7464;
email: davislester86@yahoo.com;
Eddie Furay, 937-313-5163;
Kathy Ellis, 937-750-3599;
www.oldtimersclub.com
See our ad on page 229

**63 Barnesville Pumpkin Festival
Tractor Cruise**
Sept. 28   Barnesville
Tacoma, on the east side of
Barnesville, at the TJ Jefferis' field on
St. Rt. 147 just east of Michelli Drive.
Contact: Mel Kemp, 40895
Bethesda Belmont Rd., Bethesda, OH
43719; 740-484-4042;
email:
info@barnesvillepumpkinfestival.com
www.barnesvillepumpkinfestival.com

**66 Malabar Farm State Park
Heritage Days**
Sept 28-29   Lucas
Malabar Farm State Park,
4050 Bromfield Rd.
Contact: Malabar Farm State Park,
4050 Bromfield Rd., Lucas, OH 44843;
419-892-2784;
email:
malabar.farm.park@dnr.state.oh.us
www.malabarfarm.org

**38 Pumpkin Fest with Tracks
to the Past**
Sept. 28-29   Findlay
12505 CR 99.
Contact: Jim Arras, 12505 CR 99,
Findlay, OH 45840; 419-722-0774;

Show Listings

email: nworrp@nworrp.org
www.nworrp.org

67 3rd Annual Farm Heritage Show
Oct. 5-6   Lower Salem
Feature: Farmall.
From Marietta: north on I-77 to exit 6,
right onto St. Rt. 821, north to St. Rt. 145,
north about 3 miles. Show on right.
Contact: Steve Howard, 5109
Stanleyville Rd., Whipple, OH 45788;
740-350-5090; 740-373-5090;
email: farmallman813@gmail.com

68 Harvest Happenings
Oct. 5-6   Sandusky
Features: Oliver Machinery and All
Types of Engines.
3910 E. Perkins Ave. Rt. 250 into town,
east on Perkins Avenue.
Contact: Ray Downing, 2410 CR 306,
Vickery, OH 43464; 419-684-5946;
419-504-8910;
email:
downingdeeres@roadrunner.com

24 Farm Toy Show
Oct. 6   Van Wert
Feature: Collector Toys.
Van Wert County Fairgrounds,
1055 Washington St.
Contact: Lowell Morningstar,
1913 Chatfield Rd., Cable, OH 43009;
937-826-4201

**69 49th Annual Algonquin Mill
Fall Festival**
Oct. 11 13   Carrollton
234 Autumn Rd. SW, 4 miles south
on St. Rt. 332.
Contact: David L. George,
113 Pennsylvania Ave., Minerva, OH
44657; 330-868-5609;
email: dgeorge113@yahoo.com
www.carrollcountyohio.com/history

**69 20th Annual Carroll County Antique
Power Show**
Oct. 18-20   Carrollton
Features: John Deere Tractors and
Briggs and Stratton Engines.
Carroll County Fairgrounds, St. Rt. 9,
north of town.
Contact: Robert A. Fallot, 8151
Waynesburg Dr. S.E., Waynesburg, OH
44688; 330-866-2048;
email: bbfallot1@aol.com;
www.ccacc.webs.com

**13 Paint Valley Antique Machinery Club
Fall Festival of Leaves Tractor,
Toy and Machinery Show**
Oct. 18-20   Bainbridge
Features: John Deere and Wheelhorse
Lawn Tractors.
202 N. Main St., east of the Historical
Society building.
Contact: Jim Forsythe, 1383 N. Benner
Hill Rd., South Salem, OH 45681;
740-634-2162; 270-792-8417;
email: teepeefroggy@aol.com

**70 15th Annual Education of Yesterday
Farm Show**
Oct. 19-20   Dresden
3685 Cass Irish Ridge Rd., intersection
of St. Rts. 16 and 60.
Contact: Kendra Moore-Hindel,
3695 Raiders Rd., Dresden, OH
43821; 740-754-6248;
email:
educationofyesterday@gmail.com
Facebook: Education of Yesterday

**71 2nd Annual Harrison Coal and
Reclamation Historical Park Tours
of the Age of Steam Roadhouse**
Oct. 26   Sugarcreek
Contact: Bryan Coulson, PO Box 116,
Halloway, OH 43985; 740-312-5385;
email: roundhousetour@hcrhp.org
www.hcrhp.org; www.coalpark.org
Facebook: HCRHP

8 Fall Plow Day
Oct. 26   Belpre
Call for directions. Rain date: Nov. 3.
Contact: Pat Tornes, 740-984-2516;
Blaine Melvin, 304-482-9305

**72 ROAR Day (Rural Ohio Appalachia
Revisited)**
Oct. 26   Zaleski
Hope School surrounded by Zaleski
State Forest. Located on Wheelabout
Road.
Contact: Lake Hope State Park,
740-596-0601

4 Farm Toy Show
Nov. 17   Urbana
Champaign County Fairgrounds,
384 Park Ave.
Contact: Lowell Morningstar,
1913 Chatfield Rd., Cable, OH 43009;
937-826-4201

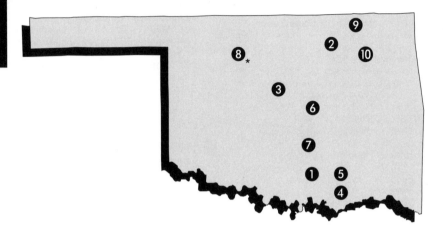

OKLAHOMA

❶ 17th Annual Marshall County Antique Iron Tractor & Implement Show

April 12-13   Lebanon
10488 Gator Rd. South on Red River Avenue, pass fire department and community center. After community center, road changes to Gator Road. Road dead ends at show grounds.
Contact: Karla Earley and Suzanne Bishop, 13570 Wilderness Way, Kingston, OK 73439; 580-380-2790; 580-564-6449;
email: karlaearley@yahoo.com
Facebook: Marshall County Antique Iron Tractor Club

❷ 53rd Annual Oklahoma Steam, Tractor and Gas Engine Show

May 3-5   Pawnee
Steam Park Grounds, 409 E. Beck Dr.
Contact: Pawnee Chamber of Commerce, 613 Harrison, Pawnee, OK 74058; 918-762-2108; Deb Hunt (arts and crafts), 620-307-6141; Chuck Sittler (flea market), 918-798-4004;
www.oklahomathreshers.org
See our ad on page 230

❸ 19th Annual Central Oklahoma Antique Tractor Club Farm and Road Show

May 18   Cashion
Feature: John Deere.
Cashion Sports Complex, west of downtown.
Contact: Mark Adams, 29226 E 850 Rd., Cashion, OK 73016; 405-627-2213;
email: hankhay@sbcglobal.net

❹ 26th Annual Golden Harvest Days

June 14-15   Achille
2174 Hendrix Rd., 5-1/2 miles east of Colbet or 1-1/2 miles west of Achille on Hwy 91, then 2 miles south on Hendrix Road.
Contact: Jim Esbenshade, 2174 Hendrix Rd., Colbert, OK 74733; 580-283-3453;
email: jones_sc@hotmail.com;
Clay Jones, P.O. Box 1164, Durant, OK 74702; 580-916-2414;
www.orgsites.com/ok/bcatc
See our ad on page 231

5 **Bryan County Antique Tractor Show**
June 14-15   Durant
Features: AGCO Heritage Brands.
Bryan County Fairgrounds,
1901 S. Ninth St., U.S. Hwy 69/75.
Contact: Clay Jones, PO Box 1164,
Durant, OK 74702; 580-916-2414;
email: clay.jones@okstate.edu
www.orgsites.com/ok/bcatc
See our ad on page 231

6 **Farming Heritage Festival**
June 21-22   Shawnee
Feed center, I-40 to Hwy 177, south
to Hardesty Road.
Contact: Karl Kozel, 7108 N. Harrison
St., Shawnee, OK 74801;
405-623-2834;
www.oktractorclub.com

7 **26th Annual Murray County Antique
Tractor and Implement Show**
Sept. 20-22   Sulphur
7 miles north on Hwy 177, then
3/4 mile east on Tractor Road.
Contact: Rick & Jayne Pender,
2146 Texas St., Healdton, OK 73438;
580-264-0500; 580-264-0300
See our ad on page 233

8 **29th Annual National Two-Cylinder
Tractor Show**
Sept. 27-28   Fairview
Features: 820-830 to 1939, the styled
years Ford/Fordson to International
Harvester.
1-1/2 miles east on Hwys 8 and 58.
Contact: PO Box 555, Fairview, OK
73737; 580-794-0089; 580-227-0202;
email: mchsok@yahoo.com
www.mchsok.net
See our ad on page 232

8 **34th Annual Major County Historical
Society Old Time Threshing Bee**
Sept. 27-28   Fairview
1-1/2 miles east on Hwys 8 and 58.
Contact: PO Box 555, Fairview, OK
73737; 405-880-0057; 580-227-2265;
www.mchsok.net
See our ad on page 232

9 **Green Country Antique Power
Association Fall Fling with
Western Heritage Weekend**
Sept. 28   Dewey
352 East Ninth St.
Contact: Randy Inlow, 1516 Cudahy,
Bartlesville, OK 74003; 918-907-1958;
email: randyracer58@yahoo.com;
Chuck Ellis, 918-534-6670

10 **29th Annual Route 66 Flywheelers
Gas Engine and Tractor Show**
Oct. 18-19   Catoosa
Features: John Deere, Baker Monitor,
Any Walk-Behind Tractors.
Rogers Point Park, Hwy 66 and
Verdigris River.
Contact: Mike Cartwright, 3310 E. 51st
St., Tulsa, OK 74135; 918-231-0135;
email: mike@route66flywheelers.org
www.route66flywheelers.org

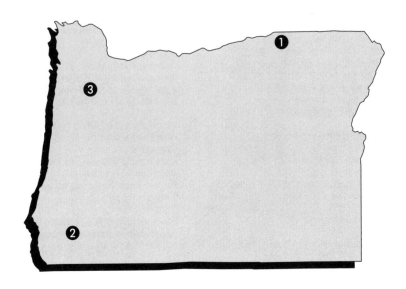

OREGON

1 Heritage Stations Old Iron Show
June 7-9   Pendleton
1100 S.W. Court. Roy Raley Park,
next to Pendleton Round-Up grounds.
Contact: Jack Remillard, 72220
Tutuilla Creek Rd., Pendleton, OR
97801; 541-310-0583;
email: jpremi@charter.net
www.heritagestationmuseum.org

**2 34th Annual EDGE&TA Branch 9
Pioneer Fair, Tractor Show and Pull**
June 15-16   Pottsville
5 miles north, Merlin exit to Monument
Drive, Pleasant Valley Road, follow
signs.
Contact: Gary Peterson, 910
S.E. M St., Grants Pass, OR 97526;
541-479-2981;
email: branch9@embarqmail.com

3 The Great Oregon Steam-Up
July 27-28 & Aug. 3-4   Brooks
3995 Brooklake Rd. N.E. From north
or south on I-5, take exit 263. Go west
on Brooklake Road N.E. 1/4 mile to
Powerland Heritage Park.
Contact: Evan Burroughs,
3995 Brooklake Rd. N.E., Brooks, OR
97303; 503-393-2424;
email:
showmanager@antiquepowerland.com
www.powerlandheritagepark.com

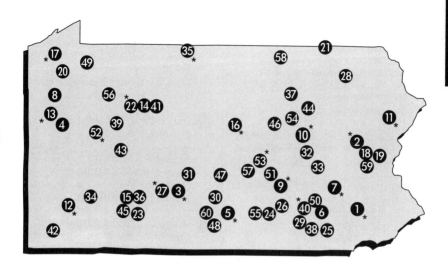

*   Indicates more than one
     show at this site.

PENNSYLVANIA

1 **Rough and Tumble Engineers Historical Mid- Winter Get Together**
Feb. 9   Kinzers
4997 Lincoln Hwy E.
Contact: Rough and Tumble, PO Box 9,
Kinzers, PA 17535;
email: info@roughandtumble.org
www.roughandtumble.org
See our ad on page 21

2 **3rd Annual Toy Show**
March 9   Kutztown
Feature: Farming Related Toys and
Collections.
Kutztown Grange, James and Kemp
streets.
Contact: Dale Leidich, 484-894-8014;
Alyse Hein, 610-914-0142; Macungie,
PA 18062;
email: otplowboys6408@aol.com

3 **Southern Cove Power Reunion Association Spring Plow Days – Antique Tractor and Engine Show**
April 20   New Enterprise
145 Cave Rd. Rain date: April 27.
Contact: George Dell, 334 Red Row Ln.,
Martinsburg, PA 16662; 814-793-3971;
email: dell1026@atlanticbb.net
See our ad on page 234

1 **Rough and Tumble Engineers Historical Antique Tractor Pull**
April 27   Kinzers
4997 Lincoln Hwy E.
Contact: Rough and Tumble, PO Box 9,
Kinzers, PA 17535;
email: info@roughandtumble.org
www.roughandtumble.org
See our ad on page 21

4 Spring Plow, Pull, Auctions and Show Day
April 27   Renfrew
Feature: Cub Cadets.
231 Beacon Rd. Directions on website.
Contact: Walter Whitfield, 135 Dobson
Rd., Mars, PA 16046; 724-799-0362;
email: wally_471@msn.com
www.chapter34.com

5 C.V. Antique Engine and Machinery Assn. Spring Fling and Flea Market
April 27-28   Chambersburg
Feature: Case.
1501 Crider's Church Rd., 4 miles west
of town, 1 mile north of U.S. Rt. 30.
Contact: J.S. Stratton, 2390
Woodstock Rd., Chambersburg, PA
17202; 717-263-8371;
email: stanlotties@pa.net
www.cvantiqueengine.org
See our ad on page 240

2 Spring Plowing Show
April 27-28   Kutztown
Features: Massey-Harris and
Massey-Ferguson.
22 Luckenbill Rd.
Contact: The Old Time Plow Boys Club,
PO Box 215, Mertztown, PA 19539;
610-683-6408;
email: otplowboys@aol.com
www.oldtimeplowboys.com

6 24th Annual Early American Steam Engine Society Spring Fling Weekend and 25th Annual Little Guys Show
May 3-5   Windsor
Feature: John Deere Tractors.
Show grounds, 1673 Manor Rd. I-83,
exit 18, 7-1/2 miles east, right on
Manor Road.
Contact: Susan Knaub, PO Box 652,
Red Lion, PA 17356; 717-244-2912;
email: steamorama@aol.com
www.steamoramapa.com
See our ad on page 237

7 "Diggin' Day" - Old Construction Day
May 4   Lititz
910 Brunnerville Rd.
Contact: Sandy Harris or Ron Snyder,
910 Brunnerville Rd., Lititz, PA 17543;
717-626-8544;
email: info@gerhartmachinery.com
www.gerhartmachinery.com

8 French Creek Valley Antique Equipment Club Plow Day
May 4   Grove City
141 Bell Rd.
Contact: Jeff Bell, 141 Bell Rd.,
Grove City, PA 16127; 724-458-4003;
email: jackie19653@verizon.net

1 Rough and Tumble Engineers Historical Spring Steam-Up Show
May 10-11   Kinzers
4997 Lincoln Hwy E.
Contact: Rough and Tumble, PO Box 9,
Kinzers, PA 17535;
email: info@roughandtumble.org
www.roughandtumble.org
See our ad on page 21

9 12th Annual Williams Grove Historical Steam Engine Spring Show
May 16-19   Mechanicsburg
1 Steam Engine Hill. 10 miles south of
Harrisburg off Rt. 15, or exit 48/49 off
Rt. 81 to Rt. 74 south for 8 miles, left
on Williams Grove Road.
Contact: Tony Thoman, 1 Steam Engine
Hill, PO Box 509, Mechanicsburg, PA
17055; 717-766-4001;
email: wghsea@yahoo.com
www.wghsea.org
See our ad on page 235

10 Middlecreek Valley Antique Association 23rd Annual Spring Antique Machinery Show
May 17-19   Selinsgrove
Features: Allis-Chalmers Tractors and
Hercules Engines.
From Rt. 522, turn onto Salem Road,
1 mile, turn right onto Old Colony Road.
Contact: Michael Clark, 570-374-9420;
email: mpclark@ptd.net
www.mvaapa.org

⑪ 33rd Annual Swap Meet and Flea Market
May 18-19   Bangor
Jacktown Grove, 1229 Richmond Rd.
Contact: Tom Buist Jr., 2260 Lake Minsi
Dr., Bangor, PA 18013; 610-588-7360;
www.jacktown.org
See our ad on page 16

⑫ National Pike Steam, Gas and Horse Association Spring Show
May 18-19   Brownsville
222 Spring Rd. Fairgrounds located
just off Rt. 40, 4 miles west of town.
Contact: 724-785-6855;
email: info@nationalpike.com
www.nationalpike.com

⑬ Spring Gas Up - Northwest PA Steam Engine and Old Equipment Association
May 18-19   Portersville
1512 Perry Hwy (U.S. Rt. 19). I-79,
exit 96, 1/2 mile north of town.
Contact: Don Fuechslin, 132 Roads End
Ln., Butler, PA 16001; 724-285-7038;
www.portersvillesteamshow.org

⑭ 18th Annual Past to Present Machinery Tractor, Equipment and Machinery Show
May 24-26   Sykesville
Feature: Garden Tractors.
Sykesville Ag and Youth Fairgrounds.
Contact: Dan McDonald,
814-590-6102;
email: djcmcdonald@comcast.net
See our ad on page 242

⑮ Chickentown Gas and Steam Show
May 25-26   Somerset
Features: Allis-Chalmers Tractors and
Hit-and-Miss Engines.
692 Chickentown Rd., 4 miles
southwest of town.
Contact: Jerry Schimpf, 814-445-8374;
email: flathead@zoominternet.net
www.chickentown.org

⑯ 45th Annual Spring Show
May 31-June 2   Centre Hall
Features: Massey-Harris, Massey-
Ferguson, and Ferguson and Wallis
Tractors.
Rt 192, 5 miles east of Centre Hall.
GPS: 222 Penns Cave Rd., Spring
Mills, PA 16875.
Contact: Robert Corman, 212
Decker Rd., Centre Hall, PA 16828;
814-777-4529;
email: rlc@psu.edu
www.nittanyantique.org
See our ad on page 236

⑰ Pioneer Steam and Gas Engine Society of Northwestern Pennsylvania Spring Gas-up and Antique Tractor Pull
June 1   Saegertown
Show grounds on Rt. 198, west off
I-79, exit 154, toward Erie.
Contact: Dave Goodwill,
814-663-1291;
email: daveg@neo.rr.com
www.pioneersteamandgas.com
See our ad on page 239

⑱ Antique Engine, Tractor and Toy Club 34th Annual Show
June 7-9   Bowers
Features: Oddballs and Orphans.
William Delong Memorial Park,
233 Bowers Rd
Contact: Richard Miller, 320 Evansville
Rd., Fleetwood, PA 19522;
610-926-6209;
email: rmiller320@msn.com

⑯ Nittany Farm Museum Show
June 8   Centre Hall
Rt. 192, toward Penn's Cave. Museum
showings by appointment.
Contact: Geo Wool, 3015 Lower Brush
Valley Rd., Centre Hall, PA 16828;
814-364-2342

⑲ 40th Annual ATCA National Meet and Flea Market
June 14-15   Macungie
Macungie Memorial Park,
50 N. Poplar St.
Contact: Antique Truck Club of America, 85 S. Walnut St., PO Box 31, Boyertown, PA 19512; 610-367-2567; email: office@antiquetruckclub.org
www.antiquetruckclub.org

⑳ French Creek Valley Antique Equipment Club Show
June 14-15   Cochranton
Features: Case and International Harvester.
Cochranton Fairgrounds.
Contact: Judy Kutruff, 2429 Reash Church Rd., Cochranton, PA 16314; 814-425-7850;
email: jjkutruff@windstream.net

㉑ 25th Annual Twin Tier Antique Tractor and Machinery Association Show
June 14-16   Rome
Feature: John Deere Tractors.
Rt. 187, 5 miles north of Wysox, or 9 miles south of Nichols, NY.
Contact: Robert Ely, 5977 Rt. 187, Sugar Run, PA 18846; 570-746-1794; 570-637-2502;
email: jdfluffy9@gmail.com
Facebook: Twin Tier Antique Association

㉒ 34th Anniversary Coolspring Power Museum Summer Exposition and Flea Market
June 13-15   Coolspring
Features: Electric Lighting Engines and Gen Sets.
179 Coolspring Rd. I-80, exit 78, 10 miles south on St. Rt. 36.
Contact: Coolspring Power Museum, 179 Coolspring Rd., Coolspring, PA 15730; 814-849-6883;
www.coolspringpowermuseum.org
See our ad on page 240

㉓ Glades Highlands Antique Iron Association 18th Tractor Show
June 14-16   Berlin
Feature: International Harvester.
2074 Huckleberry Hwy. Rt. 160, 6 miles south from Rt. 30, 6 miles north from Rt. 31.
Contact: Dan Parks, 1081 Million Dollar Hwy, Stoystown, PA 15563; 814-629-9976;
email: dpattyparks@comcast.net

㉔ 21st Annual Wheel Horse Show
June 21-22   Biglerville
Feature: Wheel Horse.
615 Narrows Rd.
Contact: Charlie Culley, 715 First Ave., Manchester, PA 17345; 717-266-2711; email: cecwh@comcast.net;
Eric Johnson (swap meet), 717-244-2317;
www.wheelhorseclub.com
See our ad on page 242

❶ International Harvester Summer Show
June 21-22   Kinzers
Features: International Harvester Tractors, Cadets, Trucks and Equipment.
Rt. 30, 15 miles east of Lancaster.
Contact: Carl H. Keeler, 1443 Perkiommenville Rd., Perkiommenville, PA 18074; 215-588-5915;
email: chkeeler@verizon.net
www.ihcc8.com

❶ Rough and Tumble Engineers Historical IHC Spring Show and Rough and Tumble Tractor Pull Show
June 21-22   Kinzers
4997 Lincoln Hwy E.
Contact: Rough and Tumble, PO Box 9, Kinzers, PA 17535;
email: info@roughandtumble.org
www.roughandtumble.org
See our ad on page 21

25 30th Annual Fawn Grove Olde Tyme Days Show
June 28-30   Fawn Grove
Features: Maryland and Pennsylvania
Manufactured Equipment.
110 N. Market St.
Contact: William Kurtz, 443-617-7304;
Alexis Thomas, 717-818-7612;
email: fawngroveotd@gmail.com
www.oldetymedays.com
See our ad on page 241

26 35th Annual Latimore Valley Fair and Tractor Pull
June 28-30   York Springs
100 Baltimore Rd. Located 1/4 mile
off U.S. Rt. 15, just north of town.
Contact: Don Bowersox, 104
Brick Church Rd., Enola, PA 17025;
717-732-2975; 717-215-7519 cell;
www.emmr.org

3 Southern Cove Power Reunion Association Tractor Ride
June 29   New Enterprise
145 Cave Rd.
Contact: George Dell, 334 Red Row Ln.,
Martinsburg, PA 16662; 814-793-3971;
email: dell1026@atlanticbb.net
See our ad on page 234

2 70th Annual Kutztown Folk Festival
June 29-July 7   Kutztown
Kutztown Fairgrounds, 450 Wentz St.
Contact: Steve Sharadin, PO Box 306,
Kutztown, PA 19530; 610-683-1597;
email: sharadin@kutztownfestival.com
www.kutztownfestival.com

27 28th Annual Ford/Fordson Collectors Association Show and Meeting
July 11-14   Alum Bank
Contact: Ted Foster, 269-470-3888;
Jim Claycum, 814-276-3533;
www.ford-fordson.org
See our ad on page 23

27 Alum Bank Community Fire Co. Antique and Classic Weekend
July 11-14   Alum Bank
Feature: Ford.
PA Turnpike to Bedford exit, left onto
Rt. 220 N to light, I-99 N to exit 3,
Rt. 56 W about 8 miles to traffic light,
right onto Rt. 96 north, show is 500
feet on right.
Contact: Paul Shaffer, 278 Miller Rd.,
Schellsburg, PA 15559; 814-733-4105;
Gerald Leppert, 1110 Blackburn Rd.,
New Paris, PA 15554; 814-830-4337;
www.alumbankvfc.org

28 26th Annual Endless Mountains Antique Power Equipment, Antique Tractor, Engine and Machinery Show
July 12-14   Tunkhannock
Features: Case Tractors and
Hercules Engines.
Lazy Brook Park, 2 miles east on
U.S. Rt. 6.
Contact: Dave Curley, 3246 Irish Hill
Rd., Montrose, PA 18801;
570-934-0947;
email: rdavidcurley@hotmail.com
See our ad on page 243

29 33rd Annual Menges Mills Historic Horse, Steam and Gas Show
July 12-14   Spring Grove
Feature: Oliver Hart-Parr Tractors and
White Rose Motorcycles.
5252 Hillclimb Rd. (near Jefferson).
Contact: Donna Sheaffer, 775
E. Walnut St., Kutztown, PA 19530;
610-683-3607;
flea market information, 717-259-7309;
email:
webmaster@mengesmillssteam.com
www.mengesmillssteam.com
See our ad on page 241

30 12th Annual Historic Burnt Cabins Grist Mill Antique Tractor Show
July 13-14   Burnt Cabins
Features: John Deere Tractors and Wheel Horse Garden Tractors.
582 Grist Mill Rd. Turnpike, exit 180. Rt. 522 North 4-1/2 miles to Burnt Cabins, 1/2 mile off Rt. 522.
Contact: Dawn Harnish, 582 Grist Mill Rd., Burnt Cabins, PA 17215; 717-987-3244;
email: info@historicmillandcamping.com
www.historicmillandcamping.com

31 2019 Antique Truck, Tractor and Machinery Show
July 19-20   Martinsburg
Morrison's Cove Memorial Park, South Walnut Street.
Contact: Tom Gardner, 2619 E. Pleasant Valley Blvd., Altoona, PA 16601; 814-937-3104;
email: teg31chevy@yahoo.com
www.keystonetrucks.org

32 27th Annual Gratz Area Antique Machinery Association Lawn and Garden Tractor Show & Tractor Pull
July 19-21   Gratz
Feature: Ford Tractors.
Gratz Fairgrounds, Rt. 25.
Contact: Edna Ferster, 6223 St. Rt. 25, Gratz, PA 17030; 717-365-3285;
Kurt, 570-809-5722;
Facebook: Gratz Area Antique Machinery Assoc. Inc.
See our ad on page 233

11 48th Annual Antique Gas Engine and Tractor Show
July 19-21   Bangor
Jacktown Grove, 1229 Richmond Rd.
Contact: Tom Buist Jr., 2260 Lake Minsi Dr., Bangor, PA 18013; 610-588-7360;
www.jacktown.org
See our ad on page 16

17 52nd Annual Pioneer Steam and Gas Engine Society of Northwestern Pennsylvania
July 19-21   Saegertown
Features: Oliver Hart-Parr and Cockshutt Tractors and Galloway Engines.
Show grounds on Rt. 198, west off I-79, exit 154, toward Erie.
Contact: Dave Goodwill, 814-663-1291;
email: daveg@neo.rr.com
www.pioneersteamandgas.com
See our ad on page 239

33 Green Acres Farm Heritage Club Show
July 19-21   Grantville
81 Pleasant View Rd. I-81, exit 80, north on 743 to stop sign, east on 443 2 miles.
Contact: Tom Holley, 804 Ritchey Rd., Everett, PA 15537; 717-439-5060;
email: superggoliver@gmail.com

34 24th Annual Fort Allen Antique Farm Equipment Association Summer Fun and Ice Cream Festival
July 20-21   Scottdale
Feature: Massey-Harris.
911 Porter Ave. Pennsylvania Turnpike, exit 75, 8 miles south on Rt. 819, 1 mile to show.
Contact: Chris Johnston, 1666 St. Rt. 217, Derry, PA 15627; 724-694-2538;
email: cjohnston.674@comcast.net
fortallen.weebly.com
See our ad on page 241

9 Williams Grove Historical Steam Engine Train Show and New/Old Stock Swap Meet
July 20-21   Mechanicsburg
10 miles south of Harrisburg off Rt. 15, or exit 48/49 off Rt. 81 to Rt. 74 S., south 8 miles, left on Williams Grove Road.
Contact: Tony Thoman, 1 Steam Engine Hill, PO Box 509, Mechanicsburg, PA 17055; 717-766-4001;
email: wghsea@yahoo.com
www.wghsea.org
See our ad on page 235

1 **John Deere Days**
July 26-27   Kinzers
Features: John Deere Crawlers and
Industrial Tractors.
4997 Lincoln Hwy.
Contact: Steve Hill, 717-529-6428;
www.waterlooboys.org

1 **Rough and Tumble Engineers**
Historical John Deere Days
July 26-27   Kinzers
4997 Lincoln Hwy E.
Contact: Rough and Tumble, PO Box 9,
Kinzers, PA 17535;
email: info@roughandtumble.org
www.roughandtumble.org
See our ad on page 21

35 **41st Annual Allegheny Mountain**
Engine and Implement Association
Show and Demonstration
July 26-28   Port Allegany
Features: Allis-Chalmers and Dairy
Industry Equipment.
4783 Rt. 155.
Contact: Peggy Cass, 716-353-2736;
email: pcass4@roadrunner.com
www.ameia.net

36 **18th Annual Stoystown Lions Club**
Antique Tractor Festival
Aug. 1-4   Stoystown
Features: Hit-and-Miss and Lesser-
known Classics.
Stoystown Lions Park, 359 N, Club Rd.
1/2 mile east of town on Rt. 30.
Contact: Seth Kaufman, 227
Four Seasons Rd., Boswell, PA 15531;
814-341-9593;
email: seth61cub1@gmail.com
www.stoystownlions.org

13 **25th Harvester Dreamland Show**
Aug. 1-4   Portersville
Feature: International Harvester
Tractors.
Portersville Steam Grounds, Rt. 19.
Contact: Tom Sharp, president,
724-992-9061;
email: antiqueacres@zoominternet.net
www.ihcwp16.club

37 **Loyalsock Valley Antique Machinery**
Association 32nd Annual Show
Aug. 1-4   Montoursville
Features: Caterpillar and All Tract
Tractors.
Lycoming County Consolidated
Sportsman's Grounds. Off I-180, Rt. 87
north 6 miles. Look for signs.
Contact: William Macinnis, 4380
Rt. 864 Hwy, Montoursville, PA 17754;
570-433-4217;
email: tritoes@aol.com;
John Easton (flea market),
570-998-9588;
Wilma Horn, 570-435-3432
See our ad on page 238

13 **Summer Show - Northwest PA**
Steam Engine and Old Equipment
Association
Aug. 1-4   Portersville
1512 Perry Hwy (U.S. Rt. 19).
I-79, exit 96, 1/2 mile north of town.
Contact: Don Fuechslin, 132
Roads End Ln., Butler, PA 16001;
724-285-7038;
www.portersvillesteamshow.org

38 **Mid Atlantic Allis Chalmers**
4th Annual Tractor Show and
Swap Meet
Aug. 3-4   Glen Rock
Feature: Allis-Chalmers B.
Wertz Power Equipment Inc ,
6877 Lineboro Rd.
Contact: Robert J. Bollinger,
4124 Thompson Rd., Needmore, PA
17238; 717-294-3669;
email: rjbjboll@yahoo.com

5 **37th Annual Steam and Gas Show**
Aug 9-11   Chambersburg
Features: Case Tractors and
New Holland Engines.
1501 Crider's Church Rd. 4 miles west
of town. 1 mile north of U.S. Rt. 30.
Contact: J.S. Stratton, 2390 Woodstock
Rd., Chambersburg, PA 17202;
717-263-8371;
email: stanlotties@pa.net
www.cvantiqueengine.org
See our ad on page 240

⑫ 39th Annual National Pike Steam, Gas and Horse Show
Aug. 9-11   Brownsville
222 Spring Rd. Fairgrounds located just off Rt. 40, 4 miles west of town.
Contact: 724-785-6855;
email: info@nationalpike.com
www.nationalpike.com
See our ad on page 22

㊲ 6th Annual Pre Dayton Fair Antique Tractor Pulls
Aug. 10   Dayton
St. Rt. 839 N. to Dayton Fairgrounds.
Contact: Bob Bresnock, 570 Sinktown Rd., Home, PA 15747; 724-397-9195;
email: rlbresnock@gmail.com
smicksburgtractorclub.webs.com

② 30th Annual Summer Show
Aug. 10-11   Kutztown
Features: Massey-Harris and Massey-Ferguson.
22 Luckenbill Rd.
Contact: The Old Time Plow Boys Club, P.O. Box 215, Mertztown, PA 19539;
610-683-6408;
email: otplowboys@aol.com
www.oldtimeplowboys.com

① 20th Annual Empire EXPO Empire Tractor Owners
Aug. 14-17   Kinzers
Feature: Empire.
4997 Lincoln Hwy E. In conjunction with the 71st Annual Threshermen's Reunion.
Contact: Carl Hering, 5862 St. Rt. 90 N., Cayuga, NY 13034; 315-253-8151;
email: info@empiretractor.net
www.empiretractor.net
See our ad on page 243

① 71st Annual Rough and Tumble Engineers Historical Threshermen's Reunion
Aug. 14-17   Kinzers
Feature: Minneapolis-Moline Tractors and Water Pumping Equipment.
4997 Lincoln Hwy E.
Contact: Rough and Tumble, PO Box 9, Kinzers, PA 17535;
email: info@roughandtumble.org
www.roughandtumble.org
See our ad on page 21

㊵ 35th Anniversary Olde Tyme Days 2019
Aug. 16-18   Dover
Feature: Allis-Chalmers.
700 E. Canal Rd. Canal and Mill Creek roads, Rt. 83 to exit 24, Susquehanna Trail south to Canal Road (Rt. 921), west to show grounds on right.
Contact: Don Kern, president, 717-577-3561; Ed Simmons, vice president, 717-870-0240;
www.oldetymedays.org
See our ad on page 239

㊶ 25th Annual Susquehanna Antique Machinery Summer Show
Aug. 17-18   Luthersburg
Feature: John Deere.
8344 Coal Hill Rd.
Contact: Steven Heuser, PO Box 78, Luthersburg, PA 15848; 814-236-0173;
email: mustng4evr@yahoo.com
See our ad on page 242

⑩ Middlecreek Valley Antique Association 23rd Annual Fall Antique Machinery Show
Aug. 23-25   Selinsgrove
Features: Allis-Chalmers Tractors and Hercules Engines.
From Rt. 522, turn onto Salem Road, 1 mile, turn right onto Old Colony Road.
Contact: Michael Clark, 570-374-9420;
email: mpclark@ptd.net
www.mvaapa.org

42 **37th Annual Mason Dixon Frontier Festival**
Aug. 24-25   Mount Morris
I-79 to Mount Morris, to Buckeye Road, to Creek Road, 1/2 mile to Mason Dixon Park.
Contact: Dave Davis, 412-751-0261; email: doubled.66@verizon.net

43 **Indiana County Fair Antique Tractor and Machinery Show**
Aug. 24-30   Indiana
Indiana County Fairgrounds, between Wayne Avenue (Old 119 S.) and South Sixth Street, near Indiana Hospital.
Contact: Robert Simpson, 31 Dales Rd., Indiana, PA 15701; 724-349-3523

9 **61st Annual Williams Grove Historical Steam Engine 9 Day Show**
Aug. 25-Sept. 2   Mechanicsburg
Features: Ford and Ferguson Tractors. 1 Steam Engine Hill. 10 miles south of Harrisburg off Rt. 15, or exit 48/49 off Rt. 81 to Rt. 74 south for 8 miles, left on Williams Grove Road.
Contact: Tony Thoman, 1 Steam Engine Hill, PO Box 509, Mechanicsburg, PA 17055; 717-766-4001; email: wghsea@yahoo.com www.wghsea.org
See our ad on page 235

44 **28th Annual Montour Antique Farm Machinery Collectors Show**
Aug. 30-Sept. 1   Washingtonville
Feature: Allis-Chalmers Tractors. Montour DeLong Fairgrounds, exit 215 off Rt. 80, east on Rt. 254, or take exit 224 off Rt. 80, west on Rt. 54, left on Rt. 254.
Contact: Ken Cotner, president, 570-437-2264; email: mafmca@verizon.net www.mafmca.org
See our ad on page 2

45 **67th Anniversary Reunion of the Farmers' and Threshermens' Jubilee**
Sept. 4-8   New Centerville
3054 Kingwood Rd., exit 110 off PA Turnpike (Somerset), 9 miles south of Somerset on Rt. 281.
Contact: Clark Brocht, 1428 Casselman Rd., Rockwood, PA 15557; 814-926-3142; www.ncrvfc.com
See our ad on page 244

16 **Annual Fall Show**
Sept. 5-8   Centre Hall
Features: Massey-Harris, Massey-Ferguson, and Ferguson and Wallis Tractors.
Rt 192, 5 miles east of Centre Hall. GPS: 222 Penns Cave Rd., Spring Mills, PA 16875.
Contact: Robert Corman, 212 Decker Rd., Centre Hall, PA 16828; 814-777-4529; email: rlc@psu.edu www.nittanyantique.org
See our ad on page 236

3 **29th Annual Southern Cove Power Reunion Association Antique Tractor and Engine Show**
Sept. 13-15   New Enterprise
Feature: Ford. 145 Cave Rd., 1 mile west of town.
Contact: George Dell, 334 Red Row Ln., Martinsburg, PA 16662; 814-793-3971; email: dell1026@atlanticbb.net
See our ad on page 234

46 **Vintage Iron Club 15th Annual Fall Festival and Show**
Sept. 13-15   Laurelton
Feature: Oliver Hart-Parr Tractors. Union County West End Fairgrounds. 1111 St. Rt. 235. From Rt 15 in Lewisburg, west on Rt. 45 toward Mifflinburg, go about 17 miles, turn left onto Fairground Road, 1 mile south to the fairgrounds (Lincoln Park).
Contact: Tanya Dietrich, 418 Snake Hill Rd., Mifflinburg, PA 17844; 570-966-2348; 570-238-1472 (cell); email: snakehil@dejazzd.com

47 17th Annual Aughwick Creek Antique Tractor Show
Sept. 20-22   Shirleysburg
Features: Ford and Ferguson Tractors.
North off exit 13 PA Turnpike, or south
off old Rt. 22.
Contact: Darleen Love, 16665
Germany Valley Rd., Shirleysburg, PA
17260; 814-542-2119;
Ed Kern (vendors), 814-542-8836

48 Two-Top Steam and Gas Show
Sept. 20-22   Mercersburg
Feature: Minneapolis-Moline Tractors.
5 miles south of Mercersburg on PA 75
South.
Contact: Richard Martin, 13182
Fort Loudon Rd., Mercersburg, PA
17236; 301-573-3768;
email: rgtin@yahoo.com
www.twotopruritan.com

49 Pioneer Steam and Gas Engine Society of Northwestern Pennsylvania Gas-up at Drake Well
Sept. 21   Titusville
Drake Well Museum, south,
follow signs.
Contact: Dave Goodwill, 814-663-1291;
email: daveg@neo.rr.com
www.pioneersteamandgas.com
See our ad on page 239

50 22nd Annual Susquehanna Old Fashioned Field Days
Sept. 21-22   Bainbridge
Features: Any and All Dairy-Related
Items.
Conoy Township Park, 10 miles north
of Rt. 30 from Columbia. 10 miles
south of Harrisburg International
Airport.
Contact: Ron Bernhard II, 609
Sunset Dr., Elizabethtown, PA 17022;
717-367-5239; 717-367-3036;
demonstrators, 717-361-8338;
crafts, 717-367-2869
See our ad on page 242

51 27th Annual Old Iron in the Grove
Sept. 27-29   Shermans Dale
Feature: International Harvester Tractors.
Lupfer's Grove, 5800 Spring Rd. (Rt. 34).
Contact: Shirley Hoffman, 400
Pleasant Valley Rd., Elliottsburg, PA
17024; 717-582-6546;
email: srhoffman@embarqmail.com
Facebook: Perry County Old Iron

52 15th Annual Burrell Township V.F.D. Tractor Ride
Sept. 28   Ford City
Intersection Cochran's Mill Road and
Garrett's Run Road. 14 miles from
town. 66 south to Alt. 66, left on Alt. 66,
left on Cochran's Mill Road to end.
Contact: Reed Schaeffer, 724-845-8794

52 19th Annual Ye Olde Autumn Festival
Sept. 29   Ford City
Intersection Cochran's Mill Road and
Garrett's Run Road. 14 miles from
town. 66 south to Alt. 66, left on Alt. 66;
left on Cochran's Mill Road to end.
Contact: Chrissy Scheffer, 724-831-7125

6 62nd Annual Early American Steam Engine Society Steam-O-Rama
Oct. 3-6   Windsor
Feature: Allis-Chalmers Tractors.
Show grounds, I-83 S. to exit 18,
east on Rt. 124 to Manor Road, right
1.3 miles.
Contact: Susan Knaub, PO Box 652,
Red Lion, PA 17356; 717-244-2912;
email: steamorama@aol.com
www.steamoramapa.com
See our ad on page 237

53 **12th Annual Fall Harvest Fest**
Oct. 4-5   Ickesburg
Features: Oliver Hart-Parr, Cockshutt
and Sear Suburban Garden Tractors.
10350 Raccoon Valley Rd. At the
intersection of St. Rt. 74 and St. Rt. 17.
Contact: Doug Urich, 412 Liberty Valley
Rd., Ickesburg, PA 17037;
717-438-3482;
email: westernflyer2@yahoo.com

54 **34th Annual Buffalo Valley Antique Machinery Autumn Exhibit**
Oct. 4-6   Lewisburg
8030 West Branch Hwy.
Contact: Mark Cromley, president,
570-524-0249
See our ad on page 243

35 **4th Annual Fall Harvest Day Event**
Oct. 5   Port Allegany
4783 Rt. 155, off of Rt. 6.
Contact: Peggy Cass, 716-353-2736;
email: pcass4@roadrunner.com

7 **Mack Day**
Oct. 5   Lititz
910 Brunnerville Rd.
Contact: Sandy Harris or Ron Snyder,
910 Brunnerville Rd., Lititz, PA 17543;
717-626-8544;
email: info@gerhartmachinery.com
www.gerhartmachinery.com

13 **Fall Fling - Northwest PA Steam Engine and Old Equipment Association**
Oct. 5-6   Portersville
1512 Perry Hwy (U.S. Rt. 19). I-79,
exit 96, 1/2 mile north of town.
Contact: Don Fuechslin, 132
Roads End Ln., Butler, PA 16001;
724-285-7038;
www.portersvillesteamshow.org

55 **South Mountain Antique Engine Association in conjunction with the National Apple Harvest Festival**
Oct. 5-6 & Oct. 12-13   Arendtsville
615 Narrows Rd., Biglerville. South
Mountain Fairgrounds, Rt. 234
west from Rt. 15. 8 miles north of
Gettysburg.
Contact: Adam Brown, 1750 Hilltown
Rd., Biglerville, PA 17307;
717-752-7381;
email: smaeassn@aol.com

56 **Central Electric Cooperative Inc. Antique Tractor Show**
Oct. 6   Clarion
650 Main St., Clarion Area Chamber
of B & I.
Contact: Tracy J. Becker, IOM, CFEE,
650 Main St., Clarion, PA 16214;
814-226-9161;
email: tracy@clarionpa.com
www.clarionpa.com

1 **Rough and Tumble Engineers Historical a Time of Harvest**
Oct. 11-12   Kinzers
4997 Lincoln Hwy E.
Contact: Rough and Tumble, PO Box 9,
Kinzers, PA 17535;
email: info@roughandtumble.org
www.roughandtumble.org
See our ad on page 21

57 **34th Annual Sherman's Valley Heritage Days**
Oct. 11-13   Blain
532 Picnic Grove Rd.
Contact: David Casner, 6182
Shermans Valley Rd., Loysville, PA
17047; 717-385-3339;
email:
david.casner@highmarkhealth.org
www.svheritagedays.com
See our ad on page 243

58 **54th Annual Fall Festival Tioga County Early Days**
Oct. 11-13   Whitneyville
Features: Orphans and Oddballs
Tractors and Hit-and-Miss Engines.
Whitneyville Fairgrounds, between
Wellsboro and Mansfield off Rt. 6.
Contact: Gary Comfort, 58 Lewis St.,
Gillett, PA 16925; 607-259-6234;
Facebook: Tioga 1904
See our ad on page 19

17 **Pioneer Steam and Gas Engine Society of Northwestern Pennsylvania Fall Harvest Show**
Oct. 12   Saegertown
Show grounds on Rt. 198, west off
I-79, exit 154, toward Erie.
Contact: Dave Goodwill, 814-663-1291;
email: daveg@neo.rr.com
www.pioneersteamandgas.com
See our ad on page 239

40 **6th Annual Smicksburg Antique Tractor, Machinery and Truck Show**
Oct. 12-13   Dayton
Feature: Ford.
Dayton Fairgrounds, St. Rt. 839, north.
Contact: Kevin Bish, 107 Rabbit Hollow
Rd., Dayton, PA 16222; 814-257-9880;
email: sales@daytontractorparts.com

59 **12th Annual Antique Power and Apple Festival**
Oct. 12-13   Oley
26 Jefferson St.
Contact: Jerry Sensenig, 610-587-4914;
www.oleyfire5.com

22 **34th Anniversary Coolspring Power Museum Fall Exposition and Swap Meet**
Oct. 17-19   Coolspring
179 Coolspring Rd. I-80, exit 78,
10 miles south on St. Rt. 36.
Contact: Coolspring Power Museum,
PO Box 19, Coolspring, PA 15730;
814-849-6883;
www.coolspringpowermuseum.org
See our ad on page 240

60 **39th Annual Grease, Steam and Rust Association Antique Tractor, Small Engine and Machinery Show**
Oct. 18-20   McConnellsburg
Feature: Minneapolis-Moline.
Fulton County Fairgrounds,
888 Lincoln Way East.
Contact: Paul Schimdt, 24105 Parks Rd.,
Orbisonia, PA 17243; 301-730-7804;
email: pschmidt@telepluscorp.com
See our ad on page 238

11 **40th Annual Fall Harvest and Sawmill Show**
Oct. 19-20   Bangor
Jacktown Grove, 1229 Richmond Rd.
Contact: Tom Buist Jr., 2260 Lake
Minsi Dr., Bangor, PA 18013;
610-588-7360;
www.jacktown.org
See our ad on page 16

16 **Massey Exposition of North America**
Sept. 5-8   Centre Hall
Features: Massey-Ferguson, Massey-
Harris, and Ferguson and Wallis
Tractors.
In conjunction with the 45th Annual
Nittany Antique Machinery Fall Show.
Penn's Cave, 222 Penns Cave Rd.
Contact: Rodger Brough, 717-677-8866;
email: rodgerb@adamsec.coop;
John Bush, 317-605-3361;
jwbush53@hotmail.com

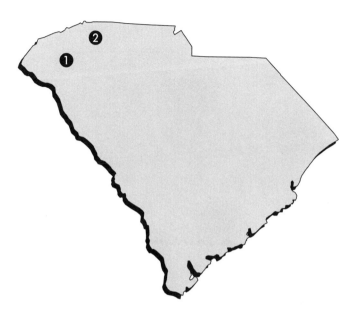

SOUTH CAROLINA

❶ Farm Day
March 30   Pendleton
120 History Ln., Hwy 76. Across from
Tri County Tech College.
Contact: Ag Museum, 120 History Ln.,
Pendleton, SC 29670; 864-646-7271;
864-643-9496;
email: nsaylors@bgamsc.org
www.pendletonhistoricfoundation.org

**❷ Power From The Past Tractor Show
and Swap Meet**
May 18   Greer
Features: Farmall and International
Harvester Tractors.
Abner Creek Baptist Church,
2461 Abner Creek Rd.
Contact: David Moss, 1450 Sharon
Rd., Greer, SC 29651; 864-680-4004;
email: david@tractorpartsbarn.org

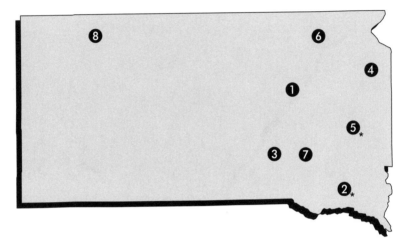

* Indicates more than one show at this site.

SOUTH DAKOTA

❶ Huron Area Antique Power Show
June 15-16   Huron
Feature: Stickney Engines.
South side of State Fairgrounds.
Contact: Roger Kropuenske,
20741 403rd Ave., Huron, SD 57350;
605-350-4434;
email: rjacres706@gmail.com

❷ WNAX Tri-State Old Iron Tractor Ride
July 11-13   Yankton
803 East Fourth St. Behind the
Chamber of Commerce Building in the
open field.
Contact: Rodger J. Harts,
3412 SD Hwy 314, Yankton, SD
57078; 605-665-9785;
email: rdharts1943@q.com;
tristateoldiron@yahoo.com

❸ Antique Tractor Pull and Fur Trader Days
Aug. 9-11   Geddes
South side of Geddes Athletic Complex.
Contact: Ron Dufek, PO Box 97,
Geddes, SD 57342; 605-337-2501;
email: dufsdfek@midstatesd.net
www.geddessd.org

❹ Twin Brooks Threshing Show
Aug. 10-11   Twin Brooks
Feature: John Deere.
From Milbank, 5 miles west and
1-1/2 miles south.
Contact: Pam Nelson, 407 W. Fifth Ave.,
Milbank, SD 57252; 605-880-2884;
email: rpnelson1@itcmilbank.com
www.threshingshow.com

**2 Riverboat Days Tractor Show and
Small Engine Display**
Aug. 16-18   Yankton
Riverside Park, by the Missouri River.
Contact: Rodger J. Harts,
3412 SD Hwy 314, Yankton, SD 57078;
605-665-9785;
email: rdharts1943@q.com;
tristateoldiron@yahoo.com

**5 35th Annual J.I. Case Collectors
Summer Convention**
Aug. 22-25   Madison
Prairie Village.
Contact: Jonathan Woodrum,
606-303-0891;
email: jwll67@yahoo.com
www.jicasecollector.com
See our ad on page 246

**5 57th Annual Historic Prairie Village
Steam Threshing Jamboree**
Aug. 22-25   Madison
2 miles west of Madison on Hwy 34.
Contact: Prairie Village Office,
PO Box 256, Madison, SD 57042;
800-693-3644;
www.prairievillage.org

**6 45th Annual James Valley Threshing
and Tractor Club Show**
Sept. 6-8   Andover
Features: Lettered John Deere Tractors
and 150 HP Case Steam Engines.
502 E. Second Ave. 30 miles east of
Aberdeen on Hwy 12, approximately
45 miles west of I-29 on Hwy 12.
Contact: Donna Anderson,
100 S. First St., Andover, SD 57422;
605-868-3242;
email: donnaanderson@yahoo.com
www.jamesvalleythreshers.com

7 Harvest Festival
Sept. 14-15   Delmont
Features: Massey-Harris and
Massey-Ferguson Tractors.
1/4 mile west of town.
Contact: Brian Weisser, 605-491-4808;
605-505-0535; 605-779-2211

**8 Coal Springs Threshing Bee and
Antique Show**
Sept. 27-29   Meadow
3 miles north of junction of SD Hwy 73
and SD Hwy 20 East.
Contact: Wade Hofer,
18867 Happy Hill Rd., Meadow, SD
57644; 605-788-2854;
email: wthofer@hotmail.com

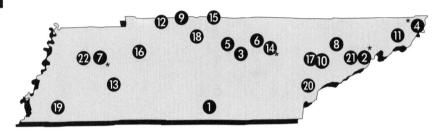

* Indicates more than one
  show at this site.

TENNESSEE

❶ 21st Annual Flint River Antique Tractor and Farm Equipment
March 30　　　　　　　Fayetteville
Lincoln County High School,
1233 Huntsville Hwy.
Contact: Clayton Brown, 332
Kelso Mulberry Rd., Mulberry, TN
37359; 931-703-2283;
email: ltbrown77@yahoo.com

❷ Spring Antique Tractor, Engine, Car & Motorcycle Show and Flea Market
April 4-6　　　　　　　Sevierville
Sevier County Fairgrounds,
754 Old Knoxville Hwy.
Contact: Eric Lampkins, 812-360-4190;
Mark Meyers, 859-679-7648

❸ Wilson Bank & Trust Antique Tractor and Engine Show
April 20　　　　　　　Alexandria
From I-40, take exit 254 (Alexandria).
Travel south on St. Hwy 53 about
8 miles to Wilson Bank & Trust. From
St. Hwy 70, turn at intersection with
St. Hwy 53 in Alexandria, Wilson
Bank & Trust on right within sight of
intersection.
Contact: Kevin Bandy, PO Box 369,
Alexandria, TN 37012; 615-529-4663;
email: kevinbandy68@gmail.com
www.bailifffamily.com

4 26th Annual Appalachian Antique Farm Show
April 25-28   Johnson City/Kingsport
Feature: Battle of the Brands.
Appalachian Fairgrounds, 100
Lakeview St., Gray, TN, I-81 to 57A,
I26 to exit 13, follow fairground signs.
Contact: Melissa Milner, 230
Rock House Rd., Johnson City, TN
37601; 423-794-6672;
email: mmilner12@chartertn.net
www.tsapa.com
See our ad on page 27

5 Tractor, Truck and Gas Engine Show
May 18   Lebanon
945 Baddour Pkwy., Ward Agricultural
Center and Fairgrounds, 30 miles east
of Nashville on I-40, exit 239, Hwy 70
west 3/4 mile.
Contact: Johnny or Debbie Mitchell,
615-444-6944;
email: jwdamitch@gmail.com

6 2019 Granville Heritage Day Antique Car and Tractor Show
May 25   Granville
I-40, exit 258 to Carthage, exit at
Hwy 53 and Hwy 70 junction toward
Cookeville. In Chestnut Mound, turn
left in front of the post office on
Hwy 53N, 5 miles ahead.
Contact: Randall Clemons, PO Box 26,
Granville, TN 38564; 931-653-4511;
email: rclemons@wilsonbank.com
www.granvilletn.com

7 Atwood Spring Tractor Show
June 1   Atwood
Show is held in park at intersection
of Hwys 70 and 79 on the west side
of town.
Contact: Jeff Oliver, 1593 Miles Rd.,
Dresden, TN 38225; 731-431-7525;
email: wtaeata@yahoo.com

4 48th Anniversary East Tennessee Crank-Up sponsored by the East Tennessee Antique Engine Association
June 6-8   Johnson City
2045 Sciota Rd., Elizabethton, TN.
From Johnson City, exit 27 off of I-26,
follow signs.
Contact: Geoff Hutchings, 2045
Sciota Rd., Elizabethton, TN 37643;
423-725-3992;
email: gkhetcu@gmail.com
www.easttennesseecrankup.org

8 Smokey Mountain Antique Engine and Tractor Association Spring Festival
June 7-8   Clinton
140 Maverick Cir., exit 122 off I-75.
Contact: John D. Wallace, 2338
Islandhome Ave., Knoxville, TN 37920;
865-776-2888;
email: deerejohn630@yahoo.com
www.smaeta.org

9 50th Annual Tennessee-Kentucky Threshermen's Show
July 19-20   Adams
U.S. Hwy 41.
Contact: Robert Mitchell, 615-887-0509;
Charlie Bumpus, 931-624-3893
See our ad on page 244

2 3rd Annual Smoky Mountain Flywheelers Show
Aug. 1-3   Seviorville
Features: International Harvester
Tractors and Engines.
1200 Dolly Parton Pkwy.
Contact: Jason Finchum,
305 Keener Rd., Seymour, TN 37865;
865-591-1705;
email: ihcollector@me.com

10 Tractor Show On The Creek
Aug. 24   Kingston
Feature: John Deere Tractors.
110 Chandley Rd.
Contact: Billy Norman,
110 Chandley Rd., Kingston, TN 37763;
865-466-1658;
email:
mrheartbeat1964@netscape.com

⓫ Greene County Antique Farm and Auto Show
Sept. 20-22   Greeneville
Feature: Ford.
Greene County Fairgrounds, Hwy 11E
behind Lowe's.
Contact: Chris Estepp, Erwin Hwy,
Afton, TN 37616; 423-620-4814;
email: carolethornburg@yahoo.com

⓬ Montgomery County Antique Tractor and Engine Club 19th Annual Show
Sept. 27-28   Clarksville
John Bartee Agriculture Center.
I-24, exit 8/Rossview Road, Hwy 237,
1.2 miles east.
Contact: Raymond Bagwell, 3301
Old Sango Rd., Clarksville, TN 37043;
931-320-0134;
email: rbagwell01@charter.net
Facebook: MCATAEC
See our ad on page 244

⓭ 24th Annual Sardis Antique Farm and Home Fall Show
Sept. 28   Sardis
City Park, 4540 Henderson Rd.
Transport entrance: 1955 Hinkle Rd.
Contact: Danny Sanderson, 950
Sanderson Rd., Sardis, TN 38371;
731-206-0858; 731-249-4106;
email: dgsanderson111@gmail.com

⓮ Fall Festival
Sept. 28   Cookeville
Hyder-Burks Agricultural Pavilion,
2390 Gainesboro Grade. From I-40,
exit 280, 7 miles north, turn right.
7 miles on the right.
Contact: Tom Tarrant, 931-260-8950

⓮ Middle Tennessee Antique Engine and Tractor Show
Sept. 28   Cookeville
Hyder-Burks Agricultural Pavilion,
2390 Gainesboro Grade.
Contact: David Qualls, PO Box 49354,
Cookeville, TN 38506; 931-526-2474;
email: dqbinder@hotmail.com

⓯ 14th Annual Days Gone By Tractor Show and Threshing
Oct. 4-5   Portland
122 Davis St.
Contact: Joey Collins, 323B Victor
Reiter Pkwy., Portland, TN 37148;
615-325-2555;
email: daysgoneby@att.net
See our ad on page 244

⓰ Fall Festival
Oct. 11-12   Waverly
Features: Allis-Chalmers, Simplicity.
Humphreys Co. Ag. Center, 234
W. Blue Creek Rd. Exit 143 north on
Hwy 13 for 13 miles.
Contact: Robin Blue, 3390 Hwy 13 S.,
Waverly, TN 37185; 931-622-2235;
email: ih1486dt@gmail.com

⓱ Three Rivers Antique Tractor and Engine Show
Oct. 11-12   Harriman
Feature: Massey-Harris Tractors.
276 Patton Ln.
Contact: Billy Norman,
110 Chandley Rd., Kingston, TN
37763; 865-466-1658;
email:
mrheartbeat1964@netscape.com

⓲ Tractors and Trucks Shackle Island Collector's Club Fall Harvest Show
Oct. 11-12   Goodlettsville
3603 Long Hollow Pike Rd.
Contact: Gary Davis, 615-504-9619;
Ron Kiecker, 615-364-6266;
email: davis500@aol.com
rkiecker@aol.com
www.tractorsandtrucks.com

❼ Atwood Fall Tractor Show
Oct. 12   Atwood
Show is held in park at intersection of
Hwys 70 and 79 on the west side of
town.
Contact: Jeff Oliver, 1593 Miles Rd.,
Dresden, TN 38225; 731-431-7525;
email: wtaeata@yahoo.com

⓳ 21st Williston Old Timers Association Show
Oct. 19   Williston
Williston Historic Square, 30 miles
east of Memphis on Hwy 194.
Contact: Tom Sheehan, 901-828-0380

20 **Starr Mountain Antique Tractor and Car Show**
Oct. 19-20   Etowah
From 411 in Etowah, take Mecca Pike (CR 310) toward Tellico, turn right on CR 881 to 4-way stop, left on CR 475, right on CR 880 to silos.
Contact: Bobby Martin, 423-462-5509; 423-263-1234

21 **4th Annual Tractor and Car Show**
Oct. 26   Seymour
959 N Knob Creek Rd.
Contact: Cliff Caldwell, 2809 Ellejoy Rd., Walland, TN 37886; 865-621-3103; email: 560farmallm1947@gmail.com

22 **Billy McKnight Memorial Antique Tractor and Engine Show**
Nov. 1-2   Trenton
Features: Farmall Tractors and John Deere Engines.
Gibson County Fairgrounds, 1242 Manufacturers Row.
Contact: Mike or Gail Privett, 561 Poplar Corner Rd., Humboldt, TN 38343; 731-487-0954; email: ellfone@bellsouth.net

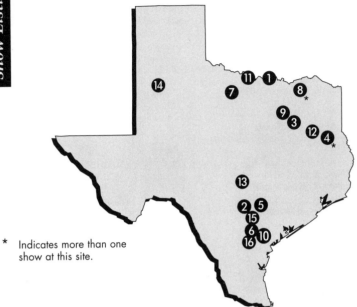

* Indicates more than one
  show at this site.

TEXAS

① 33rd Annual North Texas Farm Toy Show
March 2   Sherman
405 N Rusk. At the Sherman Municipal Ballroom.
Contact: Eugene Duperry, 251 Snider Ln., Gordonville, TX 76245; 214-914-4032;
email: toniej@yahoo.com

② Bastrop Antique Farm Show
March 2   Bastrop
American Legion Drive. "On top of the hill" across from Bastrop State Park.
Contact: Reid Sharp, PO Box 267, Bastrop, TX 78602; 512-332-6051;
email: rsharp@fnbbastrop.com
Facebook: Bastrop Antique Farm Show

③ Canton Tractor Show and Swap Meet
April 5-6   Canton
1/2 mile south of I-20 on Hwy 19.
Contact: Donna, 903-567-7897;
email: lewisautoswap@yahoo.com

④ Memories of Yesteryear
April 19-20   Henderson
Rusk County Youth Expo, FM 13, off of Loop 571 west of town. Watch for signs.
Contact: Don Reynolds, 2810 CR 342 S., Henderson, TX 75654; 903-889-2671;
email: dr48jdm@eastex.net

⑤ 30th Annual Burton Cotton Gin Festival Antique Tractor Show and Pull
April 27   Burton
Feature: 1925 16-Ton Bessemer Engine that powers the 1914 Cotton Gin fired up every year.
Texas Cotton Gin Museum, 307 N. Main. Lower field behind the 1914 Burton Farmer's Gin.
Contact: Stephanie Jarvis, 307 N. Main St., Burton, TX 77835; 979-289-3378;
email: burtoncottongin@earthlink.net
www.cottonginmuseum.org

6 South Texas Wheel Spinners and Crank Twisters Moravia Fest
May 5   Moravia
FM 957, south of Schulenburg.
Contact: Mark Hermes, 304 Buckeye
Trl., La Grange, TX 78945;
361-772-4619;
email: mark.hermes@yahoo.com

7 Jerry Askey Memorial Show
May 16-18   Decatur
From Decatur off Hwy 287, take FM
2264 and follow to CR 4530. Turning
left, follow CR 4530 approximately
2 miles to Askey Road (large gas plant
at that corner), follow private road to
1000 Acre Farm, follow signs.
Contact: Neil Mackie, general info,
1049 CR 3657, Springtown, TX 76082;
817-846-6856; 940-482-2691;
email: mackie1049@gmail.com;
Jackie Hamby, vendor info,
817-914-7010

8 Power of the Past Show and Pull
May 18   Cooper
Feature: Ferguson Tractors.
Cooper City Park, east of downtown
on Dallas Avenue.
Contact: Gus Young, 70 CR 4430,
Cooper, TX 75432; 903-401-1196;
email: gusyoung630@gmail.com

9 North Texas Antique Tractor and Engine Club Show and Pull
June 8-9   Terrell
Ben Gill Park, follow U.S. Hwy 80 east
from Dallas.
Contact: Gordon McCosh, 529
H Wallace Ln., Rockwall, TX 75032;
214-649-5478;
email: ntataec@gmail.com
www.north-texas-antique-tractor-and-
engine-club.org

10 Ricebelt Antique Tractor Show and Pull for DAV
June 14-15   El Campo
Hwy 71 S.
Contact: Debbie Chappell, 266 Palomar
Rd., El Campo, TX 77437;
979-543-4215;
email: morganchappell@att.net

11 34th Annual Cooke County Antique Tractor and Farm Machinery Show
Aug. 31-Sept. 1   Lindsay
I-35 to Gainesville, Hwy 82 west
to Lindsay, north on FM 1199 from
Lindsay, 3 miles, watch for signs.
Contact: Willie Joe Matthews,
PO Box 895, Gainesville, TX 76241;
940-736-4541; 940-665-6823

12 Lone Star Antique Tractor and Engine Show
Sept. 7   Whitehouse
At traffic light at intersection of SH 110
and FM 346, turn east. About 3 miles
on right, turn right onto Dudley Road.
Follow signs that begin at intersection
of FM 346 and SH 110.
Contact: Charles Parmley, 15246
Seven League Rd., Tyler, TX 75703;
903-571-8767;
email: cjparmley@gmail.com
www.lsatea.org

13 48th Annual State Tractor, Truck and Engine Show
Oct. 5   Temple
Features: Allis-Chalmers Tractors and
Witte Engines.
1717 Eberhardt Rd.
Contact: Dustin Marx, PO Box 1704,
Temple, TX 76503; 254-760-7358;
email: j.dustin.marx@gmail.com
texasedtea.org
See our ad on page 13

8 Delta County Cotton Harvest Festival Show
Oct. 12   Cooper
Show on northwest corner of square.
Contact: Gus Young, 903-401-1196

14 17th Annual Antique Tractor and Engine Show
Oct. 12-13   Lubbock
East Broadway and Canyon Lake
Drive. At the Bayer Museum of
Agriculture.
Contact: Lionel Patterson, 116
N. Oakridge Ave., Lubbock, TX 79416;
806-632-8003;
email: lionelp@suddenlink.net
www.spata.club

⓯ Texas Czech Heritage and Cultural Center Heritage Fest and Muziky
Oct. 18-19   La Grange
U.S. Hwy 77, north to
250 W. Fairgrounds Rd.
Contact: TCHCC/Mark Hermes,
PO Box 6, La Grange, TX 78945;
888-785-4500 (toll-free);
email: info@czechtexas.org

❹ Heritage Syrup Festival
Nov. 9   Henderson
Deport Museum, 514 N. High St.
5 blocks off Hwy 64, west on
North Mill Street going south.
Contact: Don Reynolds, 2810 CR 342 S.,
Henderson, TX 75654; 903-889-2671;
903-657-4303;
email: dr48jdm@eastex.net
www.depotmuseum.com

⓰ Texas Antique Tractor Show and Pull Kickoff
Jan. 17-18, 2020   Hallettsville
Expo Center. CR 200 and FM 957.
Contact: Mark Hermes, 304 Buckeye
Trl., La Grange, TX 78945;
361-772-4619;
email: mark.hermes@yahoo.com

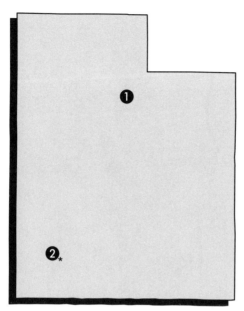

* Indicates more than one
  show at this site.

UTAH

❶ RW Erickson Antique Power Show
June 21-23   Wallsburg
Features: Over 200 Tractors;
Hit-and-Miss Engines.
50 Starks Ln. Reference signs from
Hwy 189 to ranch.
Contact: Faye Murray, PO Box 220,
50 Starks Lane, Wallsburg, UT 84082;
435-654-3570;
email: rwerickson35@yahoo.com
www.richardericksonfoundation.org

**❷ Iron County Fair Tractor Caravan,
Show and Pull**
Aug. 31-Sept. 2   Cedar City
Iron County Fairgrounds, Parowan.
Contact: Sheridan Hansen, 1021
Cedar Knolls, Cedar City, UT 84720;
435-586-7512;
email: sheridannette@q.com;
Kip C. Hansen, 345 Hillcrest,
Richfield, UT 84701; 435-592-4045

**❷ Color Country Antique Machinery
Association Cedar Heritage and
Livestock Festival**
Oct. 25-26   Cedar City
Held in conjunction with the Cedar
Livestock and Heritage Festival. Cross
Hollow Events Center.
Contact: Sheridan Hansen, 1021
Cedar Knolls, Cedar City, UT 84720;
435-586-7512;
email: sheridanette@q.com
www.cedarlivestockfest.com

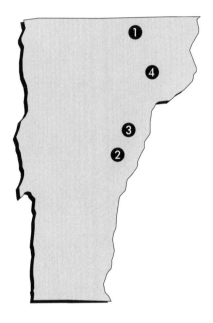

VERMONT

❶ Vermont Gas and Steam Engine Association Brownington Show
June 14-15   Brownington
Old Stone House Museum,
109 Old Stone House Rd.
Contact: Gary Howe, 1 Mountain Ave.,
Randolph, VT 05060; 802-728-9350;
email: gary05060@gmail.com

❷ Vermont Gas and Steam Engine Association Quechee Show
Aug. 2-4   Quechee
Quechee Gorge Village,
5573 Woodstock Rd.
Contact: Gary Howe, 1 Mountain Ave.,
Randolph, VT 05060; 802-728-9350;
email: gary05060@gmail.com

❸ 26th Annual Connecticut River Antique Collectors Klub (CRACK)
Aug. 22-24   Ely
Rt. 5, exit 14, 2-1/2 miles south
of Fairlee.
Contact: Ruth Driscoll, 2584 Rt. 5 S.,
Ely, VT 05045; 802-333-3243;
email:
vtantiquecollectormyfairpoint.net

❹ Vermont Gas and Steam Engine Association East Burke Fall Festival
Sept. 28   East Burke
Off the Belden Hill Road by "Dishmill
Forest Products."
Contact: Gary Howe, 1 Mountain Ave.,
Randolph, VT 05060; 802-728-9350;
email: gary05060@gmail.com

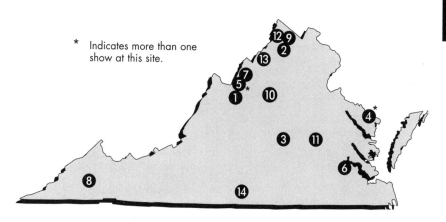

* Indicates more than one
  show at this site.

VIRGINIA

❶ Riverheads Young Farmers Farm Toy Show and Sale
March 15-16   Staunton
19 Howardsville Turnpike.
Contact: Kaitlyn Sonifrank,
19 Howardsville Rd., Staunton, VA
24401; 540-478-2719;
email:
sonifrank.km@augusta.k12.va.us

❷ Toy Show
March 22-23   Boyce
Feature: International Harvester.
Boyce Fire Hall, Rt. 340.
Contact: Chris Collis, 304-839-7011;
www.svsgea.com
See our ad on page 246

❸ 23rd Annual Powhatan Spring Antique Power Show
April 27-28   Powhatan
Yorkshire Place, 2455 Academy Rd.,
off Rt. 60.
Contact: Patsy Goodwyn,
3620 Goodwyn Rd., Powhatan, VA
23139; 804-598-4464;
email: pggoodwyn@verizon.net

❹ Opening and Planting Day
May 4   Heathsville
12705 Northumberland Hwy.
Contact: J. Rawleigh Simmons,
PO Box 789, Warsaw, VA 22572;
004-761-0892;
email: rsimmons@rivertitleva.com
www.thefarmmuseum.org

❺ 29th Annual Spring Chapter Show
May 18   Bridgewater
23 Green St.
Contact: Scott Shifflett, 2740
Old Furnace Rd., Rockingham, VA
22802; 540-478-4389;
email: greasemonkeyb61@gmail.com

❹ Spring Farm to Fork Dinner
May 18   Heathsville
12705 Northumberland Hwy.
Contact: J. Rawleigh Simmons,
PO Box 789, Warsaw, VA 22572;
804-761-0892;
email: rsimmons@rivertitleva.com
www.thefarmmuseum.org

6 29th Annual Chippokes Farm and Forestry Muse
June 1-2　　　　　　　　　Surry
Chippokes State Park, 695 Chippokes Park Rd.
Contact: 757-294-3625

7 9th Annual International Harvesters Collectors of Virginia Summer Show
June 14-16　　　　　　Harrisonburg
Feature: International Harvester.
Rockingham County Fairgrounds.
4808 S. Valley Pike.
Contact: Tinker Moats, 795 Slate Hill Rd., Weyers Cave, VA 24486;
540-246-5726;
email: pullingih@yahoo.com
www.ihcofva.com

4 Threshing Day
July 6　　　　　　　　　Heathsville
12705 Northumberland Hwy.
Contact: J. Rawleigh Simmons,
PO Box 789, Warsaw, VA 22572;
804-761-0892;
email: rsimmons@rivertitleva.com
www.thefarmmuseum.org
See our ad on page 245

5 50th Annual Bridgewater Volunteer Fire Co. Steam and Gas Meet
July 17-20　　　　　　Bridgewater
23 Green St.
Contact: Scott Shifflett, 2740 Old Furnace Rd., Harrisonburg, VA 22802; 540-478-4389;
email: greasemonkeyb61@gmail.com

8 12th Annual Summer Show
July 18-20　　　　　　　Abingdon
908 Hillman Hwy. I-81 to exit 19, north on Rt. 11, right on Hillman Hwy at stop light.
Contact: Ronald Stevenson, 14437 Prices Bridge Rd., Glade Spring, VA 24340; 276-356-5397;
email: truckman22@hughes.net
www.oldgladetractors.com

9 Pageant of Steam
July 26-28　　　　　　　Berryville
Feature: International Harvester.
890 W. Main St.
Contact: Robert Brown, 804 Minebank Rd., Middletown, VA 22645;
540-272-0931;
Barbara Heflin, 540-514-5854;
Charlie Gray, 540-533-8827;
www.svsgea.com
See our ad on page 246

10 43rd Annual Somerset Steam and Gas Pasture Party
Sept. 13-15　　　　　　　Somerset
14375 Blue Ridge Turnpike. Rt. 231.
Contact: S.S. & G.E.A., PO Box 492, Somerset, VA 22972; 540-672-3429;
email:
info@somersetsteamandgas.org
www.somersetsteamandgas.org
See our ad on page 245

11 Rockville-Centerville Steam and Gas Historical Association Field Day of the Past
Sept. 20-22　　　　　　　Richmond
Show grounds, 14 miles west of Richmond, I-64, exit 173 (Rockville-Manakin), exit south, go 1/8 mile to show grounds, follow signs.
Contact: Melinda Gammon,
PO Box 29643, Richmond, VA 23242;
804-741-8468;
email: fielddayofthepast@gmail.com
www.fielddayofthepast.net
See our ad on page 20

12 15th Annual Tri-State Antique Truck and Tractor Show
Sept. 26-28　　　　　　Winchester
Ruritan Park, I-81, exit 321 (Clearbrook), east to Rt. 11, south.
Contact: Scott Shifflett, 2740 Old Furnace Rd., Harrisonburg, VA 22802; 540-478-4389;
email: greasemonkeyb61@gmail.com
www.tri-state-antiquetruckshow.com

④ Fall Farm to Fork Dinner
Oct. 12   Heathsville
12705 Northumberland Highway.
Contact: J. Rawleigh Simmons,
PO Box 789, Warsaw, VA 22572;
804-761-0892;
email: rsimmons@rivertitleva.com
www.thefarmmuseum.org

⑬ 50th Annual Page County Heritage Festival
Oct. 12-13   Luray
Page County Fairgrounds,
15 Fairlane Dr.
Contact: Wayne Waters, steam and
gas, 471 Mt. Carmel Road, Luray, VA
22835; 540-743-4161;
Ronnie Kauffman, arts and crafts,
Kauffman's Mill Road, Luray, VA
22835; 540-244-9739;
www.pagecountyheritage.com
See our ad on page 245

④ Fall Harvest Festival
Oct. 26-27   Heathsville
12705 Northumberland Hwy.
Contact: J. Rawleigh Simmons,
PO Box 789, Warsaw, VA 22572;
804-761-0892;
email: rsimmons@rivertitleva.com
www.thefarmmuseum.org

④ Plowing Day
Nov. 2   Heathsville
12705 Northumberland Hwy.
Contact: J. Rawleigh Simmons,
PO Box 789, Warsaw, VA 22572;
804-761-0892;
email: rsimmons@rivertitleva.com
www.thefarmmuseum.org
See our ad on page 245

⑭ 16th Annual Halifax County Heritage and Antique Machinery Festival
May 3-4   South Boston
Halifax County Fairgrounds, Hwy 360 E.
Contact: 434-572-6879;
email: lucyconner40@gmail.com
www.halifaxcountyheritagefestival.org
See our ad on page 245

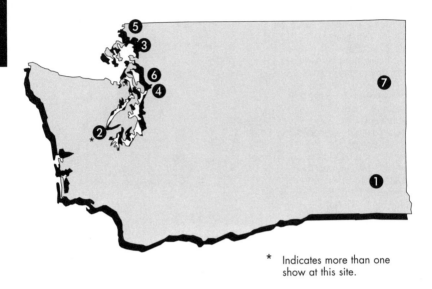

* Indicates more than one
show at this site.

WASHINGTON

❶ Spring Farming Days
April 6-7   Pomeroy
99 Fairground Rd. Approximately
1 mile east of town on Hwy 125 east,
then south on Fairground Road, watch
for and follow signs and flags.
Contact: David Ruark, 509-843-3506;
Jay Franks, 509-566-7027;
274 Malone Hill Rd., Pomeroy, WA
99347;
email: pvpercherons@msn.com
www.co.garfield.wa.us/museum

**❷ EDGETA #245 Annual Spring
Swap Meet**
April 27   Shelton
Old Iron Event Center,
11 E. Johns Creek Dr.
Contact: April Campbell, 11
E. Johns Creek Dr., Shelton, WA
98584; 360-490-8441;
email: mytractorclub@aol.com
www.exhaustfumes.org
Facebook: Early Day Gas Engine &
Tractor Association Branch 245

❸ 36th Gas-Up
May 11   Mount Vernon
Skagit County Fairgrounds,
West Hazel Street. In conjunction
with Master Gardener Plant Sale.
Contact: Morrie Robinson, 31445
Barben Rd., Sedro Woolley, WA
98284; 360-826-3782;
email: antiquetractor@yahoo.com

**❷ 2019 NorthWest Regional "Pioneer
Power of the Pacific NorthWest"**
July 12-14   Shelton
Old Iron Event Center.
11 E. Johns Creek Dr.
Contact: Dale Fye, 11 E. Johns Creek
Dr., Shelton, WA 98584;
360-426-9299; 360-490-8441;
email: mytractorclub@aol.com
www.exhaustfumes.org
Facebook: Early Day Gas Engine &
Tractor Association Branch 245

4 **Annual Show and 35 Mile Drive**
July 20-21　　　　　Carnation
Rockin R Ranch, 32317 N.E. 11th St.,
about 3 miles south of town on
St. Hwy 203.
Contact: Phil Scott, 21313 SE 215th
St., Maple Valley, WA 98038;
206-388-9895;
email: pascott41@msn.com
www.edgeta.com/event/branch-36-
annual-antique-tractor-show

5 **48th Annual Steam and Gas Show**
July 31-Aug. 3　　　　　Lynden
Feature: Steam Tractors.
8837 Berthusen Rd.
Contact: Lee & Shelly Van Beek,
194 Bay Lyn Dr., Lynden, WA 98264;
360-354-3462;
email: svanbeek1979@gmail.com
www.psatma.com

6 **Threshing Bee and Tractor Show**
Aug. 9-11　　　　　Monroe
Feature: Minneapolis-Moline Tractors.
Show grounds, Hwy 203 south, right
on Tualco Road, follow signs.
Contact: Ron Chew, 10420
159th Ave. N.E., Granite Falls, WA
98252; 360-631-2843;
email: gorrchew@gmail.com

7 **Spokane Inter State Fair**
Sept. 6-15　　　　　Spokane Valley
Feature: International Harvester
Tractors.
Fairgrounds. From I-90 West on
Broadway to Havana Street.
Contact: Harold Kellams, 1424
S. Eastern Rd., Spokane Valley, WA
99212; 509-536-5381;
email: firemanhal@comcast.net

2 **EDGETA #245 Annual Fall
Swap Meet**
Oct. 26　　　　　Shelton
Old Iron Event Center,
11 E. Johns Creek Dr.
Contact: April Campbell, 11
E. Johns Creek Dr., Shelton, WA
98584; 360-490-8441;
email: mytractorclub@aol.com
www.exhaustfumes.org
Facebook: Early Day Gas Engine &
Tractor Association Branch 245

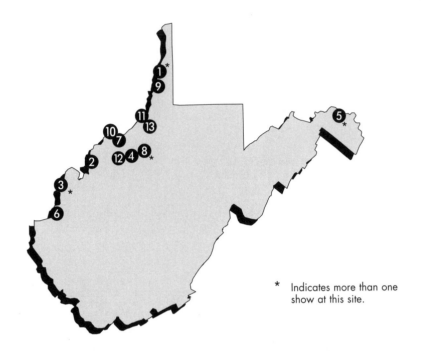

* Indicates more than one show at this site.

WEST VIRGINIA

❶ Spring Swap Meet
March 30 McMechen
From Rt. 2, turn west at "12th St. McMechen" exit, dead end at river, turn left to park.
Contact: Gary Shreve, 422 Little Grave Creek Dr., Glen Dale, WV 26038; 304-845-746;
email: maytag287@comcast.net
See our ad on page 251

❷ Wood County Flywheelers Bill Graham Plow Day
April 13 Belleville
Robinhood Road. Call for directions. Rain date April 21.
Contact: Carla Knapp, 724 Murphytown Rd., Davisville, WV 26142; 304-480-9762;
email: cknapp2314@yahoo.com;
Rick Miller, 304-481-0742;
Earl Hudkins, 304-679-3403

❸ West Virginia State Farm Museum Antique Engine and Tractor Show
May 4-5 Point Pleasant
4 miles outside of town on Rt. 2 N., turn right past sign and go 1/2 mile, on right side.
Contact: Lloyd Akers, 1458 Fairground Rd., Point Pleasant, WV 25550;
304-675-5737;
email: wvsfm@wvfarmmuseum.org
www.wvfarmmuseum.org

❹ 15th Annual Engines and Wheels Festival
May 25 Cairo
Follow signs to North Bend State Park, then to Jughandle Day Use Area.
Contact: David Wilson, 1841 Staunton Turnpike, Petroleum, WV 26161; 304-628-3587;
email: adaw@zoominternet.net

Farm Collector Show Directory 2019

Show Listings

5 L. Norman Dillon Farm Museum Antique Tractor and Gas Engine Spring Show
June 1-2 Hedgesville
Exit 16W off I-81. 3 miles on the left, across from Hedgesville High School.
Contact: Chuck Stewart, PO Box 2731, Martinsburg, WV 25402; 304-582-2279; email: leeroy487@hotmail.com

6 West Virginia Antique Engine and Tractor Association Mac's Fun Show
June 1-2 Ashton
Rivers Edge Campground, 25 miles north of Huntington on Rt. 2, or 20 miles south of Point Pleasant on Rt. 2.
Contact: Jim Bess, 6147 Coal River Rd., Tornado, WV 25202; 304-727-4878

7 Wood County Flywheelers One Day Show
June 15 Waverly
1014 Volcano Rd. Mountwood Park, 12 miles east of Parkersburg on St. Rt. 50,
Contact: Carla Knapp, 724 Murphytown Rd., Davisville, WV 26142; 304-480-9762; email: cknapp2314@yahoo.com;

1 25th Annual Gas Engine Show
June 21-22 McMechen
Feature: International Harvest Tractors. From Rt. 2, turn west at "12th St. McMechen" exit, dead end at river, turn left to park.
Contact: Gary Shreve, 422 Little Grave Creek Dr., Glen Dale, WV 26038; 304-845-7461; email: maytag287@comcast.net
See our ad on page 251

8 Boston's Antique Engine Show
July 12-13 Pennsboro
461 Boston Dr. Rt. 50 to Cunningham Run Road (mile marker 39.5). Go 1.5 miles to Boston Drive on the right.
Contact: Johnnie Boston, 461 Boston Dr., Pennsboro, WV 26415; 304-481-3687; email: kathyb1333@gmail.com
www.johnnieboston.com

9 10th Anniversary Antique Tractor Show
July 22-29 Moundsville
Marshall County Fairgrounds, 12th Street.
Contact: Tabitha O'Bannon, 12th Street, Moundsville, WV 26041; 540-359-5639; email: tabithaobannon@hotmail.com

10 Henderson Hall One Day Antique Engine Show
Aug. 3 Williamstown (Boaz)
Old River Road, off St. Rt. 14.
Contact: Carla J Knapp, 724 Murphytown Rd., Davisville, WV 26142; 304-480-9762; email: cknapp2314@yahoo.com

11 51st Annual West Virginia Oil and Gas Festival
Sept. 12-14 Sistersville
City park, McCoy Avenue, beside Ohio River. Entrance at ferry boat landing.
Contact: Barbara Vincent, PO Box 25, Sistersville, WV 26175; 304-652-2939; Fred Anderson, 304-771-0537

12 31st Annual Wood County Flywheelers Volcano Days Antique Engine Show and Festival
Sept. 27-29 Walker
Mountwood Park, 12 miles east of Parkersburg on St. Rt. 40 on Volcano Road.
Contact: Carla Knapp, 724 Murphytown Rd., Davisville, WV 26142; 304-480-9762; email: cknapp2314@yahoo.com

13 Middle Island Harvest Festival
Oct. 4-6 Middlebourne
4 Tyler County Fair Dr.. 3 miles south of town on Rt. 18.
Contact: Joseph Smith, PO Box 193, Middlebourne, WV 26149; 304-771-4098; email: joe.smith@tylercountyfair.org
tylercountyfair.org

❸ Fall Festival West Virginia State Farm Museum
Oct. 5-6   Point Pleasant
4 miles outside of town on Rt. 2 N.,
turn right past sign and go 1/2 mile,
on right side.
Contact: Lloyd Akers, 1458 Fairground
Rd., Point Pleasant, WV 25550;
304-675-5737

❺ L. Norman Dillon Farm Museum Antique Tractor and Gas Engine Fall Show
Oct. 12-13   Hedgesville
Exit 16W off I-81. 3 miles on the left
across from Hedgesville High School.
Contact: Chuck Stewart, PO Box 2731,
Martinsburg, WV 25402; 304-582-2279;
email: leeroy487@hotmail.com

❶ Fall Swap Meet
Nov. 2   McMechen
From Rt. 2, turn west at "12th St.
McMechen" exit, dead end at river,
turn left to park.
Contact: Gary Shreve, 422
Little Grave Creek Dr., Glen Dale, WV
26038; 304-845-7461;
email: maytag287@yahoo.com
See our ad on page 251

❽ Boston's Antique Engine Show
Nov. 8-9   Pennsboro
Rt. 50 to Cunningham Run Road (mile
marker 39.5). Go 1-1/2 miles to Boston
Drive on the right.
Contact: Johnnie Boston, 461
Boston Dr., Pennsboro, WV 26415;
304-481-3687;
email: kathyb1333@gmail.com
www.johnnieboston.com

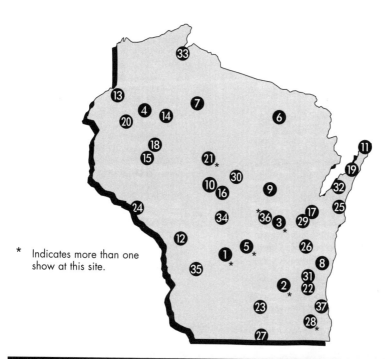

* Indicates more than one
show at this site.

WISCONSIN

❶ Badger Steam and Gas Engine Club
Spring Swap Meet
May 3-5   Baraboo
Feature: Auction Saturday, May 4,
10 a.m.
S3347 Sand Rd. I-90/94, exit 92,
Hwy 12 east 3 miles to Hwy 33,
exit 215, west 1/2 mile to Sand Road,
north 1/2 mile.
Contact: Robert Mattson, PO Box 255,
Baraboo, WI 53913; 608-393-3021;
www.badgersteamandgas.com
See our ad on page 247

❷ Ixonia Vintage Tractor Expo
May 24-26   Ixonia
Feature: J.I. Case Collectors
Spring Convention.
Ashippun Firemen's Park,
W2665 Oak St.
Contact: Curt Pernat, N7771 Hwy F,
Ixonia, WI 53036; 920-988-0857;
email: downhomecollect@att.net
www.ixoniavintagetractorexpo.com
See our ad on page 11

❷ J.I. Case Collectors Annual Spring
Convention
May 25-26   Ixonia
Ixonia Firemen's Show.
Contact: Jonathan Woodrum,
606-303-0891;
email: jwll67@yahoo.com
www.jicasecollector.com
See our ad on page 246

❸ Pickett Independence Pull
June 29   Pickett
7 miles south of Oshkosh or
4-1/2 miles north of Rosendale,
W9975 Olden Rd. (west of Hwy 26).
Contact: Bud Kaufmann, president,
920-426-0814;
email: fkaufmann@new.rr.com
www.pickettsteamclub.org
See our ad on page 250

4 50th Annual Show Hungry Hollow Steam and Gas Engine Club Inc.
June 29-30   Rice Lake
From Barron, Hwy 25 north to 19th Avenue. From Rice Lake, Hwy 48 west to Hwy 25 south to 19th Avenue. Follow signs.
Contact: Mike Messner, 2213 18 1/2 St., Rice Lake, WI 54868; 715-234-8423;
email: messfam39@yahoo.com
www.hungryhollowclub.com
See our ad on page 250

3 Pickett Engine Show
July 6   Pickett
7 miles south of Oshkosh or 4-1/2 miles north of Rosendale, W9975 Olden Rd. (west of Hwy 26).
Contact: Bud Kaufmann, president, 920-426-0814;
email: fkaufmann@new.rr.com
www.pickettsteamclub.org
See our ad on page 250

5 50th Anniversary John Deere Patio (Custom Colors)
July 11-14   Portage
300 Superior St., I-39, exit 87, Hwy 33 east into Portage to first stop light, turn right onto Hwy 51 S. for 1 mile, turn left on Wauona Trail for 2 blocks, left onto Townsend Street, turn right into main gate at Veterans Memorial Field-Columbia County Fairgrounds.
Contact: Bret Esse, 608-297-7400;
email: bestfabtractorparts@yahoo.com
Facebook: Annual Garden Tractor Daze Portage, Wisconsin

5 Garden Tractor Daze
July 11-14   Portage
Feature: Wheelhorse.
300 Superior St., I-39, exit 87, Hwy 33 east into Portage to first stop light, turn right onto Hwy 51 S. for 1 mile, turn left on Wauona Trail for 2 blocks, left onto Townsend Street, turn right into main gate at Veterans Memorial Field-Columbia County Fairgrounds.
Contact: Bret Esse, 608-297-7400;
email: bestfabtractorparts@yahoo.com
Facebook: Annual Garden Tractor Daze Portage, Wisconsin

5 National Case Colt Ingersoll Collectors Convention at Annual Garden Tractor Daze
July 11-14   Portage
300 Superior St., I-39, exit 87, Hwy 33 east into Portage to first stop light, turn right onto Hwy 51 S. for 1 mile, turn left on Wauona Trail for 2 blocks, left onto Townsend Street, turn right into main gate at Veterans Memorial Field-Columbia County Fairgrounds.
Contact: Bret Esse, 608-297-7400;
email: bestfabtractorparts@yahoo.com
Facebook: Annual Garden Tractor Daze Portage, Wisconsin

6 Wabeno Steam-Up Days
July 12-14   Wabeno
Downtown Wabeno.
Contact: Travis Tucker, 827 MacArthur, Wabeno, WI 54566; 715-889-4166;
email: bigttruckingllc@yahoo.com
Facebook: Wabeno Antique Power Association

7 11th Annual Antique Tractor Expo
July 20-21   Phillips
Expo at Price County Fairgrounds. From St. Hwy 13, turn onto CR H and drive 1 mile to the fairgrounds.
Contact: Steve Janacek, W6201 N. Loop Rd., Phillips, WI 54555; 715-339-3652;
www.pricecountyantiqueassociation.org

8 26th Annual Wisconsin Antique Power Reunion Show
July 20-21   Saukville
Features: Allis-Chalmers Tractors and Equipment including Allis Garden, Allis-Chalmers D-12 Raffle Tractors. 4880 Cty. Rd. "I" Hwy "33" to CTH "I" 4 miles north.
Contact: William Hinckley, 921 Birchwood Dr., West Bend, WI 53095; 262-365-9734;
email: williamh921@charter.net
www.waprtractorclub.com

9 52nd Annual Union Threshermen's Club Thresheree and National Antique Tractor Pull
July 26-28　　　　　Symco
Features: Minneapolis-Moline Tractors and Foreign Engines.
3-1/2 miles north of Manawa on Hwy 22 heading to town.
Contact: Gary Knuth, 920-757-6995;
Jerrod Werth, 920-596-1803;
www.symcoutc.com
See our ad on page 249

10 Sherry Tired Iron Tractor Show
July 27　　　　　Sherry
Anderton Park, 2-1/2 miles south on County Road F, off St. Hwy 10 (Blenker exit), between Marshfield and Stevens Point.
Contact: Fritz Miller, 715-572-8296;
email: sherrytirediron@gmail.com

11 Antique Tractor and Art/Craft Show
July 27-28　　　　　Ellison Bay
Hwy 42 on the south side of town.
Contact: Dave Westen, 10697 Sumac Ln., Sister Bay, WI 54234;
630-981-7844;
email: dcwesten@gmail.com
www.libertygrovehistorical.org

12 48th Annual Show Coulee Antique Engine Club
Aug. 2-4　　　　　Westby
Feature: Massey-Harris (State Show).
2 miles north of town or 4 miles south of Cashton on Hwy 27 (31061).
Contact: John Wangen, 608-606-0103;
email: jjcox86@yahoo.com
www.couleeantiqueengineclub.com

13 51st Annual Dodge County Antique Power Show
Aug. 2-4　　　　　Burnett Corners
Features: Oliver Hart-Parr and Cletrac Tractors.
1/2 mile south on St. Hwy 26, 1/2 mile west on CR B.
Contact: Bill Frank, 815-219-0537;
Darrell Pollesch, 920-928-2392;
920-296-0876;
www.dcapc.org
See our ad on page 248

14 3rd Annual Golat Implement Days, Tractor and Implement Show
Aug. 3-4　　　　　Ladysmith
Feature: Allis-Chalmers.
W7910 CR P. 3 miles south of town on Hwy 27 to CR P, east 1 mile. Show grounds on north side.
Contact: Chet and Deb Golat, W7910 CR P, Ladysmith, WI 54848;
715-532-6623;
email: paintballbcd@webtv.net

15 56th Annual Chippewa Valley Antique Engine and Model Club Pioneer Days
Aug. 9-11　　　　　Eau Claire
Features: Oliver Hart-Parr Tractors and Small Engines.
S9464 Porterville Rd., corner of Hwys 37 and 85.
Contact: Dan Goulet, 702 Cedar St., Chippewa Falls, WI 54729;
715-723-9524; Daryl Dehnke, 3641 Stein Blvd., Eau Claire, WI 54701; 715-559-5597;
email: harriet.dehnke@att.net
www.pioneer-days.org

16 Rudolph Old Tractor Club Show
Aug. 10　　　　　Rudolph
Community park, 8 miles north of Wisconsin Rapids on Hwy 13/34.
Contact: David Repinski, 3211 Reber Dr., Wisconsin Rapids, WI 54494;
715-423-8403;
email: rudolpholdtractorclub@gmail.com

17 67th Annual Wisconsin Steam Engine Show
Aug. 10-11　　　　　Chilton
Features: Massey-Harris Tractors and Logging Equipment.
Calumet County Fairgrounds.
Contact: Paul Reckelberg, N3212 CR AB, Luxemburg, WI 54217;
920-845-2908;
email: cny81677@centurytel.net
www.wisteam-engine.com

18 10th Annual Eau Claire Big Rig Truck Show
Aug. 16-18   Chippewa Falls
Located at the Northern Wisconsin
State Fairgrounds, 225 Edward St.
Contact: Terry Biddle, 2425 Seymour
Rd., Eau Claire, WI 54703;
715-832-6666;
email: terry@ectruckshow.com
www.ectruckshow.com

1 56th Annual Badger Steam and Gas Engine Club Show
Aug. 16-18   Baraboo
Features: Minneapolis-Moline Tractors.
S3347 Sand Rd. I-90/94, exit 92,
Hwy 12 east 3 miles to Hwy 33,
exit 215, west 1/2 mile to Sand Road,
north 1/2 mile.
Contact: Tyler Roudebush,
608-843-2652; Peter Holzmand,
608-635-7772;
www.badgersteamandgas.com
See our ad on page 247

19 Valmy Thresheree
Aug. 16-18   Sturgeon Bay
Feature: Farmall, International Tractors
and Equipment.
5005 N. Country View Rd., 6 miles
north on Hwy 42 to Whitefish Bay
Road, east 2 miles to Country View
Road.
Contact: Ralph Bochek, 4289
S. Country View Rd., Sturgeon Bay, WI
54235; 920-559-0466;
email: bocheksales@hotmail.com
www.valmythresheree.org

20 35th Annual Moon Lake Threshermen's Threshing Bee and Minneapolis Moline Summer Convention
Aug. 17-18   Turtle Lake
George Sollman's, 862 2/38 St. 5 miles
south of town on Hwy K.
Contact: Tim Sollman, 715-948-2533;
715-781-5566;
email: cliprfix@amerytel.net
www.moonlakeshow.org
See our ad on page 9

21 46th Annual North Central Wisconsin Antique Steam and Gas Engine Club Show
Aug. 23-25   Edgar
Feature: John Deere.
22 3755 Steam Hill Dr.
Contact: Greg Szemborski, 4958
Thomas Hill Rd., Edgar, WI 54426;
715-302-2311
email: gregsz2001@yahoo.com
www.edgarsteamshow.com
See our ad on page 248

22 61st Annual Sussex Engine Show
Aug. 24-25   Sussex
Hwy VV (Main Street).
Contact: George Becker, N. 64 W.
12929 Mill Rd., Menomonee Falls, WI
53051; 262-250-7223 (day);
262-252-3187 (night);
email: georgeb@glenroy.com

23 63rd Reunion of the Rock River Thresheree
Aug. 30-Sept. 2   Edgerton
Feature: International Harvester
Tractors.
51 E Cox Rd. From Edgerton, Hwy 51
south to Hwy M. From Janesville,
Hwy 51 north to Hwy M. From Milton,
Hwy M west.
Contact: Bill Werfal, 51 E. Cox Rd.,
Edgerton, WI 53534; 608-868-2814;
email: werf706@gmail.com
www.thresheree.com
See our ad on page 249

24 Fountain City Old Time Farm Fest
Aug. 31-Sept. 1   Fountain City
Feature: Case.
4 miles east on Hwy 95.
Contact: Jerry Dekan, N26051
Myers Valley Rd., Arcadia, WI 54612;
608-323-7401;
email: jerryg@centurytel.net
www.farmfestlions.com

3 Pickett Truck and Tractor Pull
Sept. 6   Pickett
7 miles south of Oshkosh or
4-1/2 miles north of Rosendale,
W9975 Olden Rd. (west of Hwy 26).
Contact: Bud Kaufmann, president,
920-426-0814;
email: fkaufmann@new.rr.com
www.pickettsteamclub.org
See our ad on page 250

㉕ 21st Annual Mid-Lakes Thresheree and Tractor Show
Sept. 7-8   Manitowoc
Feature: Oliver Hart-Parr.
Pinecrest Historical Village. From I-43: exit 152 to Waldo Boulevard, west 3 miles. From Fox Valley: Hwy 10 east to CR S in Whitelaw, south on S to CR JJ, turn left and go 2 miles.
Contact: Steve Kress, 3715 N. 50th St., Sheboygan, WI 53083; 920-946-0706; email: skress1955@gmail.com
www.mid-lakesrusticiron.org

❸ 33rd Annual Pickett Steam and Gas Engine Show
Sept. 7-8   Pickett
Features: Minneapolis-Moline and Oliver Hart-Parr Tractors, Fuller Johnson and Wisconsin-made Engines.
7 miles south of Oshkosh or 4-1/2 miles north of Rosendale, W9975 Olden Rd. (west of Hwy 26).
Contact: Bud Kaufmann, president, 920-426-0814;
email: fkaufmann@new.rr.com
www.pickettsteamclub.org
See our ad on page 250

㉖ Early Farm Days
Sept. 8   Kewaskum
1202 Parkview Dr., just off Hwy 28, by the bridge.
Contact: Bill Vrana, 262-689-7919; email: billyv25t@gmail.com
Facebook: Kewaskum Historical Society

㉗ Friends of Beckman Mill Heritage Day
Sept. 8   Beloit
5 miles west of Beloit on St. Road 81, 1 mile south of CR H.
Contact: Kevin Johnson, 7309 W. State Rd. 81, Beloit, WI 53511; 608-295-1194;
email: info@beckmanmill.org
www.beckmanmill.org

㉘ 28th Annual Fall Harvest Days
Sept. 13-15   Union Grove
Feature: Allis-Chalmers (The Gathering of the Orange).
Racine County Fairgrounds, 19805 Durand Ave.
Contact: Bill Schwartz, 262-331-4246; www.fallharvestdays.com
See our ad on page 250

㉘ Gathering of the Orange 2019
Sept. 13-15   Union Grove
Contact: 715-268-4632;
email: oldallisnews@amerytel.net
www.fallharvestdays.com

㉙ 31st Annual R.S. Vintage Steel Steam and Gas Engine Show
Sept. 14-15   Calumetville
Feature: Minneapolis-Moline.
Intersection of Hwy 151 and CR HHH.
Contact: Dennis and Shirley Lefeber, W2593 CR Q, Malone, WI 53049; 920-795-4531; 920-960-6157;
email: 4lefeber@gmail.com

㉚ 8th Annual Glacier Ridge Antique Tractor Show
Sept. 21-22   Shantytown
Features: Massey-Harris and Massey-Ferguson.
201282 CR J, Rosholt.
Contact: Robert Ostrowski, 715-572-1548;
Jim Hilger, 715-341-1308; PO Box 84, Rosholt, WI 54473;
email: bobssmalljobs@yahoo.com;
Karen (free vendor space), 715-498-2155;
Facebook: Glacier Ridge Antique Tractor Club

㉛ 21st Annual Richfield Historical Society Thresheree and Harvest Festival
Sept. 21-22   Richfield
1896 Hwy 164, 1/2 mile north of Hwy 167 (Holy Hill Road).
Contact: Herb Lofy, 4434 Pleasant Hill Rd., Richfield, WI 53076; 262-297-1546;
email: hsl1725@yahoo.com
www.richfieldhistoricalsociety.org

32 26th Annual Agricultural Heritage Days
Sept. 21-22   Luxemburg
Feature: Case Tractors.
Kewaunee County Fairgrounds.
Contact: Dale Swoboda, PO Box 174, Kewaunee, WI 54216; 920-323-3323; Jim Junion, 920-660-6562; www.agriculturalheritage.org

33 Northern Aged Iron Tractor and Threshing Show
Sept. 21-22   Highbridge
Feature: Oliver Hart-Parr Tractors.
38565 St. Hwy. 13.
Contact: Diana Rea, 21370 Kallgren Rd., Mason, WI 54856; 715-746-2710; email: dianamrea@gamil.com www.northernagediron.com

34 16th Annual Fall Harvest Festival
Sept. 27-29   Friendship
Feature: John Deere Tractors.
West of Friendship on CR J, about 4 blocks on Hwy 13.
Contact: Dennis Erickson, 1559 18th Ave., Arkdale, WI 54613; 608-564-7378
See our ad on page 250

21 Steam School
Sept. 27-29   Edgar
W4255 Hilldale Dr.
Contact: Jeff Bloemers, 5903 Cart Path Rd., Sheboygan, WI 53081; 920-287-1146; email: jwbsteam@gmail.com www.whsea.org

35 Wheels of Time
Oct. 4-6   Richland Center
Feature: John Deere and Trucks of All Kinds.
Richland County Fairgrounds. Take Hwy 80 north out of town and follow the signs.
Contact: Paul Paasch, 23328 County Hwy DD, Richland Center, WI 53581; 608-647-8064; email: hillcountrycp@yahoo.com

36 Berlin Antique Equipment Show
Oct. 5-6   Berlin
Feature: Oliver Hart-Parr and Simplicity Garden Tractors.
Riverside Park, 217 W. Cumberland Ave.
Contact: Joe Smith, W7626 Short St., Wautoma, WI 54982; 608-302-5585; email: redejsmity@centurytel.net

36 Berlin Area Antique Equipment 4th Annual Tractor Show
Oct. 5-6   Berlin
Features: Oliver Hart-Parr, Cockshutt and Related Tractors, Engines and Equipment.
Riverside Park, 217 W. Cumberland Ave., Huron Street to Wisconsin Street, north to Cumberland, west to show.
Contact: Marlan Rusch, 920-410-6623; email: baaeclub@gmail.com

37 Pioneer Farm Days
Oct. 12-13   Oak Creek
Features: International Harvester and Farmall Frolic Tractors.
American Legion Park, 9327 S. Shepard Ave., 6 miles south of Milwaukee. Exit I-94 at Ryan Road (Hwy 100), go east 2 miles to Shepard Avenue, north to show grounds.
Contact: Dave Chvilicek, PO Box 472, Oak Creek, WI 53154; 414-768-8580; email: pfmc@wi.rr.com www.pioneerfarmdays.com

2 Ixonia Vintage Tractor Expo Plow Day
Oct. 19   Ixonia
Pernat Farm, N7771 Hwy F. First farm 1/2 mile south of town on Hwy F.
Contact: Curt Pernat, N7771 Hwy F, Ixonia, WI 53036; 920-988-0857; email: downhomecollect@att.net www.ixoniavintagetractorexpo.com

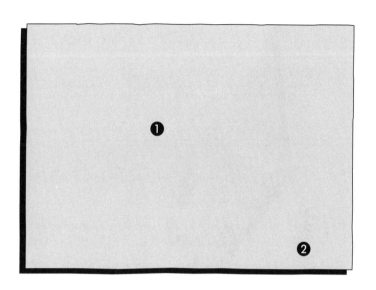

WYOMING

1 **24th Anniversary Don Layton**
Annual Memorial Antique Tractor
and Engine Show
June 8-9   Shoshoni
Park at east side of Shoshoni.
Contact: Carlta Witthar, 014
N. Sixth St. E., Riverton, WY 82501;
307-856-1164;
email: cmaule@wyoming.com
Facebook: Wind River Flywheelers

2 **Laramie County Fair**
Aug. 3-4   Cheyenne
Archer Fairgrounds
Contact: Brad Hays, 9303 CR 124,
Carr, CO 80612; 970-481-5755;
email: haysranch@hotmail.com

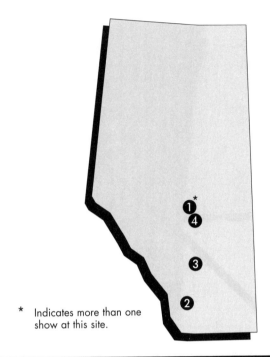

*   Indicates more than one
    show at this site.

ALBERTA

1 Leduc West Antique Society Spring Tractor Pull and Swap Meet
May 25   Leduc
5 kilometers west of Leduc on Hwy 39,
1 kilometer north on Range Road 260.
Contact: Ron Bodnar, 780-446-7652;
email: ronbodnar@hotmail.com
www.leducwestantique.com

1 29th Annual Leduc West Exposition
July 20-21   Leduc
5 kilometers west of Leduc on Hwy 39,
1 kilometer north on Range Road 260.
Contact: Ron Bodnar, 780-446-7652;
email: ronbodnar@hotmail.com
www.leducwestantique.com

2 Heritage Acres Annual Show
Aug. 2-5   Pincher Creek
Feature: Massey and Massey-Harris
Stationary.
Located 15 kilometers northeast of
town. Travel on Hwy 3 to secondary
Hwy 785 and north 8.4 kilometers to
the museum. See map on website.
GPS: 49.574895 - 113.864518.
Contact: Garry Visser, Box 2514,
Pincher Creek, AB T0K 1W0;
403-339-0552;
email: garryvisser@gmail.com
www.heritageacres.org

3 50th Annual Pioneer Acres Show
Aug. 9-11   Irricana
Northeast of Calgary, just off Hwy 9.
House No. 263178, Township Rd.,
274 Rocky View Cou.
Contact: Dorothy Weigum, Box 58,
Irricana, AB T0M 1B0; 403-935-4357;
email: curator@pioneeracres.ab.ca
www.pioneeracres.ab.ca

❹ Harvest Festival Reynolds-Alberta Museum
Aug. 31-Sept. 1   Wetaskiwin
Feature: 1922 Sawyer Massey Steam Traction Engines.
6426 40 Ave. 2 kilometers west of town on Hwy 13.
Contact: Jim Takenaka, 6426 40th Ave., Wetaskiwin, AB T9A 2G1; 780-312-2065;
email: jim.takenaka@gov.ab.ca
www.reynoldsmuseum.ca

❶ Leduc West Antique Society Provincial
Sept. 14   Leduc
5 kilometers west of Leduc on Hwy 39, 1 kilometer north on Range Road 260.
Contact: Ron Bodnar, 780-446-7652;
email: ronbodnar@hotmail.com
www.leducwestantique.com

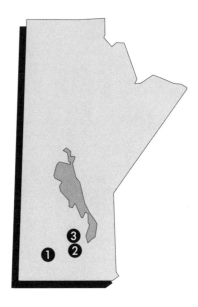

MANITOBA

❶ Pioneer Power and Equipment Club Summer Show
June 16   Brandon
Commonwealth Air Training Plan Museum at Brandon Airport, 1 mile north of the Trans Canada Hwy on PTH 10, west side.
Contact: Barry Bromley, Box 33, RR 2, Brandon, MB R7A 5Y2; 204-728-7503; email: barrybromley@inetlink.ca

❷ 65th Annual Manitoba Threshermen's Reunion and Stampede
July 25-28   Austin
3 kilometers south of the intersection of the Trans-Canada and 34 Hwys near Austin.
Contact: Museum Office, Box 10, Austin, MB R0H 0C0; 204-637-2354; email: agmuseum@mymts.net
ag-museum.mb.ca

❸ Threshing Days and Toy Show
Sept. 21-22   Gladstone
1/4 mile west of Gladstone on Hwy 16.
Contact: Doug McBride, Box 524, Gladstone, MB R0J 0T0; 204-872-0303; email: mcbridef@live.com

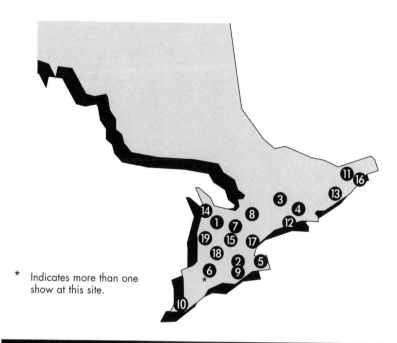

* Indicates more than one show at this site.

ONTARIO

1 Bruce County Heritage Association Toy Show
March 31   Mildmay
Knights of Columbus Hall,
1658 Hwy 9 S.
Contact: Paul Flynn, 519-927-3581;
email: bchatoyshow@gmail.com
www.bruceheritage.com

2 Haldimand County Vintage Farm Equipment & Collectibles Tour
May 18-20   Hagersville
3910 Hwy 3.
Contact: Jim Heaslip, 3910 ON-3,
Hagersville, ON N0A 1H0;
905-512-6711

3 41st Annual Heritage Show
June 15-16   Lindsay
Feature: Massey-Harris.
354 Angeline St. S. From Toronto,
east on Hwy 401 to Hwy 35/115,
north to Hwy 35. West on Hwy. 7,
right on Angeline St./CR 4, right into
fairgrounds.
Contact: Gail Jordan, 47 Killarney Bay
Rd., Cameron, ON K0M 1G0;
705-374-5023;
email:
info@kawarthaantiquepower.com
www.kawarthaantiquepower.com

4 23rd Annual Father's Day Smoke and Steam Show
June 16   Keene
Lang Pioneer Village Museum.
104 Lang Rd. Registration, 8:30 a.m. to
noon. Open to public, 10 a.m. to 4 p.m.
Contact: Elizabeth King, 866-289-5264;
email: info@langpioneervillage.ca
www.langpioneervillage.ca

5 **Niagara Antique Power Heritage Display**
June 29-July 1   Sherkston
Feature: Cockshutt and Oliver Hart-Parr.
1957 Wilhelm Rd., 21 kilometers west
of Peace Bridge, 10 kilometers east of
Port Colborne, 2 kilometers north of
Hwy 3, on Wilhelm Road; coordinates
to show grounds: north 42 degrees
54.471' west 079 degrees 07.926'.
Contact: Barbara Mittlestead, 1903
Miller Rd., RR 1, Port Colborne, ON
L3K 5V3; 905-835-8902;
email: sbm1@lastmilenet.ca

6 **Heritage and Antique Show**
July 12-14   Ilderton
Feature: Case Tractors.
Ilderton Fairgrounds, 195 King St.,
10 miles northwest of London, Ontario.
Contact: Bev Hughes, 22679
Wonderland Rd. N. RR 3, Ilderton, ON
N0M 2A0; 519-666-0452;
email: heritageclub@ilderton.ca
www.ilderton.ca/heritageclub

6 **Vintage Garden Tractor Club of America Canadian Regional Show**
July 12-14   Ilderton
Ilderton Fairgrounds and Arena.
Contact: Doug Tallman, 804 N. Trimble
Rd., Mansfield, OH 44906;
419-545-2609;
email: dtallman@accnorwalk.com
www.vgtcoa.com

7 **27th Anniversary Upper Canada Two-Cylinder Club Show**
July 26-28   Grand Valley
Feature: Allis-Chalmers Tractors.
Grand Valley Fairgrounds.
Contact: Jim Hulse, 311371 16th Line,
East Garafraxa, ON L9W 7C7;
519-941-0178;
www.uppercanadatwocylinderclub.com

8 **54th Annual Georgian Bay Steam Show**
Aug. 2-5   Cookstown
Feature: Cockshutt Farm Equipment.
4635 Victoria St. W.
Contact: Gary Frampton, president,
905-778-9315; Shirley Corbyn,
secretary, 705-357-2531;
109-36 Church St., Sunderland, ON
L0C 1H0; 705-357-2531;
www.steamshow.ca
See our ad on page 251

9 **Heritage Days in Jarvis**
Aug. 3-5   Jarvis
2050 Hwy 6, 1/2 mile south of
intersection of Hwys 3 and 6. Take
Hwy 6, on the left.
Contact: Larry Moyer, RR 1, Jarvis,
ON N0A 1J0; 519-587-2601

10 **34th Annual Essex County Steam and Gas Engine Show**
Aug. 9-11   McGregor
11081 11th Concession, Co-An Park.
Walker Road South from Windsor for
12 minutes, left at 11th Concession,
1/2 mile, 25 minutes from U.S. border
Contact: Gary Struhar, 1604 CR 22,
RR 3, Belle River, ON N0R 1A0;
519-791-0321;
email: gary.struhar@honeywell.com
www.essexsteamandgasengine.com

11 **Merrickville Agricultural Fair and 45th Annual Steam and Antique Collectibles Show**
Aug. 9-11   Merrickville
See website.
Contact: Wayne Poapst, PO Box 595,
Merrickville, ON K0G 1N0;
613-269-3405;
email: wpops@sympatico.ca

12 **Antique Machinery Show**
Aug. 10-11   Port Hope
Between Port Hope and Cobourg, or
Hwy 2 or Dale Road between Port Hope
and Cobourg. Watch for signs; easily
accessible from 401 thruway.
Contact: Earl Ashby, 5077 Country
Rd. 10, Canton, Port Hope, ON
L1A 3V5; 905-753-2387;
email: earl@ashbyfarmequipment.com
www.hahclub.com

⑬ Gathering of the Orange 2019
Aug. 15-18   Forest
Contact: 715-268-4632;
email: oldallisnews@amerytel.net
steamthreshers.com

⑭ 26th Annual Bruce County Heritage Farm Show
Aug. 16-18   Paisley
2 kilometers south of Paisley on
CR 3.
Contact: Dale Woelfle, PO Box 28,
Paisley, ON N0G 2N0; 519-373-1666;
email: bruceheritage@gmail.com
www.bruceheritage.com

⑮ Waterloo County Steam Threshers' Reunion
Aug. 23-24   Wallenstein
Features: Minneapolis-Moline Tractors.
7590 Line 86.
Contact: Leon Martin, 7590 Line 86,
Wallenstein, ON N0B 2S0;
844-88STEAM (844-887-8326);
email: president @
waterloocountysteamthreshers.com
www.waterloocountysteamthreshers.com

⑯ Antique Wheels in Motion 24th Annual Harvest Days
Aug. 24-25   Roebuck
                          (Augusta Township)
5877 CR 18.
Contact: Al Slater, 3900 Lords Mills Rd.,
RR 2, Prescott, ON K0E 1T0;
613-925-2100

⑰ Steam-Era
Aug. 30-Sept. 2   Milton
Country Heritage Park,
8560 Tremaine Rd.
Contact: Candice Welch, Moffat, ON
L0P 1J0; 905-854-2460;
email: candice.welch@hotmail.com
www.steam-era.com

⑱ Tractor and Engine Antique Show
Aug. 31-Sept. 1   Mitchell
Features: Minneapolis-Moline and
Waterloo Manufacturing Co. Tractors.
Mitchell Fairgrounds, Wellington Street
North. 40 miles northwest of London.
Contact: Cecil Rose, 75 Sylvia St.,
PO Box 925, Mitchell, ON N0K 1N0;
519-348-4993;
email: cecilrose@quadro.net

⑲ Blyth Steam Show
Sept. 6-8   Blyth
Features: Allis-Chalmers (Rumley).
Threshers Campground, 86 Blyth Rd.
Contact: Jackie Lantinga, PO Box 239,
Blyth, ON N0M 1H0; 226-523-9100;
email: hptha@tcc.on.ca
www.blythsteamshow.on.ca

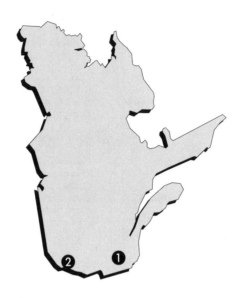

QUEBEC

❶ Exposition 2019
Aug. 17-18   Compton
La Fromagerie de la Station,
440 chemin de Hatley (Rt. 208). From
Rt. 147 in Compton Village, in front
of the town hall, take Rt. 208 west
(chemin de Hatley) for about
5 kilometers.
Contact: Gordon Barnett, 5785
Rte. 147, Waterville, QC J0B 1H0;
819-837-2261;
email: barnettg@axion.ca
www.machinesdantan.com

**❷ Chateauguay Valley Antique
Association Show**
Aug. 24-25   Rockburn
Hwy 202 to Rockburn, south at
Rennies Side Road. 2 kilometers
to show.
Contact: Rene Labelle, 986 Rte. 138A,
Ormstown, QC J0S 1K0;
450-829-3962;
email: atrlabelle@hotmail.com
www.cvantiqueassociation.com

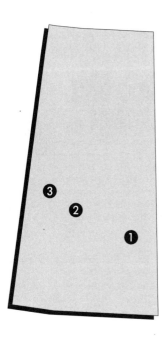

SASKATCHEWAN

1 Yorkton Farm Toy Show
Feb. 9-10   Yorkton
240 Wellington Ave.
Contact: Jeremy and Kim Mehrer,
Box 547, Churchbridge, SK S0A 0M0;
306-742-7888;
email: jkmehrer@hotmail.com

2 Pion-Era 2019
July 13-14   Saskatoon
2610 Lorne Avenue.
Contact: Brenda Mundell, 2610 Lorne
Ave., Saskatoon, SK S7J 0S6;
306-931-1910;
email: bmundell@wdm.ca
www.wdm.ca

**3 Western Development Museum
"Those Were the Days"**
Aug. 17-18   North Battleford
Features: More than 35 working
tractors; Case 110 & 75 and Nicholas
Sheppard Steam Engines.
Junction of Hwys 16 and 40.
Contact: Cheryl Stewart-Rahm,
Box 2223, North Battleford, SK
S9A 2Y1; 306-937-7225;
email: c.rahm@sasktel.net
www.wdm.ca

RECOMMENDED PRODUCTS FOR THE VINTAGE FARM COLLECTOR

COOLSPRING PACKAGE

For more than 25 years, the Coolspring Power Museum in Coolspring, Pennsylvania has been recognized as housing the world's finest collection of early and historically significant internal combustion engines. The museum boasts a collection of more than 250 engines in 20 buildings, 40 of which are profiled in Vol. I, with an additional 39 profiled in Vol. II. You can also get the accompanying visual guide with our Vol. I, II, & DVD package!

Item #5442	Vol I	~~$19.95~~	$17.95
Item #8395	Vol II	~~$19.95~~	$17.95

BARN FIND ROAD TRIP

It's barn-find freestyle! Roaming the Southeast, auto archaeologist Tom Cotter, car collector Brian Barr, and photographer Michael Alan Ross embark on a 14-day collector-car-seeking adventure with no predetermined destinations. They document their day-to-day car search in photos and through stories and interviews. If you love tales of automotive adventure, this book is for you!

Item #7783 ~~$35.00~~ $29.99

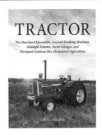

FARMALL: THE RED TRACTOR THAT REVOLUTIONIZED FARMING

In this inclusive guide, the history of the Farmall is traced from the first tractor, developed in the early 1920s, through its evolution to the new models. The book includes photos of restored machines, as well as color and black-and-white archival photography. Trace all of the tractor models, variations, improvements, engine and hydraulic advances, and accompanying implements through every Farmall generation.

Item #7813 ~~$40.00~~ $37.99

FAIRBANKS MORSE: 100 YEARS OF ENGINE TECHNOLOGY 1893-1993

This book by C.H. Wendel includes more than 300 pictures to help tell the history of Fairbanks Morse. It includes extensive coverage of various models including patents, serial numbers, and company chronology as appendices.

Item #1080 ~~$24.95~~ $22.95

TRACTOR: RED EDITION

This book has the same content as Tractor (above), just with a different color on the cover for those that bleed red! This rollicking ride into machine history follows the innovators, entrepreneurs, and hucksters who transformed our world with farm machines. Starting with the turn-of-the-century visionaries who saw that four wheels and a motor could replace the horse, the book moves swiftly through key early developments to cover the power farming movement of the latter part of the 20th century.

Item #9096 ~~$29.95~~ $24.99

**Limited
Quantities**

OLD FASHIONED FARM TOOLS SET

Farm Collector has put together a two-book set dedicated to old-fashioned farm tools and implements, plus the skills and techniques to make them. This set includes nearly 400 pages of cast-iron field rollers, broadcast seeders, and corn harvesters, along with how to make straight forming tools, re-flute worn cutters, grind curved surfaces, and more!

Item #8047 ~~$29.99~~ $26.99

FARM COLLECTOR T-SHIRTS

Perfect for the proud *Farm Collector* reader, this charcoal gray cotton T-shirt features the magazine's vintage logo. Show off your favorite magazine to the world, especially at antique tractor pulls, spring swaps, or annual meetings.

Item #8042-#8045 S-XL ~~$15.00~~ $13.99
Item #8046 2XL ~~$17.00~~ $15.99
Item #8905 3XL ~~$17.00~~ $15.99

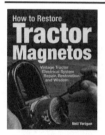

HOW TO RESTORE TRACTOR MAGNETOS

How to Restore Tractor Magnetos is the essential guide to farm tractor electrical systems and offers the tractor restorer all the information needed to restore, repair, and diagnose magnetos. Authored by the late Neil Yerigan, who was a master of working with vintage electronics, the book comprehensively covers how magnetos function as well as how to troubleshoot and repair common problems.

Item #6384 ~~$24.95~~ $21.95

THE JOHN DEERE CENTURY

Iconic John Deere tractors ranging from the spartan Waterloo Boy to the Model AOS, and from German and Argentine models to the acclaimed New Generation tractors are featured in this celebration of industrial tractor design. Loaded with photographs, both modern and vintage, and excellently written info, this hardcover book is perfect for John Deere fans.

Item #8804 ~~$40.00~~ $37.95

FARM COLLECTOR TRUCKER HAT

Wear your *Farm Collector* hat proudly! This soft mesh cap has a 100 percent cotton twill front and soft nylon mesh back. The fabric velco closure makes adjusting the fit simple and easy, and the mesh back offers refreshing and unbeatable airflow on hot summer days. This brown and natural hat features the classic *Farm Collector* logo, adorned in red and white thread.

Item #8944 ~~15.00~~ $13.99

**To order,
call toll-free
1-866-624-9388
(outside the United States
and for customer service,
call 785-274-4366,
or go to
FarmCollector.com/Recommended
Mention code MFCPAJZ8**

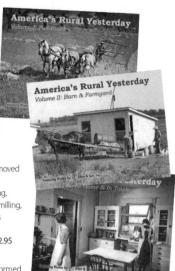

RECOMMENDED PRODUCTS FOR THE VINTAGE FARM COLLECTOR

AMERICA'S RURAL YESTERDAY VOLUME 1: FIELDWORK

America's Rural Yesterday transports the reader to another time, when life moved slower and family and community was important. More than 100 photos by famed photographer J.C. Allen show fieldwork, including planting, tilling, harvesting, and more. Also included are shots of threshing, corn shelling, milling, and haystacking. Horses, mules, oxen, vintage tractors, and steam engines provided the power back when rural life was the norm.

Item #7554 $~~$24.95~~ $22.95

VOLUME 2: BARN & FARMYARD

Volume 2 of America's Rural Yesterday includes photos of farmwork performed in dairy, poultry, and hog barns, as well as the wide variety of tasks performed in the barnyard: ensilaging, stock feeding and watering, haymow loading, threshing, corn grinding, butchering, collecting eggs, root cellaring, and much more. Item #7555 $~~$24.95~~ $22.95

VOLUME 3: AT HOME & IN TOWN

This book, the third in the three-volume series, showcases what people did when they weren't working in the fields, barns, or farmyards in the 1920s-1940s. More than 120 photos show rural families in their kitchens, parlors, and dining rooms. There are photos of going to town and spending time at the library, grocery and general stores, the school and doctor's office, and more. Item #7556 $~~$24.95~~ $22.95

FARM COLLECTOR FIELD GUIDE TO MYSTERY FARM TOOLS

If you like the "What Is It?" section in each issue of *Farm Collector*, you're going to love this special edition dedicated solely to mystery tools from farm country. Packed with super photos, patent drawings and collector resources, it's a jim-dandy for anybody interested in antique farm equipment.

Item # 4850 $~~$7.99~~ $2.99 *NEW LOWER PRICE*

FARM ENGINES AND HOW TO RUN THEM

This book fully describes every part of a farm engine and boiler, giving complete directions for the safe and economical management of both. Included are chapters on farm engine economy (with special attention to traction and gasoline farm engines) and a chapter on the science of successful threshing. The book abounds with precision artwork and cutaway illustrations showing the different parts of a boiler and engine, and nearly every make of traction engine (including those made by Case, Nichols and Shepard, and Buffalo Pitts).

Item #8263 $~~$12.95~~ $11.95

ULTIMATE GUIDE TO FARM MECHANICS

The book is divided into three parts: the first covers general skills such as woodworking and blacksmithing, the second is dedicated to farm engines and how to run them, and the third teaches readers how to construct classic labor-saving devices such as an effective milking stool, plowing gear for a kicking mule, and a nest for egg-eating hens. Readers are taught to mend broken tools, make fertilizer and corn fodder, buy engine parts, and manage gasoline engines safely and economically.

Item #7578 $~~$17.95~~ $16.95

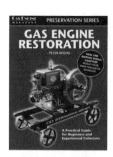

GAS ENGINE RESTORATION

From start to finish, Peter Rooke's newly revised, easy-to-follow narrative will impress and educate both new and experienced hobbyists with exhaustive coverage of the process. In 112 pages, Rooke meticulously leads you from stripping an engine through rebuilding each component — from bearings to cylinder head to ignition. Tips along the way cover everything from repairing damaged threads to removing rust and zinc plating.

Item #5463 $19.95 $17.95

MORE GAS ENGINE RESTORATION

A follow-up to his highly regarded first book this newest gas engine restoration guide from veteran vintage engine restorer Peter Rooke offers a wealth of information for both the new and experienced engine hobbyist. Drawing from his experience repairing and restoring gas engines, Rooke shares the tips and techniques he's acquired to aid engine restorers in almost every facet of the restoration process.

Item #7949 $19.95 $17.95

TRADITIONAL TOOLMAKING

With the collective wisdom of a past generation of craftsmen, Traditional Toolmaking provides an in-depth record of the skills and techniques that made the mass production revolution of the 20th century possible. It includes timeless practices as well as methods by master toolmakers, including how to make straight forming tools, grind curved surfaces, gauge the angle of a thread, and much more! With detailed descriptions of every procedure, this book is an invaluable reference for those with an interest in toolmaking.

Item #8287 $14.95 $13.95

THE FARMALL DYNASTY

The *Farmall Dynasty* recounts the dramatic story of the developmental history of tractors built by International Harvester, the dominant agricultural manufacturer of the early 20th century. The book includes well-researched accounts of the development of the original Farmall, the Letter Series, the 4100, Cub and other legendary IHC tractors, with firsthand accounts from factory engineers describing the challenges they faced.

Item #6382 $19.95 $16.99

METALWORKING

With more than 2,000 black-and-white illustrations and clear, practical instructions, *Metalworking* offers everything you need to know to turn a chunk of metal into a useful and well-crafted product. Included here is information on working sheet metals, gold, and silver; building a dynamo and electric motor; making a vertical steam engine; and more!

Item #5453 $17.95 $15.95

To order, call toll-free
1-866-624-9388
(outside the United States and for customer service, call **785-274-4366**, or go to
FarmCollector.com/Recommended
Mention code MFCPAJZ8

FARM COLLECTOR
SHOW DIRECTORY
2019

SHOW
ADVERTISING

CUMMING STEAM
ANTIQUE TRACTOR AND GAS ENGINE SHOW
—— NOVEMBER 8 & 9, 2019 ——

Cumming is home to some of the finest steam engines, antique tractors and hit-and-miss engines in the South, not to mention the expert entrepreneurs who maintain and safely operate the engines for our community's very special parades and shows. Working demonstrations within the Heritage Village portion of the fairgrounds include: sawmill, cotton gin, hay baling and Baker fan.

Parade of Power on Saturday • Exhibitors Welcome (free admission)
Campsites Available • "Barn Supper"

So ... Come join us for Cumming's 19th Annual Steam and Gas Exposition 2019

CUMMING FAIRGROUNDS
235 Castleberry Road, Cumming, GA.
Ph: (770) 316-2925
www.capa-ga.com

The Cumming Fairgrounds is a drug and alcohol free family entertainment site and aggressively promotes safety in all demonstrations and events.

The 57th Annual Reunion of
THE WILL COUNTY
THRESHERMEN'S ASSOCIATION

2019 Show will be at *14151 W. Joliet Rd., Manhattan, IL 60442*

The show is located at 1/2 mile
East of Wilton Center, IL on Rt 52

SHOW DATES:
JULY 18-21, 2019

FEATURE: OLIVER, WHITE,
CLETRAC TRACTORS & EQUIPMENT

SCHEDULE OF EVENTS
Flea Market • Crafts • Real Working Steam Engine
Food & Concessions • Antique Tractor Pull
Garden Tractor Pull • Wheat Harvesting

Please see web-site for more information
www.steamshow.org or call (815) 467-3004

Show Advertising

33rd Annual Show
Oblong Antique Tractor & Engine Association Inc.

August 9-11, 2019

Antique tractors, engines, automobiles, threshing, baling and too much more to mention. Large flea market, arts & crafts and great food on the grounds.

FEATURING:
OLIVER HART-PARR TRACTORS
NOVO ENGINES

Crawford County Fairgrounds
State Highway 33, Oblong, Ill.

Flea Market: Wendell Gene Bridget....(618) 928-1902
Toy Show: Dave Dix.............................(618) 592-4139
General Information: Mike Garrard....(618) 546-5615

It is best to call these numbers in the early evening.

Admission: $5 for adults — Kids under 12 FREE

Several Large Engines Including:
100 hp Fairbanks-Morse • 75 hp Superior
60 hp Muncie • 60 hp Pattin Bros. • 35 hp Superior
25 hp Superior • Pull a Working Power and More!

—The Friendly Show—

30TH ANNUAL
ANTIQUE POWER DAYS
Presented by the Southern Illinois Antique Power Club
SEPT. 5-8, 2019
County Fairgrounds Route 37 South Salem, IL

FEATURING: McCormick-Deering International Harvester

FEATURE CHAIRMEN: DOUG TELFORD 618-267-6384
RICK GARNER 618-339-4518

ALL MAKES WELCOME

CONSIGNMENT AUCTION:
September 5th 9:00 AM
www.antiquepowerdays.com
FEATURING MCCORMICK-DEERING
INTERNATIONAL HARVESTER
Marion County Fairgrounds Salem, IL
Admission $5 FFA/4-H Members FREE 14 & Under FREE
Flea Market, Toy Show & Auction, Tractor Pulls, Parade of Power, Lawn & Garden Tractor Pull, Pedal Pulls, Equipment Demonstrations, Church & Memorial Service

FEATURE CHAIRMEN:
DOUG TELFORD 618-267-6384
RICK GARNER 618-339-4518
SEAN EARLE · GENERAL INFO 618-322-3978
JIM SELLERS · CAMPING 618-315-4578
EMAIL: jlsellers@charter.net
EMAIL: antiquepowerdays@yahoo.com

 LIKE US ON FACEBOOK:
Southern Illinois Antique Power Club

52ND ANNUAL SHOW
WESTERN ILLINOIS
THRESHER'S BEE CRAFT SHOW AND FLEA MARKET
Hamilton, IL.

AUG. 2, 3, 4, 2019

FEATURING:
INTERNATIONAL HARVESTER
Primitive camping $5 per weekend
Exhibitor camping FREE
Electric hookups 20 or 30 Amps
Free parking 2 miles north, on 19th St.

FRIDAY: Tractor Games, Sanctioned Tractor Pull 6 p.m. (Exhibition Only), Kids Pedal Tractor Pull, Country Music, Steak Supper

SATURDAY: Draft Horse Plowing, Biscuits & Gravy Breakfast, Antique Tractor & Car Parade, Country Music, Pork Chop Supper

SUNDAY: Antique Tractor Pull (Exhibition Only), Biscuits & Gravy Breakfast, WCAZ Fun & Games for Kids, Antique Tractor & Car Parade, Tractor & Quilt Raffle
Church on grounds Sunday

Danny Buckert (217) 219-0049
976 E. County Rd. 1650 N., Hamilton, IL 62341
FLEA MARKET:
Rob Coyle (217) 847-3293
www.westernillinoisthreshers.org

15TH ANNUAL
FARM HERITAGE
DAYS
JULY 26-28, 2019
AMERICAN FARM HERITAGE MUSEUM • GREENVILLE, IL
45 MILES EAST OF ST. LOUIS ON I-70 - EXIT 45

FEATURING:
INTERNATIONAL HARVESTER TRACTORS, TRUCKS, EQUIPMENT & FARM ENGINES
www.americanfarmheritagemuseum.org

FRIDAY: Tractorcade
DAILY: Parades
Flea Market * Vendors
Farm Toys * Crafts * Children's Activities
Daily Pedal Pulls * Live Entertainment * Sawmill
Threshing * Lil Red Barn Museum Displays

GREENVILLE
ILLINOIS

Wheat Threshing • Baling
Combining • Field Demos
Train Rides

CONTACTS:
General Info 618-664-9733
Vendors 618-664-9733
Camping 217-825-8443
Tractorcade 618-664-3522

44TH ANNUAL
LANESVILLE
HERITAGE WEEKEND
Lanesville, Ind.

HOSTING THE INDIANA
MASSEY COLLECTORS
ASSOCIATION STATE SHOW

SEPTEMBER
12-15, 2019

Steam & Gas Engine Show
Antique Tractor Pull • Toy Show
Antique Tractor Display • Crafts &
Demonstrations • Food • Rides • Parade
Truck & Tractor Pull • Contests • Threshing
Sawmill • Musical Entertainment
Flea Market • Free Admission & Parking

FEATURING:
Massey-Harris/Massey Ferguson Tractors,
Massey- Ferguson Lawn & Garden Tractors, Sandow
Gas Engines and Orphan & Oddball Steam Engines

Only 15 minutes west of Louisville, Ky.,
on I-64 West, Exit 113 to Hwy 62.

FOR INFORMATION CALL:
Kenny Acton, chairman
P.O. Box 313, Lanesville, IN 47136
(812) 952-2027
www.LanesvilleHeritageWeekend.com
www.Facebook.com/lanesvilleheritageweekend

Homespun Handcrafters Market

VISIT WEBSITE FOR SPRING & FALL BARN MARKET EVENTS

SEPTEMBER 5-8, 2019

Located on Highway 57-Daviess County Fairgrounds at Elnora, IN
(Located within 2 hours of Indianapolis, Evansville, Terre Haute & Louisville)

FEATURING: CO-OP, COCKSHUTT AND LEADER TRACTORS, REEVES ENGINES

DEMONSTRATIONS FRIDAY & SATURDAY INCLUDE:

Belt-Driven Machinery-Threshing-Sawmill-Hay Presses
Shingle Mill-Baker Fans-Blacksmith & Machine Shops
Horse Drawn Machinery-Working Grist Mill
One Room School in session-Antique Cars & Trucks
Church Services Daily
There will be limited demonstrations on Thursday & Sunday

WE WILL BE MAKING:

Cider, Sorghum, Apple Butter, Ham & Beans, Lye Soap,
Hand Dipped Candles, Homemade Ice Cream, Cornmeal, Quilts

DISPLAYS INCLUDE:

600+ Tractors-Hand Tools and other Collections
Horse Carriages-House of Yesteryear-General Store-Quilts
Hardware Store-Homestead-Toy Display & Dealers

HUGE FLEA MARKET
VARIETY OF FOOD VENDORS AVAILABLE
SOMETHING GOING ON ALL THE TIME!

All Exhibitors must be members-Admission $5 per person
Children under 12 admitted free
No Alcoholic Beverages-Camping available-Plenty of parking

For more information phone:
812-692-7800
visit our website: www.wrvaa.org

Winter Tractor Show

Winter Tractor and Gas Engine Show
Auburn, Indiana
March 2019

KIDS PEDAL PULL CONTEST

KIDS PEDAL TRACTOR EXHIBIT & PARADE!

NEW DAYS!! Thurs. 14th, Fri. 15th, Sat. 16th

Featuring: THE PRAIRIE GOLD RUSH

HOURS
Thursday & Friday: 9am - 6pm
Saturday: 9am - 5pm

All makes & models WELCOME!

HOSTED BY:

MINNEAPOLIS-MOLINE
MODERN MACHINERY

FPC

FARM POWER CLUB

MM AUCTION!
Saturday Morning 9:30.
Please bring your MM stuff -
limit of 15 items.

BANQUET
Friday, 6:30pm
Seating is Limited,
Call for Tickets!

LOCATION
Indoors at
Auburn Auction Park
AUCTIONS AMERICA

I-69 & CR 11A
EXIT 326

ADMISSION
$7 Day Pass/$10 3-Day Pass
FREE PARKING

SPECIAL AREA FOR MUSCLE TRACTORS 1960'S AND UP!!

SPECIAL EVENTS
Swapmeet
Toy Show
(Farm Toys, Collectables & Nascar)
Craft Show
Seminars
Tours
Trading Post
(Call 260-925-0855 for Info)

FOOD AVAILABLE
Pancake & Sausage
Breakfast Daily
7am-10am
•
Lunch Available
Daily

For More Information Contact:
Farm Power Club Inc.
Bruce Bell: 260-925-0855
Bill Hand: 260-414-9368

Host Hotel - Auburn Inn
260-925-6363
(mention tractor show when calling)

NO PETS - SERVICE ANIMALS ONLY • PRODUCED IN COOPERATION WITH THE DEKALB COUNTY VISITORS BUREAU

Show Advertising

28TH ANNUAL SHOW
INDIANA'S JOHNSON COUNTY ANTIQUE MACHINERY ASSN.

JUNE 13-16, 2019

FEATURING:
LESSER KNOWN CLASSICS, ALL MUSCLE TRACTORS, CONSTRUCTION & INDUSTRIAL EQUIPMENT & OIL FIELD ENGINES

PLEASE PLAN TO ATTEND A FAST GROWING TRACTOR, MACHINERY & ENGINE SHOW! ORIGINAL TRACTORS & EQUIPMENT WELCOME!

Special tent & area for featured equipment • Flea Market and Swap Meet
Limited Electricity • Farm Tractor Pull Thurs Eve, Antique Pull Fri. Eve, Horse Pull Sat. Eve

DAILY DEMOS INCLUDE: THRESHING • BAKER FAN • ROCK CRUSHING • HORSE POWERED EQUIPMENT • CORN SHELLING SAWMILL • CORN SHUCKING • GAS ENGINES • STEAM ENGINES • OLD CARS & TRUCKS • WOMEN'S ACTIVITY AREA

FANTASTIC SHOW GROUNDS & DISPLAY AREA
Plenty of food & camping onsite. Must be a member to show, exhibit & pull.
$10⁰⁰ Family Membership Annually. $3⁰⁰ Daily Admission

GOLF CART REGISTRATION REQUIRED WITH PROOF OF INSURANCE

–SEE US AT JCAMACH.ORG–
At 600-acre Johnson County Park,
From I-65 Exit 80 west onto S.R. 252
approx. 4 miles then follow signs
at US 31 & 252 at Edinburgh, IN.

CONTACT: Consignment Sale:
Fred Price ....(317) 403-2510
Vendors/Flea Market/Swap Meet /General Info/Equipment:
Dwayne Hansford ....(317) 512-0493

38TH ANNUAL ANTIQUE
FARM POWER STEAM & GAS SHOW

AUGUST 8-10, 2019
4-H Fairgrounds in LaGrange, Indiana
1030 E 075 North, LaGrange, IN 46761
Antique Steam & Gas Engines, Tractors, Machinery & Tools
FEATURING: Lesser Known Classics, Doodlebugs and Port Huron

FEATURE EXHIBITORS WILL RECEIVE A COLLECTOR BUTTON

Steam Plowing – Threshing – Sawmills – Model Engine Tables – 125 hp 13"X16" Erie Steam Engine
Large Parade 5 PM Fri. & Sat. – Baker Fans – Buy & Sell Trading Post – Antique Truck
Large Flea Market & Indoor Arts & Crafts Area – Toy Show – Garden Tractors – Displays
Tractor Activities – Ferguson (FENA) area – Ladies programs on Fri. & Sat., Evening Entertainment Fri. & Sat.
Fun Tractor Pull for Exhibitors Sat. 9 AM – Weigh In Fri. after Parade to 9 PM and Sat. to 9 AM
plus much more. **Northern Indiana Garden Tractor Club Displays** – Old Gas Engines

Show Info 260-463-3639		Concessions 260-444-7828	
Flea Markets 574-238-0849		Toy Show 260-925-0855	
Arts & Crafts 260-499-0878		Feature Area 574-304-4213	

EVERYONE WELCOME!
Good food and camping on grounds. Motels nearby – Admission $5.00
All exhibitors FREE admission & an exhibitor plaque.

888-277-3184 • www.visitshipshewana.org

2020 SHOW AUGUST 13-15 • FEATURING: OLIVER HART-PARR, LEADER

Two GREAT SHOWS you CAN'T MISS!

29TH ANNUAL

NATIONAL
TOY TRUCK–N–CONSTRUCTION
SHOW AND AUCTION

AUGUST 23-25, 2019
WYNDHAM INDIANAPOLIS
WEST HOTEL

INDIANAPOLIS, IN

42ND ANNUAL

NATIONAL

FARM TOY SHOW
NOVEMBER 1-3, 2019
❖ Beckman High School
❖ The National Farm Toy Museum
❖ The Commercial Club Park

DYERSVILLE, IA

CALL 1-800-533-8293 FOR MORE INFO
www.toytrucker.com • (701) 883-5206 • www.toyfarmer.com

10TH ANNUAL
JACKSON COUNTY ANTIQUE MACHINERY SHOW

MAY 9-11, 2019

FEATURING: MASSEY-HARRIS, MASSEY-FERGUSON
AND FERGUSON BUILT TRACTORS, GARDEN TRACTORS,
ENGINES AND EQUIPMENT, INDIANNA BUILT ENGINES

ADMISSION ADULTS $ 2.00
VETERANS FREE GATE THURSDAY
VINTAGE EQUIPMENT & WORKING GAS ENGINES DISPLAYS
PEDAL TRACTOR PULL & BARREL TRAIN RIDES
SWAP MEET & FLEA MARKETS & SILENT AUCTIONS
LIVE MUSIC & HAM AND BEAN DINNER
TRACTOR DRIVE AND GAMES & GARDEN TRACTOR PULL
OPEN CRUISE IN & ARTS & CRAFTS - BASKET WEAVING,
BLACKSMITH & WOODWORKING DEMONSTRATIONS
ANTIQUE TRACTOR PULL, FEATURING CUMMINS, TOY SHOW

FALL SWAP MEET NOVEMBER 2, 2019

DIRECTIONS: BROWNSTOWN S.R. 50 AND S.R. 250 EAST,
1/2 MILE TO THE COUNTY FAIRGROUNDS.
NOT RESPONSIBLE FOR ACCIDENTS

JACKSON COUNTY FAIRGROUNDS
476 East Co Rd., 100 South, Brownstown, IN 47220

CONTACT INFO ....812-523-3246 or 812-523-3594
DAY OF SHOW 812-216-5597

Like us on facebook

BROWN COUNTY ANTIQUE ENGINE AND TRACTOR SHOW

Nashville, Ind. 1/4-mile east on Old State Route 46 at 4-H Fairgrounds

SEPTEMBER 13-14, 2019

FEATURING FOR 2019 INTERNATIONAL HARVESTER

Antique Tractors • Gas Engines
Stationary Hay Baler • Sawmill
Old Farm Equipment • Hand Tools
Cornmeal Grinding • Beans & Cornbread
Crafts • Barrel Rides • Pedal Tractor Pull
Kids Area • Tractor Parade

AUCTION SATURDAY • 2 PM
LUMBER, PLAYHOUSE, RAILS

ACROSS INDIANA TRACTOR DRIVE JUNE 23-25, 2019
Exhibitors Welcome

INFO CONTACT:
Randy Barrett, President (812) 325-6722
Visit Our Website at www.bcama.net

23rd Annual Swap Meet - May 4 & Oct 26, 2019
Tractor Drive - July 23, 2019

Hosting IHC Chapter 7 State Show
Flea Market • Food • Setup Fee

MAUMEE VALLEY ANTIQUE STEAM & GAS ASSOCIATION

Annual Summer Show
Since 1978
42ND ANNIVERSARY SHOW

AUGUST 15-18, 2019

East of New Haven, IN, at 1720 Webster Road between U.S. 24 and U.S. 30

MASSEY HARRIS   Wheel Horse
JOHN DEERE   MASSEY FERGUSON

FEATURE: John Deere & Massey-Harris/Ferguson tractors and equipment with special feature the Wheel Horse garden tractors plus all other brands of Garden tractors.
ALL OTHER EXHIBITORS ARE WELCOME.

Plowing, Threshing, Sawing with steam engines & tractors, Baker Fan, Shingle mill, Steam Engines, Antique Tractors, Gas Engines, Car and Truck Display, Garden Tractors, 125 hp Buckeye Oil Engine, Stationary Steam Engines, Tractor Pulls Friday & Saturday, Horse and Mule Demonstrations and Hayrides Friday and Saturday, Working Blacksmith Ship, Steamed Sweet Corn, Good Food, Quilt Show, Trading Post, Spark Show Friday and Saturday after dark, Camping with limited electrical hookups

President	260-414-9489	Tractor Pull	260-760-2420
Flea Market & Camping	260-341-4805	Quilt Show	260-580-5285
Trading Post, Cell	260-460-0569	Garden Tractors	
Model Engine Show	260-485-9104	& Gas Engines	419-769-9635
Exhibitors	260-580-5416		

www.maumeevalley.org for map and more information. FREE PARKING

MID-AMERICA Threshing & Antiques Inc.
(A Non-Profit Organization)

CELEBRATING OUR 45TH ANNIVERSARY SHOW

At Tipton County 4-H Fairgrounds, Tipton, IN

AUGUST 8-11, 2019

FEATURING: CASE

Large Steam Engines • Model Steam Engines
Antique Gas Engines • Tractors • Caterpillars
Sawmill • Two Fans • Tractor Driving Permitted
Antique Farm Machinery Threshing Wheat &
Baling Straw at Intervals • Flea Market • Parade of
Machinery • Trailer Parking • Camping $20 per night
Meals on Grounds • Antique Tractor Pull Friday
Evening at 6:00 p.m. and Saturday at 1:00 p.m.
Plowing Demo • Flea Market Space Available!

FOR MORE INFORMATION CONTACT:
Rick Bennett, pres. ....(765) 491-7312
Paul Powel, v. pres. ....(765) 620-0936

FOOD VENDOR & FLEA MARKET CONTACT:
Jenna Burger, Vendor ....(765) 437-0542
Terry Dunn, Food ....(317) 966-2539

45th   *Exhibitors Welcome!*   45th

27TH ANNUAL SHOW & SWAP MEET
JUNE 22-23, 2019

Swap Meet – April 20, 2019 – "Daylight to ?"

EVERYONE WELCOME!
Morgan Co. Fairgrounds

State Routes 37 & 252, Martinsville, Ind.
Free admission. Exhibitor must be member.
Memberships are available at show. Food concessions.
Free primitive exhibitor camping – electric hook-up fee.

ANTIQUE GAS ENGINES & TRACTORS • STEAM ENGINES
ANTIQUE MACHINERY IN USE • SPECIAL FEATURES
AUCTION SUNDAY @ 1:00 • LARGE FLEA MARKET (space still available)

MORGAN COUNTY ANTIQUE MACHINERY ASSOCIATION

SHOW INFORMATION:
PRESIDENT: Dave Zoller ....(765) 537-2750
FLEA MARKET: Sandy Fields ....(812) 988-6103
AUCTION: Harris Craven ....(765) 342-0055
SWAP MEET INFO: John Schoolcraft ....(765) 318-7571
CAMPING: Dave Zoller ....(765) 537-2750

Northern Indiana Power from the Past Inc.

CELEBRATING OUR 42ND YEAR
JULY 18-21, 2019

City Park, Winamac, Indiana

THIS YEAR'S FEATURED ATTRACTIONS:
GRAHAM-BRADLEY TRACTORS AND
EQUIPMENT, HIT AND MISS ENGINES,
LAWN AND GARDEN EQUIPMENT

*Huge Flea Market, Working Displays
& Kids Games Each Day
Live Entertainment Nightly*
Adults $3, Under 12 Free

INFORMATION
GENERAL INFO:
(574) 242-9164
FLEA MARKET INFO:
(574) 946-3206
catfishm@pwrtc.com
www.winamacpowershow.com

JUNE 7, 8, & 9, 2019

VANDERBURGH 4-H CENTER
201 E Boonville-New Harmony Rd.
Darmstadt, IN 47725 Evansville, IN

FEATURING JOHN DEERE TRACTORS, HERCULES
AND OTHER EVANSVILLE BUILD ENGINES,
AND CAST IRON SEAT COLLECTORS.

Toy Show – Flea Market – Vendors – Camping
Lawn & Garden Tractors – Demonstrations
Pedal Tractor Pulls – Live Music and Much More!

For general show information, contact
Brad Fromm at **812-983-3300** or visit
www.siamclassiciron.com
Southern Indiana Antique Machinery Club

FULTON COUNTY
HISTORICAL POWER SHOW
ROCHESTER, IND.
JUNE 14-16, 2019

Admission Charged for Adults (12 and up) • Free Parking

Farm & Garden Tractors - Gas Engines
Farm Machinery - Trucks
Kiddie Tractor Pull - Trading Post
Tractor Pulls - Sawmill and Other Demonstrations
Parade - Outdoor Craft & Flea Market - Swap Part
Vendors - Toy Show - Food & Drink Concessions
Museum, Round Barn & Living History Village

Co-sponsored by
Fulton County Historical Power Assn.
and Fulton County Historical Society.
Held on FCHS property, 4 miles north
of Rochester, Ind., on U.S. 31
and Tippecanoe River.

FEATURE: LESSER KNOWN CLASSICS OR ODD BALLS

CONTACT: Secretary Melinda Clinger
(574) 223-4436 • melinda@rtcol.com

24TH ANNUAL
CEDAR VALLEY MEMORIES
AUGUST 10-11, 2019
SATURDAY & SUNDAY
HOME OF THE SMOLIK EXHIBIT
FEATURING: OLIVER

Located 2 miles west of Osage, Iowa, on Hwy. 9.

EXHIBITORS ARE WELCOME!

DEMONSTRATING: Steam Engines • Threshing
Baling • Plowing • Gas Engines • Antique Tractors
Shingle Mill • Corn Shelling • Sawmill • Quilting
Rug Hooking Weaving • Spinning Wheel • Tatting
Hardanger • Knitting Machines • Blacksmith
Flea Market • Tractor Pull on Saturday
LUNCH ON GROUNDS

For More Information: (641) 330-2017
www.facebook.com/MitchellCounty

PIONEER HARVEST FIESTA

63RD Year 1956-2019
OCTOBER 18-20, 2019

ADMISSION FOR THREE DAYS - $5.00

FEATURE TRACTOR
FORD

FEATURE ENGINE
HERCULES

PARADE DOWNTOWN THURS., OCT. 17, 2019
FORT SCOTT, KANSAS

Antique Tractor Display • Steam Engine Display
Gas Engine Display • Corn–Wheat Threshing • Baling
Sawmill Operation • Rock Crushing • Flea Market
Planing Mill Demo • Quilt Show • Live Music
Arts & Crafts Show • Antique Tractor Pull Saturday
Classic Tractor Pull Sunday

SWAP MEET - May 10-11, 2019

FOR SHOW INFORMATION CONTACT:
Allen Warren ......(620) 224-7761
awarren@cebridge.net

www.pioneerharvestfiesta.com

K and O STEAM & GAS ENGINE ASSOCIATION INC.
Winfield, Kansas

38TH ANNUAL SHOW
AUGUST 16-18, 2019
WINFIELD FAIRGROUNDS
1105 West 9th
Winfield, KS

Camping available on grounds

FEATURING:
MASSEY–HARRIS
MASSEY–HARRIS ENGINES
*** OLD CAR SHOW ***

www.kosgeclub.com
Les Yung ....(620) 441-8320
Billy Metzinger ...(620) 506-7246

66TH ANNUAL SHOW

JULY 25-27 2019
Bird City, KS
Something for Everyone

FEATURING
INTERNATIONAL HARVESTER

20 Buildings • 10 Steam Engines
200 Antique Tractors • Sod House • Country
School • Print Shop • Cook Shack • Antique
Museums • Tractors • Automobiles • Trucks
Toys • Quilts • Barbed Wire • Furniture
Carpenter & Mechanic Tools • Homemaker
Items • Daily Parade & Demonstrations
Blacksmithing • Saw Mill • Shingle Making
Printing • Corn Shelling & Grinding
Wheat Binding, Combining & Threshing
Steam Engine & Antique Tractor Plowing
& Pulling • 100 Pedal Toys • Petting Zoo
Playground • Free Bingo • Bar-B-Que
Horseshoes • Corn Hole • Chuck Wagon Breakfast

CONTACT: Brendon Haack, President;
785-332-4120 • bmhaack@eaglecom.net
www.threshershow.org
785-734-2291 Association Phone

21ST ANNUAL
WILSON COUNTY OLD IRON DAYS

WILSON COUNTY OLD IRON CLUB EST. 1999

SEPTEMBER 26-29, 2019

Location: Fredonia, KS. Close to intersection of US-400 & KS-47

Feature Tractor: Oliver • All Tractors Welcome

Show Admission: $5 Children 12 & under FREE

Saturday: Parade of Power 3:30 p.m.

Garden Tractor Pull 1 p.m.
Contact Wilbur Schwatken 620-330-7394

Tractor Pull 5 p.m.
Contact Kelley Starbuck 620-330-4264
Sunday Church Service, 8:30 a.m.
No smoking/alcohol allowed on the grounds.

FEATURING more than 35 Working Farm and Domestic Demonstrations, Rock Crushing, Laundry & More!

Swap Meet & Flea Market: 620-378-3684
Camper Hookups Avaiable: 620-332-7199
Show Information: Jeff Walker 620-212-8309
E-mail: oldironclub@gmail.com
www.oldironclub.org
Find us on Facebook & Twitter

MERIDEN ANTIQUE ENGINE AND THRESHERS ASSOCIATION
THRESHING SHOW
July 19-21, 2019
FALL FESTIVAL & SWAP MEET
September 28-29, 2019

Garden Tractor Pulls, Live Music, Flour Mill, Blacksmith Shop, Sawmill, and Big Engine. Chuckwagon, camping and modern restrooms.

FEATURED TRACTOR:
Massey-Harris
FEATURED ENGINE:
New Holland

8275 K-4 Hwy
Meriden, KS 66512
www.meridenthreshers.org

19TH ANNUAL
SANTA FE TRAIL TIRED IRON SHOW

OCTOBER 12 & 13, 2019
9 am to 5 pm both days
Located 2 miles west of Larned on K-156 Hwy

FEATURING: Antique Tractors & Gas Engines and Classic & Antique Cars

Wheat Threshing & Corn Shelling Demos
Anvil Shoot • Steam Traction Engine
Kids Activities • Working Sawmill
Horse Drawn Plow Demo
Cowboy Mounted Shooting
.... and MUCH MORE!

CONTACT: 620-285-2054
museum@santafetrailcenter.org
www.santafetrailcenter.org
Food vendors on the grounds both days

41ST ANNUAL
CENTRAL MD
ANTIQUE TRACTOR CLUB
Frederick, MD
JUNE 7-9, 2019

LOCATED: Gladhill Tractor Mart, 5509 Mt. Zion Rd
www.cmatc.org
Facebook.com/CMATC

Central Maryland ANTIQUE Tractor Club

FREE ADMISSION.
PRIMITIVE CAMPING ON GROUNDS.
FLEA MARKET & CRAFTS.
HOME COOKED
FOOD & BREAKFAST
SATURDAY & SUNDAY

FRIDAY:
June 7th will be set up day and Antique & Collectible Auction at 5:30 p.m.
Cake Auction and Clayton Lenhart & Dave Boyer Memorial Scholarship 7 p.m.

SATURDAY:
Antique Tractor Pull, Sanctioned by CMATC 10 a.m.
Kiddie Pedal Pull 1 p.m.

SUNDAY:
Lawn & Garden Tractor Pull 10 a.m.
Tractor Parade 12 p.m.
Kiddie Pedal Pull 1 p.m.
Slow Tractor Race 2 p.m.

FRIDAY & SATURDAY:
Hay Wagon Rides
Kids Barrel
Train Ride

CONTACT FOR FURTHER INFORMATION:
SHOW INFORMATION:
Jeremiah Herbst .... (443) 286-7843
8104 Ray Smith Rd., Frederick, MD 21704
FLEA MARKET:
Carla Brown ....(301) 748-4193

THE BUTLER COUNTY ANTIQUE ENGINE AND TRACTOR CLUB
Presents
THE 13TH ANNUAL TRACTOR SHOW AT THE MORGANTOWN, KY CITY PARK
AUGUST 2 & 3, 2019

BUTLER COUNTY
Antique Engine and Tractor Club
Morgantown, Ky

FEATURING: ALLIS-CHALMERS TRACTORS, ALLIS-CHALMERS /SIMPLICITY LAWN AND GARDEN TRACTORS & ALMO ENGINES

ALL LAWN AND GARDEN TRACTORS AND FLEA MARKET VENDORS ARE WELCOME

EVENTS: TRACTOR AND ENGINE SHOW • TRACTOR GAMES
PEDAL TRACTOR RAFFLE • TRACTOR PARADE • GUN RAFFLE

LOCATION	CONTACTS	
LOCATION CHARLES BLACK CITY PARK 150 HELM LANE MORGANTOWN, KY 42261	**CONTACTS** TROY DUNN 270-570-4927 ROGER TANNER 270-726-5155	**FREE PARKING** NO ADMISSION FEE VENDORS WELCOME LIKE US ON FACEBOOK

57th Annual Steam & Gas Round-Up
Mason-Dixon Historical Society Inc.

Special Features: Minneapolis Moline & Sears, David Bradley

CARROLL COUNTY FARM MUSEUM
500 SOUTH CENTER ST, WESTMINSTER, MD, 21157

Exhibitors Welcome!!   **SEPT. 6-8, 2019** (SETUP DAY SEPT. 5, 2019)   **FREE ADMISSION!!**

Consignment Auction Thursday Sept. 5, 2019 at 8:30am
Antique Farm Machinery & Tractors • Steam Engines • Gas Engines
Antique Cars • Sawmilling • Shingle Sawing • Threshing & Baling
Baker Fan • Flea Market • Kids Pedal Pulling • ATM on Premises
Devotional Services Sunday

General Info: Shane Ey...(410)913-5627
Flea Market Info: Joe Rogers...(410)274-0447

MARYLAND STEAM HISTORICAL SOCIETY, INC

64TH ANNUAL
STEAM & GAS ENGINE SHOW
September 12, 13, 14, 15, 2019
FEATURING:
RARE AND UNUSUAL TRACTORS AND ENGINES

Fire Company Grounds, 16060 Arcadia Avenue,
Arcadia (Upperco), MD 21155
3 miles south of Hampstead, MD, 5 miles
north of Reisterstown, MD, off MD Route 30

Website: www.marylandsteam.org
E-mail: mdsteamhistoricalsociety@gmail.com

**Food available all day - including homemade
bean soup, vegetable soup, barbeque**

DAILY: Steam Engines, Antique Farm Machinery,
Sawmilling, Shingle Sawing, Baker Fan, Antique
Gasoline Engines, Rock Crushing, Daily Parade
of Equipment, Flea Market/Craft Vendors, Grain
Threshing, Antique Cars/Trucks (Sat. only)

SPECIAL EVENTS

THURSDAY: Consignment Sale, 10:00 AM
FRIDAY EVENING: Spark Show at Dusk
SATURDAY: Kids' Pedal Pull, 12 Noon
Garden Tractor Pull 4 PM
Spark Show at Dusk

General Info 410-374-2595
Flea Market 443-789-2508
Steam Engines 717-235-7170
Gas Engines 443-375-6222

EASTERN SHORE THRESHERMEN & COLLECTORS ASSN. INC.

• • • • • 59TH ANNUAL • • • • •

OLD-TIME WHEAT THRESHING, STEAM & GAS ENGINE SHOW

AUG. 2, 3, 4, 2019

On Route 313 between
Denton and Federalsburg, Md.

GPS ADDRESS:
5806 Federalsburg Hwy., Federalsburg, MD 21632
Free Admission • Free Parking
Free Entertainment Each Evening
Plenty of Good Food
Large Flea Market • Daily Parade

EXHIBITORS WELCOME!

FOR FURTHER INFORMATION CONTACT:
Brenda Stant, secretary
6101 Harmony Rd.
Preston, MD 21655
(410) 673-2414
email: threshermen@gmail.com
Visit our website: www.threshermen.org

Michigan Flywheelers Museum's

SWAP MEET

Over 160 Sellers!!

& Flea Market

Friday, June 7, 2019
Saturday, June 8, 2019

06285 68th St.
SOUTH HAVEN, MI

Admission- $2. 12 & under free.
Selling fee- $20 includes both
days. PTVs (golf carts etc) $15.
No dogs with pd. admission. Set
up starts Thursday, June 6. No
pre-registration. 269-639-2010.

ANTIQUE FARM POWER CLUB
28th Annual
ANTIQUE TRACTOR & ENGINE SHOW
JUNE 6-7-8, 2019

Muskegon County Fairgrounds, 6621 HTS/Ravenna Road, Fruitport, MI 49415

FEATURING:
Oliver Tractors
& Garden Tractors

ENGINES:
Anything you want
to bring, bring

Antique Truck Show by West Michigan Chapter A.T.H.S.
FEATURING: TRUCKS OF THE DECADES

Daily Threshing, Corn Shelling & Baling • Antique Engines, Tractors, Garden Tractors, Trucks &
Equipment Demonstrations & Exhibits • Antique Tractors, Farm Stock, Pickup, Pedal & Garden
Tractor Pulls • Valve Cover Derby • Flea Market • Churning • Candle Making • Quilting - Broom
Making • Wood Carving • Loom Weaving Spinning • Antique Exhibits & More • Kids Games • Tractor
& Equipment Parades • Tractor Games • Farm Toy Show • Free Primitive Camping for Exhibitors •
Parts Corral • Pony Pulling • 2nd Annual Cubfest • Doodlebug Pulls • Cab Tug • Port Side Model A

INFORMATION:
Mark Scholten, (616) 293-1961 • Dan Engel, (616) 887-7462
Flea Market - Wally Weber, (231) 853-2882

Kalamazoo Valley Antique Engine & Machinery Club

40th Annual Show
Father's Day weekend
June 14-16, 2019

Featuring all 1940s era tractors & equipment in celebration of our 40th anniversary!
all makes & models welcome

FREE DAILY ADMISSION

Show hours:
Friday & Saturday 9 am- 5 pm
Sunday 9 am- 1 pm

FREE RUSTIC CAMPING
(no electric or water hookups available)

Show Highlights!

Some of our daily events are listed below

Daily raffle drawings, daily tractor parade, blacksmith demos, sawmill demos, kid's area and games, kid's pedal pull and much more!

NEW SHOW GROUNDS!

Tillers International
located at

10515 OP Ave E
Scotts, MI 49088

Tillers International was founded in 1981. Tillers International is a non-profit organization dedicated to improving the lives of people in rural areas around the world.
www.tillersinternational.org

Please contact our club with questions.

Email us at: kalvalleyclub@aol.com
Call our club president Tim Andrews at (269) 207-1006.

More information can be found at our website: www.kalvalleyclub.org

ST. JOE VALLEY
OLD ENGINE ASSOCIATION INC.
JONES, MI

59TH ANNUAL AUG. 2-4, 2019

Gates open 9 a.m. each day
Easy to reach location! Boot Hill Ranch
Bair Lake St., 1-1/2 miles east of Jones

FEATURING: ALLIS-CHALMERS AND RUMELY

STEAM ENGINES • TRACTORS • GAS ENGINES • GARDEN
TRACTORS • ANTIQUE MACHINERY • SAW MILL OPERATION
PARADES DAILY • LIVE MUSIC FRI. & SAT.

FOOD AVAILABLE ON THE GROUNDS

DONATION $5 • FREE PARKING • CHILDREN UNDER 12 FREE
WITH ADULT • SUNDAY: NO ADMISSION CHARGE

THURS., AUG. 1ST – 14TH ANNUAL 10 MPH TRACTOR TOUR
FOR DETAILS CALL: Terry Bowby ....(269) 476-2724

Flea Markets & Antique Dealers Welcome
Contact Mary Shirk ....(269) 278-4965
Cell ....(269) 506-5941
Daily charge $10 per space or $25 for 3 days

FEATURE FOR 2020 OLIVER & CLETRAC
JACOBSEN GARDEN TRACTORS

35TH ANNUAL MICHIANA ANTIQUE
ENGINE & TRACTOR SWAP MEET

Fri & Sat. May 3-4, 2019 • Boot Hill Ranch
Sponsored by: St Joe Valley Old Engine Assn. Inc.
$15 setup fee • Grounds Open Wednesday, May 1st @ noon;
94 Vendors in 2018 • Donation: $2 per person
FOR SHOW AND SWAP MEET INFO CONTACT:
Tim Rossman (269) 651-4878 & David Machan (269) 625-7232
FIND US ON FACEBOOK OR THE WEB: SJVOEA.ORG

MICHIGAN STEAM ENGINE & THRESHERS CLUB

61st ANNUAL REUNION
JULY 26, 27 & 28, 2019
(Three day show always starting the last Friday in July)
- *SPECIAL FEATURE*-

CASE EQUIPMENT
Over 30 Steam Engines in operation daily

Antique Sawmill

Teeter Totter

Steam Crane

Gas Engines

Threshing

Shingle Mill

Steam Plowing

Gas & Oil Tractors

Clean Restrooms

Food on Grounds

Big Flea Market

Church Service

Parade Daily

Baker Fan

Transfer Sled

Adults $10.00/day

$20.00/weekend

12 & Under Free

Gates open at 8:00 a.m.
Friday is Senior Citizen Day (65 & over) $5.00
3 miles South of Mason, MI on US-127, Northeast corner of Barnes Rd. Exit

All Boilers are State of Michigan Inspected

Show Information:	Concessions:	Flea Market:
Todd & Cindy Luks	Maddison Chatfield	Susie Chatfield
toddluks@aol.com	maddschatfield@gmail.com	smckchat@aol.com
517-628-2635	517-202-7769	517-202-0666

www.michigansteamengineandthreshersclub.com
NO Golf Carts or Motorized Vehicles EXCEPT for Handicapped Guests

Celebrating 36 years!

Michigan Flywheelers Museum's

ANTIQUE ENGINE & TRACTOR SHOW

Hundreds of Tractors & Engines on display! Working Sawmill & Shingle Mill! Flea Market! Tractor Pulls! Consignment Auction! South Haven Tractor Cruise! Blacksmith! Music! Parades! Steamed Corn! Valve Cover Races! Kids Activities & much more!

Thursday, Sept. 5 - Sunday, Sept. 8, 2019

SOUTH HAVEN, MI

Admission - $7. Thursday- Senior Day. Admission $3 for 62 and over. Exhibitor/ Camper/Flea Market registration starts Tuesday, Sept. 3. Registration hours 8 a.m. - 8 p.m. Do not line up before Sunday at 8 a.m. Pets allowed only with exhibitors/ campers /vendors and must stay at camp site. PTV (golf carts etc) Registration - $15. No ATVs, dirt bikes, mini bikes, or firearms.

Good Food On Grounds

45th Annual Show

August 16 - 18, 2019

MMOGTA Souvenirs

Tractor Pulls

Working Displays

MID MICHIGAN

OLD GAS TRACTOR ASSN, INC.

Michigan's Largest Gas Tractor Show!

Featuring: International Harvester

17180 West Ferden Road • Oakley, MI 48649
10 Miles North of Owosso

Gates Open at 7:00am Daily,
Donations: Adults $10,
Students 13 - 18 years $5,
Kids 12 & Under Free,
Senior Day $5 (Friday Only),
3 Day Pass $20

Live Harvesting & Tilling Demo
Cider Mill • Steam Engines
Blacksmith Shop • Handle Mill
Veneer Mill • Saw Mill
Tractor Raffle • Bingo
Flea Market • Arts & Crafts
Kids Crafts • Petting Zoo

Exhibitors: 2 Free Passes
No ATV's Except Handicap
No Pets on Grounds
No Camping With Displays
Primitive Camping Only
Free Parking

For Information Contact Jody Schlicklin (517) 625-3263
Or Visit www.mmogta.org

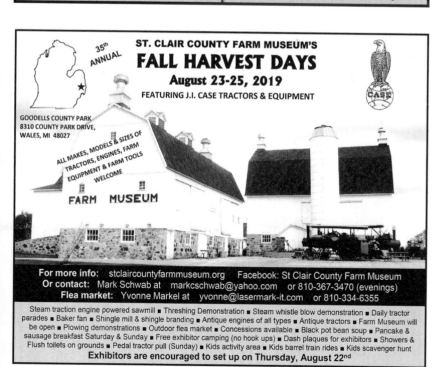

THE THUMB AREA OLD ENGINE & TRACTOR ASSN.

44TH ANNUAL SHOW
AUGUST 9-11, 2019

TUSCOLA CO. FAIRGROUNDS • 188 PARK DRIVE • CARO, MICH.

FEATURING: FORD & ANYTHING MADE IN MICHIGAN

FARM TOY SHOW & SALE AUGUST 10

Live Music • Flea Market • Sunday Church Service • Food Available

ADULTS $5 ADMISSION • 12 AND UNDER FREE

ALL EXHIBITORS WELCOME!
FREE PRIMITIVE CAMPING FOR EXHIBITORS
FEE FOR ELECTRICITY
CAROTRACTORSHOW.COM

Flea Market & Crafts
Diane Wilder: (989) 670-7210
3337 Cedar Run Road, Cass City, MI 48726

Exhibitors
Corey Will: (989) 325-1176
4425 Leix Rd., Mayville, MI 48744

44TH ANNUAL SHOW
Labor Day Weekend

The U.P. Steam & Gas Engine Association

August 30–September 2, 2019
U.P. State Fairgrounds
U.S. Highway 2 & 41, Escanaba Michigan

FEATURING: FLYWHEEL ENGINES AND JOHN DEERE TRACTORS

MANY ATTRACTIONS
Antique Village • Museum • Flea Market • Knife & Gun Show
• Large Auction Sunday No charge for exhibitors
• Camping with hook-ups available

FOR MORE
INFORMATION CONTACT
U.P. Steam & Gas Engine Association
P.O. Box 954, Escanaba, MI 49829
www.UPSteamAndGasEngine.org

QUESTIONS
Bob, 906-789-1257
robwillis@charter.net

Sault Ste Marie
ESCANABA
Wausau
Green Bay
Madison
Lake Michigan
Grand Rapids
Detroit
Chicago
South Bend
Toledo

Show Advertising

43RD SHOW
MID-MICHIGAN ANTIQUE MACHINERY ASSOCIATION AT CLIO FIREMAN'S PARK
1170 W. Wilson Road, Clio, MI 48420

SEPTEMBER 20-22, 2019

Tractor Fun Pull	**MID-MICHIGAN**	Purse Auction
Free Camping for Exhibitors	**ANTIQUE MACHINERY ASSOCIATION**	Sunday Service Held 8 a.m.
	CLIO, MICH.	
Consignment Auction Friday at 4 p.m.	**GATES OPEN AT 7 A.M.**	Adults $5, 12 & Under FREE

Open-Kettle Bean Soup to Benefit Charity • Sawmill
Tractor Parade (Fri., Sat. & Sun.) • Antique Cars, Trucks & Tractors
Gasoline & Steam Engines • Games
Entertainment • Food Put On by Club.

HUGE FLEA MARKET
Flea Market Setup is $30 per site; first come, first serve.

Exhibitors Free • Come Join Us!
Club Pres., Bob Watson
(989) 871-2467 • (810) 513-0369 Cell
Exhibitors: Peggy Lawerance,
(810) 429-8044
Flea Market • Setup fee $30
Flea Market: Leo Sutherland,
(810) 523-0318
Reservations June 1st - Sept. 5th

SPRING SWAP MEET • SAME LOCATION
(810) 513-0369 Cell
(989) 871-2467 Home
APRIL 19-20, 2019
mmamaclio@gmail.com • mmama.org

Northern Michigan Antique-Flywheelers
32ND ANNUAL SHOW

July 25-28, 2019

FEATURING:
Walk Behind
Tractors
and
Power Plants
Gas and Electric

WALLOON LAKE MICHIGAN

• Free Primitive Camping for Exhibitors •

Flea Market • Music • Arts & Crafts
Working Demonstrations • Kids Activities
All You Can Eat Breakfast Buffet
Gates Open 7 a.m. • Opening Ceremony 9 a.m.
Parade of Power each day at 2 p.m.

• www.walloonlakeflywheelers.com •

Show Information: Bob DeVol, president
(231) 564-1617 or flywheelersclub@gmail.com
Flea Market: Jim Stamm (231) 758-6484
Arts and Crafts: Jackie Capelin (231) 582-9490
Location: 00145 U.S. 131 Boyne Falls, MI
4 miles south of Walloon Lake on U.S. 131 Hwy.

PIONEER POWER OF WEST BRANCH, MI
26TH ANNUAL SHOW, FLEA MARKET & CRAFTS

BRING YOUR TRACTORS, ENGINES & CRAFTS TO SHOW & DEMONSTRATE.

Exhibitors FREE
Primitive Camping

Spectator Camping:
$10 per night

JULY 18-21, 2019

Food Vendors
on Grounds

Setup on July 17, 2019
All exhibitors welcome!
SWAP MEET
May 2-4, 2019

Quiet Time
10:00 p.m.

Admission $5
Under 12 FREE

Tractors ~ Gas Engines ~ Antique Cars ~ Shingle Mill
Purse Auction ~ Threshing ~ Working Exhibits

5 miles east of West Branch on M-55
Large Flea Market

Flea market spaces 30' Frontage x 30' Deep $30
No pets or bikes in show area.

Flea Market & Crafts:
Gloria Schmitt ....(989) 345-0189
Diane Philbrick ....(989) 327-7014
Marie Gibson ....(989) 345-2723
Gas Engines, Tractors and Show Info:
Walt Sappington ....(989) 240-3687
www.facebook.com/pioneerpower

SOUTHEAST MICHIGAN ANTIQUE TRACTOR & ENGINE ASSOCIATION INC.
30TH ANNUAL SHOW
JULY 18-20, 2019

NIKE PARK-NEWPORT RD., MONROE, MICHIGAN
Exit 21 off I-75, 2-1/2 miles west to park.

FEATURING: MINNEAPOLIS-MOLINE, COCKSHUTT TRACTORS AND HIT & MISS GAS ENGINES

SATURDAY NIGHT FIREWORKS

FLEA MARKET, MODEL AIRPLANE DEMONSTRATIONS,
FABULOUS FOOD VENDORS, FREE PARKING

ALL ARE WELCOME TO EXHIBIT

THURSDAY - Tractor Games, Tractor Baseball, Parade, Food & Fun

FRIDAY - AM Tractor Drive, Tractor Games, Tractor Baseball, Evening Entertainment, Food & Fun

SATURDAY - AM Auction, Tractor Games, Tractor Baseball, Parade, Entertainment, Fireworks

EACH DAY - all color tractor display, gas engine and equipment displays, rustic camping, Flea market, food and so much more!
For complete schedule-visit—www.smatea.org

FARM CONSIGNMENT AUCTION SAT. 9 AM
Mark Oberly 734-279-2233

FOR SHOW INFORMATION:
General Info: Lee Eggert, President 734-279-1202
Brian Hoppert, V. President 734-777-9611
Flea Market: Brian Hoppert 734-777-9611

49TH ANNUAL
NOWTHEN
THRESHING SHOW
AUGUST 16, 17 & 18, 2019
7415 Old Viking Blvd., Nowthen, Minn.
Only 45 Minutes NW of Minneapolis/St. Paul!

SHOW FEATURE:
MASSEY-HARRIS TRACTORS

Restored 1920s Red Crown Gas Station • Steam Traction Engines • Hundreds of Tractors • Gas Engines • Antique Cars & Trucks • Shingle Mill • Plowing • Sawmill • Lathe Mill • Threshing • Other Antique Machinery • Children's Barnyard • General Store • Pottery • Weaving • Quilting Print Shop • Free Train Rides • Blacksmith Shop • Primitive Camping Available On Site • Large Flea Market • Log House & Barn • Historical Church & School Restoration Milwaukee Road Depot & Memorabilia • Food & Beverage Vendors • Pancake Breakfast Served Daily • Live Music & Entertainment Daily • Daily Parade of Power at 2 p.m. • Tractor Pull Friday Night at 6 p.m. & Saturday Night at 6 p.m. • Sunday Church Service at 9 a.m.

• • • • SHOW INFORMATION • • • •

Also at the Nowthen Threshing Show Grounds June 2019

SPRING TRACTOR PULL EVENT

FALL TRACTOR PULL EVENT

GENERAL SHOW INFO
Contact Joe Lewerenz
(763) 744-7290

Nowthen Historical Power Association
P.O. Box 43
Rogers, MN 55374
www.nowthenthreshing.com

Orange Spectacular
July 26, 27 & 28, 2019

McLeod County Fairgrounds
Hutchinson, Minnesota

ExploreHUTCHINSON.com
#MuchinHutch

WIN

1962 ALLIS-CHALMERS D10 SERIES I

A-C

ALLIS-CHALMERS

FREE ADMISSION · FREE PARKING
CHILDREN'S ACTIVITIES · WOMEN'S ACTIVITIES
FEATURING A-C 220 TRACTORS
HUGE SWAP MEET · FIELD DEMOS EACH DAY
LARGE TOY SHOW · LAWN & GARDEN DISPLAY

ALL ALLIS-CHALMERS TRACTOR,
MACHINERY AND TOY SHOW

For camping, motel & much more information
check out the website: www.orangespectacular.com
Upper Midwest A-C Club
or contact: Darrell Grams, Sr. 612-280-3397

2019 **CASE** EXPO
AUGUST 30 - SEPTEMBER 2

WESTERN MINNESOTA STEAM
THRESHERS REUNION
Rollag, MN | www.rollag.com

ALMELUND
THRESHING SHOW
AUGUST 9-11, 2019
*****FEATURING*****
COCKSHUTT

BRANTFORD CANADA

COCKSHUTT
FARM EQUIPMENT

17th Annual Tractor Caravan August 4th

ATTRACTIONS AND EXHIBITS

TRACTOR PARADES · GAS ENGINE ALLEY
BLACKSMITH SHOP · HISTORIC COURTHOUSE
LOG BUILDINGS · TRACTOR PULLS
PIONEER BUILDING · HUGE FLEA MARKET
KIDS PLAY AREA · AND LOT'S MORE
COME ENJOY THE SHOW!

17760 ST CROIX TRAIL,
TAYLORS FALLS, MN 55084
651-583-2083
www.almelundthreshingco.org

MINNESOTA ASSOCIATION
OF ANTIQUE POWER SHOWS
(MAAPS)
Surrounding States are Invited to Attend!

An organization designed to help all antique power shows work together to define best practices for these events. The leaders and/or board of directors of the antique power shows in the state of Minnesota meet twice a year to share ideas, concerns and suggestions about how antique power shows and/or threshing shows can do a better job of sharing the functions of threshing, sawing, shingles, cooking and the other things we do at these shows to educate and reminisce the ways of those times.

With the continued growth of our organization we are **now inviting surrounding states** to attend our meetings. We believe that we have so much information to share that we want to invite more antique power shows to share and learn.

Minnesota
Association
of
Antique
Power
Shows

YOU ARE INVITED!

SPRING MAAPS MEETING
When: Saturday, May 11, 2019 – 11:00 am to 2:00 pm
Location: White Pine Logging & Threshing Show
McGrath, MN

FALL MAAPS MEETING
When: Saturday, October 5, 2019 – 11:00 am to 2:00 pm
Location: Scott-Carver Threshers Association
Jordan, MN

TO RSVP TO ONE OF THE MEETINGS:
Contact: Jody Hicks, President 612-940-5588
Contact: Karen Kuhnau, Secretary 218-943-5631

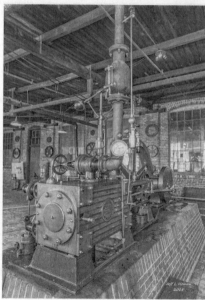

Show Advertising

The MINNEAPOLIS-MOLINE COLLECTORS

Featuring ALLIS-CHALMERS TRACTORS, ADVANCE STEAM GAS ENGINES, IH GAS ENGINES

Hosted by

LATHROP'S 41ST ANNUAL ANTIQUE CAR, TRACTOR & ENGINE SHOW

LARGEST RUSSELL SAWMILL IN OPERATION

JUNE 13-16, 2019

PARADE OF POWER
FRI & SAT-4 P.M. & SUN- 1:00 P.M.
FEATURE TRACTORS FIRST

TRACTOR CRUISE
THUR. MORNING
HEATH HISEL 816-812-0858

✓ STEAM ENGINES   ✓ GAS ENGINES

Largest display of Fairbanks-Morse Power Plant Engines in Missouri

DEMONSTRATIONS

- STEAM ENGINES Large and Small in Operation
- BLACKSMITH SHOP
- SAW MILL
- PRINT SHOP
- CORN SHELLING
- SHINGLE MILL
- GENERAL STORE
- ROPE MAKING
- EARLY DAY GAS ENGINES
- ANTIQUE TRACTORS ON DISPLAY
- VENEER MILL
- BROOM MAKING

. . . .

CAMPING INFO:
816-528-3511

TRACTOR PULL SATURDAY MORNING

For Information on Tractor Pull & Friday Evening Banquet Tickets
Gary & Mary Olsen 15187 Nickel Ave. Altamont, MO.
660-367-2330 660-334-0733 (cell)

Not Responsible for Accidents or Theft
FOR SHOW INFORMATION CONTACT
Jim Plowman, Lathrop, MO. 816-528-3511 or 816-896-5546 Cell
ADMISSION $7 FOR A WEEKEND PASS • 12 & UNDER FREE
VISIT OUR WEBSITE AT **www.lathropantique.com**

Since 1961

Platte County Steam Engine Show

Re-visit Agricultural History

PLATTE COUNTY FAIRGROUNDS
FIRST STREET AND TREBBLE STREET
TRACY, MISSOURI 64079

AUGUST 9, 10, 11, 2019

Tractor, Truck & Engine Show (Daily)
FEATURING STATE MASSEY COLLECTORS
JIM MCCLUNG
PCSTEAMSHOW1961@GMAIL.COM

Tractor Cruise (August 8)
APPROXIMATELY 40 MILES
ALAN GOODWIN – (816) 550-0481
KIDINUS2@AOL.COM

Tractor Pull (August 9-10)
MARK MANVILLE ....(816) 646-5431

NW MO Garden Tractor Pull
RICHARD SWANK ....(641) 785-2353

PLATTECOUNTYSTEAMANDGASSHOW.COM

43RD ANNUAL

MONTGOMERY COUNTY OLD THRESHER'S SHOW

3 BIG DAYS OF EVENTS!

AUG. 16-18, 2019

FEATURE TRACTOR: FORD
FEATURE GAS ENGINE: CUSHMAN
At Fairgrounds Highway 19, Montgomery City, Mo.

Check website or call for more information
www.montgomerycountyoldthreshers.org

- Steam Engines
- Lumber Sawing
- Gas Engines
- Antique Tractors
- Antique Cars
- Antique Trucks
- Farm Equipment
- Large Flea Market
- Arts & Crafts
- Fiddle Contest: Junior, Open & Senior
- Garden Tractor
- Antique & Garden Tractor Pulls
- Lawn Mower Derby
- Good Variety of Food
- Camping & Showers
- Lots of Music
- Dutch Oven Cooking
- Other Entertainment
- Worship Service Sunday
- Parade Each Day

INFORMATION:
Howard Hollensteiner ......(573) 564-2979
Jane Johnson, sec. ....(573) 684-2645
COME VISIT US!

48TH ANNUAL
DUBLIN
GAS ENGINE
MEET

FEATURE:
LARGE ENGINES
(BUT ALL ARE WELCOME)

SEPTEMBER 6, 7, 8, 2019

We are featuring engines 6HP and over.
Most never take them out of the barn.
We will have unloading equipment on
site to assist. All entries welcomed,
especially the big boys!

**$500.00 CASH drawing
for active Sunday
exhibitors**

RAIN OR SHINE. PRIMITIVE CAMPING FOR EXHIBITORS ONLY.
Giant flea market for hobby related items only. New England's largest show.
East of Jct. 101/137 on Rt. 101, Dublin, NH
INFO: DublinNHGasEngineMeet.com or call Dave Whitney: 603-563-8067

1960-2019
THE NEW YORK STEAM ENGINE ASSN. INC.

THE
NEW YORK
Steam Engine Assn Inc

FEATURING:
RUMELY OIL PULL & NEW YORK BUILT EQUIPMENT
59th Annual Pageant of Steam
AUGUST 7, 8, 9, 10, 2019

SPECIAL DISPLAYS AND ACTIVITIES:
Antique Tractors • Parades • Steam Traction Engines • Shingle Making • Corliss Steam Engines
Grain Threshing • Antique Gas Engines • Plowing • Sawmill Demonstrations

ANTIQUE TRACTOR PULL: Wednesday, Thursday & Friday • 5 pm
GIANT CRAFT & FLEA MARKET: Ed Nageldinger, (585) 526-5358
INFO: Rick Finley (585) 721-6172 • Gary Love (585) 394-8102
CONSIGNMENT AUCTION WEDNESDAY 2 PM
www.pageantofsteam.org • e-mail: info@pageantofsteam.org
No alcoholic beverages permitted • Shoes and shirt required • Events subject to change
A non-profit organization • Food available • Exhibitors welcome

GATES OPEN: Wednesday through Saturday 7:30 am-8 pm

3349 Gehan Rd., Canandaigua, N.Y.	Tractor Pull – ESP Pull Saturday • 5 pm Garden Tractor Pull Saturday • 9 am **Tractor Pull Info:** 585-704-4312 • 585-465-9100	Adults $7 Children under 12 **FREE**

CATSKILL MOUNTAIN ANTIQUE ENGINE AND MACHINERY CLUB

30TH ANNUAL SHOW
at the
DELAWARE COUNTY FAIR
AUGUST 12-17, 2019
Walton, NY

Working antique machinery, shingle mill, operating 1930s Ireland #2 Sawmill powered by John Deere. W111 stationary engine

Welcome any and all, old and new tractors & equipment

CONTACT INFORMATION:
ART REED ....(845) 676-4622
ED BUDINE ....(607) 865-7207

42ND ANNUAL SHOW
CHEMUNG VALLEY OLD TIMERS ASSOCIATION

CHEMUNG COUNTY FAIRGROUNDS
170 Fairview RD., Horseheads, NY
Call or email for details.
JULY 19-21, 2019

FEATURES: INTERNATIONAL HARVESTER TRACTORS, ENGINES & EQUIPMENT

Demonstrations • Parades • Shingle Mill
Gas Engines • Oil Field Engine • Crafts
Invited Traction Engines • Free Primitive
Camping • Saturday Chicken BBQ
Pedal Pulls • Powder Puff Pull, Tractor Pull
Sunday Church Service • Antique Pull
Lumber Jack & Jill Competition
Model Engines
THANK YOU ALL 2018 EXHIBITORS

GENERAL INFORMATION:
Randy Brigham ....(607) 745-7349
Cory ....McCracken.Cory@yahoo.com
Call or email for details
Flea Market - Diana Henneman...(607) 624-3834
WWW.CHEMUNGVALLEYOLDTIMERS.COM

Western New York Gas & Steam Engine Assoc. Inc.

ALEXANDER, NY

53RD ANNUAL RALLY
SEPTEMBER 5, 6, 7 & 8, 2019
FEATURING - HONORING STEAM
10294 Gillate Rd., Alexander, NY 14005
Approximately 11 miles off Interstate 90, Exit 48
GATES OPEN 9 AM - 9 PM

* Antique Tractors * Steam Engines * Log Sawing
* Gas Engines * Threshing * Tractor Pulls
* Working Models * Woodworking * Flea Market
* Antique Car Display - Sunday Only * Food
* Live Music * Blacksmith Shop

Info: www.alexandersteamshow.com
Bill Dellapenta (716) 380-7061
THE WNY GAS & STEAM
ENGINE ASSOCIATION, INC.
IS A NOT-FOR-PROFIT ORGANIZATION

52ND ANNUAL
GAS UP SHOW

Acres of antique Farm Equipment, Tractors, Old Trucks, Saw Mill, Homemade Ice Cream, Shingle Mill, Antique Marine Engines, Blacksmith, Bucyrus Erie Steam Crane & Steam Engines

SHOW DATES:
JUNE 8-9 & 15-16, 2019

Shutters Corners, NY west of Albany, NY on Rte 443.
GPS location 106 Murphy Road, Schoharie, NY
I-88 to exit 23 and follow the signs.
Contact: 518-605-1926
Website: www.mysite.company/thegasup.html
Email: gasup1967@gmail.com

"THE BURGETT"

NEW YORK STATE
TWO CYLINDER ASSOCIATION
EXPO XIV

JULY 11-13, 2019
CANANDAIGUA, NEW YORK
THE WORLD'S LARGEST ANTIQUE TWO CYLINDER JOHN DEERE SHOW!
FEATURING: JOHN DEERE M SERIES

CONSIGNMENT AUCTION	DEMONSTRATIONS
SEMINARS	CAMPERS WELCOMED
HUGE VENDOR AREA	TRACTOR GAMES
TRACTOR PULLS FRI & SAT	PEDAL TRACTOR PULLS

DONATIONS: Adults $7.00/$14.00 for 3-day pass

For More Information Call: Alan Hain 585-227-1864
E-mail: alswife127@aol.com
Website: www.newyorkstateexpo.com

Presented by NYS Two Cylinder Expo Association, Inc.

OLE SMOKY
ANTIQUE TRACTOR

24TH ANNUAL SHOW

MAY 31ST - JUNE 1ST, 2019
Set up May 30th
Registration All Day May 31st - June 1st
Tractor Pull Saturday June 1st @ 10 a.m.
WEBSITE: www.olesmokytractorclub.com
HAYWOOD COUNTY FAIRGROUNDS
758 Crabtree Road, Waynesville, NC 28785

PRIMITIVE CAMPING:
Exhibitors and Vendors Only
Contact Faye Ledford 828-627-6844
or Karen Wade 828-593-8326
SHOW INFORMATION:
Courtney Smith 828-593-8330
James Dickson 828-775-5773
Darren Wade 828-593-8327
olesmokytractor@gmail.com

ASHLAND COUNTY
YESTERYEAR MACHINERY CLUB
27TH ANNUAL SHOW
SATURDAY & SUNDAY • JULY 6 & 7, 2019
Setup - July 5, 2019
HOSTING: AVERY & B.F. AVERY CLUB 25TH YEAR.
ALL GARDEN TRACTORS WELCOME. HERCULES ENGINES
Any make Tractor, Equipment & Engine also Military Vehicles are WELCOME.
Show grounds are at The Ashland County - West Holmes Career Center
1783 State Route 60, Ashland, OH 44805

Free Admission & Parking	Food Vendors	Threshing & Corn husking
Handicap Parking Spaces	Craft & Flea Market Area	"Railroad Gary" Kids Rides
Handicap Transportation on grounds	Conservation Tree Farm Wagon Tours	Kiddie pedal Pulls Sunday at 1:00 p.m.
Donation Accepted	Haflinger Wagon Tours	

SPRING SWAP MEET – APRIL 20, 2019
For information visit our website: www.yesteryearmachineryclub.org or
Visit us on Facebook at Ashland County Yesteryear Machinery Club
or Contact: General: Tom Adams - Ph: (419) 651-4109 or tkadams90@yahoo.com
Vendors: Ken Booth - Ph: (419) 606-6504 or massey444@zoominternet.com
Tractors: Jason Arnold - Ph: (419) 685-2234 or arnoldjrfn@gmail.com

30ᵀᴴ ANNUAL FARM DAYS

sponsored by:

Morrow County Antique Tractor & Equipment Assn. Inc.

at the Morrow County Fairgrounds, State Route 42, Mount Gilead, Ohio

AUGUST 2, 3 & 4, 2019

THIS YEAR FEATURING: ALLIS-CHALMERS TRACTORS & EQUIPMENT AND ALL MAKES OF HIT-AND-MISS ENGINES

Friday, August 2
Gates Open – 10 a.m.
Farm Toy Show – 10 a.m.
Flea Market & Crafts All Day
Live Entertainment – All Day
Truck Pull – 6:30 p.m.

Saturday, August 3
Gates Open – 7 a.m.
Farm Toy Show – 9 a.m.
Consignment Sale – 10 a.m.
Antique Tractor Pulls – 10 a.m.
Live Entertainment – All Day
Kids Pedal Pull – 2 p.m.
Parade – 5:30 p.m.
P.U. Truck & Auto Figure 8 Race
& Lawn Mower Derby – 6 p.m.

Sunday, August 4
Gates Open – 8 a.m.
Church Service – 9 a.m.
Farm Toy Show – 9 a.m.
Antique Tractor Rodeo – 10 a.m.
Ladies Skillet Throwing Contest – 11:30 a.m.
Kids Skillet Throwing & Wrench Toss to follow
Mens Wrench Toss
Slow Race – to follow
Live Entertainment – All Day
Pie Bakeoff Contest – 2 p.m.
Raffle/Drawing – 2:30 p.m.
Pie Auction – 2:30 p.m.
Parade – 4:00 p.m.

Gas Engine Display • Flea Markets • Crafts • Threshing & Baling
Free Entertainment • Food on Grounds • Free Parking
Camping on Grounds • Motels Nearby • Security on the Grounds
Golf Carts and ATVs w/Proof of Insurance
Admission $3 – Children 12 & Under FREE
Membership Fee $10 • Camping $20 per day

FOR MORE INFORMATION CONTACT:

FLEA MARKETS & CRAFTS:
Faith Jagger.....................(419) 946-4957
TRACTOR PULL:
John Powell.....................(419) 864-0454
TRUCK PULL:
Jeff Barker........................(419) 210-6803
TOY SHOW:
Jon Axthelm.....................(740) 225-3558

www.morrowcountytractor.com

SHOW INFO:
Larry Welch.................(419) 946-2277
Dwight Murphy.............(419) 946-8236
Jon Axthelm.................(740) 225-3558

DEMOLITION DERBYS:
Jon Axthelm.................(740) 225-3558

farmdays1@hotmail.com

The Historical Construction Equipment Association's 34th Annual

INTERNATIONAL CONVENTION
AND
OLD EQUIPMENT EXPOSITION

The Largest Earthmoving Show in North America!
Over 200 Vintage Construction Machines and Trucks!

Sept. 13–15, 2019
National Construction Equipment Museum • 16623 Liberty Hi Road • Bowling Green, Ohio
Hosted by the Museum Volunteers

FEATURING INTERNATIONAL HARVESTER!

Equipment built or powered by International Harvester will be featured. Stationary and operational equipment in any condition is welcome.

ALSO FEATURING...

Also hosting the Power of Yesteryear's annual agricultural tractor, farming and threshing show. Vintage trucks displayed by the Black Swamp Chapter of the American Truck Historical Society.

EVENTS AND HIGHLIGHTS

Live demonstrations and daily parade of dirt-moving, ground-breaking, earth-shaking antique construction equipment. The convention will also feature historical displays, memorabilia vendors, the world's largest sandbox for kids, and the Saturday night HCEA member's banquet on the Museum grounds.

SHOW HOURS:
Friday, Sept. 13: 9:00 AM to dark
Saturday, Sept. 14: 9:00 AM to 5:00 PM
Sunday, Sept. 15: 9:00 AM to 3:00 PM

ADMISSION:
$10.00 daily, or $20.00 weekend pass. Under age 16, vendors and exhibitors free.

VENDORS:
$40.00 for first 8-foot table, additional tables $35.00 each. Limited tables available for $10 each to HCEA members for historical displays only. Call the HCEA office at 419-352-5616.

HCEA BANQUET:
Saturday, Sept. 14. Social hour at 6:00 PM, dinner at 7:00 PM. Order tickets through the HCEA office at 419-352-5616. Adults, $25, 12 and under, $15.

CAMPING:
Limited primitive camping available. $20.00 fee per site for show. First come, first served.

GOLF CARTS:
Golf carts will be available. Reserve them from Welch's Golf Carts Inc., 888-310-9333 or welchsgolfcarts.com, and mention HCEA and the show dates. $5 one-time fee payable at gate for all personal transport vehicles, except for mobility scooters for the handicapped.

FOR MORE INFORMATION:
Visit www.hcea.net • HCEA 419-352-5616 • **Fax:** 419-352-6086 **email:** tberry@hcea.net

Buckeye Farm Antiques, Inc.

(NONPROFIT)
www.buckeyefarmantiques.com

THIRTIETH ANNUAL SHOW

Shelby County Fairgrounds
655 S. Highland Ave.,
Sidney, OH 45365.
Located at the I75 exit 90 (Turn East)

May 24, 25, 26, 2019
FEATURING:
Allis-Chalmers Tractors and Equipment
Indiana Made Engines
Hosting: Buckeye Allis Club

FEATURED EVENTS:

- Free Entertainment • Craft & Flea Markets
- Primitive Crafts • Blacksmith
- Threshing & Bailing Straw
- Sawmill & Shingle Mill • Parts Area
- National Kiddie Tractor Pull
- Antique & Division II Tractor Pulls
- Kids Tractor Pull & Late Model Tractor Pull
- Western Ohio Garden Tractor Pulls
- Car-Truck & Motorcycle Show, Sunday 26th

General admission

Exhibitors Free

Maint. fee
for all campers

Golf carts welcome
w/proof of insurance
with fee

MORE INFORMATION:

President	937-726-2485
Flea Market	937-726-2486
Camping	419-953-5100
Parts	419-305-0265
Crafts	419-738-8638
Entertainment & Food	937-596-6812

www.buckeyefarmantiques.com

26TH ANNUAL SWAP MEET
NOVEMBER 8 & 9, 2019

Tractor Parts & Related Items, Crafts & Flea Market
* Friday 8:00 a.m. till dark, Saturday 8:00 a.m. till 5:00 p.m. *
Food on grounds! For information call 937-726-2485
Admission: (buyer or vendor) $10 maintenance fee for camping

Greenville Farm Power of the Past

20th Anniversary

July 11 – 14, 2019

Darke County Fairgrounds
Greenville, Ohio

Allis-Chalmers, New Idea, Fractional HP Engines

Hosting The Buckeye Allis Club
& The New Idea Historic Preservation Committee

★GREENVILLE★
FARM POWER ⚙ PAST

Daily Admission $5.00 per person
Ages 12 and under are admitted FREE
Membership is $10.00 per person
Golf Cart, Gator, Etc. Registration is $5.00
Exhibitor Camping $20.00
Non-Exhibitor Camping $20.00 per Night

General Info   Von Oswalt   937-547-1845

Flea Markets & Concessions
Chuck & Kelly Zell   937-692-5798

www.greenvillefarmpower.org

cfcinc@centurylink.net

THE HISTORICAL ENGINE SOCIETY INC.
49TH ANNUAL ANTIQUE POWER EXHIBITION
FEATURING: RUMELY TRACTORS, WHEEL HORSE GARDEN TRACTORS & FAIRBANKS-MORSE ENGINES
JULY 26, 27 & 28, 2019

Century Village Museum, 14653 East Park Street, Burton, Ohio 44021

Steam Engines • Gas Engines • Gas Tractors • Excavating/Construction Equipment
Antique Cars and Trucks • Sawmill • Threshing • Baker Fan • Blacksmith
Flea Market • Parade of Machinery • Tractor Starting Demonstration • Tractor Pull
Ride the Miniature Railroad • Tour the Restored Homes and Shops of the Century Village

Location & Directions: Century Village Museum is located on the southeast side of the traffic circle in Burton at the intersection of Routes 87 & 168. Burton is located either 40 miles east of Cleveland or 45 miles west of Youngstown on Route 87. Show hours are from 8 am – 5 pm. Homes and Shops of the Century Village will be open Saturday and Sunday only. All events and equipment are subject to change without notice. The Historical Engine Society and Geauga County Historical Society are not responsible for any loss, theft or accidents of any kind should they occur.

www.historicalengine.org   (440) 669-2578   PO Box 945, Burton, OH 44021

****** 49TH ANNUAL REUNION ******
OHIO VALLEY ANTIQUE MACHINERY SHOW
Georgetown, Ohio
AUGUST 8-11, 2019

FEATURING:
INTERNATIONAL HARVESTER
& GARDEN TRACTORS

- 400 Tractors • 100 Gas Engines • Working Steam Engines • 1920 Bucyrus Steam Shovel • Antique Tractor, Garden Tractor Fun Pull • O.V.A.M. Old Time VILLAGE • Entertainment & Demonstrations Throughout the Day
- Flea Markets

Events subject to change.

O.V.A.M. SHOW GROUNDS - 1 mile west of Georgetown, Ohio
Intersection of State Route 125 & Winfield Drive
General Information: Jeff Smith ....(513) 734-6272
website: www.ovams.com

ENJOY 4TH OF JULY WEEKEND AT THE 43RD ANNUAL
VAN WERT COUNTY
OLD FASHIONED FARMERS DAYS
JULY 4, 5, 6, 2019

Van Wert County Fairgrounds • U.S. Rt. 127 South • Van Wert, Ohio
FEATURING: Ohio Built Orphans and Odd Balls, Hit-and-Miss Engines, Wheel Horse Lawn Mowers, All Brands Welcome

- Over 300 Tractors • Threshing • Trading Post • Quilt Show
- Old Machinery • Sawmill • Antique Car Show • Kids Games
- Animal Land • Kids & Adult Pedal Tractor Pull
- Antique Tractor Pull • Gas Engines • Crafts • Flea Market
- Musical Shows Every Day

ADMISSION:	CONTACT:
$3.00 Donation (Under 12 Free)	**Old Fashioned Farmers Assoc.**
Three Day Pass: $7.00	P.O. BOX 882, VAN WERT, OHIO 45891
CAMPING: 419-203-9626	Flea Market: 419-305-1984
$20.00 a day for non-exhibitors	President: 419-203-2700
	Vice President: 419-203-4159
EXHIBITORS CAMPING:	Car Show: 419-733-0055
Wed. free. $10.00 a day during show	Music Shows: 419-363-3259
Before and after show $20.00 a day	Camping: 419-203-9626

oldfashionedfarmersdays.com

SEPTEMBER 20-22

Paulding County Fairgrounds
Paulding, Ohio
419-399-5215
www.flatrockcreekfestival.com

Antique Tractor Pulls on Saturday
Draft Horse Pulls & Truck Show on Sunday
Hit and Miss Engines, Oil Pulls
Antique Farming Demonstrations

Feature Tractor & Engine
OLIVER & COCKSHUTT

Festival Entry: $5 per day $10 for all three days
Camping is available on the grounds.
Over 175 Craft, Food, and Flea Market Vendors!

S.C.R.A.P.
SANDUSKY COUNTY RESTORERS OF ANTIQUE POWER

Presents
31ST ANNUAL ANTIQUE
TRACTOR & ENGINE SHOW
Labor Day Weekend
AUG. 30-31 & SEPT. 1-2, 2019

NORTH
U.S. 20
Gibsonburg
WHITE STAR PARK → ★ U.S. 6
Helena   Fremont
960 CR60 Gibsonburg, Ohio.

Church Service at 9 a.m. • Antique Car & Truck Display • Flea Market • Crafts • Wheat Threshing
Stationary Baling • Rope Making • Corn Shredding • Blacksmithing • Quilting • Kettle Corn
Kiddie Tractor Pull • Country Music • Great Food • Exhibitors Only Primitive Camping
Parades • Pumpkin Vine • Railroad • Antique Tractor Pull • Friday Night Tractor Pull

NEW 4 DAY SHOW

All golf carts must have
VALID CERTIFICATE
of liability insurance.
$15 fee, handicapped
exempt from fee

ALL EXHIBITORS WELCOME! ADMISSION $4/DAY
CONSIGNMENT AUCTION – 9:37 A.M. LABOR DAY
FEATURING: MCCORMICK-DEERING & FARMALL
HOSTING INTERNATIONAL CHAPTER 6 STATE SHOW

FOR MORE INFORMATION CONTACT: Elwood Dick ....(419) 307-4265
FOR FLEA MARKET INFORMATION CONTACT: Pat Perry ....(419) 637-2678
FOR FEATURE TRACTOR INFORMATION CONTACT: Steve Smith ....(419) 618-0017

NO DOGS ALLOWED – PARK RULE

——— 57TH ANNUAL ———
STUMPTOWN STEAM THRESHERS CLUB
REUNION & SHOW

Saturday and Sunday	September 7-8, 2019

Harrison County Fairgrounds, 550 Grant St., Cadiz, OH 43907

Steam & Gas Engines • Tractors • Model Engines • Antique Cars
Threshing • Baling • Grinding Corn • Sawing Lumber
Making Shingles • Antique Farm Equipment • Ladies Aux. Bazaar
Thresherman & Queen Awards • Flea Markets • Good Food

SATURDAY EVENTS:
Slow Engine Race at 1 p.m.
Pedal Pull Contest at 3 p.m.
Live Entertainment

SUNDAY EVENTS:
Church Service at 8:30 a.m.
Tractor Contest at 1 p.m.
Quilt Drawing at 2:30 p.m.
Kiddie Coin Hunt at 2:45 p.m.
Grand Parade at 4 p.m.

SHOW INFORMATION:
Gary Wellendorf
8465 Valleybrook S.E.
East Canton, OH 44730
330-265-3659

PLAQUES AWARDED TO ALL EXHIBITORS!
Camping & admission FREE to all exhibitors.
Spectator primitive camping available.
Activities subject to change.
No alcoholic beverages, firearms or
ATVs permitted on the grounds.

National Threshers Association
75th Anniversary Reunion, June 27-30, 2019
Fulton County Fairgrounds, Wauseon, Ohio

Featuring: Port Huron Steam Engines - Caterpillar Equipment - Novo Gas Engines
Contact: Michele Johnson, Sec. @ 419-666-1884
Michele.Johnson.NTA@gmail.com
Come spend the weekend with us! Great Camping-Great Entertainment & Great Fun!
Visit us on the web@ www.NationalThreshers.com

THE ASHTABULA COUNTY ANTIQUE ENGINE CLUB INC.

38TH ANNUAL 3-DAY SHOW

FEATURING:
CASE TRACTORS & WISCONSIN BUILT ENGINES
AGRICULTURE HERITAGE MUSEUM, RAILROAD MUSEUM,
COUNTRY STORE AND ONE-ROOM SCHOOL

Show Grounds – 4026 St. Rt. 322, Wayne Township,
Ashtabula County, OH. 3-1/2 miles east of Route 11.

July 5-7, 2019

$5 Donations for Admission to Show
Free for Members, Exhibitors & Children under 12
Senior Citizen Day - Friday • Free Parking
Wheelchair & Handicap Transport Available.

FOR MORE INFORMATION:
DAVE COVER
29 S Outer Dr., Vienna, OH 44473
(330) 507-9078

Spring Gas-Up ⟶ May 11, 2019
Fall Show ⟶ Sept. 21 & 22, 2019

PLEASE VISIT OUR WEBSITE:
www.ashtabulaantiqueengineclub.com

Continuous Displays of Operating Equipment
Parades & Tractor Pulls - Sat. & Sun.
BIG FLEA MARKET:
Contact Gary Goodge (440) 285-2419
Crafts • Country, Gospel & Old-Time Music
Food & Refreshments on Grounds

MID OHIO ANTIQUE FARM MACHINERY SHOW

41 YEARS OF FARM SHOW EXPERIENCE

JULY 26-28, 2019

RICHWOOD INDEPENDENT FAIRGROUNDS
Richwood, Ohio

FEATURING: COCKSHUTT/CO-OP
WELCOMING: BUCKEYE REGIONAL
COCKSHUTT/CO-OP CLUB

ADMISSION $3.00
Children 12 and under FREE
when accompanied by adult.
ON SITE CAMPING

FOR MORE INFORMATION CONTACT:
PRESIDENT:
Tom Myers...................(740) 225-2301
FEATURE INFO:
Caleb Schwartz............(740) 262-3987

OLD TIMER'S DAYS
49TH ANNUAL
XENIA, OHIO
Greene County Fairgrounds • Xenia, Ohio

SEPTEMBER 27-29, 2019

Ice cream, beans and cornbread, threshing,
antique tractors "one of the largest in the state
of Ohio," gas engines, tractor pull, sawmill,
lumber auction, flea markets, arts & crafts,
antique dealers and much more! Welcome steam
engines, antique engines, tractors and related parts.

FEATURING: OLIVER HART-PARR,
MINNEAPOLIS-MOLINE AND WHITE

PARADE ON SATURDAY
Camping is available 8:00 a.m. Monday, September 23rd
Sunday church service
Exhibitors – Free Entertainment – Fri. & Sat. Tractor Pull
Arts & Crafts – Adult/Children Games – Vendors welcome

FOR MORE INFORMATION CONTACT:
President, Lester Davis 937-789-7464
V.P., Eddie Furay 937-313-5163
2nd V.P., Kathy Ellis 937-750-3599
davislester86@yahoo.com
www.oldtimersclub.com

TUSCARAWAS VALLEY PIONEER POWER Assoc.

56th ANNUAL SHOW

AUGUST·16-17-18

Featuring Massey Harris Ferguson

Friday Night Garden Tractor Pull

General Inquires:
Call Emily Weldon
330-844-5415

Saturday Evening Tractor Pull

Daily Features
& Educational Opportunities

TUSC. COUNTY FAIRGROUNDS
JUST OFF OF I-77 IN DOVER, OHIO

www.doversteamshow.com

FAIRFIELD COUNTY
ANTIQUE TRACTOR CLUB
2019 SHOW

Fairfield County Antique Tractor Club
Is Proud to Feature

ALLIS-CHALMERS AND HIT & MISS ENGINES
Tractors, Equipment and Memorabilia

The show will be held at the
FAIRFIELD COUNTY FAIRGROUNDS
157 East Fair Avenue Lancaster Ohio 43130

AUGUST 16-18, 2019

Bring the whole family and enjoy the show.
Tractors, Memorabilia, Flea Market, Crafts
Steam Engines, Corn Sheller, Saw Mill,
Buzz Saw, Threshing Wheat, Stationary Bailer,
Hit and Miss Engines, Corn Shredding,
Rope Making, Ensilage Cutting & Blowing,
Raffles, 3rd Annual Women's Pan Toss
& Men's Wrench Toss, Farm Animals,
Food Vendors, Thomas the Train, 2nd Annual
Little Miss & Mr Antique Tractor Club Pageant

CAMPING AVAILABLE CALL
Geb Bader 740-304-4170
NEED MORE INFORMATION, CALL
Doug Shaw 740-407-2347
Mike Bowers 740-243-7096

2019 ICCI SPRING MEET

MARK YOUR CALENDAR!

APRIL 12-13-14, 2019
SCHOENBRUNN INN
NEW PHILADELPHIA, OH

BANQUET

SATURDAY, APRIL 13, 2019
$30/person - $25 UNDER 18
Make check payable
to ICCI and mail to:
Caleb Schwartz
200 Saint James St
Marion, OH 43302
resshowtractors@yahoo.com
Phone: (740) 262-3987
Cash Bar
Go to www.cockshutt.com
for more information.

53RD ANNUAL

STEAM & GAS ENGINE SHOW

Pawnee, Oklahoma

MAY 3, 4, 5, 2019 Fri.-Sat.-Sun.

FEATURED TRACTOR: INTERNATIONAL HARVESTER
FEATURED GAS ENGINE: INTERNATIONAL HARVESTER
FEATURED GARDEN TRACTOR: INTERNATIONAL HARVESTER
FEATURED STEAM ENGINE: MINNEAPOLIS

Antique Cars • Camping • Antique Machinery
Wheat Threshing • Straw Baling • Plowing
Saw Mill Operation • Shingle Mill • Corn Meal
Grinding • Blacksmith • Prony Brake • Daily Parade
Toy Show • Crafts • Flea Market • Food
Sanctioned Kids Tractor Pull • Entertainment
Trading Post • Exhibitors Welcome

CONTACT INFORMATION
INFORMATION: Pawnee Chamber of Commerce
(918) 762-2108
ARTS & CRAFTS: Angie Bengston ..(918) 212-6511
FLEA MARKET: Chuck Sittler ......(918) 798-4004
Website: www.OklahomaThreshers.org
OST&GEA Inc. is a non-profit organization.

All Steam Engines Must Be State of Oklahoma
Inspected (405) 528-1500 Ext. 243
For personal transportation needs see website.

Show Advertising

Major County
Historical Society

34TH

ANNUAL OLD TIME THRESHING BEE

OKLAHOMA TRAVELOK.COM

Red Carpet Country.com

SEPTEMBER 27-28, 2019

Fairview, Okla.

For more Information: (405) 880-0057; (580) 227-2265
P.O. Box 555, Fairview, OK 73737; www.mchsok.net
Steam Engines • Old-Time Equipment • Daily Parade
Antique Tractors/Tractor Pull • Stationary Straw Baler • Corn
Shelling • Plowing • Grain Milling • Stationary Gas Engine Show
While you're in Red Carpet Country, visit the
Glass Mountains & Roman Nose State Park.
BE SURE TO TOUR OUR:
Museum • Veteran's Memorial • Pioneer School, House & Church
Railroad Depot • Blacksmith Shop

29TH ANNUAL
NATIONAL
Two-Cylinder Tractor Show
Sept. 27-28, 2019

★ TWO CYLINDER SHOW

Sponsored by the Oklahoma Two-Cylinder Club

FEATURE: JOHN DEERE 1939, THE STYLED YEARS
GUEST TRACTOR: INTERNATIONAL HARVESTER

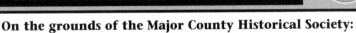

On the grounds of the Major County Historical Society:
Live Demonstrations • Memorabilia • Arts & Crafts
Parade of Tractors & Equipment • Food • Swap Meet • Toy Show
Slow Races • Plowing • Baling • Threshing • Corn Shelling

Call for information on tractor drawing
P.O. Box 555, Fairview, OK 73737
580-794-0089 • 580-227-0202 • www.oktcclub.com • MCHSOK@yahoo.com

Show Advertising

SOUTHERN COVE POWER REUNION ASSOCIATION

29TH ANNUAL
ANTIQUE TRACTOR & ENGINE SHOW

SEPT. 13-15, 2019

Located 1 mile west of New Enterprise, Pa., along Cave Road.
P.O. Box 175, 145 Cave Road, New Enterprise, PA 16664
(814) 766-2100

FEATURING: FORD
GAS & HIT-N-MISS ENGINES • STEAM ENGINES • TOYS

Flea Market • Tractor Pulls Sat. at 5:00 p.m. • Kid's Tractor Pulls & Games
Plenty of Flea Market & Camping Space on the Show Grounds
Antique Tractor Pulls Friday at 5:00 p.m.
DAILY EVENTS: Threshing • Sawmill • Shingle Mill • Tractor Games
Tractor Parades at 1 p.m. • Apple Butter • Basket Raffle
Musical Entertainment • And A Lot More
Plenty of Good Food • Church Service Sunday at 8:30 a.m.
FOR INFO. PLEASE CONTACT: Flea Market: Chris McCauley (814) 414-6470
Nathan Hershberger ....(814) 766-2887
TRACTOR RIDE JUNE 29, 2019

SPRING PLOW DAYS
ANTIQUE TRACTOR AND ENGINE SHOW

APRIL 20, 2019
RAIN DATE:
April 27, 2019

DAILY EVENTS:

Plowing Demonstrations with Tractors & Teams of Horses and
Mules • Antique Tractor Pulls • Kids Tractor Pull & Games
Tractor Games • Tractor Parades • Musical Entertainment
• Flea Market • Lots of Good Food & Fun

CONTACT:
Nathan Hershberger ......(814) 766-2887

NITTANY ANTIQUE MACHINERY ASSOCIATION INC. OF CENTRAL PENNSYLVANIA

45TH ANNUAL SHOW

FOUNDED 1975

www.nittanyantique.org

Penns Cave – Route 192 – 5 miles east of Centre Hall, Pa.
222 PENNS CAVE ROAD, SPRING MILLS, PA 16875

SPRING SHOW MAY 31 & JUNE 1 & 2, 2019

ANTIQUE FARM EQUIPMENT • TRACTORS • STEAM & GAS ENGINES
Consignment Sale (Related Items ONLY)
JUNE 1ST AT 9 A.M.
CONSIGNMENT ITEMS CALL: (814) 692-8738 & (814) 238-1097
Antique Tractor Pull (1976 & Older) For Fun May 31 & June 1, at 5:30 P.M.

Tractors & Steam/Gas Engines on Display • Craft/Flea Markets • Camping Available on Grounds (NO HOOK-UPS) • Square Dancing • Food Available on Grounds - Bean Soup, Pot Pie & Apple Butter by Steam • Cider Pressing • Homemade Ice Cream & Peanuts
Dogs are not allowed on show grounds or Flea Market.

ANNUAL FALL SHOW

SEPT. 5-8, 2019
4 BIG SHOW DAYS!
This is one show you don't want to miss!

You've Seen us on RFD-TV

STEAM TRACTION ENGINES • GASOLINE & STEAM ENGINES • OVER 900 TRACTORS • BAKER FAN SHINGLE MILL TOY SHOW & SALE • THRESHING MACHINE • STATIONARY HAY BALER MODEL STEAM TABLES • CHAIN SAW ARTIST • HORSE-DRAWN WAGONS • SAWMILL ANTIQUE CARS & TRUCKS • HORSE POWER DEMONSTRATIONS DOUBLE DECKER BUS • 150 HP CORLISS ENGINE • CORN HUSKING & CHOPPING • HIT-AND-MISS ENGINES CALLIOPE • NEWLY BUILT GRIST MILL WILL BE OPEN FOR TOURS & GRINDING CORN MEAL

FEATURING: MASSEY FERGUSON, MASSEY-HARRIS, FERGUSON & WALLIS

DAILY EVENTS: Special Events for Kids • Equipment Parades • Sawing Logs into Lumber Sawing Wood Shingles • Straw Baling • Threshing Grain • Steam & Gas Engines and Antique Tractors in Operation • Blacksmith Shop • Homemade Ice Cream • Cider Pressing & Apple Butter Made by Steam • Homemade Bean Soup & Pot Pie by Steam • Model Tables • Broom Making • Hot Roasted Peanuts Antique Tractor Pulls for Fun (Sept. 5-7 at 5:30 p.m., Garden Tractor Activites to be announced) Special Live Entertainment Every Day • Equipment Parades • Calliope • Tractor Pull Square Dancing (Friday & Saturday Evenings) • Exhibitors Always Welcome! Over 800 Craft/Flea Markets • Arts & Crafts Demos • Food Available on Grounds • Camping Available on Grounds (No Hook-ups) • Dogs are not allowed on show grounds or Flea Market.

FOR MORE INFORMATION CONTACT:
Doug Leitch, President, 107 Cooper Street, Spring Mills, PA 16875 • (814) 360-4975
Ken Clouser, 1st Vice President, PO Box 76, 128 Mustang Alley, Madisonburg, PA 16852 (814) 571-1025
Robert L. Corman, Sec., 704 Penns Cave Road, Spring Mills, PA 16875 • (814) 777-4529, bobc@psu.edu
Heather Benner, Flea Market, PO Box 498, Centre Hall, PA 16828 • hezbenner@gmail.com

A NON-PROFIT ORGANIZATION

39TH ANNUAL SHOW
GREASE, STEAM & RUST ASSOCIATION, INC
ANTIQUE TRACTOR & MACHINERY SHOW
OCTOBER 18, 19, 20, 2019
Fulton County Fairgrounds, McConnellsburg, PA

SPECIAL FEATURE
Minneapolis-Moline

An invitation is hereby extended to all Minneapolis-Moline exhibitors, collectors and enthusiasts to participate in the 39th annual Grease, Steam and Rust Association antique tractor and engine show to be held at the Fulton County fairgrounds in McConnellsburg, PA. We place special emphasis on equipment as we would like to show our crowd what these tractors really did on the farm. Minneapolis-Moline tractors and equipment will take center stage in our display area and lead the annual Main Street parade held Saturday 10:30 AM, rain or shine, in conjunction with the annual Fulton Fall Folk Festival, a county wide event.

Show Activities include: A 2-hour Main Street parade Saturday 10:30 AM rain or shine, a 4x4 pickup and semi–truck pull Friday evening, Farm Stock tractor pull Saturday evening, Antique & Classic tractor pull Sunday afternoon, farm toy show, threshing and saw mill operating with steam engines, hit-and-miss engines, pedal pulls and activities for kids, flea market, great food and tractor parts vendors. Primitive camping is available on a first come first serve basis.

Feature Tractor Area: We will have a tent reserved for Minneapolis-Moline feature items, i.e. toys, literature and other memorabilia. If you are a vendor of Minneapolis-Moline items, parts, literature, etc. please let us know so we can allocate space for you.

If you need any additional information regarding the show please contact your host, the Grease, Steam and Rust Association, 717-485- 4581 Other Show Info or 717-485- 5192 Flea Market or check out our website www.gsandr.com or like us on Facebook.

DAILY ADMISSION $2.00 • SORRY NO PETS, SERVICE ANIMALS ONLY
ADMISSION PRICE $5.00 AFTER 5 P.M. FRIDAY NIGHT

LOYALSOCK VALLEY ANTIQUE MACHINERY ASSN. INC.

32ND ANNUAL REUNION
AUGUST 1-4, 2019
FEATURE TRACTOR FOR 2019 CATERPILLAR & ALL TRACK TYPE TRACTORS

Easy access off I-180 Montoursville, Route 87 north, 6 miles to the scenic Loyalsock Valley at the Lycoming County Consolidated Sportsman Grounds. Antique Farm Tractors; Machinery; Antique Cars; Gas, Steam & Hit-and-Miss Engines; Horse-Drawn Equipment; Lumberjack Show, Large Quality Flea Market; Camping on the Grounds (No Hookups); Lots of Shade

EXHIBITORS MORE THAN WELCOME!

DAILY EVENTS:

Demonstrations of sawmill, threshing machine & baler Antique tractor & equipment parade • Antique tractor pull Thursday, Friday & Saturday • Garden tractor pull Friday & Saturday • Entertainment Thursday - Saturday nights Free plaques & buttons for exhibitors • Crafts being made Security on grounds • Lots of good food

2020 - CASE   2021 - MASSEY-HARRIS

Open at Noon on Thursday $5,
Friday & Saturday $5 - Sunday Free Under 12 FREE
Flea market stand: $60/4 days
We are a non-profit organization dedicated to the preservation, restoration and public display of our nearly forgotten heritage. No alcoholic beverages permitted on premises. All dogs in camping area only must be on a leash and cleaned up after.

Come out, relax, and step back in time!

2020 SHOW DATES: July 30-31 August 1-2, 2020
SHOW LOCATION: 6386 St., Rt. 87, Williamsport, PA 17701
FACEBOOK: Loyalsock Valley Antique Machinery Inc.
FOR MORE INFORMATION CONTACT:
L.V.A.M.A., P.O. Box 391, Montoursville, PA 17754
www.lvamassoc.org

William Macinnis, Pres., (570) 433-4217 • 4380 Rt 864 Hwy, Montoursville, PA 17754
John Easton, Vice Pres., (570) 998-9588
Wilma Horn, Flea Market Chairperson, (570) 435-3432
Vernice Vaughn, Sec., (570) 323-5038

SEARS GARDEN TRACTORS AND ATTACHEMNTS AND ALL PA BUILT ENGINES

34TH ANNIVERSARY CELEBRATION
COOLSPRING POWER MUSEUM
Presents
Expos 2019

FEATURING ELECTRIC LIGHTING ENGINES & GEN SETS

SUMMER EXPOSITION & FLEA MARKET
~ JUNE 13, 14 & 15 ~
FALL EXPOSITION & SWAP MEET
~ OCTOBER 17, 18 & 19 ~
LOCATED IN COOLSPRING, PA

Open Days with Select Running Displays &
Guided Tours ~ (No Flea Market) 10 a.m.-5 p.m.
- April 20 & 21
- May 18 & 19
- July 20 - History Day and Antique Car, Truck, & Tractor Show
- July 21
- August 17 & 18
- September 21 & 22

For Complete Details – Visit Our Web Site or Call

Coolspring Power Museum
179 Coolspring Rd., Coolspring, PA 15730
(814) 849-6883
www.coolspringpowermuseum.org
A NON-PROFIT ORGANIZATION

GPS Coordinates:
41° 02' 35" N
&
79° 08' 09" W

FEATURING:
CASE Tractors
and
New Holland
Engines

C.V. Antique Engine
& Machinery Assn Inc.
STEAM & GAS SHOW
37th Annual Show
AUGUST 9, 10, 11, 2019
Twin Bridges Show Grounds
1501 Criders Church Rd., Chambersburg, PA 17202
4 miles west of Chambersburg, Pa.,
& 1 mile north of U.S. Route 30.

Daily Parades • Machinery Operating
Threshing • Baling • Sawmill
Shingle Making • Blacksmith
Flea Market • Food Available
Contact: 717-369-9937
CV.Ant.Eng@PA.Net • cvantiqueengine.org
Free Admission & Parking - Both Shows

Antique Tractor Pull
Friday & Saturday,
August 9 & 10
Garden Tractor Pull
Kiddie Pedal Pulls Daily
Gas Engines in
the Woods

Spring Show & Flea Market • APRIL 27 & 28, 2019
Consignment Sale: Fri., April 26, 2019
FEATURING: JOHN DEERE GARDEN TRACTORS
Vendors wanted. No alcoholic beverages on grounds please. No camping on show grounds.
Camping at Twin Bridge Camp Grounds
Contact: (717) 369-2216

Show Advertising

PPMA
PAST TO PRESENT MACHINERY ASSOCIATION
~ 18TH ANNUAL ~
TRACTOR~EQUIPMENT & MACHINERY SHOW
MAY 24-26, 2019

FEATURING GARDEN TRACTORS

At the Sykesville Ag & Youth Fairgrounds, Sykesville, PA

Friday the 24th is set up & registration day

CONSIGNMENT AUCTION, SATURDAY, 25TH AT 9:00 A.M.

ALL MAKES OF TRACTORS, TRUCKS, CARS & ENGINES WELCOME

Tractor pulls, kids pedal pulls, tractor games, antique machinery demonstrations, consignment auction & other events

FOR MORE INFORMATION

Fred Reed (814) 590-6551 • Dan McDonald (814) 590-6102

Website: pasttopresent.org　　**Email:** dsreed4@verizon.net

PPMA
PO BOX 123, SYKESVILLE, PA 15865

Primitive camping available on the grounds

Not responsible for loss, damage or accidents

25TH ANNUAL SHOW
SUSQUEHANNA ANTIQUE MACHINERY ASSN.
Setup Aug. 16, 2019
AUGUST 17-18, 2019

8344 COAL HILL RD, LUTHERSBURG, PA 15848

5 miles south of DuBois, 1 mile south of Luthersburg 219 S

FEATURE TRACTOR: JOHN DEERE

Tractor, Pedal & Garden Pulls
Working Displays • Parades
Food & Homemade Ice Cream
Primitive Camping • Flea Market
Church Service is Sunday 9 a.m.
FREE ADMISSION & PARKING
Like us on Facebook:
Susquehanna Antique
Machinery Association

GENERAL INFORMATION:

Ray ...(814) 762-8735　Steve ....(814) 236-0173

Fred ....(814) 583-5313

No alcoholic beverages on premises. Not responsible for lost or damaged items. A non profit organization dedicated to preserving the past for the future.

22ND ANNUAL
SUSQUEHANNA OLD FASHIONED
FIELD DAYS

Sept. 21-22, 2019

Route 441, Conoy Twp. Park Bainbridge, Pa.

10 miles north of Route 30 from Columbia;

10 miles south of Harrisburg International Airport

FEATURING:
ANY AND ALL DAIRY RELATED ITEMS

Antique Tractors
Old Fashioned Apple Cider Pressing
Hit-and-Miss Engines
Operation of Old Fashioned Machinery
Food • Music
Auction of Handcrafted Collectibles
Homemade Ice Cream Making
Chainsaw Carving Demonstrations
Colonial Time Period Demonstrations
Revolutionary War Military Encampment
and Reenactment

Machinery Info.: .....(717) 367-5239 or (717) 367-3036

Demonstrators: ....(717) 361-8338

Crafts: ....(717) 367-2869

A HOMETOWN FRIENDLY SHOW

"WHERE THE WHOLE FAMILY HAS FUN TOGETHER!"

21ST ANNUAL
WHEEL HORSE
SHOW
www.wheelhorseclub.com

SOUTH MOUNTAIN FAIRGROUNDS
615 Narrows Rd., Biglerville, PA 17307

Rain or shine with indoor and outdoor exhibit areas
On-site camping (no hook-ups) Restrooms • Showers
Large horse trading • swap meet area
Tractor games for young and old

NO ARRIVAL OR SETUP
BEFORE 9 A.M. THURSDAY

JUNE 21-22, 2019
FRIDAY & SATURDAY ONLY
SET UP DAY IS JUNE 20, 2019

FOR MORE	**CHARLIE CULLEY**
INFORMATION	GENERAL INFO
CONTACT:	(717) 266-2711
ERIC JOHNSON	**RANDY CULLEY**
SWAP MEET AREA	CAMPING INFO
(717) 244-2317	(717) 418-0845

67TH ANNIVERSARY REUNION

★ JUBILEE ★

SEPT. 4-8, 2019

New Centerville, Pa.,
Exit 110 off PA Turnpike,
9 miles south of
Somerset on Route 281.
GPS ADDRESS:
3054 Kingwood Rd.
Rockwood, PA 15557

Steam-powered sawmill
& shingle making. Flailers
& horse power with the
tumbling shaft machine. Tread
power & first steam engine
threshing with hand feeding,
self-feeding threshing. Baling
of straw, dog-powered butter
churning. Steam engine
plowing (weather permitting).
Corn shredding, corn shelling,
blacksmithing, broom making,
cement block machine, steam
powered cider mill, other
demonstrations to see also.
Home of the "Outhouse Dash."

**Daily Parade of
Antique Equipment**

- Live Country &
  Bluegrass entertainment
- Lots of Good Food
- Many Contests to see
- Craft items for sale
- Quilt show at Fire Hall
- Tractor, Truck, A.T.V.,
  Semi-Truck & Horse Pulling
- Steam Engine Games
  Thursday afternoon
  (weather permitting)

4 FALL FESTIVALS
www.4fallfestivals.com

For more information on schedule of
events, bus tours and free brochures.
CONTACT: Farmers & Threshermens Jubilee
1428 Casselman Road, Rockwood, PA 15557
PHONE: (814) 926-3142
Visit our website: **www.ncrvfc.com**

50TH ANNUAL
TENNESSEE-KENTUCKY
THRESHERMEN'S SHOW
JULY 19-20, 2019

US Hwy. 41 • Adams, Tenn.

Steam Traction Engines • Sawmill
Steam Models • Gas Engines
Possum Trot Blacksmith
Forge • Mule Pull
Antique Tractors • Wheat Threshing
Arts & Crafts • Antique Cars
Antique Farm Equipment
Entertainment Saturday Night
Tractor Pull • Flea Market

*See start and running of giant
diesels every hour on the hour!*

CONTACT:
Robert Mitchell (615) 887-0509
Charlie Bumpus (931) 624-3893

14th Annual
Days Gone By
TRACTOR SHOW & THRESHING
October 4-5, 2019

122 Davis Street
Portland, Tn
37148

ANTIQUE TRACTORS
ARTS & CRAFTS
BUGGIES & WAGONS
OLD GAS ENGINES
HORSE DRAWN EQUIPMENT
FLEA MARKET *BOOTH*

ADMISSION:
$5 one-day pass

Children 10 & under FREE

days.goneby@att.net

ALL 4-WHEELERS, GOLF CARTS
& POWERED VEHICLES
**MUST REGISTER
&
OBTAIN A PERMIT**

MONTGOMERY
COUNTY
Antique Tractor & Engine Club

19TH ANNUAL SHOW
September 27-28, 2019

**John Bartee Agriculture Center
Clarksville, Tennessee**
I-24 Exit 8/Rossview Road, Hwy. 237. 1.2 miles East

**Hosting National Leader Tractor Club
Annual Meeting 2019**
Live Demonstration & Craft Skills Farm Animals &
Children's Activites Tractor Parade, Games & Awards

**Vendors wanted for Flea Market
Tools, Tractor Parts, Etc.**

FOR MORE INFORMATION CONTACT:
**Raymond Bagwell
(931) 320-0134
rbagwell01@charter.net
David Clark
(931) 217-2605
Jerry Verkler
(931) 206-1429**

LIKE US ON
FACEBOOK AT
MCATAEC

H·A·L·I·F·A·X C·O·U·N·T·Y V·I·R·G·I·N·I·A

16TH ANNUAL HERITAGE & ANTIQUE MACHINERY FESTIVAL

HALIFAX COUNTY FAIRGROUND Hwy. 360 East, South Boston, VA

May 3-4, 2019 FRI. 9 - 9 & SAT. 9 - 9

* Admission $7
* Food all day on grounds
* Milk Cow
* Rides for Kids
* Petting Zoo
* Korn Box
* Antiques
* Art & Crafts
* Music
* No Alcohol Permitted

EXHIBITS
* Threshing Wheat
* Working Sawmill
* Rock Crusher
* Shingle Mill
* Honey & Bee
* Forestry
* Mining
* Tobacco

FEATURING:

* Old Motorcycles
* Hit & Miss Engines
* Spencer Lumber Co. Steam Engines
* Antique Cars & Trucks

* Corn Shucking
* Corn Grinding
* Blacksmith
* Pedal Tractor Pull
* Quarter Scale Pull
* Antique Tractor Pull

* Moonshine Still
* Primitive Craftsmen
* Power Saw Demo
* Wood Carving
* One-of-a-Kind Tool Collection

For Information visit www.halifaxcountyheritagefestival.org
or call (434) 572-6879
Email: lucyconner40@gmail.com or ccole@embarqmail.com
For Vendor Information ....(434) 579-7340
For Camping Information ....(434) 476-3300 ext. 3323

NORTHERN NECK FARM MUSEUM THRESHING DAY

JULY 6, 2019
9:00 – 4:00

**12705 NORTHUMBERLAND HIGHWAY
HEATHSVILLE, VA 22473**

**THRESHING MACHINE
COMBINES
TRACTORS
WORKING SAWMILL
ANTIQUE EQUIPMENT
FOOD**

PLOW DAY NOVEMBER 2ND

FOR MORE INFORMATION CONTACT:
GENERAL INFORMATION: (804) 761-5952
VENDOR OR EXHIBITORS: (804) 761-0892

WWW.THEFARMMUSEUM.ORG

PAGE COUNTY HERITAGE FESTIVAL

*******50TH YEAR*******

held at
**PAGE COUNTY
FAIRGROUNDS
LURAY, VA.**

WWW.PAGECOUNTYHERITAGE.COM

OCTOBER 12-13, 2019

SAWMILL
GAS ENGINE & TRACTOR DISPLAYS
ARTS & CRAFTS
APPLE BUTTER COOKING
KIDS CORNER
LIVE MUSIC
KIDDIE TRACTOR PULL

STEAM & GAS SHOW INFO:
Wayne Waters ....(540) 743-4164
471 Mt. Carmel Road, Luray, VA 22835

ARTS & CRAFTS INFORMATION:
Ronnie Kauffman ....(540) 244-9739
Kauffman's Mill Road, Luray, VA 22835

Please join us for the
43rd Annual Steam & Gas Pasture Party
September 13-15, 2019
14375 Blue Ridge Turnpike (Rt. 231)
Somerset, VA 22972

Steam Engines	Gas Engines	Tractors
Antique Cars	Models	Saw Mill
Shingle Mill	Wheat Threshing	Straw Baling
Corn Chopping	Excelsior Mill	Steam Plowing
Blacksmiths	Old World Crafts	"Tug-for-Fun" Pull
Consignment Sale		Lawn & Garden Pull
Flea Markets		Live Bands

Admission: $10/day
For More Information Contact:
S.S & G.E.A.
P.O. Box 492
Somerset, VA 22972
General information/Flea market/vendors/crafts:
(540) 672-3429
Email: info@somersetsteamandgas.org
www.somersetsteamandgas.org

 Find us on Facebook

Shenandoah Valley Steam & Gas Engine Show

July 26-28, 2019

890 W. Main St., Berryville, VA

- Gates open 7 AM rain or shine.
- Steam Traction Engines
- Gas Engines & Tractors
  - Threshing
  - Sawmilling
  - Shingle Making
- Parades of Machinery
  - Hobby Displays
  - Arts & Crafts
  - Blacksmith Shop
  - Antique Trucks
- Plenty of Shade & Food
- All Vendors by Prior Arrangement Only!
- Horse Pull & Country Music Saturday Night
- Auction Saturday 8:30 a.m.

TOY SHOW

Fri. Mar 22, 2019
(6-9 p.m.)
Sat. Mar 23, 2019
(9 a.m. - 3 p.m.)
Firehall • Boyce, VA

TOYS: Chris Collis
(304) 839-7011

FOR INFORMATION CONTACT:
Robert Brown, President
804 Minebank Rd
Middletown, VA 22645
(540) 272-0931
Flea Markets: Barbara Heflin
(540) 514-5854
Tractor Pull: Charlie Gray
(540) 533-8827
www.svsgea.com

JI CASE COLLECTORS ASSOCIATION, INC.

SPRING CONVENTION
MAY 25-26, 2019
Ixonia, WI

SUMMER CONVENTION
AUGUST 22-25, 2019
Madison, SD

For J.I.C.C.A. contact Jonathan Woodrum
606-303-0891 – jwll67@yahoo.com
www.jicasecollector.com

BADGER STEAM & GAS ENGINE CLUB BARABOO, WIS.

56th Annual Show
August 16 – 18th, 2019
7 a.m. - 5p.m.
264 Acre Show Site
Wooded Building & Exhibit Areas
29 Acres of Free Parking
3 Level Loading Dock

"The Great Minneapolis Feature"

Join us in 2019 as we feature Minneapolis-Moline and the companies that preceded it, including Minneapolis Threshing Machine Co., Twin City, Moline Plow and others.

For more information, or to participate, please contact the following:
Steamers and Prairie Tractors — Tyler Roudebush, 608-843-2652.
Tractors and Implements — Peter Holzman, 608-635-7772.

Primitive camping for exhibitors only. All vehicles other than scooters and powered wheel chairs used by the disabled require proof of insurance.

See Antique Machines in Action
Steam Engines-Antique Tractors-Antique Engines-1901 Keystone Steam Well Drilling Rig-Sawmills-Threshing-Silo Filling-Rock Crushing-Straw Baling-Horse Powered Rock Picker– Blacksmith Shop-Woodworking Shop-Model Engines-Old Cars & Trucks-Fuller & Johnson Museum-Building With Displays For The Ladies-Parade Saturday & Sunday-Huge Flea Market-Arts & Crafts-Books & Decals For Sale-Free Shuttle Rides Around Grounds-Good Food-Home Made Pie & Ice Cream.

Driving Directions:
Exit #92 off I-90/94, Hwy. 12 East 3.8 miles to Hwy. 33 (Exit 215).
West on 33 for 1/2 mile to Sand Road, north on sand road 1/2 mile to S3347 Sand Road.

Spring Swap Meet
May 3rd — 5th, 2019
Auction Saturday, May 4th at 10:00 AM
Show Information: P.O. Box 255, Baraboo, WI 53913 608-522-4905
Spring Swap Meet and Show Flea Market Info:
Robert & Robert Mattson, 608-393-3021
www.badgersteamandgas.com

THE 51ST ANNUAL
DODGE COUNTY
ANTIQUE POWER SHOW
Burnett Corners, WI
AUGUST 2-4, 2019
1/2 mile south of Burnett on Highway 26,
then 1/2 mile west on County B.

FEATURING: OLIVER, WHITE, CLETRAC, HART-PARR
Bill Frank 815-219-0537
11TH ANNUAL ECONOMY/POWER KING REUNION
CAMPING AVAILABLE • 8-5 DAILY

SECOND FEATURE:
BOLENS 100TH ANNIVERSARY

FREE ADMISSION FOR VETERANS WITH PROPER ID.
PROOF OF INSURANCE ON ALL GATORS & GOLF CARTS

FEATURE CONTACT
John Kosmiski 920-387-3376
Scott Feucht 920-296-9321
Bob Dukstra 920-210-5533
Bill Madison 920-319-2105

WOMEN'S CENTER
Featuring spinning wheels
Michelle Zahn 920-386-2565

FLEA MARKET
Troy Brugger 262-269-6130

FOR INFORMATION
(920) 210-6744 • (920) 296-2650
Also, for tractor pull and camping
Matt Feucht at (920) 319-2281
www.dcapc.org
Check us out on Facebook

46TH ANNUAL
NORTH CENTRAL WISCONSIN ANTIQUE STEAM & GAS ENGINE CLUB INC.
EDGAR, WIS. ANTIQUE SHOW & FLEA MARKET
AUGUST 23, 24, 25, 2019

LOCATION: Kurt Umnus Farm, Edgar, Wisconsin
16 miles west of Wausau, Wis., on State Highway 29 to County Highway H.,
3 miles south to County Highway N., 3 miles west on County Highway N.
2019 SHOW FEATURE: JOHN DEERE

Sawmill, threshing machines powered by steam engines & gas tractors, model steam engines, gas tractors, gas engines, crawler tractors, teeter-totter for steam engines, log cabin, shingle mill, stone crusher, resawmill, blacksmith shop, old-time gas station, planer, general store.

SPECIAL ATTRACTIONS:	Plowing with steam engines (weather permitting), crafts & demonstrations, large flea market, shuttle wagons, log house, play area for children, pioneer skills demonstrations.
GOOD TIME MUSIC:	Friday evening, all day on Saturday & Sunday afternoon. Two large dance floors for dancing. Country Western & Polka music.
PARADE:	Sunday at 1 p.m. (weather permitting).
FIELD DEMOS:	On Saturday
PANCAKE BREAKFAST:	Buckwheat pancakes served daily from 6 a.m.-noon. Lunch and refreshments served daily. Fun for young and old • Free parking

JOIN US FOR OUR ANNUAL SWAP MEET SEPTEMBER 13 & 14, 2019
SWAP MEET CONTACT CHAD 715-223-5263

Website: Visit us at www.edgarsteamshow.com
For information, contact: Greg Szemborski, (715) 352-7722
North Central Wisconsin Antique Steam & Gas, P.O. Box 272, Edgar, WI 54426

Show Advertising

HUNGRY HOLLOW STEAM & GAS ENGINE CLUB INC.

50TH ANNUAL SHOW

JUNE 29-30, 2019

FEATURING: FORD

From Barron, WI – Hwy. 25 N to 19th Ave.
From Rice Lake, WI – Hwy 48 W to Hwy
25 South to 19th Ave. – Follow signs.

1509 19th Ave.
Rice Lake, WI 54868

**Tractor, Steam & Gas Engine Exhibits
Flea Market • Tractor Pull • Food
Antique and Working Exhibits**

**INFORMATION: MIKE MESSNER
(715) 234-8423
www.hungryhollowclub.com**

Southeast Wisconsin Antique Power
and Collectible Society presents

FALL HARVEST DAYS

SEPTEMBER
13, 14, 15, 2019
9 am to 5 pm

A-C
ALLIS-CHALMERS

**Featuring
The Gathering
Of the Orange**
This is a National Show
Racine County Fairgrounds,
19805 Durand Ave., Union Grove, WI

ALLIS-CHALMERS EQUIPMENT DISPLAYS,
HIT AND MISS ENGINES, WORKING
DEMONSTRATIONS, INDOOR/OUTDOOR
FLEA MARKET, CRAFTS, FARM TOYS,
KIDS ACTIVITES, MODEL TRAINS
SATURDAY NIGHT TRACTOR PULL

**MORE INFORMATION AT
www.fallharvestdays.com
OR CALL BILL 262-331-4246**

16th Annual

Fall Harvest Festival

SEPTEMBER 27-29, 2019

Sponsored by
**THE OLD FARMER'S ANTIQUE
CLUB OF ADAMS COUNTY**

FEATURING
JOHN DEERE TRACTORS AND EQUIPMENT

FEATURE CONTACT
NEIL STONE ....(608) 254-7195

- Silent Auction
- Antique Cars,
  Trucks & Tractors
- Flea Market
- Music
- Harvest
  Demonstrations
- Hit & Miss Engines

PANCAKE BREAKFAST
Saturday & Sunday 7 a.m. – 10 a.m.
BARN DANCE
Saturday 6:30 p.m. – 8:30 p.m.
FRIENDSHIP, WI
West of Friendship on County Road J about 4 blocks

FOR MORE INFORMATION CONTACT:
Dennis Erickson ....(608) 564-7378
Bill Schroeder ....(608) 548-6959
**THRESHING AND LUMBER
SAWING WITH STEAM ENGINES**

THE 33RD ANNUAL PICKETT STEAM AND GAS ENGINE SHOW

SEPTEMBER 7TH & 8TH 2019

7 Miles South of Oshkosh or 4 1/2 Miles North of
Rosendale, N9975 Olden Rd. (West of Highway 26)

**FEATURING MINNEAPOLIS-MOLINE
AND OLIVER HART-PARR TRACTORS
FULLER & JOHNSON ENGINES
AND WISCONSIN MADE**

**HORSE PULL SATURDAY
ANTIQUE TRACTOR PULL SUNDAY
KIDS PEDAL PULL SUNDAY
FLEA MARKET • SAW MILL
THRESHING • SHINGLE MILL
EXHIBITS EACH DAY**

**OTHER PICKETT STEAM CLUB
AND PICKETT PULLERS EVENTS**
JUNE 29 – INDEPENDENCE PULL
JULY 6 – ENGINE SHOW
SEPTEMBER 6 – TRUCK AND TRACTOR PULL
SEPTEMBER 7 & 8 – 33RD ANNUAL SHOW

Haunted Hospital - October weekends
Facebook @ Picket Steam Club Pickett Pullers
www.pickettsteamclub.org

NOTES:

FARM COLLECTOR
SHOW DIRECTORY
2019

NATIONAL
CLUBS AND
PUBLICATIONS

■ Allis-Chalmers
Old Allis News
471 70th Ave., Clayton, WI 54004;
Contact: Dave Clausen,
email: oldallisnews@amerytel.net
https://oldallisnews.com

Allis-Chalmers Connection
913 N. Main St., Abingdon, IL 61410;
Contact: Mike Anderson,
email: barma@frontier.com
www.theallisconnection.com

■ B.F. Avery
B.F. Avery
2030 Wood Rd.,
Marlette, MI 48543;
Contact: Gary Duff, www.bfavery.com

■ Bungartz
Bungartz Tractor Owners Registry
Box 7583, Newark, DE 19714;
Contact: AK Kissell,
302-353-7993

■ Case
J.I. Case Collectors Assn.
Contact: Jonathan Woodrum,
email: jwll67@yahoo.com
www.jicasecollector.com

Case J.I. Case Heritage Foundation
9374 Roosevelt St., Crown Point, IN 46307;
Contact: Mark Corson,
email: caseheritage@aol.com
www.caseheritage.org

■ Caterpillar
Antique Caterpillar Machinery Owner's Club
7501 N. University, Suite 117, Peoria, IL 61614; email: cat@acmoc.org
www.acmoc.org

■ Centaur
Centaur Tractor Club
5864 Coder Road, Attica, OH 44807;
Contact: Jason Tallman,
email: mrandmrstallman@yahoo.com

■ Cletrac
California Oliver Cletrac Club
3380 Ferry St., Eugene, OR 97405;
Contact: Richard Borgaro,
email: coccinfo@calolivercletrac.org
www.calolivercletrac.org

Cletrac and Oliver Crawlers
21092 N. Norrisville Rd.,
Conneautville, PA 16406;
Contact: Blake Malkamaki,
email: blake@cletrac.org
www.cletrac.org

■ Cockshutt
International Cockshutt Club
Contact: Caleb Schwartz,
email: resshowtractors@yahoo.com
www.cockshutt.com

■ Empire
Empire Tractor Newsletter
5862 St. Rt. 90 N., Cayuga, NY 13034;
Contact: Carl Hering,
email: info@empiretractor.net
www.empiretractor.net

■ Ford
Ford/Fordson Collectors Assn.,
Inc. P.O. Box 506, Buchanan, MI 49107;
Contact: Ted Foster,
email: info@fordtractorcollectors.com
www.ford-fordson.org

■ Gravely
Gravely Tractor Club of America
403 S. Mill St., New Knoxville, OH 45871;
Contact: Doug Hoelscher,
email: dhoelscher@nktelco.net
www.GTCOA.com

■ Huber
Huber Machinery Museum
email: hubermuseum@aol.com
www.hubermuseum.com

■ International Harverster
International Harvesters Collectors Club
18221 County Rd 25A, Watakoneta, OH 45895;
Contact: Douglas Etzkorn,
www.nationalihccollectors.com

■ Massey
Massey Collectors Association
1975 N. Washington St.,
Danville, IN 46122-9595;
Contact: Gary T. Emsweller,
email: masseyh@aol.com
www.masseycollectors.com

National

■ Minneapolis-Moline
Minneapolis-Moline Enthusiasts
4380 Rt. 864 Hwy., Montoursville, PA 17754;
Contact: Bill MacInnis,
email: tritoes@aol.com

■ New Idea
New Idea Engine Registry
P.O. Box 43, Somonauk, IL 60552;
Contact: Ray Forrer,
email: rncforrer@juno.com

■ Porsche
Porsche-Diesel Owners Registry
Box 7583, Newark, DE 19714; ‐
Contact: AK Kissell
302-353-7993

■ Rawleigh
Rawleigh-Schryer, Ziegler-Schryer and Rawleigh Gas Engine Registry
7879 St. Rt. 309, Galion, OH 44833;
Contact: Michael E. McCracken,
419-462-1362

■ Rumely
Rumely Products Collectors
5455 Elizabethtown Rd., Palmyra, PA 17078;
Contact: Keith Kuhlengel,
email: krkhulengel@comcast.net
www.rumelycollectors.com

■ Sandwich
Sandwich Engine Registry
P.O. Box 43, Somonauk, IL 60552;
Contact: Ray Forrer,
email: rncforrer@juno.com
www.oldengine.org/Members/sandwich

■ Schools
Heritage Park of North Iowa Steam School
Contact: Jarred Ruble,
email: steamschool@heritageparkofnorthiowa.com
www.heritageparkofnorthiowa.com

■ Shaw
Shaw Du-All Collectors Club
Contact: Doug Tallman,
email: dtallman@accnorwalk.com

■ Toy
Toy Farmer Magazine
496 106th Ave. S.E., La Moure, ND 58458;
Contact: Lori Aberle,
email: laberle@toyfarmer.com
www.toyfarmer.com

Toy Trucker & Contractor Magazine
7496 106th Ave. S.E., La Moure, ND 58458;
Contact: Lori Aberle,
email: laberle@toyfarmer.com
www.toyfarmer.com

■ Watch Fob
International Watch Fob Assn, Inc.
107 Karl St., Berea, Ohio 44017;
Contact: Chuck Sword,
email: chuck@dhsdiecast.com
www.watchfob.com

■ Wheel Horse
Wheel Horse Collectors Club
715 1st Ave., Manchester, PA 17345;
Contact: Charlie Culley,
email: cecwh@comcast.net
www.wheelhorsecc.com

■ Miscellaneous/Publications
Antique Truck Historical Society
10380 N. Ambassador Drive Suite 101, Kansas City, MO 64190;
Contact: Lea Ann Reed,
email: leaann@aths.org www.aths.org

Cast Iron Seat Club
Contact: Tom Wilson,
email: qctrax@frontiernet.net

Corn Items Collectors Assn.
Contact: David Vandenboom,
641-919-2042

Corn Shredding Autumn Harvest Club
64245 355th Avenue, Lake City, MN 55041;
Contact: Dwain Gerken,
email: farming@cornshreddingharvest.com
www.Cornshreddingharvest.com

Engineers & Engines Magazine
PO Box 10, Bethlehem, MD 21609;
Contact: Brenda Stant,
email: stant@threshermen.org
www.engineersandengines.com

National

Red Power Magazine
PO Box 245, Ida Grove, IA 51445;
Contact: Dennis & Sallie Miesner,
email: dmiesner@netlic.net
www.redpowermagazine.com

Vintage Garden Tractor Club of America
804 N. Trimble Rd., Mansfield, OH 44906;
Contact: Doug Tallman,
email: dtallman@accnorwalk.com
www.vgtcoa.com

Vintage Tractor Digest
PO Box 10, Bethlehem, MD 21609;
Contact: Brenda Stant,
email: stant@threshermen.org
www.vintagetractordigest.com

National

FARM COLLECTOR
SHOW DIRECTORY
2019

SHOW
FEATURES

■ AGCO
OK   Bryan County Antique Tractor Show June 14-15

■ Allis-Chalmers
DE   First State Antique Tractor Club Show June 14-15
IA   28th Annual The Allis Connection "All Allis" Father's Day Weekend Show
     June 15-16
IL   18th Annual Clark County Antique Power Club Tractor and Engine Show
     Aug. 16-18
IL   21st Annual ECIA Summer Show July 18-20
IL   25th Annual Antique Tractor Show Sponsored by the Triple A Tractor Club, Inc.
     March 14-17
IL   38th Annual Mill Road Thresherman's Show Aug. 9-11
IL   Rantoul Half Century of Progress Show Aug. 22-25
IL   Thee Olde Time Farm Show July 5-7
IN   25th Annual Franklin County Antique Machinery Show Sept. 26-29
IN   8th Annual Wolf Lake Onion Days Farm & Garden Tractor Show Aug. 2-3
IN   Antique Steam and Gas Engine Club Fall Show Oct. 11-13
IN   Antique Steam and Gas Engine Club Summer Show July 26-28
IN   Greentown Lions Club Pioneer Village Tractor & Engine Show July 8-13
IN   Rumely Allis Chalmers La Porte Heritage Center Tractor Show Sept. 20-22
IN   Wildcat Creek Antique Tractor and Engine Show June 7-9
KY   11th Annual Sycamore Flats Flywheelers Show at the Ag Center May 10-11
KY   12th Annual Show at the Park Oct. 5
KY   13th Annual Tractor Show Aug. 2-3
KY   24th Annual South East Kentucky Antique Tractor Show Oct. 3-5
KY   49th Annual Central Kentucky Antique Machinery Association Show July 26-27
KY   Sycamore Flats Flywheelers 11th Annual Show at the Ag Center May 10-11
KY   Tractor and Engine Show Sept. 20-21
MI   21st Annual Big Rapids Antique Farm & Power Club Swap Meet
     and Flea Market July 26-27
MI   59th Annual Show Aug. 2-4
MI   Big Rapids Antique Farm & Power Club Swap Meet and Flea Market June 7-8
MI   Wellington Antique Tractor & Engine Club Aug. 9-11
MN   36th Annual Farming of Yesteryear Threshing Festival Sept 7-8
MN   56th Annual Scott-Carver Threshers Harvest Festival Aug. 2-4
MN   Days of Yesteryear Aug. 10-11
MN   Orange Spectacular July 26-28
MN   Park Rapids Antique Tractor and Engine Club Field Days Aug. 3-4
MO   39th Annual Macon County Flywheel July 25-28
MO   41st Annual Lathrop Antique Car, Tractor & Engine Show June 13-16
OH   20th Annual Planting Time Show June 1-2
OH   30th Annual Buckeye Farm Antiques Show May 24-26
OH   30th Annual Morrow County Antique Tractor and Equipment Farm Days Aug. 2-4
OH   Fairfield County Antique Tractor Club
     and Truck Show Aug. 16-18
OH   Greenville Farm Power of the Past July 11-14
OH   Watch Fob and Vintage Equipment Show April 26-27
ON   27th Anniversary Upper Canada Two-Cylinder Club Show July 26-28
ON   Blyth Steam Show Sept. 6-8
PA   28th Annual Montour Antique Farm Machinery Collectors Show Aug. 30-Sept. 1
PA   35th Anniversary Olde Tyme Days 2019 Aug. 16-18
PA   41st Annual Allegheny Mountain Engine and Implement Association Show &
     Demonstration July 26-28
PA   62nd Annual Early American Steam Engine Society Steam-O-Rama Oct. 3-6
PA   Chickentown Gas and Steam Show May 25-26
PA   Mid Atlantic Allis Chalmers 4th Annual Tractor Show and Swap Meet Aug. 3-4
PA   Middlecreek Valley Antique Assn. 23rd Annual Fall Antique Machinery Show
     Aug. 23-25
PA   Middlecreek Valley Antique Assn. 23rd Annual Spring Antique Machinery Show
     May 17-19
TN   Fall Festival Oct. 11-12

Feature

TX 48th Annual State Tractor, Truck & Engine Show Oct. 5
WI 26th Annual Wisconsin Antique Power Reunion Show July 20-21
WI 28th Annual Fall Harvest Days Sept. 13-15
WI 3rd Annual Golat Implement Days, Tractor and Implement Show
  Aug. 3-4

■ BF Avery
AZ 2019 Winter Meeting - Apache Junction, AZ. March 9-10
On 2018 BF Avery Summer Show July 6-7

■ Bolens
MA Retired Iron Tractor Show July 6-7

■ Case
CA World AG Expo Feb. 12-14
FL International Harvester Collectors Club, Florida Chapter 27 at the 27th Annual
  Florida Flywheelers Engine & Tractor Show Feb. 20-23
IL 58th Annual Antique Engine and Tractor Working Farm Show Sept. 13-15
IL River Valley Antique Tractor Show Aug. 24-25
IN 29th Annual Keck Gonnerman Antique Machinery Association Show Aug. 2-4
IN 37th Annual Noble County Gas and Steam Show and Noble County Community
  Fair July 14-20
IN 45th Mid-America Threshing and Antiques Aug. 8-11
IN 71st Annual Reunion Pioneer Engineers   Aug. 1-4
IN Hoosier Heritage Fest July 26-28
IN Markleville Jamboree Aug 1-3
KY 20th Annual Greenup Old Tractors, Engines and Machinery Show Oct. 3-5
MA Charter Day Antique Tractor Pull & Show June 9
MI 35th Annual St. Clair County Farm Museum Fall Harvest Days August 23-25
MN 37th Annual Antique Engine & Tractor Show July 19-21
MN 45th Annual Pioneer Days Threshing Show Sept. 13-15
MN Forest City Threshers Show Aug.17-18
MO 55th Annual Northwest Missouri Steam and Gas Engine Association Annual
  Show Aug. 16-18
NE 23rd Annual Antique Tractor and Farm Machinery Show Aug. 2-4
NY 26th Annual Long Island Antique Power Assn. Show July 13-14
OH 12th Annual Coshocton County Antique Power Association Summer Show
  July 13-14
OH 38th Annual Ashtabula County Antique Engine Club Three-Day Show ,July 5-7
OH 48th Annual Northwest Ohio Antique Machinery Show Aug. 1-4
OH Antique Tractor & Machinery Show May 31-June 2
OH Clinton County Corn Festival Sept. 6-8
ON Heritage & Antique Show July 12-14
PA 26th Annual Endless Mountains Antique Power Equipment Antique Tractor,
  Engine and Machinery Show July 12-14
PA 37th Annual Steam and Gas Show Aug 9-11
PA C.V. Antique Engine & Machinery Assn. Spring Fling Aug. 9-11
PA French Creek Valley Antique Equipment Club Show June 14-15
SD 45th Annual James Valley Threshing & Tractor Club Show Sept. 6-8
SK Western Development Museum "Those Were the Days" Aug. 17-18
WI 26th Annual Agricultural Heritage Days Sept. 21-22
WI Fountain City Old Time Farm Fest Aug. 31-Sept 1
WI Ixonia Vintage Tractor Expo May 24-26

■ Caterpillar
NC 2019 ACMOC National Show Nov. 1-3
OH 75th Annual National Threshers Reunion June 27-30
PA Loyalsock Valley Antique Machinery Assn. 32nd Annual Show Aug. 1-4

■ Cockshutt
IA Homer Threshing Bee Aug. 24-25
IN 24th Annual Steuben County Antique Power Association Antique Farm
  Equipment Show June 14-15

Feature

IN   35th Annual White River Valley Antique Antique Show Sept. 5-8
MI   30th Annual Southeast Michigan Antique Tractor & Engine Show July 18-20
MN   2018 Annual Almelund Threshing Show Aug. 9-11
OH   24th Annual F.A.R.M. Inc FARM Tractor Show July 26-28
OH   Flat Rock Creek Fall Festival Sept. 20-22
OH   Mid-Ohio Antique Farm Machinery Show July 26-28
OH   Old Iron Power Club & Appalachian Foot Hills Fall Festival Sept. 21-22
ON   54th Annual Georgian Bay Steam Show Aug. 2-5
ON   Georgian Bay Steam Show Aug. 2-5
ON   Niagara Antique Power Heritage Display June 29-July 1
PA   12th Annual Fall Harvest Fest Oct. 4-5
PA   52nd Annual Pioneer Steam and Gas Engine Society of Northwestern
      Pennsylvania July 19-21
WI   Berlin Area Antique Equipment 4th Annual Tractor Show Oct. 5-6

■ Co-op
IA   Homer Threshing Bee Aug. 24-25
IN   24th Annual Steuben County Antique Power Association Antique Farm
      Equipment Show June 14-15
IN   35th Annual White River Valley Antique Antique Show Sept. 5-8
OH   Mid-Ohio Antique Farm Machinery
      Show July 26-28

■ Cub Cadet
MO   JP's 18th Midwest Cub-Arama Sept. 26-28
PA   International Harvester Summer Show June 21-22
PA   Spring Plow, Pull, Auctions and Show Day April 27

■ Ecomony
IA   Cedar Valley Engine Club Threshers Reunion Aug. 31-Sept. 2
IN   23rd Annual S.E. Indiana F.A.R.M. Club's Antique Machinery Show June 27-29
MI   Port Hope Antique Gas Engine and Tractor Show July 5-7
MN   Pioneer Power Good Old Days & Threshing Show Aug. 3-4

■ Empire
PA   20th Annual Empire EXPO Empire Tractor Owners Aug. 14-17

■ Fairbanks-Morse
FL   International Harvester Collectors Club, Florida Chapter 27
      Lake Wales Pioneer Days Oct. 26-27
IL   Olden Days Aug. 24-25
MI   Olde Tyme Plow Days and Swap Meet April 27-28
MN   56th Annual Scott-Carver Threshers Harvest Festival Aug. 2-4
NV   Antique Tractor and Engine Show Aug. 30-Sept. 1
OH   49th Annual Historical Engine Society's Antique Power Exhibition July 26-28

■ Farmall
AL   Jasper Heritage Festival Oct. 19
IA   Northeast Iowa Antique Engine and Power Show Aug. 10-11
IL   Amboy Depot Days Tractor Show Aug. 24
IL   Rock Falls Antique Tractor and Engine Show July 13
LA   IHC LA Chapter #31 Tractor and Engine Show May 2-4
MA   Retired Iron Tractor Show July 6-7
MD   Hampstead Day Tractor Show May 25
MD   Rural Heritage Spud Fest & Antique Tractor Show Aug. 24-25
MI   21st Annual Coopersville Tractor Show Aug. 7-10
MN   45th Annual Rice County Steam and Gas Engines Show Aug. 30-Sept. 1
NE   Pierce Old Time Threshers Bee Sept. 7-8
NY   Mohawk Valley Power of the Past Ole Time Power Show May 31-June 2
OH   12th Annual Coshocton County Antique Power Association Summer Show
      July 13-14
OH   3rd Annual Farm Heritage Show Oct. 5-6

Feature

SC   Power From The Past Tractor Show and Swap Meet May 18
TN   Billy McKnight Memorial Antique Tractor and Engine Show Nov. 1-2
WI   Pioneer Farm Days Oct. 12-13
WI   Valmy Thresheree Aug. 16-18

■ Ford/Fordson
IL   23rd Annual County Line Sod Busters Prairie Days July 19-21
IL   32nd Annual Marshall-Putnam Antique Tractor and Engine Show June 8-9
IL   34th Annual Edwards River Antique Engine Show Sept. 21-22
IL   43rd Annual Argyle Antique Gas Engine Show Aug. 30-Sept. 2
IL   Fall Festival Sept. 21-22
IL   Spring Festival May 25-26
IN   24th Annual Steuben County Antique Power Association Antique Farm
       Equipment Show June 14-15
IN   38th Annual Illiana Antique Power Association Show July 19-21
IN   Greensburg Power of the Past 29th Annual Reunion Aug. 15-18
KS   25th Annual Power of the Past Antique Engine and Tractor Show Sept. 13-15
KY   14th Annual Shopville Community Park Antique Tractor
       and Small Engine Show May 4
ME   24th Eliot Antique Tractor & Engine Show July 26-28
MI   16th Annual Farm Collectibles and Toy Show Feb. 23
MI   22nd Annual Hartford Old Engine and Tractor Show Aug. 9-Sept. 1
MI   44th Annual Thumb Area Old Engine and Tractor Association Show Aug. 9-11
MN   66th Annual Lake Region Pioneer Thresherman - LRPTA - Dalton Threshing
       Sept. 6-8
MN   Heritage Hill Threshing Show Aug. 16-18
MO   Osage River Antique Power Engine Show Aug. 23-25
NE   23rd Annual Antique Tractor and Farm Machinery Show Aug. 2-4
NV   Antique Tractor and Engine Show Aug. 30-Sept. 1
OH   63rd Annual Darke County Steam Threshers Show July 4-7
OH   Antique Tractor Club of Trumbull County Ohio Fall Show Aug. 16-18
OH   Antique Tractor Club of Trumbull County Ohio Tractor, Car, Truck & Motorcycle
       Show June 9
OK   29th Annual National Two-Cylinder Tractor Show Sept. 27-28
PA   17th Annual Aughwick Creek Antique Tractor Show Sept. 20-22
PA   27th Annual Gratz Area Antique Machinery Association Lawn and Garden
       Tractor Show & Tractor Pull July 19-21
PA   29th Annual Southern Cove Power Reunion Association Antique Tractor and
       Engine Show Sept. 13-15
PA   61st Annual Williams Grove Historical Steam Engine 9 Day Show
       Aug. 25-Sept. 2
PA   6th Annual Smicksburg Antique Tractor, Machinery & Truck Show Oct. 12-13
PA   Alum Bank Community Fire Co. Antique & Classic Weekend July 11-14
TN   Greene County Antique Farm & Auto Show Sept. 20-22

■ Gravely
MD   Gravely Tractor Club of America Mow-In 2019 Aug. 22-24

■ Hit and Miss
IL   60th Annual Steam, Gas and Threshing Show Aug. 14-18
IN   42nd Annual Northern Indiana Power from the Past Antique Show July 18-21
IN   Greensburg Power of the Past 29th Annual Reunion Aug. 15-18
MI   21st Annual Big Rapids Antique Farm & Power Club Swap Meet and Flea
       Market July 26-27
MI   30th Annual Southeast Michigan Antique Tractor & Engine Show July 18-20
MI   Big Rapids Antique Farm & Power Club Swap Meet and Flea Market June 7-8
OH   43rd Annual Old Fashioned Farmers Days July 4-6
PA   54th Annual Fall Festival Tioga County Early Days Oct. 11-13
PA   Chickentown Gas and Steam Show May 25-26
UT   RW Erickson Antique Power Show June 21-23

Feature

■ International/International Harvester/Farmall/Cub Cadet

AL	Jean's on the River Antique Tractor Show Oct. 12
AL	Southland Flywheelers Fall Festival and Harvest Exhibits Oct. 26
AR	20th Annual Tractor, Implement, and Engine Show May 31-June 1
CA	ATHS Show April 27
CA	California Antique Farm Show April 12-14
CA	International Harvester Sierra Fall Rallye Oct. 4-6
CA	Winter Meeting Feb. 23
CA	World AG Expo Feb. 12-14
FL	12th Annual Tractor Show Feb. 14-16
FL	International Harvester Collectors Club, Florida Chapter 27 3rd Annual Fort Christmas School Students Farm Show Oct. 3-4
FL	International Harvester Collectors Club, Florida Chapter 27 at the 12th Annual Tractor Show at Paquette's Historical Farmall Museum Feb. 14-16
FL	International Harvester Collectors Club, Florida Chapter 27 at the 27th Annual Florida Flywheelers Engine & Tractor Show Feb. 20-23
FL	International Harvester Collectors Club, Florida Chapter 27 at the 32nd Annual Antique Engine and Tractor "Swap Meet" Show Jan. 16-19
FL	International Harvester Collectors Club, Florida Chapter 27 Cracker Christmas Antique Engine & Tractor Show Dec. 7-8
FL	International Harvester Collectors Club, Florida Chapter 27 Lake Wales Pioneer Days Oct. 26-27
IA	35th Annual Steam Threshing and Plowing Show Aug. 2-4
IA	35th Annual Threshing Bee July 19-21
IA	Northeast Iowa Antique Engine and Power Show Aug. 10-11
IL	30th Annual Southern Illinois Antique Power Club Antique Power Days Sept. 5-8
IL	52nd Annual Western Illinois Thresher's Bee, Craft Show and Flea Market Aug. 2-4
IL	Annual Heritage Days Show July 26-28
IL	Historic Farm Days July 11-14
IN	37th Annual Noble County Gas and Steam Show and Noble County Community Fair July 14-20
IN	Brown County Antique Engine and Tractor Show Sept. 13-14
KS	Caney Valley Antique Power Assn. Pioneer Days May 31-June 2
KS	Heritage Day Festival Oct. 5
KY	33rd Annual Farm Festival Oct. 5-6
LA	IHC LA Chapter #31 Tractor and Engine Show May 2-4
MD	Rural Heritage Spud Fest & Antique Tractor Show Aug. 24-25
MI	21st Annual Coopersville Tractor Show Aug. 7-10
MI	26th Annual Farmer's Antique Tractor and Engine Spring Show May 18-20
MI	34th Annual Farmer's Antique Tractor and Engine Fall Show Sept. 20-22
MI	45th Annual Mid-Michigan Old Gas Tractor Show Aug. 16-18
MI	48th Annual Antique Gas and Steam Engine Show July 12-14
MN	45th Annual Rice County Steam and Gas Engines Show Aug. 30-Sept. 1
MN	Atwater Threshing Days Sept. 7-8
MO	41st Annual Lathrop Antique Car, Tractor & Engine Show June 13-16
MO	43rd Old Timers' Day May 25-26
MO	JP's 18th Midwest Cub-Arama Sept. 26-28
MO	Mark Twain Old Threshers July 11-13
NE	23rd Annual Antique Tractor and Farm Machinery Show Aug. 2-4
NE	Pierce Old Time Threshers Bee Sept. 7-8
NY	26th Annual Long Island Antique Power Assn. Show July 13-14
NY	42nd Annual Chemung Valley Old Timers Show July 19-21
OH	34th Annual International Convention and Old Equipment Exposition Sept. 13-15
OH	49th Annual Reunion Ohio Valley Antique Machinery Show Aug. 8-11
OK	29th Annual National Two-Cylinder Tractor Show Sept. 27-28
PA	25th Harvester Dreamland Show Aug. 1-4
PA	Glades Highlands Antique Iron Assn. 18th Tractor Show June 14-16
PA	International Harvester Summer Show June 21-22
SC	Power From The Past Tractor Show and Swap Meet May 18
TN	3rd Annual Smoky Mountain Flywheelers Show Aug. 1-3

VA	9th Annual International Harvesters Collectors of Virginia Summer Show June 14-16
VA	Pageant of Steam July 26-28
VA	Toy Show March 22-23
WA	Spokane Inter State Fair Sept. 6-15
WI	63rd Reunion of the Rock River Thresheree Aug. 30-Sept. 2
WI	Pioneer Farm Days Oct. 12-13

■ John Deere

CA	California Antique Farm Equipment Show April 12-14
FL	International Harvester Collectors Club, Florida Chapter 27 Lake Wales Pioneer Days Oct. 26-27
FL	North Florida Antique Tractor Club with the Dudley Farms Florida State Park March 1-2
IA	Midwest Old Threshers Reunion Aug. 29-Sept. 2
IL	48th Annual Engine, Tractor, and Toy Show June 29
IL	Hamilton County Ageless Iron July 6
IL	Sublette Farm Toy and Antique Tractor Show March 16-17
IN	42nd Annual Summer Show - Maumee Valley Steam and Gas Association Aug. 15-18
IN	43rd Annual Northern Indiana Historical Power Association Fall Harvest Festival and Antique Equipment Show Sept. 27-29
IN	Southern Indiana's Antique and Machinery Club Classic Iron Show June 7-9
KS	62nd Annual McLouth Threshing Bee Sept. 20-22
KS	Goessel Country Threshing Days Aug. 2-4
MA	Retired Iron Tractor Show July 6-7
MD	Hampstead Day Tractor Show May 25
MI	30th Annual Clarksville Steam and Gas Engine Tractor Show Aug. 22-24
MI	44th Annual U.P. Steam and Gas Engine Show Aug. 30-Sept. 2
MN	27th Annual Field Days, Swap Meet & Auction May 4-5
MN	29th Annual Little Log House Antique Power Show July 26-28
MN	Butterfield Steam and Gas Engine Show Aug. 17-18
MO	32nd Annual Northeast Missouri Old Threshers Sept. 12-15
MO	Livingston County Steam and Gas Association Old Time Harvest Days Sept. 27-28
MO	Western Missouri Antique Tractor & Machinery Association June 28-30
MT	North Central Montana Antique Show May 31-June 2
NE	37th Annual Old Trusty Antique Engine and Collectors Show Sept. 7-8
NE	40th Annual Mid-States Antique Tractor & Engine Show July 27-28
NY	New York State Two-Cylinder Expo XIV July 11-13
OH	19th Annual Crawford Farm Show June 20-22
OH	20th Annual Carroll County Antique Power Show Oct. 18-20
OH	Medina County Antique Power Association EDGETA br 192 Show July 12-13
OH	Paint Valley Antique Machinery Club Fall Festival of Leaves Tractor, Toy & Machinery Show Oct. 18-20
OH	Summer Show - Bainbridge July 26
OK	19th Annual Central Oklahoma Antique Tractor Club Farm and Road Show May 18
OK	29th Annual Route 66 Flywheelers Gas Engine and Tractor Show Oct. 18-19
PA	12th Annual Historic Burnt Cabins Grist Mill Antique Tractor Show July 13-14
PA	24th Annual Early American Steam Engine Society Spring Fling Weekend and 25th Annual Little Guys Show May 3-5
PA	25th Annual Susquehanna Antique Machinery Summer Show Aug. 17-18
PA	25th Annual Twin Tier Antique Tractor and Machinery Association Show June 14-16
PA	John Deere Days July 26-27
SD	45th Annual James Valley Threshing & Tractor Club Show Sept. 6-8
SD	Twin Brooks Threshing Show Aug. 10-11
TN	Billy McKnight Memorial Antique Tractor and Engine Show Nov. 1-2
TN	Tractor Show On The Creek Aug. 24
WI	16th Annual Fall Harvest Festival Sept. 27-29

Feature

WI   46th Annual North Central Wisconsin Antique Steam and Gas Engine Club Show Aug. 23-25
WI   Wheels of Time Oct. 4-6

■ Leader
IN   35th Annual White River Valley Antique Antique Show Sept. 5-8

■ Massey-Ferguson/Massey-Harris
AB   Harvest Festival Reynolds-Alberta Museum Aug. 31-Sept. 1
AB   Heritage Acres Annual Show Aug. 2-5
IA   49th Annual Albert City Threshermen and Collectors Show Aug. 9-11
IL   23rd Annual County Line Sod Busters Prairie Days July 19-21
IL   50th Annual Steam Show and Fall Festival Sept. 27-29
IL   71st Annual Central States Threshermen's Reunion Aug. 29-Sept. 2
IL   Adams County Olde Tyme Threshing Show July 26-29
IL   Fall Festival Sept. 21-22
IL   Olden Days Aug. 24-25
IL   Spring Festival May 25-26
IN   10th Annual Jackson County Antique Machinery Show May 9-11
IN   23rd Annual S.E. Indiana F.A.R.M. Club's Antique Machinery Show June 27-29
IN   27th Annual Warren Area Antique Tractor and Engine Show July 4-6
IN   42nd Annual Summer Show - Maumee Valley Steam and Gas Association Aug. 15-18
IN   44th Annual Lanesville Heritage Weekend Sept. 12-15
KS   38th Annual Kansas and Oklahoma Steam and Gas Engine Association Show Aug. 16-18
KS   41st Annual Fall Festival and Swap Meet Sept. 28-29
KS   43rd Annual Threshing Show July 19-21
KY   27th Annual Antique Tractor & Engine Show July 20-21
MA   Charter Day Antique Tractor Pull & Show June 9
MN   49th Annual Nowthen Historical Power Threshing Show Aug. 16-18
MN   Pioneer Power Good Old Days & Threshing Show Aug. 3-4
MO   Platte County Steam Engine Show Aug. 8-11
OH   56th Annual Dover Steam Show Aug. 16-18
OH   Holmes County Steam & Engine Show Aug. 1-3
ON   41st Annual Heritage Show June 15-16
PA   24th Annual Fort Allen Antique Farm Equipment Association Summer Fun and Ice Cream Festival July 20-21
PA   30th Annual Summer Show Aug. 10-11
PA   45th Annual Spring Show May 31-June 2
PA   Annual Fall Show Sept. 5-8
PA   Spring Plowing Show April 27-28
SD   Harvest Festival Sept. 14-15
TN   Three Rivers Antique Tractor and Engine Show Oct. 11-12
WI   48th Annual Show Coulee Antique Engine Club Aug. 2-4
WI   67th Annual Wisconsin Steam Engine Show Aug. 10-11
WI   8th Annual Glacier Ridge Antique Tractor Sept. 21-22

■ Maytag
MO   Steam-O-Rama Sept. 12-15

■ Minneapolis-Moline
IA   30th Annual Prairie Homestead Antique Power Tractor Show Aug. 16-18
IA   36th Annual Steam Threshing Festival June 7-9
IA   Carstens Farm Days Sept. 7-8
IA   Cedar Valley Engine Club Threshers Reunion Aug. 31-Sept. 2
IL   38th Annual Mill Road Thresherman's Show Aug. 9-11
IL   43rd Annual Bond County Antique Machinery Expo Aug. 2-4
IN   Hoosier Heritage Fest July 26-28
IN   Winter Tractor and Gas Engine Show March 14-16
MD   57th Annual Steam and Gas Round-Up Mason-Dixon Historical Society Sept. 6-8

Feature

MI	30th Annual Southeast Michigan Antique Tractor & Engine Show July 18-20
MI	Twenty Lakes Antique Engine and Tractor Show June 19-23
MT	Huntley Project Threshing Bee Aug. 17-18
NE	37th Annual Antique Machinery Show Aug. 11
NE	Nebraska State Antique Tractor and Horse Plowing Bee/Rae Valley Old Threshers Reunion Aug. 24-25
NE	Tractors & Treasures Sept. 21-22
OH	49th Annual Old Timers Club Old Timer's Days Sept. 27-29
OH	49th LaGrange Engine Club Show Sept. 20-22
OH	Old Iron Power Club & Appalachian Foot Hills Fall Festival Sept. 21-22
ON	Tractor & Engine Antique Show Aug. 31-Sept. 1
ON	Waterloo County Steam Threshers' Reunion Aug. 23-24
PA	39th Annual Grease, Steam and Rust Association Antique Tractor, Small Engine, and Machinery Show Oct. 18-20
PA	71st Annual Rough and Tumble Engineers Historical Threshermen's Reunion Aug. 14-17
PA	Two-Top Steam and Gas Show Sept. 20-22
WA	Threshing Bee and Tractor Show Aug. 9-11
WI	31st Annual R.S. Vintage Steel Steam and Gas Engine Show Sept. 14-15
WI	33rd Annual Pickett Steam and Gas Engine Show Sept. 7-8
WI	52nd Annual Union Threshermen's Club Thresheree and National Antique Tractor Pull July 26-28
WI	56th Annual Badger Steam and Gas Engine Club Show Aug. 16-18

■ Oddballs and Orphans

IN	44th Annual Lanesville Heritage Weekend Sept. 12-15
IN	Greensburg Power of the Past 29th Annual Reunion Aug. 15-18
IN	YesterYear Power Club Tractor and Engine Show Aug. 3
OH	29th Annual Clermont County Antique Machinery Show Aug. 2-4
OH	43rd Annual Old Fashioned Farmers Days July 4-6
PA	54th Annual Fall Festival Tioga County Early Days Oct. 11-13
PA	Antique Engine, Tractor and Toy Club 34th Annual Show June 7-9

■ Oliver Hart-Parr

IA	24th Annual Cedar Valley Memories Aug. 10-11
IA	55th Annual Antique Acres Old Time Power Show Aug. 16-18
IL	33rd Annual Oblong Antique Tractor and Engine Assn. Show Aug. 9-11
IL	43rd Annual Bond County Antique Machinery Expo Aug. 2-4
IL	57th Annual Reunion of The Will County Threshermen's Association July 18-21
IL	60th Annual Steam, Gas and Threshing Show Aug. 14-18
IL	71st Annual Central States Threshermen's Reunion Aug. 29-Sept. 2
IL	Thee Olde Time Farm Show July 5-7
KS	21st Annual Wilson County Old Iron Days Sept. 26-29
KY	24th Annual South East Kentucky Antique Tractor Show Oct. 3-5
MD	42nd Annual Kingsdale Gas Engine Show June 1-2
MI	29th Annual Antique Farm Power Club Antique Tractor and Engine Show June 6-8
MI	Olde Tyme Plow Days and Swap Meet April 27-28
MN	46th Annual Le Sueur County Pioneer Power Show Aug. 23-25
NE	43rd Annual Camp Creek Threshers Association Show July 20-21
OH	24th Annual F.A.R.M. Inc FARM Tractor Show July 26-28
OH	49th Annual Old Timers Club Old Timer's Days Sept. 27-29
OH	49th LaGrange Engine Club Show Sept. 20-22
OH	70th Annual Miami Valley Steam Threshers Show and Reunion July 18-21
OH	Flat Rock Creek Fall Festival Sept. 20-22
OH	Harvest Happenings Oct. 5-6
ON	Niagara Antique Power Heritage Display June 29-July 1
PA	12th Annual Fall Harvest Fest Oct. 4-5
PA	33rd Annual Menges Mills Historic Horse, Steam and Gas Show July 12-14
PA	52nd Annual Pioneer Steam and Gas Engine Society of Northwestern Pennsylvania July 19-21

Feature

PA	Vintage Iron Club 15th Annual Fall Festival and Show Sept. 13-15
WI	21st Annual Mid-Lakes Thresheree & Tractor Show Sept. 7-8
WI	33rd Annual Pickett Steam and Gas Engine Show Sept. 7-8
WI	51st Annual Dodge County Antique Power Show Aug. 2-4
WI	56th Annual Chippewa Valley Antique Engine and Model Club Pioneer Days Aug. 9-11
WI	Berlin Antique Equipment Show Oct. 5-6
WI	Berlin Area Antique Equipment 4th Annual Tractor Show Oct. 5-6
WI	Northern Aged Iron Tractor & Threshing Show Sept. 21-22

■ Rumley

IN	Rumely Allis Chalmers La Porte Heritage Center Tractor Show Sept. 20-22
MI	59th Annual Show Aug. 2-4
MN	27th Annual Rumely Products Collectors Expo Aug. 31-Sept. 2
MN	41st Annual White Pine Logging & Threshing Show Aug. 31-Sept. 2
MO	Steam-O-Rama Sept. 12-15
NY	59th Annual New York Steam Engine Pageant of Steam Aug. 7-10
OH	49th Annual Historical Engine Society's Antique Power Exhibition July 26-28
ON	Blyth Steam Show Sept. 6-8

■ Silver King

MI	Waldron Antique Tractor Show Aug. 31-Sept. 2

■ Stover

IL	50th Annual Old-Time Threshing and Antique Show Aug. 2-4
IN	25th Annual Franklin County Antique Machinery Show Sept. 26-29

■ Wheel Horse

IN	42nd Annual Summer Show - Maumee Valley Steam and Gas Association Aug. 15-18
MD	46th Annual Tuckahoe Steam and Gas Engine Reunion and Show July 11-14
OH	22nd Annual Antique Tractor & Gas Engine Show and 64th Annual Richland County Steam Threshers Sept. 7-8
OH	43rd Annual Old Fashioned Farmers Days July 4-6
OH	49th Annual Historical Engine Society's Antique Power Exhibition July 26-28
OH	Antique Tractor & Machinery Show May 31-June 2
PA	12th Annual Historic Burnt Cabins Grist Mill Antique Tractor Show July 13-14
PA	21st Annual Wheel Horse Show June 21-22

FARM COLLECTOR
SHOW DIRECTORY
2019

REFERENCE

Advertising

Allis-Chalmers Old Allis News WI 251
Almelund Threshing Show MN 214
American Farm Heritage Museum IL 186
American Thresherman Association Inc. IL 28
Antique Acres IA 197
Antique Farm Power Club MI 202
Antique Steam and Gas Engine Club Inc. IN 191
Ashland County Yesteryear Machinery Club OH 220
Ashtabula County Antique Engine Club Inc. OH 229
Badger Steam and Gas Engine Club WI 247
Blue Mountain Antique Gas and Steam Engine Association Inc. PA 16
Bond County Antique Machinery Club IL 187
Bos Brothers IL 17
Brown County Antique Machinery Association IN 195
Bryan County Antique Tractor Club OK 231
Buckeye Farm Antiques Inc. OH 223
Buckeye Iron Will Club OH 231
Buffalo Valley Antique Machinery Association PA 243
Butler County Antique Engine and Tractor Club KY 200
Catskill Mountain Antique Gas Engine and Machinery Club NY 219
Central Kentucky Antique Machinery Association KY 18
Central Maryland Antique Tractor Club MD 199
Central States Threshermen IL 185
Charlton Park Antique Gas and Steam Engine Club MI 209
Chemung Valley Old Timers Association NY 219
Clay County Historical Society/Old Trusty Antique Engine and Collectors NE 217
Coolspring Power Museum PA 240
County Line Sod Busters IL 187
Cumberland Valley Antique Engine & Machinery Association PA 240
Cumming Antique Power Assn./Cumming Fairgrounds GA 184
Darke County Steam Threshers Association, Inc. OH 231
Days Gone By Tractor and Threshing Club TN 244
Deer Creek Sodbusters Inc. NE 217
Dodge County Antique Power Club WI 248
Double D Living History Farm CT 10
Early American Steam Engine and Old Equipment Society PA 237
Eastern Shore Threshermen and Collectors Assn. Inc. MD 202
Ebenshade Farms OK 231
Empire Tractor Owners Club PA 243
Endless Mountains Antique Power Equipment Association PA 243
Fairfield County Antique Tractor Club OH 230
Farm Power Club IN 190
Farmer's Antique Tractor and Engine Association MI 209
Fawn Grove Olde Tyme Days PA 241
Florida Flywheelers Antique Engine Club FL 183
Ford Fordson Collectors Association PA 23
Fort Allen Antique Farm Equipment Association Inc. PA 241
Franklin County Antique Machinery Club Inc. IN 25
Fulton County Historical Power Association c/o Fulton County Historical Society IN 196
Granite State Gas and Steam Engine Assn. NH 218
Gratz Area Antique Machinery Association Inc. PA 233
Grease, Steam and Rust Association Inc. PA 238
Greensburg Power of the Past IN 26
Greenville Farm Power of the Past OH 224

Halifax Antique Machinery Club VA 245
Heritage Park of North Iowa IA.. 197
Historical Construction Equipment Association OH..................................... 222
Historical Engine Society OH 224
Hudson Mills Old Power Club MI 211
Hudson-Mohawk Chapter Pioneer Gas Engine Association, Inc. NY 219
Hungry Hollow Steam and Gas Engine Club Inc. WI.................................. 250
I&I Antique Tractor and Gas Engine Club IL 14, 15
International Cockshutt Club Inc. OH.. 230
International Cockshutt Club Inc. ON.. 251
International J.I. Case Heritage Foundation MN.. 7
International Rumely Products Collectors Inc. MN.. 6
Ixonia Vintage Tractor Club WI..11
J.I. Case Collectors Association SD... 246
J.I. Case Collectors Association WI.. 246
Jackson County Antique Machinery Association Inc. IN.............................. 194
Johnson County Antique Machinery Association IN 192
Jugville Old Engine Club MI 211
Kalamazoo Valley Antique Tractor, Engine, and Machinery Club MI............. 203
K&O Steam and Gas Engine Association Inc. KS 198
Lanesville Heritage Weekend IN.. 188
Lathrop Antique Car, Tractor and Engine Club MO.................................... 216
Le Sueur County Pioneer Power   MN.. 213
Legacy of the Plains Museum NE 217
Little Log House Properties MN... 213
Loyalsock Valley Antique Machinery Assn. Inc. PA 238
Major County Historical Society / Red Carpet Country OK 232
Marshall County Antique Power Association WV 251
Marshall-Putnam Antique Association IL 183
Maryland Steam Historical Society, Inc. MD...201
Mason-Dixon Historical Society Inc. MD... 200
McCracken County FFA Alumni Antique Gas Engine and Tractor Club KY 4
Menges Mills Historic Horse, Steam and Gas Association PA...................... 241
Meriden Antique Engine and Threshers Association KS 199
Miami Valley Steam Threshers Association OH 225
Michigan Flywheelers Museum MI 202, 206
Michigan Steam Engine and Thresher's Club MI....................................... 205
Mid-America Threshing and Antiques Inc. IN.. 195
Mid-Florida Antique Machinery Club FL 183
Mid-Michigan Antique Machinery Association MI 210
Mid-Michigan Old Gas Tractor Association, Inc. MI.................................... 206
Mid-Ohio Antique Farm Machinery Show, Inc. OH 229
Midwest Old Settlers and Threshers Association IA 24
Mill Road Thresherman's Association IL 185
Minnesota Association of Antique Power Shows (MAAPS) MN..................... 214
Minnesota's Machinery Museum & Pioneer Power Threshing Club MN.......... 213
Mitchell County Historical Society/Cedar Valley Memories IA 196
Montgomery County Antique Tractor and Engine Club TN 244
Montgomery County Old Threshers Assn. MO 216
Montour Antique Farm Machinery Collectors Association PA 2
Moon Lake Threshermens Association, Inc. WI... 9
Morgan County Antique Machinery Association IN..................................... 195
Morrow County Tractor and Equipment Association, Inc. OH 221
Murray County Antique Tractor and Implement Association OK 233
National Pike Steam, Gas and Horse Assn. Inc. PA 22
National Threshers Association, Inc. OH 228
New Centerville and Rural Volunteer Fire Co. PA 244
New York State Two-Cylinder Expo Association, Inc. NY 220

Index

New York Steam Engine Association NY 218
Nittany Antique Machinery Association Inc. of Central Pennsylvania PA 236
North Central Wisconsin Antique Steam and Gas Engine Club Inc. WI............................ 248
Northeast Indiana Steam and Gas Association IN 192
Northern Illinois Steam Power Club IL.. 185
Northern Indiana Historical Power Association   IN 193
Northern Indiana Power from the Past Inc. IN 196
Northern Michigan Antique - Flywheelers MI..210
Northern Neck Farm Museum VA 245
Northwest Michigan Engine and Thresher Club Inc. MI... 207
Northwest Ohio Antique Machinery Association OH 225
Nowthen Historical Power Association MN 212
Oblong Antique Tractor and Engine Association Inc. IL 186
Ohio Valley Antique Machinery Club OH 226
Oklahoma Steam Threshing and Gas Engine Association OK.. 230
Old Farmers Antique Club   WI.. 250
Old Fashioned Farmers Association Inc. OH 226
Old Timers Club Inc. OH 229
Ole Smoky Antique Tractor and Engine Association NC.. 220
Page County Heritage Assoiacion VA.. 245
Past to Present Machinery Association PA 242
Paulding County Flat Rock Creek Gas and Steam   OH 227
Pickett Steam and Gas Engine Club WI 250
Pioneer Engineers Club IN 193
Pioneer Harvest Fiesta Inc. KS.. 198
Pioneer Power Antique Tractor and Gas Engine Club MI..210
Pioneer Steam and Gas Engine Society of Northwestern Pennsylvania Inc. PA............. 239
Platte County Steam Engine Show, Inc. MO.. 216
Platte Valley Antique Machinery Association NE 217
Prairie Homestead Antique Power Club IA 197
Rock River Thresheree Inc. WI 249
Rockville-Centerville Steam and Gas Historical Association VA.. 20
Rough and Tumble Engineers Historical Association PA 21
Rust N Dust Steam & Gas MI..211
S.E. Indiana F.A.R.M. Club IN... 191
Sandusky County Restorers of Antique Power   OH... 227
Santa Fe Trail Center Museum KS.. 199
Scott-Carver Old Threshers MN.. 213
Scotts Olde Tyme Power and Equipment Association MI 211
Shenandoah Valley Steam and Gas Association VA 246
Sherman's Valley Heritage Days, Inc. PA 243
Somerset Steam and Gas Engine Association VA... 245
Soulé Live Steam Mississippi Industrial Heritage Museum MS...................................... 215
South Central Pennsylvania Historical Lifestyle and Power Society PA........................ 239
Southeast Michigan Antique Tractor and Engine Association MI 210
Southeastern Wisconsin Antique Power and Collectibles Society WI............................. 250
Southern Cove Power Reunion Association PA 234
Southern Illinois Antique Power Club IL.. 186
Southern Indiana's Antique and Machinery Club Inc. IN 196
St. Clair County Farm Museum MI 207
St. Joe Valley Old Engine Association MI 204
Stephenson County Antique Engine Club IL 187
Stumptown Steam Threshers Club OH.. 228
Susquehanna Old Fashioned Field Days PA 242
Tennessee-Kentucky Threshermen's Association, Inc. TN 244
Texas Early Day Tractor & Engine Assn. TX.. 13

Index

Thumb Area Old Engine and Tractor Association of Michigan MI 208
Tioga County Early Days PA 19
Toy Farmer Ltd. IA 194
Tri-State Antique Engine and Thresher Show KS 198
Tri-State Antique Power Association TN 27
Tri-State Gas Engine and Tractor Association, Inc. IN ....IFC
Triple A Tractor Club Inc. IL 187
Tuckahoe Steam and Gas Engine Association   MD 29
Tuscarawas Valley Pioneer Power Association   OH 230
U.P. Steam and Gas Engine Association MI 208
Union Threshermen's Club WI 249
Upper Midwest Allis-Chalmers Club MN 214
Western Illinois Threshers   IL 186
Western Minnesota Steam Threshers Reunion Inc. MN 214
Western New York Gas and Steam Engine Association Inc. NY 219
Wheel Horse Collectors Club PA 242
White River Valley Antique Association IN 189
Will County Threshermen's Association IL 184
Williams Grove Historical Steam Engine Association PA 235
Wilson County Old Iron Club KS 199

Commercial

Astragal Press 32
Dakotah Toys 31
Evergreen Restoration 32
Great Lakes Agri Marketing / All States Ag Parts .... IBC
Great World Buttons .... OBC
Heritage Farm Power 32
Joel P Auctions 30
Nixon Auctioneers 5
PM Research, INC. 12
Rallye Productions 3
Steiner Tractor Parts 8
N-News 31
Weaver's Magneto Repair 30, 31
Zimmerman Oliver Cletrac 32

Show Listings

January
4	IL	Illini Farm Toy Show and Auction
12	KY	Winter Antique Tractor Show
16	FL	Florida Flywheelers Antique Engine Club 32nd Annual Antique Engine & Tractor "Swap Meet"
16	FL	International Harvester Collectors Club, Florida Chapter 27 at the 32nd Annual Antique Engine and Tractor "Swap Meet" Show
17	TX	Texas Antique Tractor Show and Pull Kickoff
25	FL	20th Annual Tractor and Truck Pull
26	CA	Table Top Auction
30	NC	Southern Farm Show

February
2	GA	Hog Killing at Old South Farm Museum
8	FL	2nd Annual Dunnellon Farm Days Antique Tractor and Engine Show
9	MD	Annual Toy Auction and Toy Show
9	PA	Rough and Tumble Engineers Historical Mid-Winter Get Together
9	AZ	Sahuaro Ranch Park Winter Show
9	SK	Yorkton Farm Toy Show
12	CA	World AG Expo
14	FL	12th Annual Tractor Show
14	FL	International Harvester Collectors Club, Florida Chapter 27 at the 12th Annual Tractor Show at Paquette's Historical Farmall Museum
17	OH	Fairfield County Antique Tractor Club Toy Show
20	FL	Florida Flywheelers Antique Engine Club 27th Annual Antique Engine and Tractor Show
20	FL	International Harvester Collectors Club, Florida Chapter 27 at the 27th Annual Antique Engine and Tractor Show
20	FL	International Harvester Collectors Club, Florida Chapter 27 at the 27th Annual Florida Flywheelers Engine & Tractor Show
23	MI	16th Annual Farm Collectibles and Toy Show
23	MN	North Central Minnesota Farm and Antique Association Horse Drawn Sleigh Rides
23	CA	Table Top Auction
23	CA	Winter Meeting
28	FL	51st Annual Pioneer Park Days

March
1	KY	25th Annual Meade County Farm Toy Show & Sale
1	KY	5th Annual Tollesboro Treasure Days and Flea Market
1	FL	North Florida Antique Tractor Club with the Dudley Farms Florida State Park
2	TX	33rd Annual North Texas Farm Toy Show
2	TX	Bastrop Antique Farm Show
2	FL	Mid-Florida Antique Machinery Club Display of Antique Machines & Tractors Spring Show
3	IL	26th Annual ROWVA FFA and Alumni Toy Show Auction
8	IL	ECIA Antique Tractor Show
9	AZ	2019 Winter Meeting - Apache Junction, AZ.
9	KY	23rd Butler County FFA Farm Toy and Antique Tractor Show
9	PA	3rd Annual Toy Show
9	AZ	Arizona Junction Spring Show
9	AZ	Vintage Garden Tractor Club of America Southwest Regional Show
10	OH	28th Annual Union Local FFA Farm Toy Show
14	IL	25th Annual Antique Tractor Show Sponsored by the Triple A Tractor Club, Inc.
14	IN	Winter Tractor and Gas Engine Show
15	AZ	35th Annual Arizona Flywheelers Show
15	VA	Riverheads Young Farmers Farm Toy Show & Sale

Index

16 LA   Jena Spring Tractor Show and Pull
16 AR   Rusty Wheels Old Engine Club Jonquil Festival
16 AL   Southland Flywheelers Spring Show and Swap Meet
16 IL   Sublette Farm Toy and Antique Tractor Show
22 VA   Toy Show
23 CA   Table Top Auction
30 TN   21st Annual Flint River Antique Tractor and Farm Equipment
30 NC   Cotton Ginning Days Swap Meet
30 SC   Farm Day
30 WV   Spring Swap Meet
31 ON   Bruce County Heritage Assn. Toy Show

April

4   TN   Spring Antique Tractor, Engine, Car & Motorcycle Show and Flea Market
5   IN   16th Annual White River Valley Antique Swap Meet and Barn Market
5   TX   Canton Tractor Show and Swap Meet
6   IN   Franklin County Antique Machinery Club Swap Meet
6   MD   Friends of the Agricultural History Farm Park Gas and Steam Engine Show
6   WA   Spring Farming Days
12 OK   17th Annual Marshall County Antique Iron Tractor & Implement Show
12 CA   California Antique Farm Equipment Show
12 CA   California Antique Farm Show April 1 2 IL Corn Items Collectors Spring Meeting
12 OH   International Cockshutt Club Spring Meeting
12 MO   PC Antique Swap and Flea Market
12 NC   Spokes & Cleats Swap Meet
13 NC   10th Annual Union County Farm Show and Festival
13 AL   April Fest - Sponsored by Lawrence County Tractor Club
13 MO   Early Day Gas Engine and Tractor Assn. Branch 16 Swap Meet
13 IN   S.E. Indiana F.A.R.M. Club's Spring Swap Meet
13 WV   Wood County Flywheelers Bill Graham Plow Day
14 OH   33rd Annual Farm Toy Show
19 AR   26th Annual Spring Show
19 MI   43rd Spring Swap Meet
19 TX   Memories of Yesteryear
20 IN   4th Annual Crank-Up Gas Engine Show
20 OH   Ashland County Yesteryear Machinery Club Swap Meet
20 IN   Morgan County Antique Machinery Spring Swap Meet
20 AL   Snead Case IH Show
20 PA   Southern Cove Power Reunion Association Spring Plow Days – Antique Tractor
            and Engine Show
20 KS   Spring Crank Up! Tractor Show
20 TN   Wilson Bank & Trust Antique Tractor and Engine Show
25 KY   17th Annual Hillbilly Flywheelers Gas Engine and Tractor Show
25 TN   26th Annual Appalachian Antique Farm Show
26 CA   Early Day Gas Engine and Tractor Association Spring Gas-Up
26 MN   Le Sueur County Pioneer Power Swap Meet
26 MS   Mississippi Valley Flywheelers Spring Show
26 IN   Spring Show
26 OH   Watch Fob and Vintage Equipment Show
27 VA   23rd Annual Powhatan Spring Antique Power Show
27 TX   30th Annual Burton Cotton Gin Festival Antique Tractor Show & Pull
27 CA   ATHS Show
27 WA   EDGETA #245 Annual Spring Swap Meet
27 MI   Olde Tyme Plow Days and Swap Meet
27 PA   Rough and Tumble Engineers Historical Antique Tractor Pull
27 PA   Spring Plow, Pull, Auctions and Show Day
27 PA   Spring Plowing Show
28 CT   45th Annual Belltown Antique Engine & Tractor Meet

May

2	NC	Antique Farm Equipment Days
2	LA	IHC LA Chapter #31 Tractor and Engine Show
2	MI	Pioneer Power Antique Tractor and Gas Engine Swap Meet
3	NC	12th Annual Spring Valley Hills Antique Power Club Swap Meet
3	VA	16th Annual Halifax County Heritage and Antique Machinery Festival
3	PA	24th Annual Early American Steam Engine Society Spring Fling Weekend and 25th Annual Little Guys Show
3	MI	35th Annual Michiana Antique Engine and Tractor Swap Meet
3	OK	53rd Annual Oklahoma Steam, Tractor, and Gas Engine Show
3	WI	Badger Steam and Gas Engine Club Spring Swap Meet
4	KY	14th Annual Shopville Community Park Antique Tractor and Small Engine Show
4	IN	23rd Annual Brown County Antique Machinery Spring Swap Meet
4	MN	27th Annual Field Days, Swap Meet & Auction
4	MD	28th Annual Antique Tractor Show
4	IL	American Farm Heritage Museum Annual Swap Meet and Spring Fling Festival
4	CT	Annual Spring Power-Up
4	PA	"Diggin' Day" - Old Construction Day
4	PA	French Creek Valley Antique Equipment Club Plow Day
4	VA	Opening & Planting Day
4	IL	Swap Meet
4	WV	West Virginia State Farm Museum Antique Engine & Tractor Show
4	CT	Zagray Farm Museum Spring Gas-up and Swap Meet
5	OH	4th Annual Harrison Career Center FFA Tractor, Truck, Engine and Car Show
5	MA	Dunstable Show
5	TX	South Texas Wheel Spinners and Crank Twisters Moravia Fest
5	IL	Spring at the Farm
9	IN	10th Annual Jackson County Antique Machinery Show
10	KY	11th Annual Sycamore Flats Flywheelers Show at the Ag Center
10	PA	Rough and Tumble Engineers Historical Spring Steam-Up Show
10	MO	Spring Show - Ozarks Older Iron
10	KS	Pioneer Harvest Fiesta Swap Meet
11	OH	25th Annual Harrison Coal and Reclamation Historical Park Dinner- Auction
11	WA	36th Gas-Up
11	OH	Dean Becker - Bill Atkinson Memorial Tractor Ride
11	OH	Kidron Antique Power Show
11	MN	Spring Meeting Minnesota Association of Antique Power Shows (MAAPS)
11	OH	Spring Show - South Salem
11	KY	Sycamore Flats Flywheelers 11th Annual Show at the Ag Center
12	OH	Ashtabula County Antique Engine Club Annual Spring Gas-Up
15	IN	37th Annual Tri-State Gas Engine and Tractor Swap and Sell
15	MO	Missouri River Valley Steam Engine Ozark Flint Knappers Spring Show
16	PA	12th Annual Williams Grove Historical Steam Engine Spring Show
16	TX	Jerry Askey Memorial Show
17	IA	27th Annual Swap Meet
17	MI	37th Annual Buckley Old Engine Spring Swap Meet
17	PA	Middlecreek Valley Antique Assn. 23rd Annual Spring Antique Machinery Show
18	IL	10th Annual AJ's Garden Tractor Jamboree
18	IN	31th Annual Tractor Supply Show
18	OK	19th Annual Central Oklahoma Antique Tractor Club Farm and Road Show
18	NC	19th Annual Foothills Antique Power Show
18	MI	26th Annual Farmer's Antique Tractor and Engine Spring Show
18	PA	33rd Annual Swap Meet and Flea Market
18	CT	42nd Antique Machinery Show
18	IL	Adams County Olde Tyme Spring Swap Meet and Flea Market
18	NE	Camp Creek Threshers Swap Meet
18	MD	Farm Toy Show and Sale and Antique Tractor, Truck, and Car Show
18	ON	Haldimand County Vintage Farm Equipment & Collectibles Tour

Index

18	MD	Johnsville Ruritan Spring Show
18	IA	MAGETA Steam & Gas Engine Show
18	PA	National Pike Steam, Gas and Horse Assn. Spring Show
18	SC	Power From The Past Tractor Show and Swap Meet
18	TX	Power of the Past Show and Pull
18	VA	Spring Farm to Fork Dinner
18	PA	Spring Gas Up - Northwest PA Steam Engine and Old Equipment Association
18	TN	Tractor, Truck and Gas Engine Show
18	VA	29th Annual Spring Chapter Show
19	MA	12th Annual Hillside Tractor Ride
24	PA	18th Annual Past to Present MachineryTractor, Equipment and Machinery Show
24	OH	30th Annual Buckeye Farm Antiques Show
24	WI	Ixonia Vintage Tractor Expo
25	WV	15th Annual Engines and Wheels Festival
25	MN	19th Annual Rice County Steam and Gas Engines Swap Meet and Flea Market
25	TN	2019 Granville Heritage Day Antique Car & Tractor Show
25	AL	41st Annual Alabama Jubilee
25	MO	43rd Old Timers' Day
25	MN	Annual Flea Market and Swap Meet
25	MA	Bernardston Gas Engine Show and Flea Market
25	PA	Chickentown Gas and Steam Show
25	MD	Hampstead Day Tractor Show
25	OH	Historical Society & Paint Valley Antique Machinery Club Show
25	WI	J.I. Case Collectors Annual Spring Convention
25	AB	Leduc West Antique Society Spring Tractor Pull and Swap Meet
25	NY	New York Steam Engine Spring Flea Market and Tractor Pull
25	IL	Spring Festival
26	MN	Forest City Threshers Spring Antique Tractor Pull
31	AR	20th Annual Tractor, Implement, and Engine Show
31	NC	24th Annual Ole Smoky Antique Tractor and Engine Show
31	MI	27th Annual Hudson Mills Old Power Antique Gas Engine and Tractor Show
31	PA	45th Annual Spring Show May 3 1 OH Antique Tractor & Machinery Show
31	KS	Caney Valley Antique Power Assn. Pioneer Days
31	NY	Mohawk Valley Power of the Past Ole Time Power Show
31	MT	North Central Montana Antique Show
31	AL	SAATEC Plow Days
31	NV	ATHS National Convention and Truck Show

June

1	OH	20th Annual Planting Time Show
1	VA	29th Annual Chippokes Farm and Forestry Museum Steam and Gas Engine Show
1	IN	3nd Annual Kent Vintage Tractor Drive
1	MD	42nd Annual Kingsdale Gas Engine Show
1	OH	43rd Annual Columbia Station Engine Show
1	KY	5th Annual Salt River Antique Power Tractor Drive
1	NH	87th Annual Gas & Steam Spring Show
1	TN	Atwood Spring Tractor Show
1	MO	CAFMO June Tractor Pull and Swap Meet
1	MI	Clinton Summerfest & Antique Tractor Show
1	WV	L. Norman Dillon Farm Museum Antique Tractor and Gas Engine Spring Show
1	PA	Pioneer Steam and Gas Engine Society of Northwestern Pennsylvania Spring Gas-up & Antique Tractor Pull
1	NE	Tractor Relay Across Nebraska
1	WV	West Virginia Antique Engine and Tractor Association Mac's Fun Show
2	IL	27th Annual Gateway Two Cylinder Club Antique Tractor, Gas Engine & Toy Show
2	CT	6th Annual Spring Tractor Show and Farm Open House
6	MI	29th Annual Antique Farm Power Club Antique Tractor and Engine Show
6	TN	48th Anniversary East Tennessee Crank-Up Sponsored by the East Tennessee Antique Engine Association

Index

7	IA	36th Annual Steam Threshing Festival
7	MD	41st Annual Central Maryland Antique Tractor Club Gas Engine and Tractor Show
7	PA	Antique Engine, Tractor and Toy Club 34th Annual Show
7	KY	Antique Farm Machinery & Craft Show
7	IN	Cast Iron Seat Club Annual Meeting
7	OR	Heritage Stations Old Iron Show
7	IN	La Fontaine Ashland Days
7	AR	North Arkansas Rusty Wheels Old Engine Club Spring Show
7	TN	Smokey Mountain Antique Engine and Tractor Association Spring Festival
7	IN	Southern Indiana's Antique and Machinery Club Classic Iron Show
7	IA	Summer Farm Toy Show
7	MI	Swap Meet & Flea Market
7	IN	Wildcat Creek Antique Tractor and Engine Show
8	OH	14th Annual Antique Tractor & Power Show
8	WY	24th Anniversary Don Layton Annual Memorial Antique Tractor and Engine Show
8	IL	32nd Annual Marshall-Putnam Antique Tractor and Engine Show
8	NY	37th Annual Spring Antique Gas & Steam Engine Exhibition
8	NY	52nd Annual Hudson-Mohawk Chapter Pioneer Gas Engine Gas-Up Show
8	MI	Big Rapids Antique Farm & Power Club Swap Meet and Flea Market
8	MT	Central Montana Flywheelers Pioneer Power Days
8	PA	Nittany Farm Museum Show
8	TX	North Texas Antique Tractor & Engine Club Show & Pull
8	IN	Owen County Antique Machinery Show
8	NE	Planting Festival
8	OH	Power of Yesteryear Spring Show
8	MD	Strawberry Festival
9	OH	Antique Tractor Club of Trumbull County Ohio Tractor, Car, Truck & Motorcycle Show
9	MA	Charter Day Antique Tractor Pull & Show
13	IN	14th Annual Collector Show
13	IN	28th Annual Johnson County Antique Machinery Show
13	MO	41st Annual Lathrop Antique Car, Tractor & Engine Show
14	NC	1st Annual T-ville Vintage Power Show
14	IN	24th Annual Steuben County Antique Power Association Antique Farm Equipment Show
14	PA	25th Annual Twin Tier Antique Tractor and Machinery Association Show
14	OK	26th Annual Golden Harvest Days
14	PA	34th Anniversary Coolspring Power Museum Summer Exposition and Flea Market
14	PA	40th Annual ATCA National Meet and Flea Market
14	VA	9th Annual International Harvesters Collectors of Virginia Summer Show
14	NE	All Nebraska Tractor Ride
14	OK	Bryan County Antique Tractor Show
14	DE	First State Antique Tractor Club Show
14	PA	French Creek Valley Antique Equipment Club Show
14	IN	Fulton County Historical Power Show
14	PA	Glades Highlands Antique Iron Assn. 18th Tractor Show
14	TX	Ricebelt Antique Tractor Show and Pull for DAV
14	VT	Vermont Gas and Steam Engine Association Brownington Show
15	IL	10th Annual Amish Country Tractor Cruise
15	NY	20th Anniversary Barber Homestead Antique Tractor Show
15	IA	28th Annual The Allis Connection "All Allis" Father's Day Weekend Show
15	OR	34th Annual EDGE&TA Branch 9 Pioneer Fair, Tractor Show and Pull
15	ON	41st Annual Heritage Show
15	OH	8th Annual Ohio Vintage Truck Jamboree
15	NC	Annual Harvest Wheat, Binding, & Threshing Show
15	CA	Antique Engine & Tractor Show
15	KY	Clark County Antique Tractor & Machinery Show
15	MN	Farming of Yesteryear Horse and Mule Show

Index

15 SD   Huron Area Antique Power Show
15 IN   Randolph County Antique Garden Tractor Pull, Show, and Old Iron Swap Meet
15 MN   University of Rollag Steam Traction Engineering Course
15 WV   Wood County Flywheelers One Day Show
16 ON   23rd Annual Father's Day Smoke & Steam Show
16 MB   Pioneer Power & Equipment Club Summer Show
16 OH   Washboard Music Festival Antique Tractor/Vehicle Show
19 NE   Homestead Days
19 MI   Twenty Lakes Antique Engine and Tractor Show
20 OH   19th Annual Crawford Farm Show
21 PA   21st Annual Wheel Horse Show
21 WV   25th Annual Gas Engine Show
21 KS   31st Annual Tractor and Engine Show
21 NE   51st Annual JayHusker Swap Meet & Show
21 OK   Farming Heritage Festival
21 PA   International Harvester Summer Show
21 PA   Rough and Tumble Engineers Historical IHC Spring Show and Rough and Tumble
           Tractor Pull Show
21 UT   RW Erickson Antique Power Show
22 IN   27th Annual Morgan County Antique Machinery Show
22 CA   Antique Engine & Tractor Show
22 NE   Cortland Antique Tractor Show
22 MD   Howard County Summer Fest
22 IL   Marbold Farmstead Antique Show & Farm Fest
26 IN   29th Annual Hoosier Flywheelers Show
27 IN   23rd Annual S.E. Indiana F.A.R.M. Club's Antique Machinery Show
27 OH   75th Annual National Threshers Reunion
28 IL   15th Annual Railroad Days Spoon River Antique Agriculture Association Toy and
           Tractor Show
28 PA   30th Annual Fawn Grove Olde Tyme Days Show
28 PA   35th Annual Latimore Valley Fair and Tractor Pull
28 MI   AuSable Valley Engine and Tractor Show
28 OH   Highland County Antique Machinery Show
28 NY   Kreiner/Loomis Antique Gas Engine and Tractor
28 IN   Olde Time Engine and Tractor Show
28 IL   Tractor Parade Through Sandwich
28 MO   Western Missouri Antique Tractor & Machinery Association
29 IN   17th Annual Covered Bridge Antique Power Tractor Tour
29 MA   43nd Annual Central Mass Steam Gas & Machinery Association Yankee
           Engine-uity Show
29 IL   48th Annual Engine, Tractor, and Toy Show
29 WI   50th Annual Show Hungry Hollow Steam and Gas Engine Club Inc.
29 PA   70th Annual Kutztown Folk Festival
29 ON   Niagara Antique Power Heritage Display
29 WI   Pickett Independence Pull
29 MT   Pioneer Days
29 PA   Southern Cove Power Reunion Association Tractor Ride
30 IL   Tractor Ride - Sandwich Early Day Engine Club

July

2   NC   49th Annual Southeast Old Threshers' Reunion
2   AL   Piney Chapel American Farm Heritage Days
4   IL   12th Annual Carmi Lions Tractor, Truck and Car Show
4   OH   22nd Annual Beverly Lions Club Antique Tractor & Engine Show
4   IN   27th Annual Warren Area Antique Tractor and Engine Show
4   OH   43rd Annual Old Fashioned Farmers Days
4   OH   63rd Annual Darke County Steam Threshers Show
4   KS   Kaw Valley Engine Truck & Tractor Club

Index

5	OH	38th Annual Ashtabula County Antique Engine Club Three-Day Show
5	NY	Antique Tractors and Engines working for Diabetes
5	MI	Port Hope Antique Gas Engine and Tractor Show
5	IL	Thee Olde Time Farm Show
6	OH	14th Annual Outville Power Show
6	ON	2018 BF Avery Summer Show
6	OH	27th Annual Ashland County Yesteryear Machinery Club Show
6	ME	Antique Engine & Outboard Meet
6	NE	Grover Cleveland Alexander Days Antique Tractor Display, Games, and Parade
6	IL	Hamilton County Ageless Iron
6	WI	Pickett Engine Show
6	MA	Retired Iron Tractor Show
6	KY	Sycamore Flats Flywheelers Lakefest Historic Machinery Show
6	VA	Threshing Day
6	NY	Tri-County Old Time Power Gas Engine Show Representing 42 Years
6	IN	Vigo County Fair Antique Tractor, Threshing and Gas Engine Show
7	MT	Miracle of America Museum Live History Days
7	IN	Vigo County Fair
8	IN	Greentown Lions Club Pioneer Village Tractor & Engine Show
11	PA	28th Annual Ford/Fordson Collectors Association Show & Meeting
11	MD	46th Annual Tuckahoe Steam and Gas Engine Reunion and Show
11	WI	50th Anniversary John Deere Patio (Custom Colors)
11	PA	Alum Bank Community Fire Co. Antique & Classic Weekend
11	WI	Garden Tractor Daze
11	OH	Greenville Farm Power of the Past
11	IL	Historic Farm Days
11	IL	I&I Antique Tractor and Gas Show
11	MI	Jugville Old Engine Club Annual Show
11	MO	Mark Twain Old Threshers
11	WI	National Case Colt Ingersoll Collectors Convention at Annual Garden Tractor Daze
11	NY	New York State Two-Cylinder Expo XIV
11	SD	WNAX Tri-State Old Iron Tractor Ride
12	WA	2019 NorthWest Regional "Pioneer Power of the Pacific NorthWest"
12	PA	26th Annual Endless Mountains Antique Power Equipment Antique Tractor, Engine and Machinery Show
12	PA	33rd Annual Menges Mills Historic Horse, Steam and Gas Show
12	IN	35th Annual Antique Farm & Tractor Show
12	MI	3rd Annual Antique Tractor and Equipment Show
12	MI	3rd Annual Heart of Michigan Antique Tractor Club Show
12	MI	48th Annual Antique Gas and Steam Engine Show
12	WV	Boston's Antique Engine Show
12	ON	Heritage & Antique Show
12	OH	Medina County Antique Power Association EDGETA br 192 Show
12	OH	Ohio Hills Folk Festival
12	ON	Vintage Garden Tractor Club of America Canadian Regional Show
12	MI	Vintage Garden Tractor Club of America National Expo 2019
12	WI	Wabeno Steam-Up Days
12	MN	Waverly Daze Tractor Show
12	NE	Windmiller's Trade Fair
13	OH	12th Annual Coshocton County Antique Power Association Summer Show
13	PA	12th Annual Historic Burnt Cabins Grist Mill Antique Tractor Show
13	IA	20th Annual Tractor Tour
13	NY	26th Annual Long Island Antique Power Assn. Show
13	ND	Fort Ransom Sodbuster Days
13	MN	North Central Minnesota Farm and Antique Association Gearhead Car Show
13	SK	Pion-Era 2019
13	IL	Rock Falls Antique Tractor and Engine Show
13	IA	Threshing Day

Index

14	MI	31st Annual Midland Antique Engine
14	IN	37th Annual Noble County Gas and Steam Show and Noble County Community Fair
14	MI	Summer Show at the Barry County Fair
15	NY	Allegany County Fair
17	VA	50th Annual Bridgewater Volunteer Fire Co. Steam and Gas Meet
18	VA	12th Annual Summer Show
18	IL	21st Annual ECIA Summer Show
18	MI	26th Annual Pioneer Power Antique Tractor and Gas Engine Show, Flea Market and Crafts
18	MI	30th Annual Southeast Michigan Antique Tractor & Engine Show
18	IN	42nd Annual Northern Indiana Power from the Past Antique Show
18	IL	57th Annual Reunion of The Will County Threshermen's Association
18	OH	70th Annual Miami Valley Steam Threshers Show and Reunion
18	MI	Riverbend Steam & Gas Show
19	PA	2019 Antique Truck, Tractor, and Machinery Show
19	IL	23rd Annual County Line Sod Busters Prairie Days
19	NC	27th Annual Early Farm Days Antique Engine and Tractor Show
19	PA	27th Annual Gratz Area Antique Machinery Association Lawn and Garden Tractor Show & Tractor Pull
19	IA	35th Annual Threshing Bee
19	MN	37th Annual Antique Engine & Tractor Show
19	IN	38th Annual Illiana Antique Power Association Show
19	NY	42nd Annual Chemung Valley Old Timers Show
19	KS	43rd Annual Threshing Show
19	PA	48th Annual Antique Gas Engine and Tractor Show
19	TN	50th Annual Tennessee-Kentucky Threshermen's Show
19	PA	52nd Annual Pioneer Steam and Gas Engine Society of Northwestern Pennsylvania
19	MO	Gasconade County Threshers aka Owensville Threshers 57th Steam and Threshing Show
19	PA	Green Acres Farm Heritage Club Show
19	MI	Olde Tyme Tractor and Steamer Show
19	IN	Randolph County Antique Club Tractor, Gas Engine, and Equipment Show
19	IN	White County 4-H Fair and Antique Power Show
20	WI	11th Annual Antique Tractor Expo
20	PA	24th Annual Fort Allen Antique Farm Equipment Association Summer Fun and Ice Cream Festival
20	WI	26th Annual Wisconsin Antique Power Reunion Show
20	KY	27th Annual Antique Tractor & Engine Show
20	AB	29th Annual Leduc West Exposition
20	IL	41st Annual Bureau Valley Antique Club Ol' Fashun Threshun Days
20	NE	43rd Annual Camp Creek Threshers Association Show
20	IN	4th Annual Orscheln's Tractor Show at North Vernon
20	WA	Annual Show and 35 Mile Drive
20	NY	Coon Hollow Engine & Tractor Show
20	MI	River Valley Antique Summer Show
20	IL	Waterman Lions Summerfest and Antique Tractor and Truck Show
20	PA	Williams Grove Historical Steam Engine Train Show and New/Old Stock Swap Meet
20	CT	Zagray Farm Museum Summer Show
22	WV	10th Anniversary Antique Tractor Show
23	NY	Saratoga County Fair
24	NY	55th Annual Pioneer Gas Engine Reunion Show
25	MI	32nd Annual Show
25	MO	39th Annual Macon County Flywheel
25	MB	65th Annual Manitoba Threshermen's Reunion & Stampede
25	KS	66th Annual Tri-State Antique Engine and Thresher Show

Index

25 OH   69th Annual Brookville Community Picnic
25 NC   High Country Crank-Up
25 OH   Steam, Tractor, and Gas Engine Reunion
26 MI   21st Annual Big Rapids Antique Farm & Power Club Swap Meet and Flea Market
26 OH   24th Annual F.A.R.M. Inc FARM Tractor Show
26 ME   24th Eliot Antique Tractor & Engine Show
26 ON   27th Anniversary Upper Canada Two-Cylinder Club Show
26 MN   29th Annual Little Log House Antique Power Show
26 PA   41st Annual Allegheny Mountain Engine and Implement Association Show & Demonstration
26 KY   49th Annual Central Kentucky Antique Machinery Association Show
26 OH   49th Annual Historical Engine Society's Antique Power Exhibition
26 WI   52nd Annual Union Threshermen's Club Thresheree and National Antique Tractor Pull
26 IL   Adams County Olde Tyme Threshing Show
26 IL   Annual Heritage Days Show
26 IN   Antique Steam and Gas Engine Club Summer Show
26 IL   Bos Brothers Old Fashioned Threshing Bee
26 IN   Hoosier Heritage Fest
26 PA   John Deere Days
26 OH   Mid-Ohio Antique Farm Machinery Show
26 MN   Orange Spectacular
26 VA   Pageant of Steam
26 PA   Rough and Tumble Engineers Historical John Deere Days
26 IL   Summer Harvest
26 OH   Summer Show - Bainbridge
27 MO   17th Annual River Hills Antique Tractor Club Adventure Ride
27 NV   25th Annual Northern Nevada Antique Power Show
27 NE   40th Annual Mid-States Antique Tractor & Engine Show
27 CT   Annual Antique Engine Show
27 WI   Antique Tractor and Art/Craft Show
27 AZ   Beat the Heat
27 OH   DHS Annual Open House
27 IL   Grandpa's Day
27 MI   Michigan/Wisconsin Antique Power Association
27 MN   Rose City Threshing and Heritage Festival
27 WI   Sherry Tired Iron Tractor Show
27 OR   The Great Oregon Steam-Up
28 CA   Outdoor Consignment Auction
28 MO   Weingarten Picnic, Antique Tractor and Steam Engine Expo
31 WA   48th Annual Steam and Gas Show

August

1 PA   18th Annual Stoystown Lions Club Antique Tractor Festival
1 PA   25th Harvester Dreamland Show
1 TN   3rd Annual Smoky Mountain Flywheelers Show
1 MI   46th Annual Old Engine and Tractor Show
1 OH   48th Annual Northwest Ohio Antique Machinery Show
1 IN   71st Annual Reunion Pioneer Engineers
1 OH   Holmes County Steam & Engine Show
1 PA   Loyalsock Valley Antique Machinery Assn. 32nd Annual Show
1 IN   Markleville Jamboree
1 IN   Randolph County Antique Club State Line Heritage Days
1 OH   Silver King Festival
1 PA   Summer Show - Northwest PA Steam Engine and Old Equipment Association
2 KY   13th Annual Tractor Show
2 NE   23rd Annual Antique Tractor and Farm Machinery Show
2 OH   29th Annual Clermont County Antique Machinery Show

Index

2	IN	29th Annual Keck Gonnerman Antique Machinery Association Show
2	OH	30th Annual Morrow County Antique Tractor and Equipment Farm Days
2	IA	35th Annual Steam Threshing and Plowing Show
2	OH	3rd Annual Chandlersville Homecoming Tractor and Power Show
2	IL	3rd Annual Steam Threshing Days
2	IL	43rd Annual Bond County Antique Machinery Expo
2	WI	48th Annual Show Coulee Antique Engine Club Aug. 0 2 IL 509th Annual Old-Time Threshing and Antique Show
2	WI	51st Annual Dodge County Antique Power Show
2	IL	52nd Annual Western Illinois Thresher's Bee, Craft Show and Flea Market
2	ON	54th Annual Georgian Bay Steam Show
2	MN	56th Annual Scott-Carver Threshers Harvest Festival
2	MD	59th Annual Eastern Shore Threshermen and Collectors Assn. Old-Time Wheat Threshing, Steam and Gas Engine Show
2	MI	59th Annual Show
2	IN	8th Annual Wolf Lake Onion Days Farm & Garden Tractor Show
2	CO	Ault Engine and Machinery Show
2	ON	Georgian Bay Steam Show
2	KS	Goessel Country Threshing Days
2	AB	Heritage Acres Annual Show
2	GA	Trains, Trucks & Tractors
2	VT	Vermont Gas and Steam Engine Association Quechee Show
2	IL	Western Illinois Threshers
3	MD	12 Annual Wheat Threshing
3	OH	18th Annual Vintage Truck Show
3	WI	3rd Annual Golat Implement Days, Tractor and Implement Show
3	CO	Chaffee County Fair Tractor Pull and Engine Show
3	WV	Henderson Hall One Day Antique Engine Show
3	ON	Heritage Days in Jarvis
3	NE	Heritage Power Assn. Tractor Show
3	OH	Jon Amundson Crossroads of America Memorial Antique Tractor Tour
3	MN	Lake of the Woods Steam & Gas Show
3	WY	Laramie County Fair
3	IL	Living History Antique Equipment Assn. Show
3	PA	Mid Atlantic Allis Chalmers 4th Annual Tractor Show and Swap Meet
3	MN	Park Rapids Antique Tractor and Engine Club Field Days
3	MN	Pioneer Power Good Old Days & Throching Show
3	SK	Threshermen's Show and Seniors' Festival
3	IN	Wingate Antique Tractor, Gas Engine and Old Truck Show
3	IN	YesterYear Power Club Tractor and Engine Show
4	MN	Lake Lillian Fun Days Tractor Pull
4	OH	Olmsted Historical Society Antique Engine Show
6	NY	Empire Farm Days
7	MI	21st Annual Coopersville Tractor Show
7	NY	59th Annual New York Steam Engine Pageant of Steam
8	IN	38th Annual Northeast Indiana Steam and Gas Antique Farm Power Show
8	IN	45th Mid-America Threshing and Antiques
8	OH	49th Annual Reunion Ohio Valley Antique Machinery Show
8	IL	63rd Annual Northern Illinois Steam Power Club Sycamore Steam Show
8	MN	Heritage Days
8	MO	Platte County Steam Engine Show
8	MI	Rust n Dust Antique Steam & Gas Show
9	MN	2018 Annual Almelund Threshing Show
9	MI	22nd Annual Hartford Old Engine and Tractor Show
9	NC	28th Annual Spokes & Cleats Antique Engine and Tractor Show
9	IL	33rd Annual Oblong Antique Tractor and Engine Assn. Show
9	ON	34th Annual Essex County Steam and Gas Engine Show
9	PA	37th Annual Steam and Gas Show
9	IL	38th Annual Mill Road Thresherman's Show

Index

9	PA	39th Annual National Pike Steam, Gas and Horse Show
9	AR	42nd Annual Rusty Wheels Engine and Tractor Show
9	MI	44th Annual Thumb Area Old Engine and Tractor Association Show
9	IA	49th Annual Albert City Threshermen and Collectors Show
9	AB	50th Annual Pioneer Acres Show
9	WI	56th Annual Chippewa Valley Antique Engine and Model Club Pioneer Days
9	MI	Alpena Antique Tractor and Steam Engine Show
9	SD	Antique Tractor Pull and Fur Trader Days
9	PA	C.V. Antique Engine & Machinery Assn. Spring Fling
9	ON	Merrickville Agricultural Fair and 45th Annual Steam and Antique Collectibles Show
9	WA	Threshing Bee and Tractor Show
9	MI	Wellington Antique Tractor & Engine Club
10	NE	13th Annual Tractor Show and Summer Fair
10	IL	18th Annual South Fulton Antique Tractor Show (Sunday Tractor Ride)
10	IA	24th Annual Cedar Valley Memories
10	KY	2nd Annual Sycamore Flats Flywheelers Tractor Show and Farmer's Market
10	PA	30th Annual Summer Show
10	MN	35th Annual Steam and Threshing Show
10	MA	40th Annual Straw Hollow Engine Works Show
10	WI	67th Annual Wisconsin Steam Engine Show
10	PA	6th Annual Pre Dayton Fair Antique Tractor Pulls
10	ON	Antique Machinery Show
10	MN	Days of Yesteryear
10	IA	Northeast Iowa Antique Engine and Power Show
10	CO	Pikes Peak Antique Machinery Days Show and Museums Makers Fair
10	WI	Rudolph Old Tractor Club Show
10	SD	Twin Brooks Threshing Show
10	MO	Warren County Farm Heritage Days
11	NE	37th Annual Antique Machinery Show
11	OH	Annual Car & Power Show
12	NY	30th Annual Catskill Mountain Antique Engine and Machinery Show at the Delaware County Fair
14	PA	20th Annual Empire EXPO Empire Tractor Owners
14	IL	60th Annual Steam, Gas and Threshing Show
14	PA	71st Annual Rough and Tumble Engineers Historical Threshermen's Reunion
15	IN	42nd Annual Summer Show - Maumee Valley Steam and Gas Association
15	MI	52 Annual Buckley Old Engine Show
15	ON	Gathering of the Orange 2019
15	IN	Greensburg Power of the Past 29th Annual Reunion
16	WI	10th Annual Eau Claire Big Rig Truck Show
16	IL	18th Annual Clark County Antique Power Club Tractor and Engine Show
16	ON	26th Annual Bruce County Heritage Farm Show
16	IA	30th Annual Prairie Homestead Antique Power Tractor Show
16	PA	35th Anniversary Olde Tyme Days 2019
16	NE	36th Annual Antique & Collector Show - Platte Valley Antique Machinery
16	KS	38th Annual Kansas and Oklahoma Steam and Gas Engine Association Show
16	MO	43rd Annual Montgomery County Old Threshers Show
16	MI	45th Annual Mid-Michigan Old Gas Tractor Show
16	MN	49th Annual Nowthen Historical Power Threshing Show
16	IA	55th Annual Antique Acres Old Time Power Show
16	MO	55th Annual Northwest Missouri Steam and Gas Engine Association Annual Show
16	WI	56th Annual Badger Steam and Gas Engine Club Show
16	OH	56th Annual Dover Steam Show
16	NY	Allen's Adirondack Gas Engine Show
16	OH	Antique Tractor Club of Trumbull County Ohio Fall Show
16	OH	Fairfield County Antique Tractor Club and Truck Show
16	MN	Heritage Hill Threshing Show
16	MN	Lake Itasca Region Pioneer Farmers 44th Annual Show

Index

16	SD	Riverboat Days Tractor Show and Small Engine Display
16	WI	Valmy Thresheree
17	KY	15th Annual Vette City Lions Motorfest
17	NY	19th Annual Roseboom Antique Power Days
17	PA	25th Annual Susquehanna Antique Machinery Summer Show
17	WI	35th Annual Moon Lake Threshermen's Threshing Bee & Minneapolis Moline Summer Convention
17	CT	Annual Antique Marine Engine Exposition
17	MN	Butterfield Steam and Gas Engine Show
17	QC	Exposition 2019
17	MN	Forest City Threshers Show
17	OH	Harlem Township Days Annual Show
17	MT	Huntley Project Threshing Bee
17	NY	The Way It Was Antique Club
17	KY	Warren County Antique Tractor & Engine Club at the 15th Annual Vette City Lions Motor Fest
17	SK	Western Development Museum "Those Were the Days"
18	IL	Day at the Farm
20	IN	54th Antique Engine and Tractor Show
20	IN	Tri-State Gas Engine Show & Tractor Show
22	MI	30th Annual Clarksville Steam and Gas Engine Tractor Show
22	SD	35th Annual J.I. Case Collectors Summer Convention
22	MD	Gravely Tractor Club of America Mow-In 2019
22	IL	I&I Antique Tractor and Gas Engine Club at the Half Century of Progress
22	IL	Rantoul Half Century of Progress Show
22	VT	26th Annual Connecticut River Antique Collectors Klub (CRACK)
23	IN	29th Annual Toy Truck-N Construction Show and Auction
23	MI	35th Annual St. Clair County Farm Museum Fall Harvest Days
23	IN	37th Leota Country Frolic
23	MN	46th Annual Le Sueur County Pioneer Power Show
23	WI	46th Annual North Central Wisconsin Antique Steam and Gas Engine Club Show
23	KS	55th Annual Southwest Kansas Antique Engine and Thresher Show
23	MN	58th Annual Lakehead Harvest Show
23	MN	England Prairie Pioneer Days
23	MO	Osage River Antique Power Engine Show
23	PA	Middlecreek Valley Antique Assn. 23rd Annual Fall Antique Machinery Show
23	MN	St. Charles Gladiola Days Tractor Show
23	ON	Waterloo County Steam Threshers' Reunion
24	PA	37th Annual Mason Dixon Frontier Festival
24	MN	44th Annual Finn Creek Summer Folk Festival
24	MN	54rd Annual Donnelly Threshing Bee
24	WI	61st Annual Sussex Engine Show
24	IL	Amboy Depot Days Tractor Show
24	ON	Antique Wheels in Motion 24th Annual Harvest Days
24	QC	Chateauguay Valley Antique Assn. Show
24	IA	Farm Days in the Village
24	IA	Heritage Park of North Iowa Horse & Mule Event
24	IA	Homer Threshing Bee
24	PA	Indiana County Fair Antique Tractor and Machinery Show
24	NE	Nebraska State Antique Tractor and Horse Plowing Bee/Rae Valley Old Threshers Reunion
24	IL	Olden Days
24	IL	River Valley Antique Tractor Show
24	MD	Rural Heritage Spud Fest & Antique Tractor Show
24	TN	Tractor Show On The Creek
24	MN	White Oak Antique Farm Show
25	PA	61st Annual Williams Grove Historical Steam Engine 9 Day Show
25	ND	NE North Dakota Pioneer Machinery Threshing Show

Index

28	OH	58th Annual Canfield Fair Antique Equipment Pageant
29	IL	71st Annual Central States Threshermen's Reunion
29	IL	Illinois Massey Collectors State Show29 IA Midwest Old Threshers Reunion
29	MN	Western Minnesota Steam Threshers Reunion
30	PA	28th Annual Montour Antique Farm Machinery Collectors Show
30	OH	31st Annual Antique Tractor & Engine Show
30	MN	33rd Annual JI Case Exposition
30	IL	43rd Annual Argyle Antique Gas Engine Show
30	MI	44th Annual U.P. Steam and Gas Engine Show
30	MN	45th Annual Rice County Steam and Gas Engines Show
30	WI	63rd Reunion of the Rock River Thresheree
30	NV	Antique Tractor and Engine Show
30	IN	Hesston Steam & Power Show
30	ON	Steam-Era
30	NY	Yates Antique Tractor and Engine Society
31	OH	14th Annual Mad River and Nickel Plate Railroad Museum Truck & Car Show
31	MN	27th Annual Rumely Products Collectors Expo
31	TX	34th Annual Cooke County Antique Tractor and Farm Machinery Show
31	NY	37th Annual Fall Harvest Days and Exhibition
31	NC	41st Annual Old-Fashioned Farmers' Day
31	MN	41st Annual White Pine Logging & Threshing Show
31	IA	Cedar Valley Engine Club Threshers Reunion
31	WI	Fountain City Old Time Farm Fest
31	AB	Harvest Festival Reynolds-Alberta Museum
31	MI	Hudson Mills Old Power Fall Antique Tractor Pulls
31	OH	6th Annual Capital City Chrome & Customs Special Olympics Benefit Truck Show
31	UT	Iron County Fair Tractor Caravan, Show and Pull
31	ON	Tractor & Engine Antique Show
31	MI	Waldron Antique Tractor Show

September

4	PA	67th Anniversary Reunion of the Farmers' and Threshermens' Jubilee
5	IL	30th Annual Southern Illinois Antique Power Club Antique Power Days
5	IN	35th Annual White River Valley Antique Antique Show
5	NY	53rd Annual Rally Western New York Gas and Steam Engine
5	PA	Annual Fall Show
5	MI	Antique Engine & Tractor Show
6	NC	19th Annual Justice Community Antique Tractor, Car and Engine Show
6	AR	27th Annual Fall Show
6	SD	45th Annual James Valley Threshing & Tractor Club Show
6	NH	48th Annual Dublin Engine Meet
6	MD	57th Annual Steam and Gas Round-Up Mason-Dixon Historical Society
6	MN	66th Annual Lake Region Pioneer Thresherman - LRPTA - Dalton Threshing
6	ON	Blyth Steam Show
6	OH	Clinton County Corn Festival
6	KY	Hopkinsville Antique Tractor & Small Engine Show
6	KY	Old Time Machinery Show
6	WI	Pickett Truck and Tractor Pull
6	IN	Rentown Old Fashion Days
6	WA	Spokane Inter State Fair
6	IL	Stearman Fly-In with Spoon River Antique Agriculture Association Show
7	IL	15th Annual Tractors for Charity
7	OH	16th Annual Old Construction & Mining Equipment Show
7	IL	1st Annual Viola Heritage Fest
7	WI	21st Annual Mid-Lakes Thresheree & Tractor Show
7	OH	22nd Annual Antique Tractor & Gas Engine Show and 64th Annual Richland County Steam Threshers
7	AR	27th Annual Antique Tractor and Engine Show
7	WI	33rd Annual Pickett Steam and Gas Engine Show

7	MN	36th Annual Farming of Yesteryear Threshing Festival
7	NE	37th Annual Old Trusty Antique Engine and Collectors Show
7	OH	57th Annual Stumptown Steam Threshers Club Reunion and Show
7	MN	Andersons' Rock Creek Relics Threshing and Sawing Show
7	MN	Atwater Threshing Days
7	IA	Carstens Farm Days
7	NY	Dan Rion Memorial Antique Engine Jamboree & Powerfest
7	ND	Drake Threshing Show
7	NC	Foothills Antique Power Annual Swap Meet
7	ND	Fort Ransom Sodbuster Days
7	TX	Lone Star Antique Tractor and Engine Show
7	OH	Ohio Antique Power Club Gathering
7	KS	Old Albany Days
7	NE	Pierce Old Time Threshers Bee
7	OH	Pioneer Days Tractor & Machinery Show
7	IL	Slow Boys Antique Tractor & Farm Equipment Show
7	ND	Yesterday's Farmers Threshing Bee
8	ND	26th Annual Pembina County Historical Society Pioneer Machinery Show
8	WI	Early Farm Days
8	WI	Friends of Beckman Mill Heritage Day
9	NY	14th Annual Marilla Ag Day
10	OH	Wyandot County Fair Show
12	MO	32nd Annual Northeast Missouri Old Threshers
12	IN	44th Annual Lanesville Heritage Weekend
12	WV	51st Annual West Virginia Oil and Gas Festival
12	MD	64th Annual Steam and Gas Engine Show
12	OH	Old Machinery Days
12	MO	Steam-O-Rama
13	NY	17th Annual Oneida Lake Ole-Tymers Antique Engine & Tractor Show
13	KS	25th Annual Power of the Past Antique Engine and Tractor Show
13	WI	28th Annual Fall Harvest Days
13	PA	29th Annual Southern Cove Power Reunion Association Antique Tractor and Engine Show
13	OH	34th Annual International Convention and Old Equipment Exposition
13	CT	39th Annual Gas, Steam, and Machinery Meet
13	VA	43rd Annual Somerset Steam and Gas Pasture Party
13	MN	45th Annual Pioneer Days Threshing Show
13	IL	58th Annual Antique Engine and Tractor Working Farm Show
13	IN	Brown County Antique Engine and Tractor Show
13	IL	Corn Items Collectors Association, Inc at the Antique Engine and Working Farm Show
13	GA	Farm Days of Yesteryear
13	WI	Gathering of the Orange 2019
13	IL	Moline Universal Tractor and Plow Co. Reunion
13	PA	Vintage Iron Club 15th Annual Fall Festival and Show
14	WI	31st Annual R.S. Vintage Steel Steam and Gas Engine Show
14	IL	5th Annual Vintage Farm Equipment Show
14	NE	Camp Creek Threshers Miniature Railroad Show
14	IL	Farm & Family Day
14	OH	Green Camp Fireman's Festival Tractor and Car Show
14	SD	Harvest Festival
14	AB	Leduc West Antique Society Provincial Finals Tractor Pull and Fall Harvest
14	IN	Tip Wa Antique Tractor and Engine Show
14	IL	Vintage Garden Tractor Club of America Illinois Regional Show
15	IL	6th Annual "All About Allis-Chalmers" Farm Days
19	KY	42nd Annual McCracken County FFA Alumni Antique Gas Engine & Tractor Show
19	KY	42nd Annual McCracken County FFA Alumni Antique Gas Engine and Tractor Show
19	MO	50th Annual Lincoln County Old Threshers

Index

19	MO	Mid-Missouri Antique Power and Collectible Show
19	IN	Nappanee Apple Festival Antique Tractor, Engine and Toy Show
20	PA	17th Annual Aughwick Creek Antique Tractor Show
20	OK	26TH Annual Murray County Antique Tractor and Implement Show
20	GA	2nd Annual Antique Tractor Show
20	MI	34th Annual Farmer's Antique Tractor and Engine Fall Show
20	MI	43rd Annual Fall Show
20	OH	49th LaGrange Engine Club Show
20	KS	62nd Annual McLouth Threshing Bee
20	MO	CAFMCO Fall Show
20	ND	Central North Dakota Steam Threshers Reunion
20	NJ	Days of the Past
20	OH	Flat Rock Creek Fall Festival
20	TN	Greene County Antique Farm & Auto Show
20	AL	Hartselle Depot Days
20	IA	Plagman Barn Show Days
20	VA	Rockville-Centerville Steam and Gas Historical Assn. Field Day of the Past
20	IN	Rumely Allis Chalmers La Porte Heritage Center Tractor Show
20	KY	Tractor and Engine Show
20	PA	Two-Top Steam and Gas Show
21	AUS	2018 Clarendon Classic Rally
21	IN	21st Annual Albion Harvest Fest
21	WI	21st Annual Richfield Historical Society Thresheree & Harvest Festival
21	PA	22nd Annual Susquehanna Old Fashioned Field Days
21	WI	26th Annual Agricultural Heritage Days
21	IL	34th Annual Edwards River Antique Engine Show
21	IA	54th Annual Fall Festival
21	WI	8th Annual Glacier Ridge Antique Tractor
21	IN	8th Annual Kent Vintage Tractor Show at Leroy's
21	NY	8th Annual Pioneer Gas Engine Fall Division Tractor Pull and Gas-Down Running Class A & &C
21	IL	Adams County Olde Tyme Fall Swap Meet and Flea Market
21	OH	Ashtabula County Antique Engine Club 23nd Annual Fall Show
21	IL	Fall Festival
21	IN	From the Seat of a Tractor - Tractor Drive
21	KY	Greensburg Rotary Club's Cow Days, Antique Tractor and Gas Engine Show
21	NE	Harvest Festival
21	MI	Harvest Festival Tractor Show
21	WI	Northern Aged Iron Tractor & Threshing Show
21	OH	Old Iron Power Club & Appalachian Foot Hills Fall Festival
21	OH	Oldtime Farming Festival
21	PA	Pioneer Steam and Gas Engine Society of Northwestern Pennsylvania Gas-up at Drake Well
21	IN	Pleasant View Heritage Day
21	MT	TASGA Threshing Bee
21	MB	Threshing Days and Toy Show
21	NE	Tractors & Treasures
22	MN	23rd Annual West Central Antique Power Collectors Tractor Pull
26	VA	15th Annual Tri-State Antique Truck and Tractor Show
2	KS	21st Annual Wilson County Old Iron Days
26	IN	25th Annual Franklin County Antique Machinery Show
26	MI	35th Annual Fall Swap Meet
26	OH	56th Annual Barnesville Pumpkin Festival
26	MO	JP's 18th Midwest Cub-Arama
27	WI	16th Annual Fall Harvest Festival
27	PA	27th Annual Old Iron in the Grove
27	OK	29th Annual National Two-Cylinder Tractor Show
27	WV	31st Annual Wood County Flywheelers Volcano Days Antique Engine Show and Festival

27 OK 34th Annual Major County Historical Society Old Time Threshing Bee
27 OH 37th Annual Luckey Fall Festival
27 IN 43rd Annual Northern Indiana Historical Power Association Fall Harvest Festival and Antique Equipment Show
27 OH 49th Annual Old Timers Club Old Timer's Days
27 IL 50th Annual Steam Show and Fall Festival
27 MI 6th Annual Fall Harvest Festival & Tractor Show
27 CT Annual Fall Festival
27 SD Coal Springs Threshing Bee & Antique Show
27 MO Livingston County Steam and Gas Association Old Time Harvest Days
27 MS Mississippi Valley Flywheelers Fall Show
27 TN Montgomery County Antique Tractor & Engine Club 19th Annual Show
27 WI Steam School
27 IL Stillman Valley Fall Festival Hit and Miss Engine and Antique Tractor Show
27 AL Winfield Mule Day
28 CT 11th Fall Tractor Ride and Tractor Show
28 PA 15th Annual Burrell Township V.F.D. Tractor Ride
28 MN 20th Annual Corn Shredding Autumn Harvest Days
28 TN 24th Annual Sardis Antique Farm and Home Fall Show
28 KS 41st Annual Fall Festival and Swap Meet
28 ND 59th Annual Makoti Threshing Show
28 OH Barnesville Pumpkin Festival Tractor Cruise
28 AL Eva Frontier Days
2 TN Fall Festival
28 IA Fall-der-all Antique Tractors & Engines Festival
28 OK Green Country Antique Power Association Fall Fling with Western Heritage Weekend
28 OH Malabar Farm State Park Heritage Days
28 TN Middle Tennessee Antique Engine and Tractor Show
28 OH Pumpkin Fest with Tracks to the Past
28 VT Vermont Gas and Steam Engine Association East Burke Fall Festival
29 PA 19th Annual Ye Olde Autumn Festival

October
3 KY 20th Annual Greenup Old Tractors, Engines and Machinery Show
3 KY 24th Annual South East Kentucky Antique Tractor Show
3 PA 02nd Annual Early American Steam Engine Society Steam-O-Rama
3 FL International Harvester Collectors Club, Florida Chapter 27 3rd Annual Fort Christmas School Students Farm Show
4 PA 12th Annual Fall Harvest Fest
4 NC 12th Annual Fall Valley Hills Antique Power Club Tractor Show
4 NC 13th Annual Harvest Show Lord Granville Agricultural Heritage Association
4 TN 14th Annual Days Gone By Tractor Show and Threshing
4 PA 34th Annual Buffalo Valley Antique Machinery Autumn Exhibit
4 CA International Harvester Sierra Fall Rallye
4 WV Middle Island Harvest Festival
4 WI Wheels of Time
5 KY 12th Annual Show at the Park
5 FL 30th Annual Jay Peanut Festival - Sponsored by Gabbert Farm
5 KY 33rd Annual Farm Festival
5 OH 3rd Annual Farm Heritage Show
5 IN 3rd Annual Orscheln's Tractor Show at Scottsburg
5 IL 43rd Annual Knox County Scenic Drive Spoon River Antique Agriculture Association Show
5 TX 48th Annual State Tractor, Truck & Engine Show
5 PA 4th Annual Fall Harvest Day Event
5 NY Antique Tractor and Engine Show
5 IL Autumn on Parade Tractor Show

Index

5	WI	Berlin Area Antique Equipment 4th Annual Tractor Show
5	MD	Catoctin Antique Gas Engine Show
5	MI	Fall Festival and Swap Meet
5	WV	Fall Festival West Virginia State Farm Museum
5	PA	Fall Fling - Northwest PA Steam Engine and Old Equipment Association
5	MN	Fall Meeting Minnesota Association of Antique Power Shows (MAAPS)
5	OH	Harvest Happenings
5	KS	Heritage Day Festival
5	PA	Mack Day
5	IL	Marshall-Putnam Antique Swap Meet
5	AL	October Fest
5	MI	Olde Tyme Harvest Festival
5	PA	South Mountain Antique Engine Association in conjunction with the National Apple Harvest Festival
5	CT	Zagray Farm Museum Fall Festival and Swap Meet
5	WI	Berlin Antique Equipment Show
6	PA	Central Electric Cooperative, Inc. Antique Tractor Show
6	OH	Farm Toy Show
10	IN	15th Annual Tri-State Gas Engine and Tractor Fall Swap Meet
10	IN	Annual Hoosier Flywheelers Fall Swap Meet
11	MO	27th Antique Car, Tractor & Steam Engine Association
11	PA	34th Annual Sherman's Valley Heritage Days
11	OH	49th Annual Algonquin Mill Fall Festival
11	PA	54th Annual Fall Festival Tioga County Early Days
11	KS	Annual Swap Meet
11	IN	Antique Steam and Gas Engine Club Fall Show
11	NC	Cotton Ginning Days Show
11	TN	Fall Festival
11	MO	Fall Show - Ozarks Older Iron Club
11	AR	North Arkansas Rusty Wheels Old Engine Club Fall Show
11	PA	Rough and Tumble Engineers Historical A Time of Harvest
11	TN	Three Rivers Antique Tractor and Engine Show
11	TN	Tractors and Trucks Shackle Island Collector's Club Fall Harvest Show
12	PA	12th Annual Antique Power and Apple Festival
12	TX	17th Antique Tractor and Engine Show
12	IN	19th Annual Model Engine, Gas Engine, and Tractor Pull Fall Show
12	KS	19th Annual Santa Fe Trail Tired Iron Show
12	VA	50th Annual Page County Heritage Festival
12	PA	6th Annual Smicksburg Antique Tractor, Machinery & Truck Show
12	CO	Arkansas Valley Flywheelers Antique Farm Equipment Show and Tractor Pull
12	TN	Atwood Fall Tractor Show
12	IN	Buckley Homestead Fall Festival
12	KY	Campbell County Log Cabin History and Farm Heritage Museum
12	TX	Delta County Cotton Harvest Festival Show
12	AL	Falkville Festival
12	VA	Fall Farm to Fork Dinner
12	NE	Harvest Festival
12	AL	Jean's on the River Antique Tractor Show
12	WI	Pioneer Farm Days
12	PA	Pioneer Steam and Gas Engine Society of Northwestern Pennsylvania Fall Harvest Show
12	PA	South Mountain Antique Engine Association in conjunction with the Apple Harvest Festival
12	KY	Summersville Fun Days Tractor & Old Engine Show
12	NY	The Farmer's Museum Tractor Fest
12	KY	Woodburn Antique Tractor, Engine, Truck and Car Show
17	PA	34th Anniversary Coolspring Power Museum Fall Exposition and Swap Meet
18	GA	13th Annual Gordon County Antique Engine and Tractor Show
18	KY	14th Annual Clifty Tractor 7 Car Show

Index

18	OH	20th Annual Carroll County Antique Power Show
18	OK	29th Annual Route 66 Flywheelers Gas Engine and Tractor Show
18	IL	2nd Annual Harvest To Home
18	IL	33rd Annual Annual Fall Show and Festival
18	PA	39th Annual Grease, Steam and Rust Association Antique Tractor, Small Engine, and Machinery Show
18	KS	63rd Annual Pioneer Harvest Fiesta
18	NC	Hodges Farm Antique Tractor & Engine Show
18	OH	Paint Valley Antique Machinery Club Fall Festival of Leaves Tractor, Toy & Machinery Show
18	TX	Texas Czech Heritage and Cultural Center Heritage Fest and Muziky
19	MD	11th Annual Fall Harvest
19	OH	15th Annual Education of Yesterday Farm Show
19	TN	21st Williston Old Timers Assn. Show
19	PA	40th Annual Fall Harvest and Sawmill Show
19	MA	40th Annual Waters Farm Days Fall Festival
19	CA	Antique Engine & Tractor Show
19	MO	Cedar Hill Tractor and Engine Show
19	WI	Ixonia Vintage Tractor Expo Plow Day
19	AL	Jasper Heritage Festival
19	LA	Jena Fall Tractor Show and Pull
19	TN	Starr Mountain Antique Tractor and Car Show
25	UT	Cedar Heritage and Livestock Festival
26	IN	23rd Annual Brown County Antique Machinery Fall Swap Meet
2	OH	2nd Annual Harrison Coal & Reclamation Historical Park Tours of the Age of Steam Roadhouse
26	TN	4th Annual Tractor and Car Show
26	AR	Corning Harvest Festival
26	WA	EDGETA #245 Annual Fall Swap Meet
26	GA	Fall Colors Tractor Ride
26	VA	Fall Harvest Festival
26	OH	Fall Plow Day
26	FL	International Harvester Collectors Club, Florida Chapter 27 Lake Wales Pioneer Days
26	AL	Old Tyme Farm Days
26	OH	ROAR Day (Rural Ohio Appalachia Revisited)
26	AL	Southland Flywheelers Fall Festival and Harvest Exhibits
26	GA	Wayne County Cruiser Arch Fest

November

1	NC	100 Years of Progress
1	NC	2019 ACMOC National Show
1	IA	42nd Annual National Farm Toy Show
1	TN	Billy McKnight Memorial Antique Tractor and Engine Show
1	MS	Soulé Live Steam Show
2	WV	Fall Swap Meet
2	FL	Mid-Florida Antique Machinery Club Display of Antique Machines & Tractors Fall Show
2	VA	Plowing Day
2	MS	Vardaman Sweet Potato Festival's Annual Antique Tractor Show
6	FL	24th Annual Florida Flywheelers Fall Fuel-Up
6	FL	International Harvester Collectors Club, Florida Chapter 27 at the 24th Annual Florida Flywheelers Fall Fuel Up
8	GA	19th Annual Cumming Steam, Antique Tractor and Gas Engine Show
8	WV	Boston's Antique Engine Show
9	TX	Heritage Syrup Festival
17	OH	Farm Toy Show

Index

December

7   MI   Christmas in the Village
7   IN   Farm Toy Show
7   FL   International Harvester Collectors Club, Florida Chapter 27 Cracker Christmas
         Antique Engine & Tractor Show
13 FL   Florida Flywheelers Antique Engine Club Christmas in the Village
14 GA   "Crusin' Into Christmas" Car Show

2019

January 2019
S	M	T	W	T	F	S
		1	2	3	4	5
6	7	8	9	10	11	12
13	14	15	16	17	18	19
20	21	22	23	24	25	26
27	28	29	30	31		

February 2019
S	M	T	W	T	F	S
					1	2
3	4	5	6	7	8	9
10	11	12	13	14	15	16
17	18	19	20	21	22	23
24	25	26	27	28		

March 2019
S	M	T	W	T	F	S
					1	2
3	4	5	6	7	8	9
10	11	12	13	14	15	16
17	18	19	20	21	22	23
24	25	26	27	28	29	30
31						

April 2019
S	M	T	W	T	F	S
	1	2	3	4	5	6
7	8	9	10	11	12	13
14	15	16	17	18	19	20
21	22	23	24	25	26	27
28	29	30				

May 2019
S	M	T	W	T	F	S
			1	2	3	4
5	6	7	8	9	10	11
12	13	14	15	16	17	18
19	20	21	22	23	24	25
26	27	28	29	30	31	

June 2019
S	M	T	W	T	F	S
						1
2	3	4	5	6	7	8
9	10	11	12	13	14	15
16	17	18	19	20	21	22
23	24	25	26	27	28	29
30						

July 2019
S	M	T	W	T	F	S
	1	2	3	4	5	6
7	8	9	10	11	12	13
14	15	16	17	18	19	20
21	22	23	24	25	26	27
28	29	30	31			

August 2019
S	M	T	W	T	F	S
				1	2	3
4	5	6	7	8	9	10
11	12	13	14	15	16	17
18	19	20	21	22	23	24
25	26	27	28	29	30	31

September 2019
S	M	T	W	T	F	S
1	2	3	4	5	6	7
8	9	10	11	12	13	14
15	16	17	18	19	20	21
22	23	24	25	26	27	28
29	30					

October 2019
S	M	T	W	T	F	S
		1	2	3	4	5
6	7	8	9	10	11	12
13	14	15	16	17	18	19
20	21	22	23	24	25	26
27	28	29	30	31		

November 2019
S	M	T	W	T	F	S
					1	2
3	4	5	6	7	8	9
10	11	12	13	14	15	16
17	18	19	20	21	22	23
24	25	26	27	28	29	30

December 2019
S	M	T	W	T	F	S
1	2	3	4	5	6	7
8	9	10	11	12	13	14
15	16	17	18	19	20	21
22	23	24	25	26	27	28
29	30	31				

2020

January 2020
S	M	T	W	T	F	S
			1	2	3	4
5	6	7	8	9	10	11
12	13	14	15	16	17	18
19	20	21	22	23	24	25
26	27	28	29	30	31	

February 2020
S	M	T	W	T	F	S
						1
2	3	4	5	6	7	8
9	10	11	12	13	14	15
16	17	18	19	20	21	22
23	24	25	26	27	28	29

March 2020
S	M	T	W	T	F	S
1	2	3	4	5	6	7
8	9	10	11	12	13	14
15	16	17	18	19	20	21
22	23	24	25	26	27	28
29	30	31				

April 2020
S	M	T	W	T	F	S
			1	2	3	4
5	6	7	8	9	10	11
12	13	14	15	16	17	18
19	20	21	22	23	24	25
26	27	28	29	30		

May 2020
S	M	T	W	T	F	S
					1	2
3	4	5	6	7	8	9
10	11	12	13	14	15	16
17	18	19	20	21	22	23
24	25	26	27	28	29	30
31						

June 2020
S	M	T	W	T	F	S
	1	2	3	4	5	6
7	8	9	10	11	12	13
14	15	16	17	18	19	20
21	22	23	24	25	26	27
28	29	30				

July 2020
S	M	T	W	T	F	S
			1	2	3	4
5	6	7	8	9	10	11
12	13	14	15	16	17	18
19	20	21	22	23	24	25
26	27	28	29	30	31	

August 2020
S	M	T	W	T	F	S
						1
2	3	4	5	6	7	8
9	10	11	12	13	14	15
16	17	18	19	20	21	22
23	24	25	26	27	28	29
30	31					

September 2020
S	M	T	W	T	F	S
		1	2	3	4	5
6	7	8	9	10	11	12
13	14	15	16	17	18	19
20	21	22	23	24	25	26
27	28	29	30			

October 2020
S	M	T	W	T	F	S
				1	2	3
4	5	6	7	8	9	10
11	12	13	14	15	16	17
18	19	20	21	22	23	24
25	26	27	28	29	30	31

November 2020
S	M	T	W	T	F	S
1	2	3	4	5	6	7
8	9	10	11	12	13	14
15	16	17	18	19	20	21
22	23	24	25	26	27	28
29	30					

December 2020
S	M	T	W	T	F	S
		1	2	3	4	5
6	7	8	9	10	11	12
13	14	15	16	17	18	19
20	21	22	23	24	25	26
27	28	29	30	31		

2021

January 2021
S	M	T	W	T	F	S
					1	2
3	4	5	6	7	8	9
10	11	12	13	14	15	16
17	18	19	20	21	22	23
24	25	26	27	28	29	30
31						

February 2021
S	M	T	W	T	F	S
	1	2	3	4	5	6
7	8	9	10	11	12	13
14	15	16	17	18	19	20
21	22	23	24	25	26	27
28						

March 2021
S	M	T	W	T	F	S
	1	2	3	4	5	6
7	8	9	10	11	12	13
14	15	16	17	18	19	20
21	22	23	24	25	26	27
28	29	30	31			

April 2021
S	M	T	W	T	F	S
				1	2	3
4	5	6	7	8	9	10
11	12	13	14	15	16	17
18	19	20	21	22	23	24
25	26	27	28	29	30	

May 2021
S	M	T	W	T	F	S
						1
2	3	4	5	6	7	8
9	10	11	12	13	14	15
16	17	18	19	20	21	22
23	24	25	26	27	28	29
30	31					

June 2021
S	M	T	W	T	F	S
		1	2	3	4	5
6	7	8	9	10	11	12
13	14	15	16	17	18	19
20	21	22	23	24	25	26
27	28	29	30			

July 2021
S	M	T	W	T	F	S
				1	2	3
4	5	6	7	8	9	10
11	12	13	14	15	16	17
18	19	20	21	22	23	24
25	26	27	28	29	30	31

August 2021
S	M	T	W	T	F	S
1	2	3	4	5	6	7
8	9	10	11	12	13	14
15	16	17	18	19	20	21
22	23	24	25	26	27	28
29	30	31				

September 2021
S	M	T	W	T	F	S
			1	2	3	4
5	6	7	8	9	10	11
12	13	14	15	16	17	18
19	20	21	22	23	24	25
26	27	28	29	30		

October 2021
S	M	T	W	T	F	S
					1	2
3	4	5	6	7	8	9
10	11	12	13	14	15	16
17	18	19	20	21	22	23
24	25	26	27	28	29	30
31						

November 2021
S	M	T	W	T	F	S
	1	2	3	4	5	6
7	8	9	10	11	12	13
14	15	16	17	18	19	20
21	22	23	24	25	26	27
28	29	30				

December 2021
S	M	T	W	T	F	S
			1	2	3	4
5	6	7	8	9	10	11
12	13	14	15	16	17	18
19	20	21	22	23	24	25
26	27	28	29	30	31	

Index

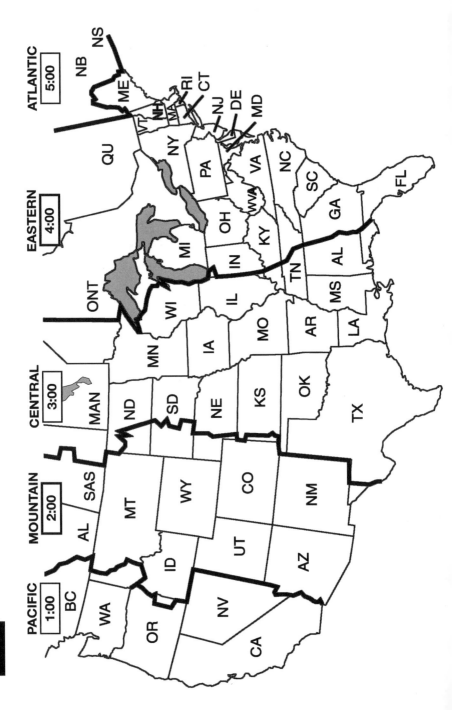

<u>NOTES:</u>

NOTES:

NOTES:

<u>NOTES:</u>